THE COMPLETE
PRO TOOLS
HANDBOOK

Pro Tools | HD • Pro Tools | 24 MIX • Pro Tools LE
for Home, Project, and Professional Studios

By José "Chilitos" Valenzuela

Backbeat
Books
San Francisco

Graphic design and editing: Ana Lorente Izquierdo
Cover design: Damien Castaneda
Front and back cover photo: Oscar Elizondo
Photographer assistant: Julian Salas
Editors: George Madaraz and Karl Coryat
Technical editors: Jon Connolly and Severine Baron
Proofreaders: Gary Glass, Andre Oliveira, Saskia Tracy,
    Vivian Khor, Hillary Beth, and Mark Dawson

Published by Backbeat Books
600 Harrison Street, San Francisco, CA 94107
www.backbeatbooks.com
email: books@musicplayer.com

An imprint of the Music Player Network
Publishers of *Guitar Player*, *Bass Player*, *Keyboard*, and other magazines
United Entertainment Media, Inc.
A CMP Information company

CMP
United Business Media

Digidesign and Pro Tools are trademarks of Digidesign, a division of Avid Technology, and names and logos are used with permission.

Distributed to the book trade in the US and Canada by
Publishers Group West, 1700 Fourth Street, Berkeley, CA 94710

Distributed to the music trade in the US and Canada by
Hal Leonard Publishing, P.O. Box 13819, Milwaukee, WI 53213

Library of Congress Control Number: 2003106344

ISBN: 0-87930-733-1

Printed in the United States of America

03 04 05 06 07   5 4 3 2 1

Please send all suggestions and questions
to the author at the following address:

AudioGraph International
Attn: José "Chilitos" Valenzuela
2103 Main Street
Santa Monica, CA 90405, USA
Tel: (310) 396-5004 • Fax: (310) 396-5882
E-mail: chilitos@audiographintl.com

Table of Contents

Dedication

I dedicate this book first to my parents, who always believed in my talent,
and for the unconditional love they have always given me.

José Valenzuela García

and

María Guadalupe Flores de Valenzuela

I also dedicate this book to one of the founders of the Instituto Tecnológico
Regional de Baja California #21, the school where I initiated my technical studies,
for believing in education and giving the opportunity to me and
so many other young people to realize their dreams and aspirations.
¡Muchas gracias, Sr. Ingeniero!

Ing. José Marquez Muñoz de Cote

(Mr. Marquez, Electronic Engineer, was the general director
of Televisa-Tijuana for more than 20 years; presently he serves
as a consultant to the current general director of
Canal 12 Televisa-Tijuana, B. C., México)

Introduction

Welcome to the world of Pro Tools

My name is José "Chilitos" Valenzuela. I am a recording/mixing engineer and have been a Pro Tools user for the last 12 years. I run a certified training school for Pro Tools ("Digidesign Authorized Pro School") in Santa Monica, CA, USA, called AudioGraph International. In my classrooms, my students receive hands-on training with Pro Tools HD TDM systems, which I feel is the very best way to learn. But I wanted to offer an alternative to those who cannot afford the time, money, or travel to be trained in a classroom, so I put this book together for you in a very simple, detailed, and visual manner. I wanted the book to read as if you were watching a video, where there are no interruptions when explaining Pro Tools concepts, menus, and functions.

If you are reading this book, it probably means that you have purchased—or are about to purchase—a Pro Tools System. For those of you who haven't yet made your purchase, this book will help you select a system that meets your needs. And once the purchase is made, this book will help you to understand, set up, and use your Pro Tools System.

A hard-disk recording and editing system

Digidesign has built a solid reputation for their hard-disk recording system known as Pro Tools. Their hardware and software package has become the gold standard in the worlds of post-production sound, broadcast, audio recording, and audio mixing and mastering.

The world of Pro Tools became possible only when personal computers were powerful enough to process sound that was represented as digital bits (ones and zeros). This new technology enabled Digidesign to design and build hard-disk editing systems whose specs met—and exceeded—those of large studio systems for a fraction of the price.

Pro Tools earned its reputation with a powerful edge on both purchase price and performance. Pristine audio, visually based editing, and random and immediate access to any locate point in the audio time line meant that hard-disk editors were able to blow away the competition when it came to show time.

Scalable DSP power

DSP is an acronym for Digital Signal Processing, and is the basis for computer-based audio editing. As you will soon see, your DSP needs will grow with the size and complexity of your projects. By offering DSP in modular units, Pro Tools enables you to expand your system to meet the needs of any sized project.

When the first Pro Tools packages were released, they were designed for Macintosh computers that already included some limited DSP capability. But the DSP needs of audio editing greatly exceeded the built-in capabilities of these computers.

Pro Tools addressed this problem by designing DSP cards that could be plugged into the computer's motherboard. These cards were populated with digital signal processing chips that added audio-processing power to the native capabilities of the Macintosh. These chips still provide the basis for the real-time processing power needed by the TDM Mixer and plug-ins in Pro Tools.

This modular approach means that Pro Tools systems are scalable. When you need more DSP power, you can add another card. The number of tracks you are recording, how many plug-ins you use, and how many audio routings, sends, and assignments you require will determine the amount of processing power you will need.

But because you can always add power to one of these systems, you won't get stuck with a heavy investment in a system that cannot grow with you.

Non-destructive editing

Prior to 1993, the Pro Tools environment was much less sophisticated. In those days, if you wanted to apply EQ to a track, you had to save a backup copy of the original material, and then export the track to a second piece of software called Sound Designer II.

When you applied an EQ operation to a track in SDII, it would modify the track permanently. After processing the track, you had to import the modified track back into Pro Tools. If you didn't like the results at that point, you had to drop back to your backup tracks, and try again.

Today, all digital processing is done in real time within Pro Tools, without ever modifying the original source material. What changes is only the list of processes that need to be applied to these audio clips when you play the session in Pro Tools—a list of start points, stop points, volume changes, plug-in changes, etc.

Non-destructive editing lets you reverse and revise any change that you make to a Pro Tools session, and provides you with a level of artistic freedom unknown before the advent of hard-disk recording.

The TDM bus and software-based plug-ins

The integrated data bus that Pro Tools utilizes is called TDM—which is an acronym for Time Division Multiplexing.

TDM is a "high-speed data highway" that routes digital signals within Pro Tools, exporting and importing signals to and from external devices, and processing and mixing them all within a single environment.

Some of the world's best digital-audio software houses have built high-end plug-ins around the TDM bus for use in the Pro Tools environment.

Pro Tools plug-ins are digital effect processors which emulate the behavior of physical boxes (such as compressors, delay units, reverb units, equalizers, etc.) by utilizing the power of Pro Tools' DSP chips.

Utilizing the combined power of the computer and Pro Tools' DSP cards, plug-ins offer the features of high-end audio hardware in a software environment. As software costs are considerably lower than hardware costs, a Pro Tools studio can provide world-class effects without taking out a loan from the bank. We will discuss the types of plug-ins you can use in a Pro Tools system, and some of the most popular plug-ins on the market today, in Chapter 10.

Pro Tools audio interfaces

In order to get audio into and out of the Pro Tools environment, Digidesign manufactures state-of-the-art ADC (analog to digital converter) and DAC (digital to analog converter) hardware. These audio interfaces have professional digital and analog audio connectors that enable Pro Tools to be integrated into professional recording environments.

We will discuss these audio "boxes" in some detail in Chapter 1.

Syncing Pro Tools to the external world

The worlds of digital audio and video are filled with timing issues. When you move into the fields of film and videotape, issues of precise timing and peripheral device control become very important. Digidesign provides a number of hardware interfaces that address the issues of timing and control of A/V equipment. We will discuss some of these connectivity issues in Chapter 9.

As a result of this integrated approach to the world of digital sound, the Pro Tools software and hardware environment presents the most comprehensive and unified system for audio on the market today.

Pro Tools software

As the power of personal computers has grown dramatically, it is now possible to utilize "light" versions of Pro Tools software that rely completely upon the native power of the computer. Although these systems have much less power than their TDM counterparts, they are truly part of this software family.

Today, the Digi 001, Digi 002, and Mbox systems offer the small project or voice-over studio a subset of the features of the larger TDM systems at a fraction of their price. If you don't have a need for a large number of tracks or extensive processing, these entry-level systems may be just the ticket for you. We will discuss these systems in Chapter 2.

Just as the DSP is scalable in the TDM systems, Pro Tools software utilizes a consistent and familiar working environment that permits users to migrate to larger systems easily. The interface in the LE (Limited Edition) software looks an awful lot like the interface of the full TDM software. The more expensive systems offer more features, but the packages look and feel very similar to the user.

In addition to the consistency of the user interface, Pro Tools has worked very hard to facilitate the movement of material between studios. This means, for example, that work done on smaller systems can be easily transferred to larger studios, where more complex processing and mastering work can be performed.

As we will see in Chapter 8, Pro Tools also makes it easy to collaborate with others—with tools that permit communication between studios, and that transfer not only audio information, but a great deal of Session information as well.

The package deal

Pro Tools offers a truly integrated hardware and software solution for the creation and editing of digital audio on personal computers. As a result of their meticulous attention to detail on all aspects of their product, Digidesign has developed a unified package that can be scaled to the end user's needs, and which can grow as those needs expand.

In my opinion, Pro Tools is the premier choice for audio and video work. And as you learn and work with this system, I am sure that you will concur.

I hope in the following pages to introduce you to the world of Pro Tools and assist you in wiring your studio, configuring your system, recording your first audio and MIDI data, transferring in synchronization using time code, importing, and exporting audio and MIDI, all the way to the burning of your first CD.

We cannot plumb the depths of Pro Tools here, but we can get you over the humps to get you started.

Where this journey ends is up to you.

Chilitos
www.audiographintl.com

CHAPTER ONE

Pro Tools TDM Concepts and Configurations

Some readers of this book have already purchased a Pro Tools TDM system and are seeking to get acquainted with their purchase. Others, having not yet made their purchase, need a little guidance in the selection of their hardware and software. Regardless of where you are, exploring Pro Tools TDM concepts and configurations will be very useful.

If you have not yet purchased your Pro Tools system, you will need to consider your specific needs. For example, are you going to record more than sixteen tracks at once? Will you concentrate solely on audio for video post-production? Will your mixes reside entirely in the Pro Tools domain? Are you producing audio books? Or, are you going to do mastering or simple editing?

In order to help purchase the Pro Tools TDM system that meets your needs, you need to have a clear understanding of Pro Tools TDM concepts and configurations and what they are capable of doing. In this chapter, we will discuss Pro Tools TDM concepts and basic terminology, and review the different TDM configurations by covering the following:

- What is a Pro Tools TDM system?
- What exactly is TDM?
- What can you do with TDM?
- What is DSP?
- What is a "Voice" in Pro Tools?
- What is a PCI card?
- Types of TDM configurations
- Different types of audio interfaces
- Computer requirements
- Compatible hard drives
- Memory requirements (RAM)
- Terminology

What is a Pro Tools TDM system?

Pro Tools TDM is a powerful and sophisticated non-linear hard disk recording and editing system manufactured by Digidesign. Using the power of a personal computer—either an Apple Macintosh or a Windows-based PC—this amazing hardware/software system lets you:

- record audio (music, sound effects, voices, etc.),
- edit the recorded or imported digital audio (copy, paste, separate, capture, etc.) without affecting the original file (non-destructive editing),
- mix and automate using internal DSP (Digital Signal Processors or plug-ins) and external (hardware) effects processors,
- master the final mix, and
- save the results to a Compact Disc, or in a wide range of file formats such as: MP3, AIFF, .WAV, and QuickTime.

If you are a composer or musician, Pro Tools also contains a full-featured MIDI sequencer which allows you to:

- record your own compositions and/or performances,
- edit the recorded MIDI information,
- control software and hardware MIDI synthesizers and samplers, and
- integrate these performances into your audio sessions.

Pro Tools is also well suited for audio/visual applications. You may:

- create audio for video post-production,
- edit and synchronize this audio with picture, and
- Playback the results to a wide variety of professional formats, including digital Beta or a ¾" tape machines, digital video by means of QuickTime movies, or Avid's Media Composer.

Just about the only thing that Pro Tools can't do in your studio is make a good cup of coffee.

What exactly is TDM?

Without being too technical, TDM stands for Time Division Multiplexing. Simply put, it is an incredibly fast 256-channel data bus with a resolution of 24 bits (in a Pro Tools 24 MIX-series).

If you are to think of TDM as a "high-speed data highway," Pro Tools would be an automated control center that routes and processes digital audio traffic using software based Plug-Ins (reverbs, EQs, delays, compressors, etc.) in real-time.

Pro Tools uses the TDM bus to internally route all connections within the digital realm, instead of cables to access external hardware. All data processing is performed using the processing power of the TDM hardware.

In order to achieve such complex real-time digital processing, TDM configurations require the installation of at least one Digidesign TDM PCI card (which is populated with dedicated DSP "chips") inside your computer.

Digidesign's latest systems—the Pro Tools HD-series—use a new and enhanced TDM II architecture which doubles the number of TDM channels ("time slots") from 256 to 512. TDM II also increases the number of connections you can make for routing signals within Pro Tools, greatly expanding Pro Tools' potential for mixing and real-time processing capabilities.

Regardless of the Pro Tools TDM hardware you choose (MIX-series or HD-series), all TDM-compatible PCI cards must be connected to one another within your computer or Pro Tools expansion chassis. To do this, MIX systems use a TDM Bus ribbon cable, while HD systems use a TDM II FlexCable. See Fig. 1.1 and 1.2 below.

Fig. 1.1 TDM Bus Ribbon cables.   **Fig. 1.2** FlexCable.

It wasn't always this good. Back in 1993, when Pro Tools software version 2.0 appeared, TDM had not been implemented. (TDM appeared with the release of Pro Tools III).

In those days, you did a lot of work one track at a time. For example, if you wanted to EQ a track, you had to export it to another piece of software known as Sound Designer II.

I also remember, you had to make a copy of the original track because any changes made to the original track in Sound Designer II were "destructive." Any change made to the original was permanent—so if you over-processed your source material, you could not return to the original (unless you had made that extra backup). After processing the track in Sound Designer II, you then had to import it back into Pro Tools to hear it in context with the other tracks.

Now, with TDM, you can do all the digital processing you want within the same software (Pro Tools) and without ever permanently modifying or destroying your original recording. All edits and plug-in settings (such as EQ or compression) are performed in real time—on all the tracks—each and every time you run a mix.

Because the source material is never changed, Pro Tools is considered to be a "non-destructive" editing system.

What can you do with TDM?

The Pro Tools mixing environment provides you with a customizable virtual mixing board (Fig. 1.3) with as many tracks (channel strips), and as many effect processors (plug-ins) as you need for your mix. The only limit is the amount of processing power available in your system.

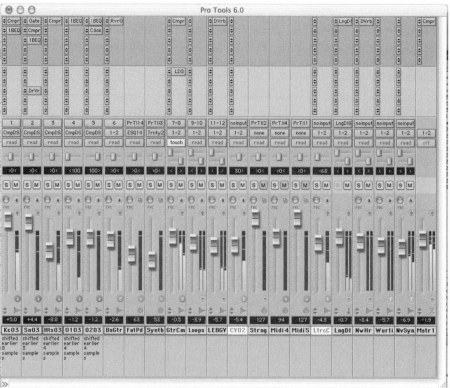

Fig. 1.3 Virtual mixing board from Pro Tools version 6.0.

If you don't know how many tracks you will need at the start of a project—or know how many of them your system can handle—just use one of the mixer templates that are supplied in the Pro Tools software installation CD-ROM (included when you purchase the system).

Each of the "channel strips" on this virtual mixing board provides you with:
- five Insert Points for signal processing—either external (outboard gear) or internal (using software processors or plug-ins),
- five Effects Sends to route any digital audio signal within Pro Tools or between Pro Tools and the outside world, and
- up to 64 internal 24-bit mix buses for complex digital signal routings and mixing. The number of buses available will depend on your Pro Tools system configuration.

When mixing on this Pro Tools virtual mixing board, you can automate:
- Volume
- Panning
- Mutes
- Send levels
- Send mutes
- Plug-in parameters
- Effects return levels from external outboard effect processors

A number of different types of faders (channel strips) can be created on the virtual mixing board, including:
- Mono and stereo audio track faders
- Master faders which can control a group of faders—such as your drum tracks—with a single fader, and without using up any DSP power
- AUX (auxiliary) input faders for use as effect returns—either for software effects (plug-ins) in Pro Tools, or external effects devices
- MIDI track faders to record and control MIDI data or import Standard MIDI Files (SMF) created in other sequencers
- Multi-channel audio tracks for surround mixing, including: LCR, Quad, LCRS, 5.0, 5.1, 6.0, 6.1, 7.0, and 7.1

What is DSP?

DSP stands for *Digital Signal Processing*. DSP is the most powerful element of Pro Tools, and is the reason you plug Pro Tools cards into your computer. The DSP chips plugged into these cards provide the real-time processing power of the TDM Mixer and the plug-ins in Pro Tools. See Fig. 1.4.

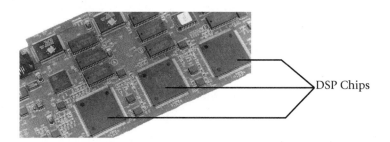

Fig. 1.4 TDM DSP Chips.

It is these DSP chips that do the work when you use plug-ins (Fig. 1.5) or digital effect processors in your session (such as compressors, delay units, reverb units, equalizers, etc.). In a sense, it is as if someone put a physical reverb unit in a box into one of the DSP chips. We'll talk more about plug-ins in Chapter 10.

Fig. 1.5 Pro Tools TDM Plug-ins.

TIP: Whenever you get software error messages—or have hardware problems—always look at the "Answerbase" document before you call Digidesign Technical Support. This file contains answers to many software and hardware problems you may encounter when using Pro Tools. You can find this document at the following location of your internal hard drive: Digidesign Folder > Pro Tools Folder > User Tools Folder > Answerbase Folder.

The more DSP chips you have in your TDM system, the more you can do in your sessions—more audio, more auxiliary inputs, more MIDI and master fader tracks, more plug-ins, more send assignments, etc.

When you do not have enough DSP power for the size of your sessions, you will see error messages like: "The plug-in could not be made active because there is not enough free DSP." When you outgrow the current capability of your system, the modular nature of Pro Tools means that you can always throw a little more hardware at the problem. Adding another DSP card will add more power to the system.

For example, when I found that I could not compress or EQ the guitar or background vocal that I had just added to a session, I just added more DSP chips to my own personal system—giving me a total of fifty-four DSP chips.

You will better understand these limitations when you start working on your first "big" gig using Pro Tools.

What is a "Voice" in Pro Tools?

The number of voices of a Pro Tools system is the number of tracks (instruments or sound effects) that the Pro Tools TDM configuration can record or play back simultaneously.

For those who have worked with old synthesizers, imagine a simple 8-voice synthesizer, which can sound only eight notes or keys at the same time. If you tried to play a ninth note, it wouldn't sound. In other words, voices are Pro Tools' polyphony.

As I mentioned earlier, depending on the configuration of a Pro Tools system, you can have from 32 to 128 voices in a system, meaning that you can record and play back from 32 to 128 mono tracks at the same time. Of course, if you use stereo or multi-channel (surround) tracks, the voice count will be reduced.

For example, in a Pro Tools | HD 1 system, you can record up to 256 tracks (96 mono tracks at a time), but you can only play back 96 tracks simultaneously—because the system is limited to 96 simultaneous voices at a sample rate of 44.1 kHz.

The number of voices available in a session is directly related to the sample rate being used. The higher the sample rate, the fewer the number of voices. For instance, if you ran a session at 192 kHz sample rate, the total number of "voiceable tracks" (previously known as "virtual tracks") would be reduced to 12 in an HD 1 system (Fig. 1.6).

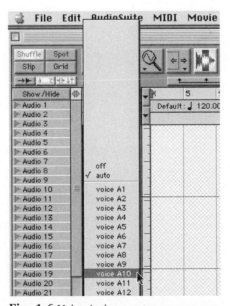

Fig. 1.6 Voice Assignment pop-up menu.

A session will often have more tracks than your system can play at one time. Since many of the tracks are not being used, you can tell the system which tracks should be played, and which should not. There are several ways to do this:

- select the track's voice assignment to "off" (Fig. 1.7a),
- make the track "inactive" in the File pop-up menu (Fig. 1.7b),
- don't assign any Output or Send to the track (Fig. 1.7c), or
- use the "track priority" technique where you can assign two tracks in the same voice, whichever track (with the same voice assigned) is in the left-most and top most position in the edit window (Fig. 1.7d) will have priority in playback.

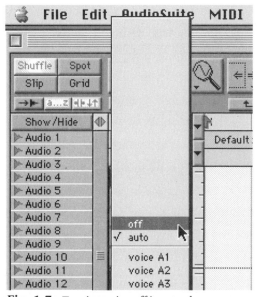

Fig. 1.7a Turning voice off in a track.

Fig. 1.7b Making a track inactive.

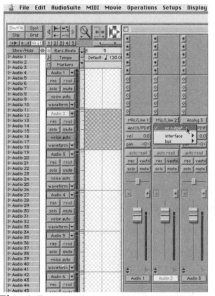

Fig. 1.7c No output assignment to a track.

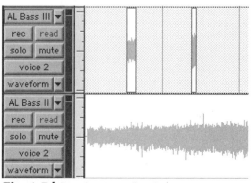

Fig. 1.7d "Track priority" technique.

By default, Pro Tools automatically assigns a voice to each newly created audio track—auto mode (Fig. 1.8). If you desire, you can bypass this assignment system using the "track priority" technique.

| off |
| √ auto |
| voice A1 |
| voice A2 |
| voice A3 |
| voice A4 |
| voice A5 |
| voice A6 |
| voice A7 |

Fig. 1.8
Track assigned to "auto mode."

What is a PCI card?

PCI is a computer bus standard for personal computers, and is an abbreviation for "Peripheral Component Interconnect." PCI provides a high-speed data path between your CPU and your peripheral components (such as video, disk, network, etc.). There are three or four slots in a computer's motherboard where the PCI cards are installed. The PCI bus comes in two sizes—32 and 64 bits—and runs at 33 MHz at 1.5 volts.

A "PCI card" is a printed circuit board that is filled with electronic components (analog and/or digital). Some of these PCI cards have an analog section and a digital section, depending on the PCI card's function.

Fig. 1.9 shows a photograph of Digidesign's SampleCell II PCI card. This card's function is a "sample player" which can play back compatible samples stored in your hard drive.

Fig. 1.9
Digidesign's
SampleCell II
PCI card.

Every Pro Tools TDM system configuration is comprised of one or more PCI cards. These cards contain the chips that add DSP power to the TDM systems.

A Pro Tools | 24 MIX system comes with one card, called the "MIX Core" card, which provides 64 tracks/16 channels of I/O 24-bit direct-to-disk recording and playback. A Pro Tools | HD 1 system comes with one card, called the "HD Core," which provides 96 tracks/32 channels of I/O (HD-series) of 24-bit direct-to-disk recording and playback.

Each of these systems can be expanded by the addition of more PCI cards. As you add more cards, you add more power to your system.

Types of TDM configurations

At the time of this writing the available Pro Tools TDM configurations are:
- Pro Tools | 24,
- Pro Tools | 24 MIX-Series (MIX, MIX Plus, and MIX3), and
- Pro Tools | HD-Series (HD 1, HD 2, and HD 3).

Pro Tools | 24

If you are looking for a simple TDM system (not Pro Tools LE), but you cannot spend too much money, and simple real-time processing tasks are all you want to do, a Pro Tools | 24 system may meet your needs.

By simple tasks, I mean functions that don't require a lot of DSP chips. This would include work such as:
- cleaning up few tracks that will be sent back to a tape machine for mixing on another analog or digital system,
- some mastering where you might only need four DSP chips,
- producing audio books, or
- working on simple ADR (Automatic Dialog Replacement), sound and/or music-editing post-production for video or TV where you have to synchronize the audio and the video with SMPTE time code.

You might only be able to buy this configuration used, as the HD systems have been introduced at the time of this writing. If you do buy a used system, make sure that you get the following items:
- two PCI cards,
- one 5-node TDM Bus ribbon cable (used to interconnect both cards),
- the Pro Tools software, and
- all of the instructional manuals.

Also, don't forget to ask for the registration card from the person or store you are buying it from. This way, you can register the system in your name to get the benefits that Digidesign offers, such as software updates.

One of Pro Tools | 24 PCI cards is known as the "d24" audio card, and the other is the "DSP Farm." See Fig. 1.10a and 1.10b.

Fig. 1.10a "d24" audio card.

Fig. 1.10b "DSP Farm" card.

The d24 audio card is designed to record direct-to-disk and play back up to 32 tracks (32 voices at 44.1 kHz) simultaneously at 24- or 16-bit resolutions, at sample rates of 44.1 kHz and 48 kHz.

With this system you have up to 32 virtual voices (voiceable tracks). If you create track #33, this track will be designated as "inactive." It won't be able to play back, unless you deactivate any one of the first 32 active tracks, or you use one of the techniques—such as track priority—that we mentioned before on page 8.

If you create a new audio track #33, Pro Tools will give you a message on the screen that reads, "There are more active audio tracks than available voices." As a result, one or more audio tracks will not play. Although you can record up to 43 tracks in Pro Tools | 24, your playback is limited to 32.

If you try to create more than 43 tracks, Pro Tools will inform you that "The maximum number of tracks already exists for the current Pro Tools configuration." Any audio track created after 43 will be automatically set to Voice Off in the voice assignment menu of the track itself. There is also a limit of 128 MIDI tracks for MIDI sequencing in Pro Tools.

As you move up through the Pro Tools system configurations (MIX and HD series) they will have more voices, and the number of audio tracks that can be recorded and played back simultaneously will increase. MIDI, though, will remain at 128 tracks regardless of configuration.

All Pro Tools TDM PCI cards—including the d24 audio card—have two types of connectors: a "DigiSerial" port and an "Audio Interface" port.

The "DigiSerial" port (See Fig. 1.11) is a serial port that can be connected to a synchronizer that outputs MIDI Time Code (MTC) such as the Universal Slave Driver I/O (MIX-series) and the SYNC I/O (HD-series)—both from Digidesign—so that Pro Tools can synchronize to external video or audio devices. This port also allows you to use a "9-pin" device for use with the Pro Tools Machine Control option.

The "Audio Interface" port (See Fig. 1.11) for the MIX-series (or the DigiLink for the HD-series) is used to connect your computer to your audio interfaces.

Audio Interfaces are rack-mounted hardware devices which convert external analog audio sources into digital form for use by Pro Tools, and which convert the Pro Tools digital data back into analog signals so you can listen to them or export them. These boxes are purchased separately.

The audio interface port gives you access to (up to) 16 digital or analog inputs and outputs (I/O's), depending upon which audio interface you use. (We will talk more about audio interfaces later.)

Using the cable that comes with your system will give you access to eight I/O's, meaning that you will be able to connect one eight I/O audio interface. (An exception is the 1622 I/O, which we will discuss later.) If you want to connect a second audio interface (for a total of 16 I/O's), you will have to connect a second interface cable to the DSP Farm PCI. (You will also have to assign the second interface in the Pro Tools software via the Playback Engine function under the Setups menu.)

Audio Interface port  DigiSerial port

Fig. 1.11 The DigiSerial and the Audio Interface ports.

If you want to connect three audio interfaces, for a total of 24 inputs and outputs, you will have to buy a 16-channel Peripheral Cable Adapter or "Y" cable. The "Y" cable goes to the d24 audio card, letting you connect two audio interfaces, and the third interface is connected on the "DSP Farm" card for a total of 24 I/O's (Fig. 1.12).

Fig. 1.12
The "Y" cable.

To an Audio Interface

To an Audio Interface

To the "d24" Audio card

The "DSP Farm" card provides the power needed for mixing, digital signal routing, real-time signal processing, and eight channels of I/O.

This card contains only four DSP chips, which limits the number of tracks on your virtual mixing board, and which will limit the number of plug-ins and effect sends you can use in a Pro Tools session. To open larger Pro Tools sessions, or to assign more plug-ins, you will need to add extra DSP Farm PCI cards (each containing another four DSP chips) to your system.

Basically, adding more DSP chips to your system will add more tracks and processing power to your Pro Tools sessions. While Pro Tools | 24 may not be the most powerful system, it may be all you need for simpler editing work.

Pro Tools | 24 MIX

If you need a slightly bigger system, you might look at the Pro Tools | 24 MIX system (Fig. 1.13). This system can play back up to 64 simultaneous audio tracks, integrate software samplers and synthesizers, perform advanced editing functions, synchronize with SMPTE time code, do surround-sound mixing, record up to 128 MIDI tracks, and perform small to medium-size mixes.

Pro Tools | 24 MIX includes:
- one PCI card called "MIX Core" (which contains six DSP chips, two more chips than Pro Tools | 24)
- the latest Pro Tools software
- all the instructional manuals.

Fig. 1.13 MIX Core PCI card.

The MIX Core PCI card's "Audio Interface" port normally lets you connect directly to one eight channel I/O device. If you need access to another eight channel device, you will have to purchase an optional "16-channel Peripheral Cable Adapter" or "Y" cable (available only for MIX-series systems).

An exception to this rule is when you utilize a 1622 I/O audio interface (16 analog inputs, two analog outputs, and two digital I/O's).

If you want to connect three audio interfaces for a total of 24 channels, then you will have to get an optional PCI card called "MIX I/O" card (Fig. 1.14), which is an I/O expansion card for 24-bit Pro Tools TDM systems. With this card you will be able to connect an additional 16 I/O channels for a total of 32 I/O's with both cards (MIX Core and MIX I/O) and using one "Y" cable with each card. Note that the MIX I/O card does not contain DSP chips; it is used only for extra audio inputs and outputs.

Fig. 1.14 The MIX I/O PCI card.

As I mentioned earlier, a MIX system has the capability to record and play back 32 or 64 simultaneous audio tracks, at sample rates of 44.1kHz and 48 kHz, and at 16 or 24 bits resolution. The system will record up to 86 audio tracks, but can only play back 32 or 64 at the same time. If you run out of "voiceable tracks," you can always use the "playlist" technique to free up voices.

Because you only have six DSP chips available in this system, you may have to monitor your DSP usage when you are working in a mix project. You can do this by looking at the "Show System Usage" window (Fig. 1.15), which is located in the "Windows" menu in the Pro Tools software.

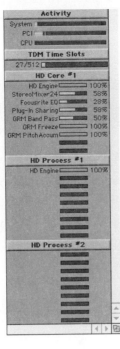

Fig. 1.15
The "Show System Usage" window shows how many DSP chips are available and used up by adding plug-ins to a Pro Tools session.

The "Show System Usage" window will help you make decisions as to what audio tracks or TDM plug-ins you need to deactivate or delete to make more DSP room to finish your mix.

If you cannot afford to expand your Pro Tools system when you need more DSP power, you also have the option of using Real Time and/or Non-Real-Time AudioSuite plug-ins. These plug-ins do not use the DSP chips on your Pro Tools PCI cards. Instead, they use the DSP power of your *host* computer, which means that your CPU or computer should be fast enough to handle the processing load. (More discussion on plug-ins, AudioSuite, and RTAS in Chapter 10.)

Pro Tools | 24 MIXplus

If a Pro Tools | 24 MIX does not meet your needs, you can purchase an additional PCI card—called "MIX Farm"—which contains six additional DSP chips for more power. Adding this card gives you a Pro Tools | 24 MIXplus system (Fig. 1.16).

A MIXplus system consists of:
- one MIX Core card,
- a MIX Farm card,
- a 5-node TDM Bus ribbon cable to interconnect both PCI cards,
- the latest version of Pro Tools software, and
- the instructional manuals.

A MIXplus system provides you with:

- 64 tracks of simultaneous audio recording and playback
- 86 virtual audio tracks
- 128 MIDI tracks
- Sample-accurate integration of audio and MIDI
- Up to 32 channels of I/O (expandable to 72 with additional cards)
- Up to five inserts and sends per track
- 64 internal mix busses
- Integrated multi-format surround mixing and processing
- DigiRack real-time and file-based plug-ins
- More than twice the DSP power of a Pro Tools|24 MIX system
- Full automation of all mixing and plug-in processing controls
- Advanced editing, tempo detection, and conforming
- DigiSerial port for connection of synchronization peripherals
- Comprehensive synchronization capabilities with the optional Universal Slave Driver (USD) or the SMPTE Slave Driver (SSD)

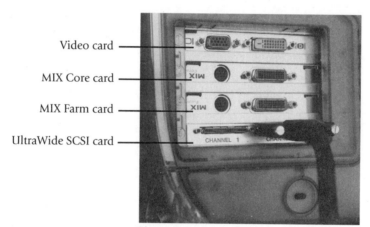

Fig. 1.16 A Pro Tools | 24 MIXplus system installed in a Macintosh G4.

All the PCI cards in the MIX-series systems contain a *DigiSerial* port and an *Audio Interface* port. If you want to connect a SMPTE generator/reader—such as the Universal Slave Driver (USD)—to your MIXplus system, you should use the MIX Core card DigiSerial connector for this purpose, and not the MIX Farm's.

The MIX Farm PCI card has another six DSP chips, making a total of 12 DSP chips for a Pro Tools | 24 MIXplus system. Of course, you can continue to add more MIX Farm cards for more DSP power and I/O channels. The two PCI cards in a Pro Tools MIXplus system will give you access to 32 analog or digital I/O's (16 per card, if you use two "Y" optional cables).

Pro Tools | 24 MIX3

A Pro Tools | 24 MIX3 system (Fig. 1.17) is designed for larger high-end music production and post-production studios. These systems are used for more complex mixing sessions that include surround sound mixing and audio for video post production.

A Pro Tools | 24 MIX3 system includes three PCI cards:

- one MIX Core audio card that is capable of recording 64 tracks simultaneously and process digital audio signals with its six DSP chips,
- two MIX Farm cards, each containing six DSP chips, making a total of 18 DSP chips in this system and having the capability to have access to 48 I/O's at the same time. That enables you to have six audio interfaces with eight I/O's each. You can expand your system to a maximum of 72 channels of I/O.

Adding a second MIX Farm card to a MIXplus system creates a Pro Tools | 24 MIX3 system.

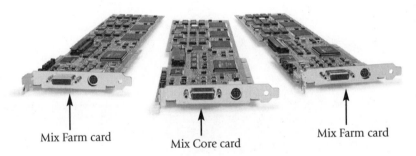

Mix Farm card   Mix Core card   Mix Farm card

Fig. 1.17 A Pro Tools | 24 MIX3 System.

Pro Tools | HD-Series

Digidesign launched a new generation of Pro Tools systems known as Pro Tools | HD (High Definition) during the Winter NAMM Show 2002.

End users started to ask me questions like, "Should I upgrade to Pro Tools HD if all I do is radio commercials?" or, "Do I really need a sampling rate of 96kHz or 192kHz for what I do?"

When I am asked these questions, I always have to ask:

a) do you have the budget,

b) do you have the storage capacity to record at 192kHz, and

c) what type of projects are you going to be working on?

Like the MIX-series, the Pro Tools HD-series comes in three different versions:
- Pro Tools | HD 1,
- Pro Tools | HD 2, and
- Pro Tools | HD 3.

The contents of a Pro Tools HD system will depend on which the system you select.

Pro Tools | HD 1

A Pro Tools | HD 1 system consists of:

- An "HD Core" PCI card,
- the latest version of the Pro Tools software, and
- the instructional manuals.

An HD 1 system (Fig. 1.18) has a total of nine DSP chips, and gives you access to up to 32 channels of I/O, and 96 simultaneous audio tracks at 44.1kHz or 48kHz sample rates.

HD Core PCI card.

Fig. 1.18 A Pro Tools | HD1 system.

Pro Tools | HD 2

A Pro Tools | HD 2 system consists of:
- An "HD Core" PCI card,
- one "HD Process" PCI card,
- one TDM FlexCable to interconnect both PCI cards,
- the latest version of the Pro Tools software, and
- the instructional manuals.

An HD 2 system (Fig. 1.19) has a total of 18 DSP chips, and gives you access to up to 64 channels of I/O, and 128 simultaneous audio tracks at 44.1kHz or 48kHz sample rates.

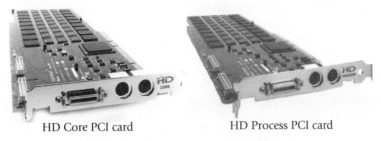

HD Core PCI card   HD Process PCI card

Fig. 1.19 A Pro Tools | HD2 system.

Pro Tools | HD 3

A Pro Tools | HD 3 system consists of:

- An "HD Core" PCI card,
- two "HD Process" PCI cards,
- two TDM FlexCables for interconnecting the three PCI cards,
- the latest version of the Pro Tools software, and
- the instructional manuals.

An HD 3 system (Fig. 1.20) has a total of 27 DSP chips, giving you access to up to 96 channels of I/O, and 128 simultaneous audio tracks.

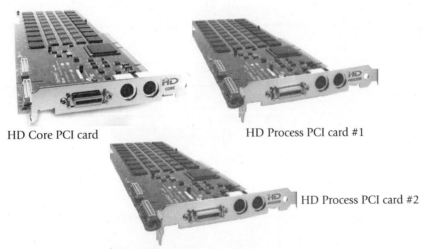

HD Core PCI card   HD Process PCI card #1

HD Process PCI card #2

Fig. 1.20 A Pro Tools | HD3 system.

Depending on Digidesign's promotional marketing strategy at the time of your purchase, you will also receive some TDM, AudioSuite, and Real Time AudioSuite (RTAS) plug-ins with your purchase of any HD system.

Of course, you can always expand your HD system by adding HD Process cards. You can use up to six HD Process cards with a single HD Core card.

Adding extra Process cards will not expand the number of audio tracks beyond the HD limit of 128 tracks, but will increase the DSP power of your system.

A side-by-side comparison of the MIX and HD series might be helpful in understanding their basic differences:

Mix Series	**HD	Series**
a) Pro Tools 24 MIX (6 DSP chips) (One Mix Core PCI card)	a) Pro Tools HD	1 (9 DSP chips) (One HD Core PCI card)
b) Pro Tools 24 MIXplus (12 DSP chips) (One Mix Core and Mix Farm PCI cards)	b) Pro Tools HD	2 (18 DSP chips) (One HD Core and HD Process PCI cards)
c) Pro Tools 24 MIX 3 (18 DSP chips) (One Mix Core and Two Mix Farm PCI cards)	c) Pro Tools HD	3 (27 DSP chips) (One HD Core and Two HD Process PCI cards)
d) Up to 64 tracks at 44.1 and 48kHz	d) Up to 128 tracks at 44.1 and 48kHz
e) 44.1kHz and 48kHz sampling rates only	e) 44.1kHz, 48kHz, 88.2kHz, 96kHz, 176.4kHz, and 192kHz sampling rates
f) Six DSP chips per PCI card	f) Nine DSP chips per PCI card
g) 16 channels of I/O from each PCI card	g) 32 channels of I/O from each PCI card
h) Can open sessions with up to 86 audio tracks	h) Can open sessions with up to 256 audio tracks
i) Can play a maximum of 64 tracks	i) Can play a maximum of 128 tracks
j) TDM Architecture with 256 time slots	j) TDM II architecture with 512 time slots (larger mixing configurations)

The track count on the HD-series will drop as you select higher sampling rates. For example, if you select a sampling rate of 192kHz on an HD | 1 system, you will only have access to 12 tracks. If you have an HD | 2 (adding an HD Process card) you'll have access to 24 tracks at the sampling rate of 192kHz.

As I mentioned earlier, you will have to make a decision to acquire an HD system based on your budget and type of projects. These systems work on both Macintosh and Windows-based PC platforms.

Different types of audio interfaces

An audio interface is a device that converts your analog sound sources into digital format for use in your digital editing system. The audio interface then converts the results of your digital edits back into analog form, so that you can listen to the results on your speakers.

None of the Pro Tools TDM system configurations mentioned above include an audio interface. You must purchase at least one audio interface in order to record or play back audio. The Digidesign audio interfaces are all given a name or number, followed by the letters "I/O," standing for Input/Output (e.g.,192 I/O, 96 I/O, 888 I/O, 1622 I/O, 882 I/O, and ADAT Bridge I/O).

The audio interface you purchase will depend upon the type of Pro Tools system series you own.

The audio interfaces for the Pro Tools 24 | MIX-series include the:
- 888 I/O (16-bit) and the 888 | 24 I/O
- 882 I/O (16-bit) and the 882 | 20 I/O
- 1622 I/O
- ADAT Bridge I/O (16-bit) and the 24-bit ADAT Bridge I/O

The audio interfaces for the Pro Tools | HD-series include the:
- 192 I/O
- 192 Digital I/O
- 96 I/O

The "Legacy" ports of the 192 and the 96 I/O boxes also enable you to utilize some of the "older" interfaces, including:
- 888|24 I/O
- 882|20 I/O
- 1622 I/O
- 24-bit ADAT Bridge I/O
- 16-bit ADAT Bridge I/O

888 I/O audio interface

The 888 I/O audio interface (Fig. 1.21) provides you with eight analog inputs and outputs (I/O's) with XLR connectors (balanced lines) at sample rates of 44.1kHz or 48kHz. You can use either the 16-bit or 24-bit versions of the 888 I/O with Pro Tools MIX-series. When you are recording, an 888 I/O can take in up to eight analog sources (such as microphones) at a time. Although most professional equipment operates a level of +4dBu, the 888 I/O can also be set to work with studio equipment operating at levels of –10dBV.

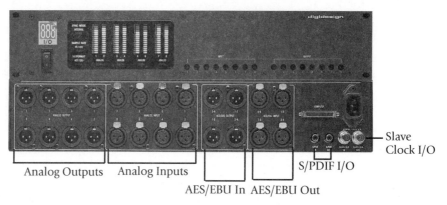

Analog Outputs   Analog Inputs   S/PDIF I/O   Slave Clock I/O

AES/EBU In AES/EBU Out

Fig. 1.21 An 888 | 24 I/O audio interface.

The 888 I/O also offers eight digital inputs and outputs (I/O's), so that you can also connect this interface to other digital equipment. You can use any combination of digital and analog I/O's, making this a very versatile box. These setups are made from within Pro Tools, in the Setups > Hardware pop-up menu.

The 888 I/O contains eight digital inputs and outputs, offering both AES/EBU and S/PDIF digital formats. You can even combine both formats, with two I/O's of S/PDIF and six of AES/EBU.

Please note that S/PDIF in the 888 I/O works only on channels 1 & 2. If you want to digitally record from, or export to, a DAT machine via S/PDIF format, assign the input or output to channels 1 & 2. Channels 5 & 6, for example, will not work with S/PDIF. Again, these assignments are made from within Pro Tools, in the Setups > Hardware pop-up menu.

One big advantage that the 888 I/O has over the other MIX-series audio interfaces is that it has eight LED meters for reading Pro Tools track output (not input) levels. You can also adjust your input and output levels with the front panel trimmers on the 888 I/O, just like we used to calibrate an analog tape machine.

Both versions have "Slave Clock In" and "Slave Clock Out" (called 256x

Super Clock) for synchronizing with other Digidesign audio interfaces within the same Pro Tools TDM system.

882 I/O audio interface

The 882 I/O (Fig. 1.22) features eight analog inputs and outputs (I/O's) with ¼" TRS connectors (balanced lines) at sample rates of 44.1kHz and 48kHz, and comes in 16- and 20-bit versions. This unit also features two S/PDIF digital I/O's. If you need to do a digital transfer from a DAT machine that has only AES/EBU digital format outputs, you will need to use a separate digital audio format converter.

Analog In — Analog Out — Slave Clock I/O — S/PDIF

Fig. 1.22
An 882 | 20 I/O
audio interface.

Like all Pro Tools audio interfaces, the 882 I/O includes the Slave Clock I/O. This is not regular word clock output signal, but 256 times the word clock, which Digidesign calls "Super Clock."

The 882 I/O does not have LED meters for reading output levels, like the 888 I/O. It does include eight LEDs (one for each channel) that display signal activity only. The inability to visually monitor Pro Tools output levels can be a serious disadvantage.

This audio interface is for those who cannot spend too much money, or for those who do not have the need for 24-bit I/O's. You can also use the 882 I/O as a digital patch bay for routing signals from Pro Tools to and from external signal processors (in the event that you don't have a good selection of plug-ins or enough DSP power for such processing).

1622 I/O audio interface

If your are a musician, a sound editor, or a sound designer who works with a lot of synthesizers, samplers, effect devices, electric guitars, or any other line level device, the 1622 I/O (Fig. 1.23) may be a good choice for you.

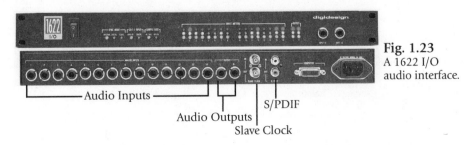

Audio Inputs — Audio Outputs — Slave Clock — S/PDIF

Fig. 1.23
A 1622 I/O
audio interface.

This audio interface has 16 channels of 20-bit analog inputs with ¼" TRS connectors, and two 24-bit analog outputs (¼" TRS). The 1622 also has two channels of 24-bit S/PDIF Digital I/O with sample rates of 44.1kHz and 48kHz.

The 1622 also includes 16 internal adjustable input gain levels controlled by the Pro Tools software, unlike any of the other TDM audio interfaces.

ADAT Bridge I/O

The ADAT Bridge I/O (Fig. 1.24) is designed for those who need to perform digital transfer to and from any Alesis ADAT, ADAT XT, M20, and other ADAT-compatible devices.

I am sure that some of you have (I know I have) recorded many projects on ADAT. The ADAT Bridge I/O is a great way to transfer those projects into Pro Tools, and to get rid of all those bulky S-VHS tapes lying around your studio.

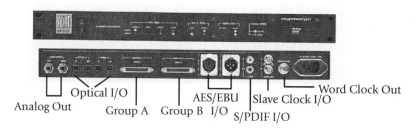

Fig. 1.24 An ADAT Bridge I/O.

An ADAT Bridge I/O can transfer 16 digital audio tracks (two S-VHS tapes) at a time, at sample rates of 44.1kHz or 48kHz. To transfer 24 tracks (three S-VHS tapes), you will need a synchronizer to align the tracks when you transfer the third tape, or you will need to purchase a second unit. Depending on the size of your Pro Tools system, you can connect up to five ADAT Bridge I/O's, for a total of 72 channels of I/O.

The ADAT Bridge I/O has two analog outputs (24-bit D/A converters) with a ¼" TRS connectors for monitoring Pro Tools. It also offers two channels of 24-bit digital ins and outs with AES/EBU or S/PDIF digital formats. These connections let you transfer two channels of digital audio at the time to and from a DAT machine, an external CD burner, or any other device with digital I/O's.

Unlike other Digidesign interfaces, the ADAT Bridge I/O offers a standard word clock output. It also has "Slave Clock In" and "Slave Clock Out" connectors with 256x "Super Clock" to synchronize your Pro Tools/ADAT system with other external synchronization sources.

The ADAT Bridge I/O has been offered in 16-bit and 24-bit versions. As of this writing, the 16-bit version has been discontinued, but you might be able to find a used one at a good price.

HD interfaces

If you just purchased—or intend to purchase—a Pro Tools HD system, you will need at least one 192 I/O or one 96 I/O audio interface in order for your HD system to operate.

You can use some of the older audio interfaces with a 192 or 96 I/O by plugging them into the "legacy" ports of these I/O's. The audio interfaces you can use with an HD system are:

- the 888|24 I/O
- the 882|20 I/O
- the 1622 I/O
- the 24-bit ADAT Bridge I/O
- the 16-bit ADAT Bridge I/O

TIP: If you are going to be using your "legacy" interfaces in conjunction with your HD system, you cannot create Pro Tools sessions above 48kHz since the highest sample rate these audio interfaces can handle is 48kHz.

Some of the older audio interfaces, which run at 16 bits, cannot be used with these "legacy" ports. They are:

- the 888 | 16 I/O
- the 882 | 16 I/O

192 I/O audio interface

The 192 I/O is a 16-channel, 24-bit audio interface for Pro Tools HD-series. This interface can record and play back at sampling frequencies of 44.1kHz, 48kHz, 88.2kHz, 96kHz, 176.4kHz, and 192kHz. It is the most advanced audio interface ever offered by Digidesign.

If you take a look at the back panel of a 192 (Fig. 1.25), you will see that it has four I/O bays with DB-25 type of connectors, instead of the typical ¼", RCA, or XLR types. At first, I viewed this as inconvenient, since you have to make or buy "snakes" (audio cables) to connect Pro Tools in your studio. To expedite studio hookup, Digidesign offers pre-made snakes that are designed for the 192 I/O, which they call "DigiSnakes."

But when I started counting up how many different connections are being made through these DB-25 connectors, I quickly realized that this is the only way they could have offered so many formats on a single machine.

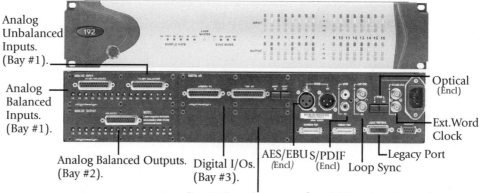

Analog Unbalanced Inputs. (Bay #1).

Analog Balanced Inputs. (Bay #1).

Optical (Encl)

Ext.Word Clock

Analog Balanced Outputs. (Bay #2).　Digital I/Os. (Bay #3).　AES/EBU *(Encl)*　S/PDIF *(Encl)*　Loop Sync　Legacy Port

Bay #4-Remains empty for additional audio card.

Fig. 1.25 192 I/O Audio Interface.

The 192 I/O Bays:

If you examine the back of the 192, you will see that it has four bays for audio ins and outs. The configuration that comes with the 192 is:

- Bay #1— Analog balanced inputs (+4dBu and –10 dBV)
- Bay #2— Analog balanced outputs (+4dBu)
- Bay #3— Digital I/O's (AES/EBU, T-DIF, and Lightpipe)
- Bay #4— The fourth bay is the blank bay in the middle, on the bottom of the interface. You can add another audio card here to expand the capabilities of your studio.

Analog Inputs

The analog input (Bay #1) has two DB-25 connectors. The connector on the left lets you connect to eight channels of 24-bit balanced inputs at +4dBu. The connector on the right lets you connect to eight channels of 24-bit balanced inputs at –10dBV.

You are able to select which of these two connectors will be used from within Pro Tools in the "Hardware Setup" menu. The Input Trim—and a Soft Clip Limiter function, which helps to avoid digital clipping—can also be selected from within Pro Tools. Pairs of dedicated Input Trims for each channel are located under the DB-25 connectors.

Analog Outputs

Bay #2 contains eight channels of 24-bit analog balanced outputs operating at +4dBu. The analog outputs also have output trims to individually calibrate each channel's output level.

If you are going to connect the 192 I/O outputs to –10dBV inputs of other equipment, Digidesign recommends the purchase of a special DigiSnake cable. If you want to make your own, be sure to use in-line transformers or resistor networks to properly pad the +4dBu outputs to –10dBV input levels.

The Digital I/O's

The Digital I/O card (Bay #3) contains:

- Eight channels of 24-bit AES/EBU digital I/O at sample rates up to 96kHz. (If you want to work at a sample rate of 192kHz, you will only get four channels.)
- Eight channels of T-DIF ins and outs at sample rates of 44.1kHz and 48kHz (for Tascam MDMs)
- Eight channels of 24-bit Lightpipe at sample rates of 44.1kHz and 48kHz (for Alesis ADATs or any ADAT compatible devices)

The 192 I/O Digital I/O card recognizes the most commonly used digital transfer formats, and provides real-time sample-rate conversion for each digital input.

This means that you can directly import a digital audio source recorded at 48kHz (DA-88, ADAT, DATs, etc.) into a Pro Tools session running at 96kHz. The digital audio will be converted to 96kHz automatically, meaning that you won't have to convert each file separately.

Enclosure Connectors [Encl]

The right side of the 192 I/O's back panel contains another set of additional digital I/O's. The ports in this section do not support real-time sample-rate conversion, so be careful when transferring digital audio through these connectors.

The connectors on the "Enclosure" section are:

- AES/EBU [Encl]—These two Cannon connectors provide 24-bit stereo AES/EBU digital I/O at sample rates up to 96kHz
- S/PDIF [Encl]—These two RCA connectors provide 24-bit stereo S/PDIF digital I/O audio sample rates up 96kHz
- Optical (ADAT) [Encl]—These two Toslink connectors provide eight tracks of digital I/O, with sample rates of 44.1kHz and 48kHz, for any Lightpipe device (such as ADATs, sound cards, or digital mixing boards). This port can also accept and deliver two channels of optical S/PDIF at sample rates up to 96kHz, if you select this mode in the "Hardware Setups" menu in Pro Tools.

Other features of the 192 I/O are:

- the 192 has input and output signal-level metering, unlike the 888 I/O, which only shows output levels on its eight LED meters
- it has a "Legacy" port to connect "old" Digidesign audio interfaces
- LOOP SYNC In and Out connectors are provided to connect several HD-series interfaces together and keep them synchronized
- the Ext. Clock In and Out connectors accept and emit a word clock signal that will synchronize the 192 I/O with any other device that requires word clock or 256x slave clock
- you can connect up to eight units for a maximum of 96 channels of I/O at 96kHz

96 I/O audio interface

If you don't want to spend too much money on an HD-series audio interface, don't need T-DIF inputs and outputs, and don't need a 192 kHz sampling rate, then the 96 I/O may be for you.

The 96 I/O (Fig. 1.26) is a 16-channel audio interface for Pro Tools HD that can record and play back sampling frequencies up to 96kHz. Other supported sampling frequencies in the 96 I/O are 44.1kHz, 48kHz, and 88.2kHz.

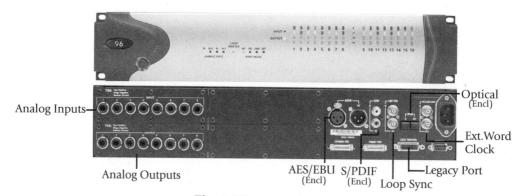

Fig. 1.26 96 I/O Audio Interface.

Analog I/O

The 96 I/O has eight balanced 24-bit analog ins with ¼" TRS connectors. Unbalanced connections are supported, and you can set the input operating levels to +4dBu or –10dBV.

The 96 I/O has eight balanced 24-bit analog outs using ¼" TRS connectors. Unbalanced connections are also supported, meaning you can select output operating levels to +4dBu or –10dBv, (unlike the 192 I/O).

Digital I/O

The 96 I/O has all the digital transfer formats found on the 192 I/O, except for T-DIF. The digital connections on the 96 I/O are:

- AES/EBU—This pair of XLR digital I/O's accepts two channels of 24-bit digital audio sources at sample rates up to 96kHz
- S/PDIF—These RCA connectors accept two channels of 24-bit digital audio at sample rates up to 96kHz
- Optical I/O—These Toslink optical connectors receive and send eight channels of Lightpipe (ADAT) digital information, at sample rates up to 48kHz. These connectors also function as a stereo input/output of S/PDIF optical. The highest sample rate supported is 96kHz

Other features of the 96 I/O include:

- sxteen LED meters can be switched to read input or output levels
- a "legacy" port to connect other MIX-series audio interfaces, just like the 192 I/O
- a word clock and loop sync inputs and outputs for synchronizing multiple 96 I/O's and 192 I/O's, and for any other device that requires word clock or 256x slave clock signals

Other requirements needed for a Pro Tools TDM system

In addition to the PCI cards, Pro Tools software, and audio interfaces discussed above, your Pro Tools TDM system will also require a number of other components, such as:

- a computer (often referred to as a CPU),
- an external hard drive (SCSI or FireWire),
- RAM requirements,
- "x" number of PCI slots,
- an external floppy disk, and
- a computer monitor, etc.

In this next section, I will discuss some of those requirements and options needed for a complete and functional Pro Tools TDM system. Of course, these components will vary depending upon the type of Pro Tools system configuration you are building, and perhaps most important, your budget.

Computer Requirements

The following information is for those of you who are contemplating the purchase of a new or used Pro Tools system.

I highly recommend that you frequently visit Digidesign's web site at www.digidesign.com to stay current with the latest system requirements and compatibility information for both Macintosh and Windows-based PC platforms (Fig. 1.27).

Fig. 1.27 Apple Macintosh Power Mac G4 867MHz Dual Processor and Compaq Presario 8000.

As of this writing, the computer and operating system requirements for Pro Tools MIX-series and HD-series systems are:

For Pro Tools | 24 MIX-series (Macintosh)

The following Mac systems are certified for use with Mix Series systems:

- Power Mac G4 Single Processor with AGP graphics or PCI graphics at 350MHz, 400MHz, 450MHz, 466MHz, 500MHz, 533MHz, 667MHz, 733MHz, 800MHz, 867MHz, or 933MHz
- Power Mac G4 (Dual Processor) at 450MHz, 500MHz, 533MHz, 800MHz, 867MHz, 1GHz, 1.25GHz.
- Power Macintosh Blue & White G3.
- Power Macintosh Beige G3.
- Power Macintosh 9500 or 9600.
- PowerBook G4 (requires a Magma two-slot or four-slot CardBus PCI Expansion System)

The Mac Operating Systems certified for use with the Mix Series include the Mac OS v9.0.4, 9.1, 9.2, 9.2.1, 9.2.2, or OS X (depending on CPU model).

For Pro Tools | HD-series (Macintosh)

The following Mac systems are certified for use with HD Series systems:
- a Power Mac G4 Single Processor with AGP graphics running at 350MHz, 400MHz, 450MHz, 466MHz, 500MHz, 533MHz, 667MHz, 733MHz, 800MHz, 867MHz, or 933MHz
- a Power Mac G4 Dual Processor running at 500MHz, 533MHz, 800MHz, 867MHz, 1GHz, or 1.25GHz
- a Titanium PowerBook G4 (with Magma CB4DRQ-D1 four-slot CardBus PCI Expansion System)

The Mac Operating Systems certified for use with the HD Series include Mac OS v9.1, 9.2, 9.2.1, 9.2.2 or OS X (depending on CPU model).

For Pro Tools | 24 MIX-series (Windows)

A PC with Pentium 3 or Pentium 4 processor is required for a Pro Tools | Mix Series with Windows.

The following computers are qualified to provide up to 64-track performance and full Pro Tools functionality:
- IBM IntelliStation M Pro—model 6850
- IBM IntelliStation E Pro—model 6846 (discontinued)
- IBM IntelliStation M Pro—model 6889 (discontinued)

Other IntelliStation M Pro & E Pro models are not qualified.

For these PC computers you need one of the following operating systems:
- Windows XP Professional Edition,
- Windows XP Home Edition, or
- Windows 2000.

For Pro Tools | HD-series (Windows)

The following computers have been qualified to provide up to 128-track performance and full Pro Tools functionality:
- Compaq EVO W8000.
- IBM IntelliStation M Pro—model 6850

For these PC computers, you need one of the following operating systems:
- Windows XP Professional Edition, or
- Windows XP Home Edition.

PCI slot considerations

The computers mentioned above vary in the number of PCI slots they come in from the factory. It is very important to know how many PCI cards your Pro Tools system will need, so you will make the right computer selection.

For example, let's say you have a new G4 with four PCI slots, and you want to install a Pro Tools | HD 3 (three PCI cards). Since Digidesign recommends the use of a SCSI (Small Computer Systems Interface) accelerator card to connect an additional external or internal hard drive for better system performance and full Pro Tools functionality, you can use the fourth slot for your SCSI controller.

But if you have a G4 with three PCI slots, and you want to install a Pro Tools | HD 3, you would need an extra PCI slot in your computer. Your choice at this point is to buy another computer, or add a PCI Expansion Chassis (Fig. 1.28.a and 1.28.b) to your system.

These expansion chassis are also used when folks want to expand their Pro Tools systems with additional process cards.

Fig. 1.28a two-slot PCI Expansion Chassis. **Fig. 1.28b** seven-slot PCI Expansion Chassis.

Hard drive requirements

Digidesign recommends the use of one (or several) external (or internal) SCSI hard drive(s) with rotational speeds of 10,000 RPM (revolutions per minute) dedicated for audio in order to simultaneously record and play back a large number of audio tracks with substantial edit densities and large amounts of cross-fades.

The following SCSI hard drives are recommended by Digidesign:

- DigiDrive from Digidesign
- rS, iS Plus, and iS Pro from Avid
- Cheetah or Barracuda from Seagate
- Ultrastar from IBM

If you bought your computer in the last three years, it is very likely that it will not have a built-in SCSI hard drive controller. This means that you will need to add a qualified SCSI HBA (Host Bus Adapter) or SCSI accelerator card to connect your external SCSI hard drive in order to maximize the track count in your Pro Tools system.

The most popular SCSI cards used for Pro Tools are made by ATTO Technology, Inc. and Adaptec (Fig. 1.29 and 1.30). Digidesign's web site keeps an updated list of all the SCSI cards qualified for use with the Pro Tools MIX-series and HD-series. Visit www.digidesign.com for more information.

Fig. 1.29 ATTO SCSI card.   **Fig. 1.30** Adaptec SCSI card.

In the best of all worlds, you would *not* use the internal boot drive of your computer for recording with Pro Tools. The intense I/O requirements of this work require frequent reformatting or de-fragging of these disks between projects.

Although it is possible to use your internal IDE/ATA hard drive for recording and playback of audio, the number of tracks may vary, and there is no guarantee of maximum Pro Tools performance.

According to Digidesign, "up to 32-track, 24-bit, 48KHz performance from one dedicated internal IDE/ATA audio drive is supported on qualified G3 and G4 Pro Tools systems." Such drives must meet the following requirements:

- disk drive rotational speed must be 7200 RPM or faster,
- average seek time must be less than 10.0ms,
- the drive must be supported by the UDMA66 controller,

- the drive must be dedicated for audio, and
- the drive should be initialized with Apple Drive Setup as HFS or HFS+ file systems.

If you must use your IDE/ATA internal drive for recording, you will want to partition your drive into two (or more) parts. One partition should be reserved for use by the operating system and all programs. The larger partition(s) can then be used for recording. This will let you de-frag your audio partitions without any concerns of damaging your operating system or your programs.

It is possible to use a FireWire hard drive (with a rotational speed of 7200 RPM) with your TDM system. The supported track count at 48KHz and 24-bit resolution is 24 tracks per drive, with a maximum of two FireWire drives being used at a time, for a total of 48 tracks.

As of this writing, one FireWire hard drive qualified by Digidesign is the DigiDrive FireWire 80 (Fig. 1.31). Digidesign maintains a list of FireWire drives made by other manufacturers that may work with Pro Tools at www.digidesign.com.

Fig. 1.31 DigiDrive FireWire.

Estimating hard disk requirements

To record and play back audio in Pro Tools, you will need a large amount of hard drive space, especially if you record at higher sample rates and require a lot of tracks.

To give you some idea of the amount of storage you will need on your hard drive, one minute of monaural audio (one track) recorded at a sample rate of 44.1kHz and at 16-bit resolution will consume five megabytes (MB) of storage. That means that 16 tracks will chew up 80 megabytes in one minute. Higher sample rates and higher resolutions will take even more.

To calculate how much storage a project will take, you need to know the sample rate you will use, how many tracks you will need, the bit rate (resolution) you want to use, and the length of the piece.

This calculation can be done by using the following formula:

Number of bytes = (samples per second) x (number of tracks) x (number of nits of resolution/8) x (number of seconds recorded (or number of minutes x 60)).

Divide the result by 1,048,576 to convert the result in bytes to megabytes.

For example, let's say we want to record five minutes of digital audio on 24 tracks at 44.1kHz and 16-bit resolution.

Plugging the numbers into the formula we get the following result:

(44100Hz) x (24 tracks) x (16-bits/8) x (5 minutes) x 60 = 635,040,000 bytes.

To convert to megabytes, divide: 635,040,000 by 1,048,576. The result is 605.62MB.

This formula will come in handy during one of your sessions if you are concerned whether or not you will have enough hard drive space for a session.

RAM requirements

You can never have too much memory (RAM) for your computer system. Depending on the configuration of your computer, the amount of RAM in your machine will vary from 128MB to 2GB.

RAM is not nearly as expensive as it was a few years ago, so I highly recommend that you install as much RAM as you can afford in your computer. The minimum RAM requirement for Pro Tools MIX-series and the HD-series is 256 MB. You will need more much more than this if your session has a lot of edits, uses a lot of plug-ins, and records and plays back more than 64 simultaneous audio tracks.

Terminology

Some terms are used over and over again in the world of Pro Tools, and can be confusing to the new user. Here are the definitions for a few terms that you will be seeing throughout this book.

Session

Whenever you start a new project by selecting the "New Session" command in the File pop-up menu in the Pro Tools software, a folder will be created with the name of the session you provided. Inside of this folder you will see two folders and a "reel tape" icon. The icon will have the name of the session. The "tape reel" icon on the right side of Fig. 1.32 is the session ("New Session").

A session is everything you see in the Pro Tools "Edit Window." This file contains all your words, all your edits, all the audio and MIDI tracks you created, all input and output assignments, and all your mixing automation, etc. This file does not contain the audio files themselves, and does not take much memory—maybe a few kilobytes. You can make many copies (backups) of this file without consuming much hard disk space.

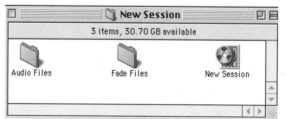

Fig. 1.32 A Pro Tools session generates an Audio Files folder, a Fade Files folder, and the session itself ("tape icon").

Audio Files

As you can see in Fig. 1.32 (above), an Audio Files folder is also created when you start a new Pro Tools session. All the recorded and imported sounds are stored in this folder in the form of audio files, which can be of any format Pro Tools can create, such as: SDII, AIFF, .WAV, MP3, QuickTime, etc. This folder is where the heavy storage goes on.

Fade Files

A Fade Files folder is also created when you start a new session. All the cross-fades, fade-ins, and fade-outs that you create in the edit window are stored in this folder.

Region

A region is the digital information (waveform) used to visually represent an entire audio or MIDI file stored in the hard drive. A region (a verse, a chorus, or the intro of a song) can be separated, captured, copied, and repeated, etc., to create an entire musical piece, if so desired. See Fig. 1.33.

Fig. 1.33 A Pro Tools audio region in an audio track.

Track

A track is where audio or MIDI information is recorded and played back. You can create additional audio or MIDI tracks when you are editing in which to place new edited audio or MIDI regions, for example. (See Fig. 1.33 and Fig. 1.34).

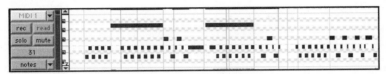

Fig. 1.34 A Pro Tools MIDI region in a MIDI track.

Channel

Channels in Pro Tools are the physical connections (input/output) on the back of your audio interface (Fig. 1.35). For example, a Pro Tools | HD 1 system can record and play back up to 96 tracks simultaneously, but could only have eight channels using one audio interface.

If you want to mix your song with an external mixing board, then you will need to use more channels. That is, you will need more than one audio interface if you want to export more than eight tracks.

Fig. 1.35 An 888 I/O rear panel showing eight analog I/O channels.

CHAPTER TWO

Pro Tools LE Systems

2

Whether you are an entry-level or an advanced Pro Tools user, a Pro Tools LE system can be an incredible digital audio recording and editing tool. A studio that uses a Pro Tools TDM system can use an LE system as a second digital audio editing station. Since files can move back and forth between TDM and LE systems, you can track in the main room using your TDM system, while your assistant "comps" vocals or auto-tunes tracks on your LE system in another room.

A Pro Tools LE system is both affordable and portable, providing an incredible "bang for the buck." All recent models have headphone outs, so you can record or edit anything and anywhere you want—in the living room, in the hotel room, even on an airplane—no kidding.

Unlike the TDM systems, LE systems perform all real-time digital audio recording, editing, mixing, routing, and processing using the DSP power of the host computer. For this reason, if you purchase an LE system, you should install it on the fastest computer you can afford. With a faster computer, you can record more audio tracks, perform more digital signal routing, and use more real-time processing (plug-ins).

LE systems can be installed on either a Macintosh (Mac OS 9.x and Mac OS X) or a PC (Windows or XP).

There are several Pro Tools LE system configurations available to choose from, including: the Digi 002, the Digi 002R, the Mbox, the Digi 001, AudioMedia III, Digi Tool/Box, or Pro Tools Free.

In this chapter we will cover configurations of the following Pro Tools LE systems:

- Digi 002,
- Digi 002R,
- Mbox, and
- Digi 001.

We will also cover the following topics related to LE systems:

- Connections and applications with the various Pro Tools LE systems.
- Pro Tools LE compatibility chart.
- Software features missing in a LE system.

Configuring Pro Tools LE systems
The Digi 002

As of this writing, the Digi 002 (Fig. 2.1) is the latest addition to the Pro Tools LE family. This LE system is a self-contained Pro Tools digital audio workstation that includes:

- Pro Tools LE software,
- up to 18 simultaneous analog and digital audio inputs and outputs,
- a MIDI interface (one in, two outs),
- four Focusrite microphone preamps,
- one headphone output,
- a stereo monitor output,
- a footswitch jack, and perhaps best of all,
- FireWire connectivity.

Firewire connectivity means higher data transfers, and you don't have to turn your computer off every time you need to connect an external hard drive or any other FireWire device! The convenience of this has to be experienced to be fully appreciated.

If you use a Mac with the 002, the Firewire connection means that you will not need to add a PCI card to your computer. If you use a PC, you will have to install a compatible FireWire card in your computer.

In addition to being used with a computer, the Digi 002 can also be used without a computer as a standalone 8x2 digital mixer, complete with four effects sends (two internal and two external), EQ, dynamics, effects, and snapshots.

This dual use makes the 002 a truly unique machine in the world of digital audio recording.

Mic/Line/Inst
Input controls

Monitor section

Console/Channel
View section

Status Indicators
and Display
controls

Keyboard
Modifiers
switches

Transport and
Navigation
controls

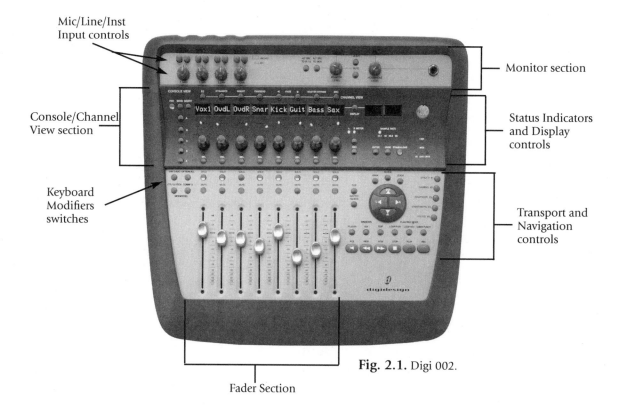

Fig. 2.1. Digi 002.

Fader Section

The Digi 002 can record and play back:

- up to 128 MIDI tracks,
- 32 audio tracks,
- with bit resolutions of 16 or 24 bits,
- with sample rates of 44.1, 48, 88.2, or 96kHz.

The Digi 002 can process digital audio using Real Time AudioSuite (RTAS) or non Real-Time AudioSuite (file-based) plug-ins. Some of these plug-ins are included when you purchase a Digi 002. Plug-in bundles are often included in the purchase price. The particular plug-ins you receive will depend upon Digidesign's promotion at the time of your purchase.

The Digi 002 is more expensive than other LE systems, but the additional cost provides a control surface that can adjust and automate the internal faders in the Pro Tools LE software. This feature is invaluable for a mixing engineer (especially for live situations).

The control surface contains eight touch-sensitive, motorized faders which can control the levels of audio and MIDI tracks, auxiliary input tracks, master fader tracks, and even the parameters of sends and plug-ins (if you use the "Flip" mode located in the "Transport and Navigation controls" section of the 002).

When you buy a Digi 002 system, you receive:

- the Digi 002 (the control surface/audio interface),
- a FireWire Cable (12'),
- a copy of Pro Tools LE Software (Version 5.3.2 as of this writing),
- DigiRack plug-ins, and
- promotional bundled software.

To use the Digi 002 with a computer, your machine will have to meet the following minimum requirements:

Requirements for Macintosh users

Computer systems:

- Power Macintosh G4 (AGP graphics).
- Apple Titanium PowerBook G4.
- Book ("Ice White" Dual-USB Models).
- Mac G4 (LCD Flat Panel Models).
- Apple FireWire PowerBook G3.

System software:

- Mac OS v9.2.2 or higher

RAM:

- 256MB minimum, 320MB recommended. The more, the better.

Computer monitor:

- Color required, with a minimum resolution of 1024 x 768

External hard drives:

For audio recording and storage on the Macintosh, Pro Tools LE requires one or more qualified ATA/IDE, SCSI, or FireWire drives (Fig. 2.2) with the following properties:

- formatted with HFS or HFS+ file system,
- data transfer rates of 3MB per second or faster,
- drive spin speed of 5,400 RPM (7,200 or faster recommended), and
- average seek time of 10.0 milliseconds or faster.

Digidesign's hard drive options include:

- DigiDrive FireWire 80,
- DigiDrive,
- DigiDrive MediaDock,
- SCSI64 Kit, and
- SCSI|128 Kit

2.2. Digidesign's 80 GB FireWire DigiDrive.

FireWire

- The Digi 002 needs a 1394 (FireWire) controller/interface to connect to your computer, and
- FireWire extensions (version 2.5 or later) must be installed.

Other requirements:

- A CD-ROM drive is needed for software installation,
- Opcode's OMS v2.3.8 or higher (supplied on software CD),
- Apple QuickTime v5.0.2 or higher (supplied on software CD),

NOTE: As of this writing, QuickTime 6 is not supported and is known to be incompatible with the Digi 002, and

- Qualified Floppy Drives.

Requirements for PC users

Computer system:

Digidesign recommends a qualified, single-processor, Windows-compatible computer with the following minimums:

- Intel Pentium 4 CPUs running at 2.0GHz (or faster), or
- AMD AthlonXP 2000+ CPUs (or faster).

The following CPUs are also compatible with the Digi 002, but may not provide the best performance:
- AMD AthlonXP 1500+ CPU (or faster), and
- AMD Athlon Thunderbird CPUs running at 800MHz (or faster).

System software:

Pro Tools LE 5.3.2 cannot be installed or used on systems running Windows 2000, NT, Me, 98, 95, or 3.1. Currently, this means you must be running:
- Windows XP Home Edition.

RAM:

- At least 256 MB (320 highly recommended). The more, the better.

Hard drives:

- Formatted with FAT16, FAT32, or NTFS file system (FAT32 or NTFS recomended),
- Data transfer rates of 3MB per second or faster,
- Drive spin speed of 5,400 RPM (7,200 or faster recommended), and
- Average seek time of 10.0 milliseconds or faster.

Digidesign's hard drive options for Hard Drives include:
- DigiDrive FireWire 80,
- DigiDrive,
- DigiDrive MediaDock,
- SCSI|128 Kit, and
- SCSI64 Kit.

Other requirements:

- Qualified FireWire PCI & CardBus Cards,
- A CD-ROM drive or equivalent drive, and
- A color monitor, with minimum resolution of 1024 x 768.

Current requirements:

Digidesign's system requirements and compatibility information are updated on a regular basis.

To get the latest requirements and compatibility information of tested and approved devices (hard drives, DVDs, CD-ROMs, etc.) for the Digi 002—or for any Pro Tools system configuration—you should visit the Digidesign web site at: www.digidesign.com.

Digi 002 connections

Rear panel connectors

There are seven different types of connectors on the Digi 002 (including the AC power connector). You may be familiar with some or all of them, but for those of you who are not, I will give an example of what you are able to plug into these connectors, including a wiring diagram.

Fig. 2.3 shows the connectors and sections of the Digi 002's rear panel, including the analog, digital, and MIDI sections. We will discuss each section.

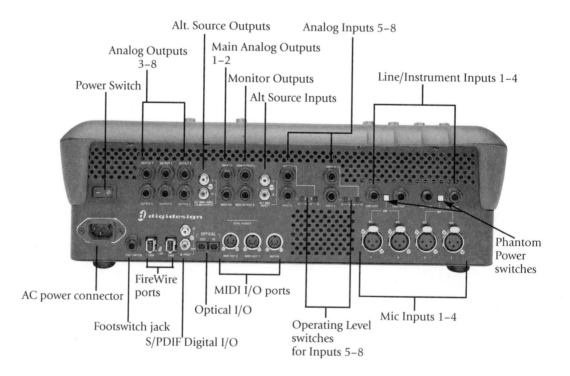

Fig. 2.3 Digi 002 back panel.

Analog input section

Halfway up on the right side of the 002's rear panel (Fig. 2.3) there are four ¼" TRS analog inputs (inputs 1–4) for line and instrument levels (LINE/INST). The operating level for these inputs is +4dBu.

Directly below the TRS inputs are four XLR connectors (Fig. 2.4). These are mic level inputs designed to connect microphones or direct boxes (DIs) to the 002. Because of the low impedance output of a DI, you can use it to plug in an electric bass or guitar (high impedance) into the 002's XLR connectors, and get a clean, powerful signal from these instruments.

The selection (LINE/INST or MIC) and gain-level adjustment for these four MIC inputs are controlled by the corresponding knobs (preamps) and black push buttons on the top panel of the Digi 002. See Fig. 2.1.

If you look carefully at Fig. 2.4, you will see two white push buttons located between the ¼" TRS connectors that allow you to provide built-in 48V phantom power needed for condenser mics (you won't need to engage these switches if you are using dynamic mics). Each of these switches enables a pair of inputs, one for inputs 1 & 2 and the other for inputs 3 & 4.

These eight inputs allow you to plug in microphones, direct boxes (XLR connectors), or any instrument such as electric guitars, electric basses, synthesizers, mixer outputs (for a synth sub-mix), external preamps, etc.

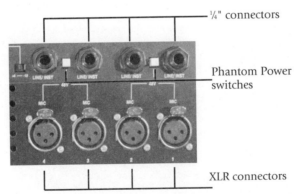

Fig. 2.4 Mic/Line/Inst Level Inputs 1–4 (back panel).

A little bit to the left of inputs 1–4, you'll find four ¼" TRS balanced line-level inputs numbered 5–8 (see Fig. 2.5). These are line-level input signals for devices that do not need pre-amplification (unlike microphones and electric guitars) such as your synthesizers, signal processors, tape decks, CD players, mixers, etc. (Take a look at Diagrams 2.1 on page 58 and 2.2 on page 66 to have a better understanding of what you can connect on any of the Digi 002 jacks.)

Each of these ¼" TRS inputs has a switch that allows you to select a +4dBu or −10dBV operating level for your incoming signal (Fig. 2.5).

These four inputs can also take ¼" TS unbalanced signal sources, if necessary. But whenever possible, you should use balanced sources to assure cleaner sonic results and better signal-to-noise performance.

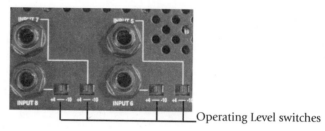

Fig. 2.5 Line Level Inputs 5–8 (back panel).

The left and right alternate source inputs or "ALT SRC INPUT" (Fig. 2.6) are unbalanced RCA inputs with an operating level of −10dBV. You can use these RCA connectors to plug a stereo device such as a CD player, a DAT machine, or a reel-to reel tape deck to the 002.

There are two push buttons on the top panel of the 002 which allow you to monitor these signals through the MON OUTPUT L and R connectors, or to route them to inputs 7 & 8 in the Pro Tools LE software, so that they can be recorded.

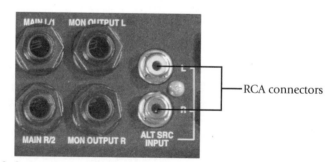

Fig. 2.6 Alt Source Input RCA jacks (back panel).

Analog Output Section

The Digi 002 has eight ¼" TRS balanced analog outputs which have an operating level of +4dBu.

The main mix of the 002 is assigned to the two jacks on the back labeled MAIN L/1 AND MAIN R/2.

To the right of the main outs is a second pair of jacks labeled MON OUTPUT

L and R. These are monitor outputs, which mirror the main outs, giving you an exact copy of any signal coming out of MAIN L/1 and R/2 (Fig. 2.7).

These monitor outs should be connected to your studio amp/monitors so you can listen to your mixes. You can control the monitor level with the knob labeled "MONITOR LEVEL" on the top panel of the Digi 002.

To the left of MAIN L/1 and MAIN R/2 outputs (Fig. 2.7) is a pair of RCA connectors (ALT MAIN UNBAL). These connectors are unbalanced outputs (–10dBV) which you can connect to devices such as a stereo tape deck, or to a stereo receiver, if you don't have a professional power amp or speakers.

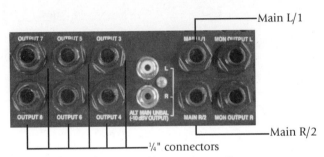

Fig. 2.7 Analog Outputs 3-8(back panel).

Outputs 3–8 (Fig. 2.7) are ¼" TRS balanced outputs with operating levels of +4dBu. You can use these to connect the 002 to a device using an unbalanced signal as well. However, if you plan to connect these outputs to –10dBV-level devices, you might want to insert a transformer-based line-level attenuator between the units. This device will reduce the high-level signal from the source (002) to the lower-level signal expected by your destination device (signal processor).

Outputs 3–8 can be used to connect external analog signal processors such as delays, reverbs, EQ's, etc., to your 002. You might also want to use a pair of these outs to connect your headphone distribution amplifier for headphone mixes, if you are doing overdubs (Diagrams 2.1 and 2.2 on pages 58 and 66).

Digital I/O section

The Digi 002's digital input and output section consist of:

- Two Toslink connectors for optical S/PDIF and Adat Lightpipe digital transfers,
- Two RCA connectors for S/PDIF digital in and out, and
- Two FireWire ports (see Fig. 2.8).

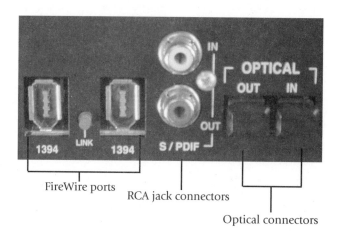

FireWire ports   RCA jack connectors

Optical connectors

Fig. 2.8 Digital Inputs/Outputs (back panel).

Using the connectors labeled "OPTICAL," you can connect an ADAT digital recorder to perform digital transfers between an ADAT and Pro Tools using the Lightpipe digital transfer format (Diagram 2.1 on page 58).

You can connect any DAT machine, CD burner/player, or digital signal processor that uses these "Toslink" connectors for S/PDIF digital transfers. When you use the "OPTICAL" connectors, you must select between the "Optical=ADAT" or "Optical=S/PDIF" option in the "Hardware Setup" dialog window (Fig. 2.9).

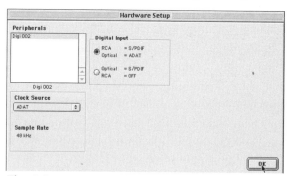

Fig. 2.9 Hardware Setup dialog window.

Using the connectors labeled "S/PDIF," you can connect any CD burner/player, DAT machine, or signal processor that uses RCA "S/PDIF" connectors to transfer data to and from the Digi 002. For this type of digital transfer, you must use a cable with 75Ω impedance to avoid the loss of data during the transfer.

The two FireWire ports labeled "1394" are used to connect the 002 to your computer and other devices such as external hard drives, digital cameras, video recorders, etc.

Although the 002 has two FireWire ports, if you are connecting your 002 to a computer, Digidesign recommends connecting your external FireWire hard drive directly to your computer instead of the 002's second FireWire port. This will avoid data errors and loss in the case the 002 is turned off.

When a connection is made between your computer and the 002, the "LINK" LED will be lit.

MIDI section

There are three 5-pin DIN connectors (Fig. 2.10) on the Digi 002, one for a MIDI input and two for MIDI out. This means that you have a total of 16 MIDI channels in the input MIDI port and 32 MIDI channels in the output port.

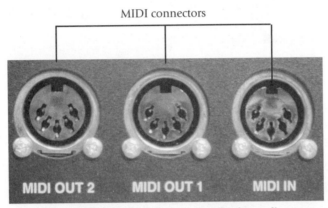

Fig. 2.10 MIDI In and Out ports (back panel).

The MIDI IN port can be directly connected to your MIDI keyboard, in order to record the MIDI data to the Pro Tools sequencer.

The MIDI Outs 1 and 2 can be plugged directly into other keyboards or sound modules, or to an I/O interface such as Digidesign's "MIDI I/O"—which has 10 MIDI inputs and 10 MIDI outputs—if you have an arsenal of MIDI keyboards and MIDI sound modules (Diagram 2.2 on page 66 shows how this setup is connected).

Footswitch jack

The footswitch jack (Fig. 2.11) comes in very useful in situations where you need more than two hands, and no one is around to help you punch-in and punch-out when you are recording audio or MIDI in Pro Tools.

There may be times when you are alone in the studio wanting to record a guitar or keyboard solo, and there is no one available to press the record button. This ¼" jack can use a "continuous on/continuous off" and "instantaneous on/off" type of footswitch pedal to make such solo recording a breeze.

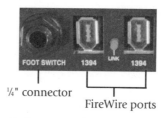

¼" connector

FireWire ports

Fig. 2.11 Footswitch jack (back panel).

How does the Digi 002 function?

Working with the Digi 002 is quite simple, once you have made your connections correctly and installed and validated (authorized) your software.

The Playback Engine (Fig. 2.12) allows you to customize various system usage parameters (such as hardware buffer size and CPU usage) and to set the size of the DAE Playback Buffer.

In most cases, the default settings for your system provide optimum performance, but you may want to adjust them to accommodate large or processing-intensive Pro Tools sessions.

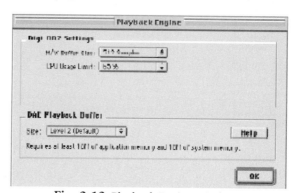

Fig. 2.12 Playback Engine window.

Now, when using the Digi 002 with Pro Tools software, you need to configure some parameters on the control surface. For example, you have to select Mic/Line/Instrument in the front panel for Inputs 1–4 (Fig. 2.13) depending on what you are using as audio source.

Mic/Line/Instrument
Selector switch

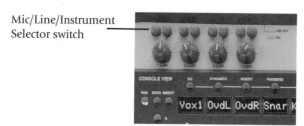

Fig. 2.13 Digi 002 Mic/Line/
Instrument Selector switches.

The Digi 002 Control Surface Views

There are three different views in the Digi 002 when working in it. These are: Home view, Console view, and Channel view. Many of the Digi 002 controls perform more than one function depending on which view you are in.

Home View

When you first open a session in Pro Tools, the Home View is set as the default view. To assign the Digi 002 to Home View, press the Pan switch located in upper left-hand corner of the Console View section. Refer to Fig. 2.14.

Console View

To set the Digi 002 to Console View, press either the Pan, Send, or Insert switch located in upper left-hand corner of the Console View section. This view allows you to toggle the 002's control surface for showing the pan position, send or insert assignments for all tracks in your Pro Tools session at the time.

The pan position and the send or insert levels for each track in the session are shown by the LED rings above the rotary encoders. The parameter showing by the LED rings will depend on which switch is lit while in the Console View.

Channel View

If you have the need to view all the plug-in assingments, send assingments, and insert names of a particular track you have selected on your session, the Channel View will allow you to do so.

Depending on which Channel View switch is lit at the moment while in the Channel View, the LED rings on top the rotary encoders will show the values for the selected control, such as insert and send levels, panning values, and plug-in parameters. Whenever any of the Dynamics, Inserts, EQ or Pan/Send selectors is lit, this means the Digi 002 is in Channel View.

To assign the Digi 002 to Channel View, press either the EQ, Dynamics, Insert, or Pan/Send switch in the Channel View section.

As I mentioned before, many of the Digi 002 controls perform more than one function depending on which view you are in. I will now explain the controls shown in Fig. 2.14 in the different views.

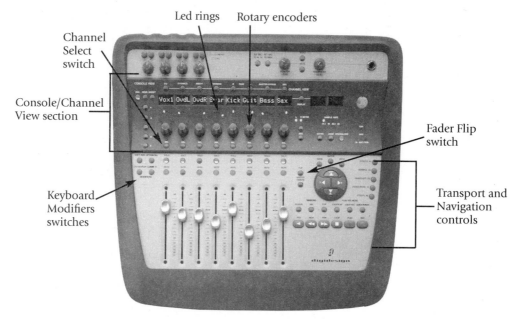

Fig. 2.14 Digi 002 Front panel view.

Channel Select Switch

- Home View: Lets you choose the selected track to be added to a group, to delete, etc., or any other track-related commands in Pro Tools.
- Console View: Allows you to select inserts on a particular track or channel strip for editing. You can also select a "Send" to be set on the pre/post-fader mode.
- Channel View: Allows you to select and edit individual send or insert settings.

Rotary Encoders

- Home View: You can control the pan position for each track using these knobs. The LED rings indicate the pan position with a single LED.
- Console View: In this view, the encoders control send levels for each track. The LED rings indicate the send levels with an expanding series of LEDs.
- Channel View: Depending on the Channel View selection, the rotary encoders control the plug-in, the pan/send, or the insert settings.

Record Enable switch

If you are ready to record, press the Record Enable switch. When you record enable a track, the "Record Enable Switch" will start flashing. For any tracks you want to enable for recording, press the Channel Select switch. Once you start the recording process, its Record Ready indicator is lit continuously. Press the Record Enable switch a second time to deactivate the Record Enable function.

Fader Flip Switch

When you press the Fader Flip switch the 002 goes into "Flip" mode, which means, that it will transfer all the control assignments from the rotary encoders to the corresponding channel faders. This will allow you to automate any parameter using the touch-sensitive faders on the Digi 002. Depending on which view you are working with on the 002, a different Flip mode type will be set.

• Home or Console View:

—*Send Flip Mode:* In this mode, the Flip switch assigns the send-level controls to the touch-sensitive faders, and the send pan controls to the rotary encoders. If using stereo tracks with stereo sends, by pressing the Encoder Mode switch you can toggle the encoder display between left and right send pan. If mono tracks with stereo sends, only the left pan indicator shows the pan position; the right pan indicator is made inactive in mono tracks.

• Channel View:

—*Plug-In Flip Mode:* I like this mode when automating plug-in parameters. By pressing the Flip switch all the plug-in control assignments will be moved from the rotary encoders to the touch-sensitive faders.

Master Fader Switch

If you are in a situation where you need to quickly do a fade-out on a master fader, by pressing the Master Fader Switch, the Digi 002 will arrange all the Master Fader tracks used in the current session on the right-hand side of the control surface.

Navigation and Zoom Buttons
  • Bank: If you have more than eight tracks in your session, and if this switch is lit, the left and right arrow keys will move eight faders at a time in the Pro Tools mixer.
  • Nudge: Unlike the Bank switch, with the Nudge switch lit, the Left and Right arrow keys will move one track at a time across the Pro Tools mixer.
  • Zoom: With the Zoom switch lit, the Left and Right arrow keys zoom the Pro Tools Edit window display horizontally, and the In and Out keys, vertically.

Navigation and Zoom Keys

- Text Entry Fields: The Left and Right arrow keys allow you to navigate through all editable fields when editing numerical values such as Selection Start, End, and Length, or Pre- and Post-Roll in the Edit or Transport windows. To increment or decrement a selected value, use the In and Out keys.
- Selection In/Out Points: When in Bank and Nudge modes, the Navigation keys have the same function as the Up and Down arrow keys on the computer keyboard. By pressing these keys during playback, you can mark the in and out points "on the fly," and be able to make selections in the Edit window. Once you have a selection in the Edit window, the Up and Down arrow keys move the selection up and down your track list.

Function/Utility switches

- F1 (Utility): Allows you to set the Digi 002's control surface and input preferences, as well as run pre-programmed diagnostic tests.
- F2 (Naming): Is for naming any channels only while the 002 is in the "stand-alone" mode only.
- F3 (Snapshot): If using the Digi 002 in a "stand-alone" mode only, you can store up to 24 mixer configurations so you can quickly recall them at any time.
- F4 (Fader Mute): Allows you to temporarily disable the fader movement on Digi 002 while working with Pro Tools, so you can monitor the audio playback without any fader noise. This won't affect any automation or volume level during playback. Press F4 while in Pro Tools mode to disable the faders. Pressing F4 a second time will restore the fader movement.
- F5 (Focus): Pressing this button will allow you to display the controls of the active plug-in window at the time on the Channel Scribble Strips just like in the Channel View. Press F5 a second time to return to the last Console view.

Keyboard Modifier Switches

- Shift/Add switch: Just like the Shift key on your computer, this switch allows you to extend a track selection or add to a group of selected items.
- Option/All switch: Is like a global command, i.e., if you want to record enable all the tracks at once, hold down this switch and the "rec" button.
- Control/Clutch switch: When you have several faders grouped and you need to move only one of the faders in the group, hold down this button and move the fader.
- Command switch: This button allows you to make fine adjustments of any control and/or automation breakpoints.

The Digi 002 Rack

The Digi 002R falls into the Pro Tools LE system category. It functions exactly the same way as the Digi 002, except for the control surface. Not having a control surface makes it portable so you can take it anywhere you want. It is a 2U rack-mountable unit.

The Mic/Line/Inst Input controls and the Monitor section, as well as the LEDs for sample rate, MIDI, and Firewire connection, are located on the front panel (Fig. 2.15a). The rear panel (Fig. 2.15b) remained the same as the original Digi 002. (Refer to page 46 for more information about the rear-panel connectors.)

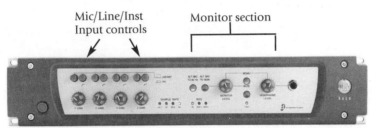

Fig. 2.15a Digi 002R front panel view.

Fig. 2.15b Digi 002R rear panel view.

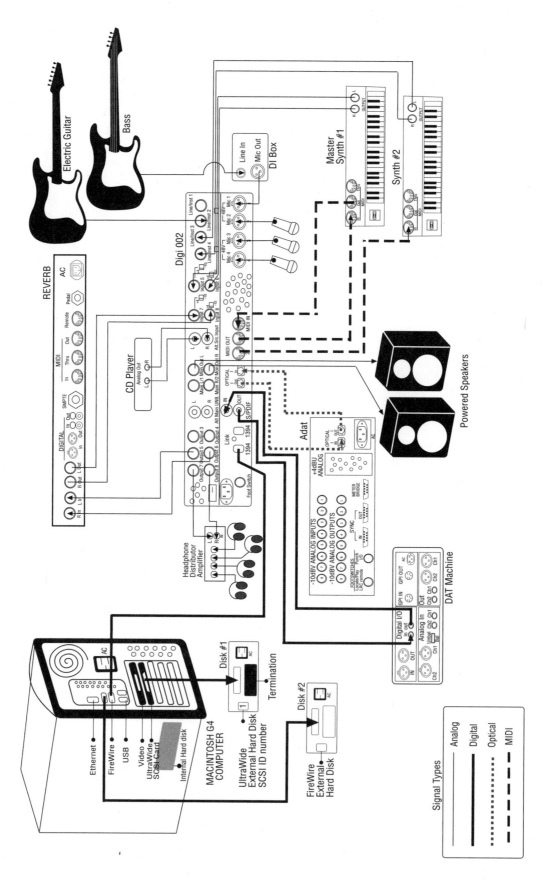

Diagram 2.1

Connecting the Digi 002

The following is just an example of what you might connect to the Digi 002. This is only a suggestion, a guideline, since you may not even have all the gear I am describing in the example.

1. Connecting External SCSI hard disks to the system.

Make sure you have installed an Ultra Wide SCSI card in your computer.

- Connect the output of the Ultra Wide SCSI card in your computer to a SCSI port of the Ultra Wide External Hard "Disk #1" (SCSI ID #1) using a SCSI cable. It is better to keep the length of the SCSI cable short due to SCSI length limitations.

- If you need to connect a second Ultra Wide SCSI drive, connect the available SCSI port of "Disk #1" to a SCSI port on the second hard "Disk #2" (SCSI ID #2). If your external hard disks are stacked together or next to each other, you can probably use a short one-foot Ultra Wide SCSI cable for this connection.

- If this is the last disk in the chain, don't forget to terminate the last SCSI port of Ultra Wide External Hard "Disk #1" or "Disk #2." When daisy chaining external hard disks together as in this example, the last unit always needs to be closed with a terminator plugged into the remaining SCSI connector.

2. Connecting a FireWire external hard disk to the system.

- Using a FireWire cable, connect an available FireWire port on your computer to the FireWire port on your external FireWire Hard Disk.

3. Connecting the computer to the Digi 002.

- Using a FireWire cable, connect the "FIREWIRE 1394" port on the rear panel of the Digi 002 to an available FireWire port located at the back of the computer.

4. Connecting a CD player to the Digi 002.

- Using an RCA cable, connect the "ANALOG OUT L" of the CD player to the "Alt. Src. INPUT L" of the Digi 002.

• Using another RCA cable, connect the "ANALOG OUT R" of the CD player to the "Alt. Src. INPUT R" on the Digi 002.

5. Connecting a DAT Machine to the Digi 002.

• Using a 75Ω RCA cable, connect the "DIGITAL I/O IN" on the DAT machine to the "S/PDIF OUT" of the Digi 002.

• Using a second RCA cable, connect "DIGITAL I/O OUT" to the "S/PDIF IN" of the Digi 002.

6. Connecting an ADAT to the Digi 002.

• Using an optical cable, connect the "OPTICAL OUT" of the ADAT to the "OPTICAL IN" on the Digi 002.

• Using another optical cable, connect the "OPTICAL IN" of the ADAT to the "OPTICAL OUT" on the Digi 002.

7. Connecting a headphone distribution amplifier to the Digi 002.

• Using a ¼" TRS male-to-male cable, connect "OUTPUT 7" of the Digi 002 to the "Left Input" on the Headphone Distribution Amplifier.

• Using another ¼" TRS male-to-male cable, connect "OUTPUT 8" of the Digi 002 to the "Right Input" on the Headphone Distribution Amplifier.

• Connect as many headphones as you need and/or as many as the headphone distribution amplifier can handle.

8. Connecting MIDI Synthesizers to the Digi 002.

• Using a ¼" TRS male-to-male cable, connect the "Left Output" of Synth #1 to "INPUT 5" on the Digi 002.

• Using another ¼" TRS male-to-male cable, connect the "Right Output" of Synth #1 to "INPUT 6" on the Digi 002.

• Using a MIDI cable, connect the "MIDI OUT" of Synth #1 to the "MIDI IN" on the Digi 002.

• Using another MIDI cable, connect the "MIDI IN" of Synth #1 to the "MIDI OUT 1" on the Digi 002.

- Using a ¼" TRS male-to-male cable, connect the "Left Output" of Synth #2 to the jack labelled "LINE/INST 3" on the Digi 002.

- Using another ¼" TRS male-to-male cable, connect the "Right Output" of Synth #2 to the jack labelled "LINE/INST 4" on the Digi 002.

- Using a MIDI cable, connect the "MIDI IN" on Synth #2 to "MIDI OUT #2" on the Digi 002. In other words, in this case Synth #1 will be your master keyboard controller.

9. Connecting an electric guitar.

- Using a ¼"-TRS-male-to-XLR-female cable, connect the jack labelled "LINE/INST 2" on the Digi 002 to the electric guitar.

10. Connecting an electric bass to the Digi 002 using a direct box.

- Using a ¼" TRS male-to-male, plug the electric bass into the "LINE IN" jack in the Direct Box (DI).

11. Connecting the DI box to the Digi 002.

- Using an XLR male-to-female cable, connect the "MIC OUT" on the DI Box to the "MIC IN 1" connector on the Digi 002.

12. Connecting three microphones to the Digi 002.

In the event that you wish to add three mics to this setup, just connect the mics using XLR-male-to-XLR-female cables and make the following connections:

- Connect the first mic to "Mic In2" on the Digi 002, since the "MIC IN 1" is used by the DI box.

- Connect the second mic to "MIC IN 3" and,

- Mic #3 to "MIC IN 4."

Note: When you are ready to use any of the mics, make sure to set the MIC/LINE button to MIC on the top panel of the Digi 002.

THE COMPLETE PRO TOOLS HANDBOOK

13. Connecting a reverb unit to the Digi 002.

- Using a ¼" TRS male-to-male cable, connect "OUTPUT 5" on the Digi 002 to the left input of the reverb unit.

- Using another ¼" TRS male-to-male cable, connect "OUTPUT 6" on the Digi 002 to the right input of the reverb unit.

- Using yet another ¼" TRS male-to-male cable, connect "INPUT 7" on the Digi 002 to the left output of the reverb unit.

- Using one last ¼" TRS male-to-male cable, connect "INPUT 8" on the Digi 002 to the right output of the reverb unit.

14. Connecting the Speakers to the Digi 002.

- Using a ¼"-TRS-male-to-¼"-TRS-male cable, connect "MON. OUT R" on the Digi 002 to the right speaker.

- Using another ¼"-TRS-male-to-¼"-TRS-male cable, connect "MON. OUT L" on the Digi 002 to the left speaker.

Software Setup

Assuming all the connections are made correctly, follow these next steps to make the proper configurations in Pro Tools LE software.

- Bear in mind that having all the equipment connected as Diagram 2.1 shows, does *not* necessarily mean you will be using all at once. For example, maybe you are doing an ADAT transfer, or maybe you want to do overdubs, or record only MIDI, or vocals. Either you use Line/Inst #2 or Mic #2, but using both at the same time is not possible.

- Same case with Line/Inst or Mic #3 and with Line/Inst or Mic #4. Also, you either record inputs 7 and 8 or the Alt.Src.Input. To record the Alt.Src.Input just press the indicate button on top of the Digi 002 control surface, if not, the Alt.Src.Input will not be recorded but will be heard through the monitors.

- So, because of this, let's assume that we are going to record a rhythm session using all the MIDI equipment, mic #1 (Bass), Line/Inst 2 to 4 (Guitar and Synth #2), Inputs 5–6 (Master Synth #1), Alt.Src.Input (Drum Loop from the CD), and the ADAT (drums previously recorded in another studio) to record into Pro Tools first then we will use mics 2 to 4 to record voices and Input 7–8 for the reverb. Finally, we will transfer the recording into the DAT Machine.

- Create a new session and then create 16 mono audio tracks and one MIDI track, or 12 mono audio tracks, two stereo audio tracks and one MIDI track.

- If you are dealing with Pro Tools version 5.3 or lower, you will need to configure your OMS Studio. Go to Setups > OMS Studio Setup to configure your OMS studio, or to Setups > OMS MIDI setup to create a "new easy setup" that will recognize all your MIDI equipment. Follow your manufacturer's information to successfully create your studio setup.

- Go to Setups > Hardware Setup and assign the Digital Input to "RCA = S/PDIF, OPTICAL = ADAT." Set the Clock Source to INTERNAL.

- Go to Setups > I/O Setup, and press the "Default" button in the Input and Output tabs. This way, you will be able to see the default names of your inputs and outputs. You can also give them different names if that's easier for you.

- Go to the Mix window and assign the inputs and outputs on your tracks following these instructions:

Track (mono)	Input	Inst/Source	Output
Audio track # 1	Analog 1	(Bass)	Analog 1–2
Audio track # 2	Analog 2	(Electric Guitar)	Analog 1–2
Audio track # 3	Analog 3	(Synth #2 L)	Analog 1–2
Audio track # 4	Analog 4	(Synth #2 R)	Analog 1–2
Audio track # 5	Analog 5	(Synth #1 L)	Analog 1–2
Audio track # 6	Analog 6	(Synth #1 R)	Analog 1–2
Audio track # 7	Analog 7	(CD Player L)	Analog 1–2
Audio track # 8	Analog 8	(CD Player R)	Analog 1–2
Audio track # 9-16	ADAT 1-8	(Drum Set)	Analog 1–2
MIDI track # 1	MIDI 1	(Synths)	MIDI OUT 1/2

(whatever channel you choose for your keyboards)

- If you choose to use two stereo tracks instead of four mono, assign Input Analog 3–4 to one of them, and Input Analog 5–6 to the other.

- Remember to set the format for Inputs 1–4 on your Digi 002 control surface to their correspondent status, set the levels for the analog inputs, and remember to press the little "Alt.Src.Input to Ch 7–8" button on the top of the Digi 002.

- Record enable the tracks on your Pro Tools session, press "record" and then "play" on the Transport window, press "play" on your CD and your ADAT, and start playing your instruments.

- On the second round, we are going to record mics 2 to 4 to record voices and Input 7–8 for the reverb, following these steps:

- Create three mono audio tracks. They will appear as Audio 17, 18 and 19. Create a stereo aux. input track as well.

- Go to the Mix window and assign the inputs/outputs as follows:

Track	Input	Inst/Source	Output
⸱ Audio track # 17	Analog 2	(Mic 1)	Analog 1–2
Audio track # 18	Analog 3	(Mic 2)	Analog 1–2
Audio track # 19	Analog 4	(Mic 3)	Analog 1–2
ST. Aux. Input	Analog 7–8	(Reverb)	Analog 1–2

- Now, on all the tracks, create a new send and set the output to Interface to "Analog 7–8", and that would be the mix sent to the headphones.

- On tracks 17, 18, and 19 (or on the tracks you want to have reverb), create another send and set the output to Interface "Analog 5–6," so the voices can be routed to the reverb, and the return will be through "Analog 7–8" already set in the Stereo Aux. Input track.

- Remember to set the format for Inputs 2–4 on your Digi 002 control surface to their correspondent status, that has changed from Line/Inst to Mic, set the levels for the analog inputs, and remember to disable the little "Alt.Src.Input to Ch 7–8" button on the top of the Digi 002; otherwise, instead of having the return of the Reverb, you will have the CD player again on the Stereo Aux. Input track and you will not hear any reverb at all.

- Record enable only tracks 17, 18, and 19 on your Pro Tools session, and press "record" and then "play" on the Transport window. Now you can sing along with the music.

- Finally, the Third Round. We will send all the recorded tracks into the DAT Machine.

- First of all, mix your recorded tracks as you like.

- Go to Setups > Hardware Setup and assign the Digital Input to "RCA = S/PDIF, OPTICAL = ADAT." Set the Clock Source to RCA (S/PDIF).

- Create a Stereo Master Fader track.

- Go to the Mix window and assign the Output of the newly created Master Fader track to "Analog 1–2, S/PDIF L–R (Stereo)."

- Enable the "REC" button on your DAT Machine, and press "Play" on the transport window in Pro Tools.

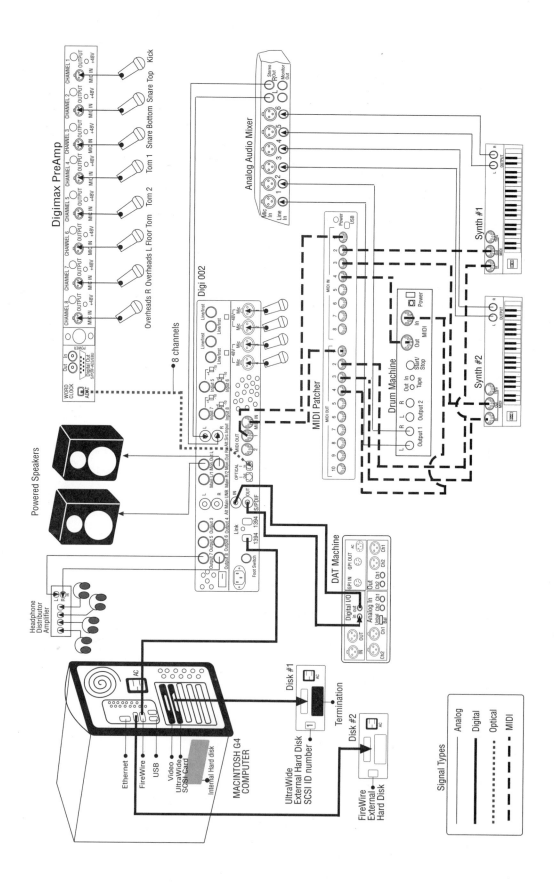

Diagram 2.2

Connections

1. Connecting external SCSI hard disks to the system.

Make sure you have installed an Ultra Wide SCSI card in your computer.

- Connect the output of the Ultra Wide SCSI card in your computer to the "SCSI IN" port of Ultra Wide External Hard Disk #1 (SCSI ID #1) using a SCSI cable. It is better to keep the length of the SCSI cable short due to SCSI length limitations.

- If this is the last disk in the chain, don't forget to terminate the last SCSI port of Ultra Wide External Hard Disk #1. When daisy chaining External Hard Disks together as in this example, the last unit always needs to be closed with a terminator plugged into the remaining SCSI connector.

2. Connecting a FireWire external hard disk to the system.

- Using a FireWire cable, connect an available FireWire port on your computer to the FireWire port on your external FireWire Hard Disk.

3. Connecting the computer to the Digi 002.

- Using a FireWire cable, connect the "FIREWIRE 1394" port on the rear panel of the Digi 002 to an available FireWire port located at the back of the computer.

4. Connecting a DAT machine to the Digi 002.

- Using an RCA cable, connect "DIGITAL I/O IN" to the "S/PDIF OUT" of the Digi 002.

- Using another RCA cable, connect "DIGITAL I/O OUT" to the "S/PDIF IN" of the Digi 002.

5. Connecting a headphone distributor amplifier to the Digi 002.

- Using a ¼" TRS male-to-male cable, connect "OUTPUT 7" of the Digi 002 to the "IN L" on the headphone distributor amplifier.

- Using another ¼" TRS male-to-male cable, connect "OUTPUT 8" of the Digi 002 to the "IN R" on the headphone distributor amplifier.

- Connect as many headphones as you need and/or as many as the headphone distributor amplifier can take.

6. Connecting the synthesizers to the audio mixer.

- Using a ¼" TRS male-to-male cable, connect the "OUTPUT L" of synth #1 to "INPUT 5" on the audio mixer.

- Using another ¼" TRS male-to-male cable, connect the "OUTPUT R" of synth #1 to "INPUT 6" on the audio mixer.

- Using a ¼" TRS male-to-male cable, connect the "OUTPUT L" of synth #2 to "LINE IN 3" on the audio mixer.

- Using another ¼" TRS male-to-male cable, connect the "OUTPUT R" of synth #2 to "LINE IN 4" on the audio mixer.

7. Connecting the synthesizers to a MIDI patcher.

- Using a MIDI cable, connect the "MIDI OUT" on Synth #1 to "MIDI IN 2" on the MIDI patcher.

- Using another MIDI cable, connect the "MIDI IN" on synth #1 to "MIDI OUT 2" on the MIDI patcher.

- Using a MIDI cable, connect the "MIDI IN" on synth #2 to "MIDI OUT 3" on the MIDI patcher.

- Using a MIDI cable, connect the "MIDI OUT" on synth #2 to "MIDI IN 3" on the MIDI patcher.

8. Connecting the drum machine to the audio mixer.

- Using a ¼" TRS male-to-male cable, connect the "OUTPUT 1 L" of the drum machine to "INPUT 1" on the audio mixer.

- Using another ¼" TRS male-to-male cable, connect the "OUTPUT 1 R" of the drum machine to "INPUT 2" on the audio mixer.

9. Connecting the drum machine to the MIDI patcher.

- Using a MIDI cable, connect the "MIDI OUT" on the drum machine to "MIDI IN 4" on the MIDI patcher.

- Using another MIDI cable, connect the "MIDI IN" on the drum machine to "MIDI OUT 4" on the MIDI patcher.

10. Connecting four microphones to the Digi 002.

Using an XLR-male-to-XLR-female, make the following connections:

- Mic 1 to "MIC IN 1" of the Digi 002.

- Mic 2 to "MIC IN 2" of the Digi 002.

- Mic 3 to "MIC IN 3" of the Digi 002.

- Mic 4 to "MIC IN 4" of the Digi 002.

11. Connecting 8 microphones to a Digimax preamp.

Using an XLR-male-to-XLR-female, make the following connections:

- "MIC IN 1" to the kick microphone.

- "MIC IN 2" to the snare top microphone.

- "MIC IN 3" to the snare bottom microphone.

- "MIC IN 4" to the tom 1 microphone.

- "MIC IN 5" to the tom 2 microphone.

- "MIC IN 6" to the floor tom microphone.

- "MIC IN 7" to the overheads left microphone.

- "MIC IN 8" to the overheads right microphone.

12. Connecting the Digimax preamp to the Digi 002.

- Using an optical cable, connect the "ADAT" port on the preamp to the "OPTICAL IN" on the Digi 002.

13. Connecting an analog audio mixer to the Digi 002.

- Using an RCA cable, connect "ALT Src. Input L" on the Digi 002 to "STEREO OUT L" on your analog audio mixer.

- Using an RCA cable, connect "ALT Src. Input R" on the Digi 002 to "STEREO OUT R" on your analog audio mixer.

14. Connecting the Digi 002 to the speakers.

- Using a ¼"-TRS-male-to-¼"-TRS-male cable, connect "MON. OUT R" on the Digi 002 to the right speaker.

- Using another ¼"-TRS-male-to-¼"-TRS-male cable, connect "MON. OUT L" on the Digi 002 to the left speaker

Software setup

Assuming all the connections are ready, follow these steps to configure your hardware in your Pro Tools session.

- Create a new session and then create 14 mono audio tracks and one MIDI track, or 12 mono audio tracks, 1 Stereo Audio tracks, and one MIDI track.

- If you are dealing with Pro Tools version 5.3 or lower, you will need to configure your OMS Studio. Go to Setups > OMS Studio Setup to configure your OMS studio, or to Setups > OMS MIDI setup to create a "new easy setup" that will recognize all your MIDI equipment. Follow your manufacturer's information to succesfully create your studio setup.

- Go to Setups > Hardware Setup and assign the digital input to "RCA = S/PDIF, OPTICAL = ADAT." Set the clock source to INTERNAL.

- Go to Setups > I/O Setup, and press the "Default" button in the Input and Output tabs. This way, you will be able to see the default names of your inputs and outputs. You can also give them different names if that's easier for you.

- Go to the Mix window and assign the inputs and outputs on your tracks following these instructions:

Track (mono)	Input	Inst/Source	Output
Audio track # 1–4	Analog 1–4	(Mic 1–4)	Analog 1–2
Audio track # 5–12	ADAT 1–8	(Digimax)	Analog 1–2
Audio track # 13	S/PDIF 1	(DAT)	Analog 1–2
Audio track # 14	S/PDIF 2	(DAT)	Analog 1–2
MIDI track # 1	MIDI 1 Ch x	(Synths/Drum. M)	MIDI OUT 1/2 Ch x

- Remember to set the format for inputs 1–4 on your Digi 002 control surface to their corresponding status, set the levels for the analog inputs.

- Now, on all the tracks, create a new send and set the output to interface to "Analog 7–8"; that would be the mix sent to the headphones.

- Record enable the tracks on your Pro Tools session, press "record" and then "play" on the Transport window, press "play" on your DAT, and start playing your instruments.

The Mbox

The Mbox (Fig. 2.16) is the smallest and most portable of all the Pro Tools LE systems, with USB connectivity and without the need of external power. You'll be surprised by all you can do with this little box, from recording, editing, and mixing music, to a post-production job. It features are:

- Pro Tools LE software,
- 24-bit stereo S/PDIF digital I/O,
- two analog inputs (Focusrite microphone preamps),
- two headphone output jacks,
- two line outputs,
- two inserts,
- phantom power, and
- USB connectivity.

As with the Digi 002, you don't have to turn your computer off every time you need to connect the Mbox.

Fig. 2.16 Mbox (front panel).

The Mbox can record and play back:
- up to 128 MIDI tracks,
- and 32 audio tracks with Windows XP or 24 tracks with Mac OS,

- with bit resolutions of 16 or 24 bits,
- with sample rates of 44.1 or 48kHz.

If you need to digitally process the audio, the Mbox can do it using Real Time AudioSuite (RTAS) or non Real-Time AudioSuite (file-based) plug-ins. You can purchase plug-in bundles as you go. The particular plug-ins you receive with your Mbox will depend upon Digidesign's promotion at the time of your purchase.

The Mbox is the least expensive and most portable of all the Pro Tools systems available. With a laptop computer, a set of headphones, and the Mbox, you can go just about anywhere and be able to record, edit, and mix in a matter of minutes. If you are a musician on the road, you'll be able to capture all your ideas while on the road.

Mbox connections

Rear panel connectors

On the Mbox, all the connections are made on the rear panel (Fig. 2.17). It may seem to you that there are not so many posibilities with this little box, but take a look at Diagram 2.3 on page 76—you will be surprised! You can even record MIDI using a USB/MIDI interface. Refer to Chapter 9 for more information about MIDI and MIDI configurations with the Mbox.

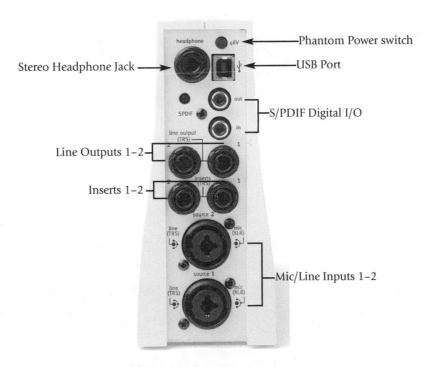

Fig. 2.17 Mbox (back panel).

Analog Input section

The Mbox contains two Neutrik-type connectors (Fig. 2.18) in the analog input section into which you can plug a microphone, or an instrument or line-level device in the same jack. If you want to use a microphone, then you have to select the mode on the Mbox's front panel.

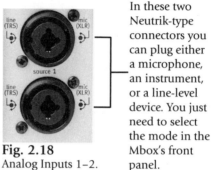

In these two Neutrik-type connectors you can plug either a microphone, an instrument, or a line-level device. You just need to select the mode in the Mbox's front panel.

Fig. 2.18
Analog Inputs 1–2.

Analog Output section

The Mbox has two ¼" TRS balanced or TS unbalanced analog outputs (Fig. 2.19). You can control the monitor level with the knob labeled "playback" on the front panel of the Mbox. These connectors can be used to connect the Mbox directly to your powered speakers or to a small analog mixing board.

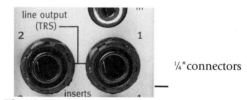

¼"connectors

Fig. 2.19 Analog Outputs 1–2.

Digital I/O section

The Mbox has a 24-bit stereo S/PDIF digital I/O (Fig. 2.20) where you can connect any DAT machine, AD and DA converter, CD burner/player, or digital signal processor that uses RCA connectors for S/PDIF digital transfers. Remember, you must use a cable with 75Ω impedance to avoid any loss of data during a digital transfer. When you assign outputs 1 and 2 to the speakers, for example, Pro Tools automatically sends them to the S/PDIF outputs as well, so you can record your mix to an external S/PDIF device.

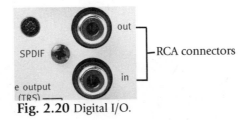

Fig. 2.20 Digital I/O.

Insert section

The Mbox has two insert points (Fig. 2.21) with ¼" connectors. You can use them to connect external effects processors.

Fig. 2.21 Inserts 1–2.

How does the Mbox function?

Working with the Mbox is really simple, once you have made your connections properly and installed and validated (authorized) your software.

The Hardware Setup window (Fig. 2.22) lets you customize various system usage parameters (such as hardware buffer size and CPU usage) and set the parameters of the session.

In most cases, you don't need to adjust any settings when working with the Mbox. You can use the default settings. If you need to make adjustments because of large or processing-intensive Pro Tools sessions, go ahead.

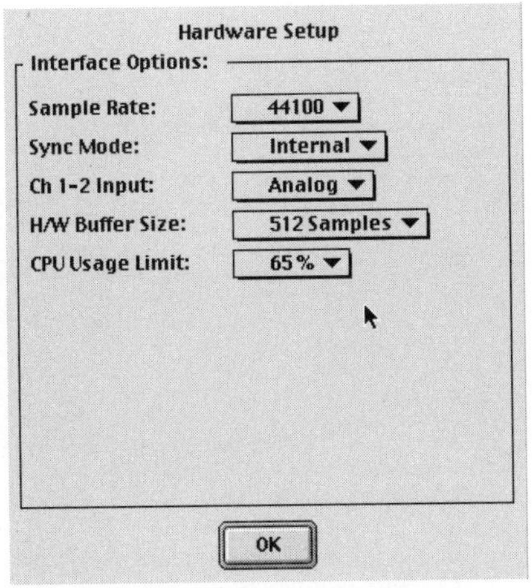

Fig. 2.22 Hardware Setup window.

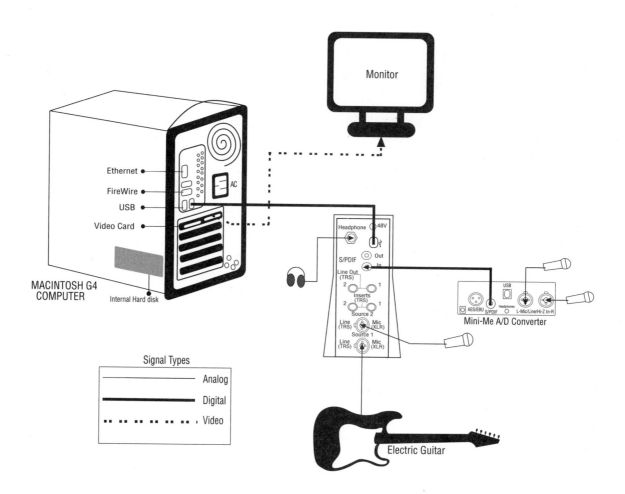

Monitor

Ethernet
FireWire
USB
Video Card
AC

MACINTOSH G4
COMPUTER
Internal Hard disk

Headphone   48V
Out
S/PDIF   In
Line Out
(TRS)
2   1
Inserts
(TRS)
2   1
Source 2
Line   Mic
(TRS)   (XLR)
Source 1
Line   Mic
(TRS)   (XLR)

AES/EBU S/PDIF   USB   Headphones   L-Mic/Line/Hi-Z In-R
Mini-Me A/D Converter

Signal Types

—————————————— Analog
—————————————— Digital
• • • • • • • • • • • Video

Electric Guitar

Diagram 2.3

Connections

1. Connecting the MBOX to the computer.

- Using a USB cable, connect the USB port on the MBOX to an available USB port on your computer.

2. Connecting a microphone to the MBOX.

- Using an XLR male-to-female cable, connect the XLR-male end of the microphone to the "SOURCE 2" MIC (XLR) input.

3. Connecting a guitar to the MBOX.

- Using a ¼"-TRS-male-to-¼"-TRS-male cable, connect an electric guitar to the "SOURCE 1" LINE (TRS) input.

4. Connecting an external A/D converter to the Mbox audio interface.

- Using good-quality RCA cables, connect the "S/PDIF IN" on the rear panel of the Mbox audio interface to the "S/PDIF OUT" of the A/D Converter.

5. Connecting two microphones to the external A/D converter.

- Using XLR cables, connect one microphone to the "Mic In L" and the other microphone to the "Mic In R" of the A/D Converter.

6. Connecting headphones to the MBOX.

- Connect the ¼" connector of the headphones to the "HEADPHONE" jack on the back of the MBOX. (If your headphones use a ⅛" connector, connect to the front of the Mbox—it has a ⅛" headphone jack.)

Software setup

Assuming all the connections are ready, follow these steps to configure your hardware in your Pro Tools session:

- Create a new session and then create two mono audio tracks.

- Go to Setups > Hardware Setup and assign the Ch 1–2 Input to "Analog." Set the Sync Mode to INTERNAL.

- Go to Setups > I/O Setup, and press the "Default" button in the Input and Output tabs. This way, you will be able to see the default names of your inputs and outputs. You can also give them different names if that's easier for you.

- Go to the Mix window and assign the inputs and outputs on your tracks following these instructions:

Track (mono)	Input	Inst/Source	Output
Audio track # 1	Analog 1	(Guitar)	Analog 1–2
Audio track # 2	Analog 2	(Mic)	Analog 1–2

- In case you are going to record in Pro Tools from the A/D Converter, create either one stereo audio track or two mono audio tracks.

- Go to the Mix window and assign the inputs and outputs on your track(s). For input, choose S/PDIF L–R if you want to record from the A/D Converter, and for output, choose Analog 1–2 to send it to the external monitors.

- Record enable the tracks on your Pro Tools session, press "record" and then "play" on the Transport window, and start playing.

The Digi 001

The Digi 001 (Fig. 2.23) is the first Pro Tools LE system that hit the market. Unlike the other LE systems, the Digi 001 needs a PCI slot in your computer to accommodate the Digi 001 PCI card. The 001 includes:

- The Pro Tools LE software,
- up to 18 simultaneous analog and digital audio inputs and outputs,
- a MIDI interface (one in and one out),
- one headphone output,
- a stereo monitor output, and
- a footswitch jack.

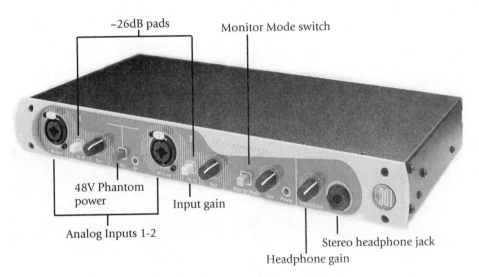

Fig. 2.23 Digi 001 front panel.

The Digi 001 can record and play back:
- up to 128 MIDI tracks,
- and up 32 audio tracks,
- with bit resolutions of 16 or 24 bits,
- and sample rates of 44.1 or 48kHz.

Digi 001 connections

Rear panel connectors

Fig. 2.24 shows the connectors and sections of the Digi 001's rear panel, including the analog, digital, and MIDI sections. Note that there are some connectors on the front panel (Fig. 2.23). See Diagram 2.4 on page 84 for a complete Digi 001 setup.

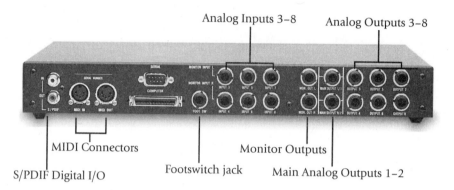

Analog Inputs 3–8   Analog Outputs 3–8

MIDI Connectors

S/PDIF Digital I/O   Footswitch jack   Main Analog Outputs 1–2

Monitor Outputs

Fig. 2.24 Digi 001 rear panel.

Analog input section

In the middle section of the 001's rear panel there are six ¼" TRS analog inputs (inputs 3–8) for line and instrument levels—LINE/INST (Fig. 2.25). Inputs 3–4 are used to connect analog audio sources or one stereo source (CD player, synth, etc.). These inputs can be monitored when assigning the 001 in "Monitor Mode." This means you can listen through the speakers whatever is coming in on inputs 3–4. To enable the "Monitor Mode," push in the switch labeled "Monitor Mode" located on the front panel. These ¼" TRS unbalanced line-level inputs are line-level input signals for devices that do not need preamplification such as synthesizers, signal processors, and CD players. The input levels for inputs 3-8 are software-adjustable by going to Setups > Hardware > Other Options.

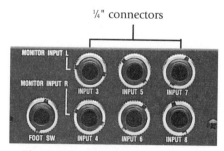

¼" connectors

Fig. 2.25 Analog Inputs 3–8.

On the front panel of the Digi 001 Audio Interface there are two Neutrik-type connectors (Fig. 2.23). These are balanced/unbalanced inputs designed to connect microphones or direct boxes (DIs), but you can use them to plug in an electric bass or guitar (high impedance) with the –26dB pad, and get a clean, powerful signal from these instruments.

The selection (LINE/INST or MIC) for these two MIC inputs are controlled via software. The gain level adjustment knobs are located on the front panel.

If you look carefully at Fig. 2.23, you will see two white push buttons located by the Neutrik connectors that allow you to attenuate the incoming signal –26dB, and one red push button that provides built-in 48V phantom power needed for condenser mics (you won't need to engage these switches if you are using dynamic mics). This switch enables inputs 1 & 2.

These two inputs allow you to plug in microphones, direct boxes (XLR connectors), or any instrument such as electric guitars, electric basses, synthesizers, mixer outputs (for a synth sub-mixes), etc.

Analog output section

The Digi 001 has ten analog outputs (Fig. 2.26). Analog outputs 1–8 use unbalanced ¼" TRS jacks for analog audio connections, while the monitor outputs are balanced ¼" TRS jacks.

The main outputs assign in the Mix window are assigned to the two jacks on the back labeled "MAIN OUTPUT L/1" and "MAIN OUTPUTR/2."

To the left side of the main outs is a second pair of jacks labeled "MON OUT L and R." These are monitor outputs, which mirror the main outs, giving you an exact copy of any signal coming out of the "MAIN L/1 and R/2" jacks.

These monitor outputs should be connected to your studio amp/monitors so you can listen to your mixes. You can control the monitor level with the knob labeled "MONITOR LEVEL" on the front panel of the Digi 001.

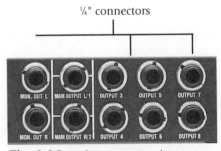

Fig. 2.26 Analog output section.

Outputs 3–8 can be used to connect external analog signal processors such as delays, reverbs, EQ's, etc., to your 001. You might also want to use a pair of these outputs to connect your headphone distribution amplifier for headphone mixes, which will be helpful when you are doing overdubs.

Digital I/O section

The Digi 001's digital input and output section consists of:

- Two Toslink connectors for optical S/PDIF and ADAT Lightpipe digital transfers, and
- Two RCA connectors for S/PDIF digital in and out.

Using the Optical connectors located on the Digi 001 PCI card (Fig. 2.27), you can plug an ADAT digital recorder to perform digital transfers between an ADAT and Pro Tools using the Lightpipe format.

You can connect any DAT machine, CD burner/player, or digital signal processor that uses these "Toslink" connectors for S/PDIF digital transfers. When you use the "OPTICAL" connectors, you must select between the ADAT or S/PDIF I/O format in your Hardware Setup window.

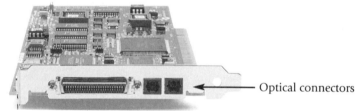

Optical connectors

Fig. 2.27 Digi 001 PCI card.

Pro Tools uses S/PDIF mirroring to automatically send main outputs 1 and 2 on the S/PDIF outputs, so you can record your mix to an external S/PDIF device. You can disable this function (if you want to use the S/PDIF outputs to send a separate signal) by going to Setups > Playback Engine and deselect the option called "Enable S/PDIF Mirroring."

Using the jacks labeled "S/PDIF" (Fig. 2.28), you can connect any CD burner/player, DAT machine, or signal processor that uses RCA S/PDIF connectors to transfer data to and from the Digi 001. For this type of digital transfer, you must use a cable with 75Ω impedance to avoid the loss of data during the transfer.

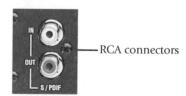

RCA connectors

Fig. 2.28 S/PDIF I/O.

MIDI section

There are two 5-pin DIN connectors (Fig. 2.29) on the Digi 001, one for MIDI input and another for MIDI output. This means that you have a total of 16 MIDI channels in the MIDI input port and 16 MIDI channels in the output port.

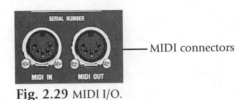 MIDI connectors

Fig. 2.29 MIDI I/O.

The MIDI In port can be directly connected to your MIDI keyboard, in order to record the MIDI data in Pro Tools' built-in MIDI sequencer.

The MIDI Out port can be plugged directly into other keyboards or sound modules, or to a MIDI interface such as Digidesign's MIDI I/O, which has 10 MIDI inputs and 10 MIDI outputs—if you have an arsenal of MIDI keyboards and MIDI sound modules. Refer to Chapter 9 for more information about MIDI and MIDI configurations with the Digi 001.

Footswitch jack

The footswitch jack (Fig. 2.30) comes in very useful in situations where you need more than two hands, and no one is around to help you punch-in and punch-out when you are recording audio or MIDI in Pro Tools.

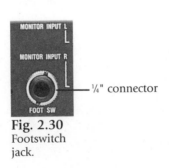 ¼" connector

Fig. 2.30 Footswitch jack.

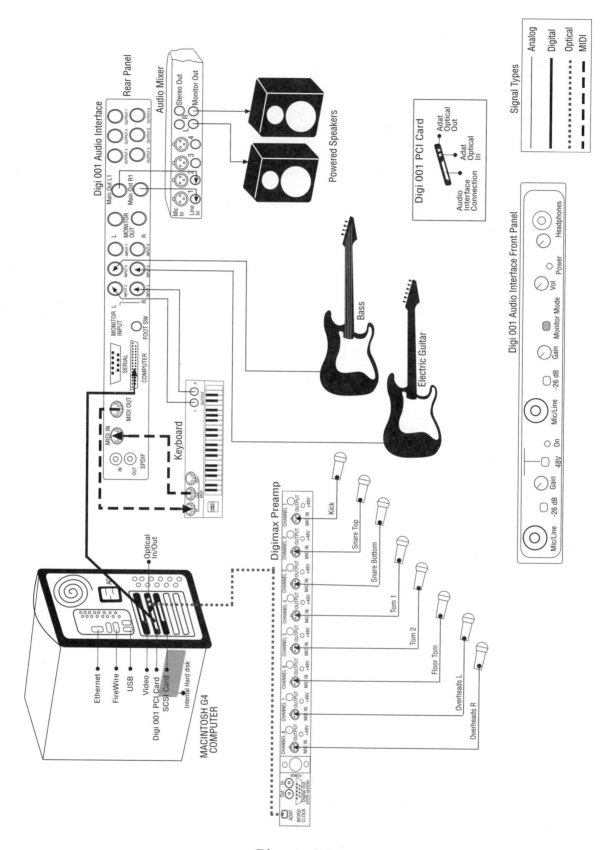

Diagram 2.4

How does the Digi 001 function?

As with the other LE systems, the Hardware Setup window (Fig. 2.31) lets you customize various system usage parameters (such as hardware buffer size and CPU usage) and set the parameters of the session.

In most cases, the default settings for your system provide optimum performance, but you may want to adjust them to accommodate large or processing-intensive Pro Tools sessions.

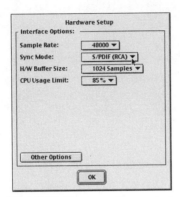

Fig. 2.31 Hardware Setup window.

Connections

1. Connecting the Digi 001 audio interface to the computer.

- Using a Digi 001 interface cable, connect the "COMPUTER" jack on the rear panel of the Digi 001 audio interface to the Digi 001 PCI card located at the back of the computer.

2. Connecting a keyboard direct to the Digi 001 audio interface.

- Using a ¼" TRS male-to-male cable, connect the "OUTPUT L" jack of the keyboard to "INPUT 3" on the Digi 001 Audio Interface.

- Using another ¼" TRS male-to-male cable, connect the "OUTPUT R" jack of the keyboard to "INPUT 4" on the Digi 001 Audio Interface.

- Using a MIDI cable, connect the "MIDI OUT" jack of the keyboard to the "MIDI IN" on the Digi 001 audio interface.

- Using a MIDI cable, connect the "MIDI IN" jack of the keyboard to the "MIDI OUT" on the Digi 001 audio interface.

3. Connecting an electric guitar.

- Using a ¼"-TRS-male-to-¼"-TRS-male cable, connect the "INPUT 6" jack on the Digi 001 audio interface to the electric guitar.

4. Connecting a bass.

- Using a ¼"-TRS-male-to-¼"-TRS-male cable, connect "INPUT 5" on the Digi 001 Audio Interface to the bass.

5. Connecting eight microphones to the Digimax preamp.

Using an XLR-male-to-XLR-female cable, make the following connections:

- "MIC IN 1" to the kick microphone.

- "MIC IN 2" to the snare top microphone.

- "MIC IN 3" to the snare bottom microphone.

- "MIC IN 4" to the tom 1 microphone.

- "MIC IN 5" to the tom 2 microphone.

- "MIC IN 6" to the floor tom microphone.

- "MIC IN 7" to the overheads left microphone.

- "MIC IN 8" to the overheads right microphones.

7. Connecting the preamp to the Digi 001.

- Using an optical cable, connect the "ADAT" connector of the Digimax preamp to the "OPTICAL IN" on the Digi 001 PCI card.

8. Connecting the Digi 001 audio interface to the audio mixer.

- Using ¼"-TRS-male-to-¼"-TRS-male cables, connect "MAIN OUT R1" on the Digi 001 Audio Interface to "LINE IN 1" on your audio mixer.

- Connect "MAIN OUT L1" on the Digi 001 Audio Interface to "LINE IN 2" on your audio mixer, using another ¼" TRS male-to-male cable.

9. Connecting the speakers to the audio mixer for monitoring.

- Connect the "MONITOR OUT L" jack on the audio mixer to the left speaker, using a ¼"-TRS-male-to-XLR-male cable. (This is the type of cable that most speakers use. However, some speakers require other types of cables, so check your manufacturer's documentation for more information.)

- Connect the "MONITOR OUT R" jack on the audio mixer to the right speaker, using another ¼"-TRS-male-to-XLR-male cable (or the type of cable needed for your speakers).

Software setup

Assuming all the connections are ready, follow these steps to configure your hardware in your Pro Tools session:

- Create a new session and then create at least 10 mono audio tracks and one stereo audio track (for the keyboard). You may also create 12 mono audio tracks and assign two of them for the keyboard left and right channels.

- Go to Setups > Hardware Setup and set the "Sync Mode" option to INTERNAL. Click OK.

- Go to Setups > I/O Setup, and press the "Default" button in the Input and Output tabs. This way, you will be able to see the default names of your inputs and outputs. You can also give them different names if that's easier for you.

- Go to the Mix window and assign the inputs and outputs on your track(s). Assign the stereo track input to Analog 3–4 (in case you decided to create one). For inputs, choose the input where the instrument you want to record is plugged in, but remember that all those microphones plugged into the Digimax will be labeled as inputs ADAT 1 through 8. For output, choose Analog 1–2 to send it to the external monitors.

Pro Tools LE compatibility chart

This chart shows the characteristics of each of the Pro Tools LE systems.

	DIGI 001	*DIGI 002/002R*	*MBOX*
Mic Preamps	2	4 Focusrite	2 Focusrite
MIDI Interface	1-In / 1-Out	1-In / 2-Out	None
Analog I/O	8-I/O	8-I/O	2-I/O
Digital I/O	10 (8-Lightpipe, 2 S/PDIF)	10 (8-Lightpipe, 2 S/PDIF)	2-S/PDIF
Computer Interface	PCI Card 1 slot	FireWire	USB
Headphone jack	Yes	Yes	Yes
Control surface	No	Yes / No	No
# of audio tracks	32	32	24
# of MIDI tracks	128	128	128
Plug-ins	AudioSuite / RTAS	AudioSuite / RTAS	AudioSuite / RTAS

Software features missing in a LE system

As of this writing, there are many features that are part of a TDM system that will not be available in an LE system. A list of some of the most important features that are missing includes:

- No Command Key Focus (only for PT 6.0 or higher)
- No Time Compression/Expansion in place
- No Copy To Send
- No Object Grabber Tools
- No Auto-Fades
- No Write-Trim Automation
- No Continuous Scrolling options
- No Region Replace
- No Repeat Paste
- No shuttling with the numeric keyboard
- No Trimmer Tool options (only for PT 6.0 or higher)
- No Trim mode
- No support to Digidesign's synchronizers (USD, SSD, VSD)
- No 9-pin Remote Machine Control or 9-pin serial
- No SMPTE time code display
- No Feet and Frames display
- No Pull-Up or Pull-Down
- No Movie Sync Offset
- No AutoSpot mode
- No support for Avoption|XL
- No AV option
- No support for PostConform
- No support for ProControl

CHAPTER THREE

Connecting Pro Tools TDM to the Outside World

3

In the last two chapters, we discussed the different Pro Tools TDM configurations available, as well as all the different types of cables needed to connect them.

In this chapter, we will briefly discuss some of the optional peripherals that you can use with your Pro Tools TDM system (MIDI interfaces, synchronizers, external effects devices, mixers, etc.), and how they are connected to a Pro Tools system.

Only time and experience will tell you which peripherals are really needed for your Pro Tools music production or post-production studio. We will not go into too much detail on these devices, as this subject itself could be the basis for an entire book.

The optional peripherals and other equipment that are often used with a Pro Tools TDM system are:

- Microphone preamplifiers

- MIDI interfaces

- Synchronizers

- MIDI keyboards and MIDI sound modules

- External effect processors

- Mixers

- Speakers

Microphone preamplifiers

If you intend to record vocals, acoustic pianos, acoustic guitars, etc., you will have to consider buying a good microphone preamplifier. The audio interfaces used in Pro Tools TDM systems (MIX-series or HD-series) have no way to "boost" microphone signal levels, and require signals at line levels of +4dBu or –10dBV.

There are many mic preamps on the market today, with many prices and features to choose from. Your choices range from solid-state and tube units whose complexity ranges from a single-channel tube unit—such as the TD-100 from Summit Audio (Fig. 3.1)—to an eight-channel, rack-mounted, remotely controlled mic preamp (such as the PRE, from Digidesign; see Fig. 3.2).

Many of today's preamps boast analog-to-digital converters, which send their mic signal inputs to Pro Tools in digital form through Toslink, XLR, or RCA connectors. PreSonus manufactures two such preamps, the DigiMax LT and the DigiMax 96k (Fig. 3.3). These are eight-channel solid-state units that convert incoming mic signals into digital streams that are sent to Pro Tools via Lightpipe (ADAT) connectors.

Apogee Electronics manufactures the Trak2 (Fig. 3.4), a 2-channel mic preamp with built-in 24-bit/96kHz analog-to-digital converters, and with AES/EBU and S/PDIF digital outs. Apogee also offers expansion cards for the Trak2 using other common digital audio transfer formats, such as T-DIF, Lightpipe, etc. We will spend some time on digital audio transfer formats later in the book in chapter 15.

Fig. 3.1 The TD-100 instrument preamp and tube direct box from Summit Audio.

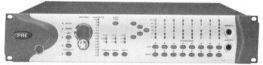

Fig. 3.2 PRE, an 8-channel remote-controllable mic preamp from Digidesign.

Fig. 3.3 The DigiMax from Presonus, an 8-channel solid-state preamp with Lightpipe digital outputs.

Fig. 3.4 Track2 from Apogee.

There are some wonderful tube mic preamplifiers on the market today that include a combination of EQ, compression, and/or limiting. Tube preamps tend to "warm up" your analog signal when sent to Pro Tools, and are favored by people who like the "analog sound." An example of such preamps are Avalon Design's Vt 737-SP mic preamp (Fig. 3.5) and Manley Electronics' Slam (Fig. 3.6).

Fig. 3.5 The Vt 737-SP. A combination of a single channel tube mic preamp with EQ and compressor from Avalon Design.

Fig. 3.6 The Slam, a stereo limiter and mic preamp from Manley.

In addition to their digital output connections, most of these high-end mic preamps accept balanced and unbalanced line/instrument levels—as well as Mic-level signals. The types of analog connectors that can be found on such devices include XLR (Cannon), ¼" TS (tip, sleeve), ¼" TRS (tip, ring, sleeve), and Neutrik™ (combination of ¼" and XLR for flexibility).

Some of these units also have MIDI (5-Pin DIN) connectors for the remote control of their parameter settings via MIDI, and some contain TRS inserts on every channel, allowing external dynamics processors or equalizers to be placed in the signal chain.

No matter what your application or budget, you will find a variety of preamps on the market that will meet your needs.

MIDI interfaces

If you want to work with MIDI synthesizers, MIDI samplers, MIDI drum modules, and MIDI control surfaces, you will have to acquire some type of MIDI interface. Your choice of a MIDI interface will depend partly upon how many MIDI channels and ports you will need in your studio.

The MIDI I/O unit from Digidesign has ten MIDI input and output ports (Fig. 3.7). The MIDI I/O utilizes USB connections, which provides increased timing accuracy and MIDI throughput, making it possible to control up to 160 MIDI channels (16 per MIDI port) in a large, complex MIDI setup.

Fig. 3.7 MIDI I/O Interface from Digidesign contains 10 MIDI inputs and outputs, offering you up to 160 MIDI channels.

Of course, if you have a small MIDI setup, you can use a simpler MIDI interface. Simpler MIDI interfaces can have two, four, or six MIDI inputs and outputs.

MIDI interfaces will require some computer connection, such as a serial or USB MIDI interface. Some smaller MIDI interfaces that use USB connectors are the Micro Express (Fig. 3.8) from Mark of the Unicorn (MOTU) and the MIDI Sport 2x2 from Midiman (Fig. 3.9).

Fig. 3.8 Micro Express from MOTU. This USB MIDI interface has four MIDI inputs and six MIDI outputs.

Fig. 3.9 Midiman's MIDI Sport 2x2. A two-input and two-output USB MIDI interface.

If you have an older computer that has a serial port—but no USB port—and have minimal MIDI needs, you might consider a MIDI interface such as the Mini Macman, which has one MIDI in and one MIDI out (Fig. 3.10).

Fig. 3.10 The Mini Macman from Midiman. A serial MIDI interface with only one MIDI in and one MIDI out.

As computers have grown more powerful, there has been a move toward software-based synthesizers. This greatly simplifies the needs for MIDI interfaces, as such connections are made within the computer.

If you will be using only software-based synthesizers in Pro Tools, you may consider an external USB MIDI controller, such as the Oxygen 8, made by Midiman (Fig. 3.11). Oxygen 8 uses a USB MIDI interface that connects directly to your computer, eliminating the need for a MIDI interface.

Fig. 3.11 Oxygen 8 by Midiman. A 25-key USB controller for software-based synthesizers.

Synchronizers

If you ever have to connect your Pro Tools TDM system to other A/V equipment, you will probably have to beg, borrow, buy, or rent some type of synchronization device. If you had to transfer 24 tracks of analog audio from a 2" tape machine to Pro Tools, you would not need a synchronizer. But if you had to transfer 48 tracks and only had one 2" machine, you would need to do the transfer in two passes. The only way to perfectly align such tracks in Pro Tools is with a synchronizer.

Synchronizers are also used in video post-production work, where you have to synchronize sound effects, dialog, and/or music to picture.

Digidesign offers the SYNC I/O unit (Fig. 3.12) for use with a Pro Tools HD system. The SYNC I/O is the only Digidesign synchronizer that works with a Pro Tools HD system.

Fig. 3.12 Digidesign's SYNC I/O.

Other manufacturers offer synchronizers (or Generic MTC readers) such as the MIDI Timepiece A/V from MOTU (Fig. 3.13) and the Unitor8 from E-Magic (Fig. 3.14).

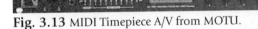

Fig. 3.13 MIDI Timepiece A/V from MOTU.

Fig. 3.14 Unitor8 from E-Magic.

These synchronizers convert SMPTE time code to MIDI time code (MTC), which is the type of time code required by Pro Tools. These units can also serve as 8x8 MIDI interfaces.

You have a wider selection among synchronizers if you own a MIX-series system. In addition to using the above mentioned devices as "generic MTC readers," you could also use the Digidesign Universal Slave Driver (Fig. 3.15) or the Digidesign SMPTE Slave Driver in conjunction with the Digidesign Video Slave Driver. These devices offer a number of added features and functions, and will be discussed later in our review of synchronization in Chapter 14.

Fig. 3.15 Digidesign's Universal Slave Driver (USD).

MIDI keyboards and MIDI sound modules

MIDI synthesizers, samplers, and sound modules are widely used by music composers and sound designers using Pro Tools.

These devices are connected to the computer and your MIDI keyboards via the MIDI interfaces we discussed earlier. This enables your Pro Tools system to record your MIDI keyboard events, and play back these MIDI events on the MIDI sound modules.

A number of manufacturers of MIDI equipment have good track records and are well thought of, including Korg (Fig. 3.16 and 3.17), Roland, Yamaha, Midiman, Alesis, and Kurzweil, among others.

Fig. 3.16 Korg's Triton Pro, a powerful music workstation.

Fig. 3.17 Triton Rack from Korg. A rack mountable MIDI sound module.

As computers grow in power, many software manufacturers have begun to offer software-based synthesizers and/or samplers. Instead of a stand-alone box which must be hooked up to your computer, these new programs offer synthesizers and samplers that reside inside your computer. Companies that offer such software include: Antares (Kantos, Fig. 3.18), Native Instruments (B4, Pro-52, and Battery—Fig. 3.19,), and Digidesign (Bruno, Reso), among others.

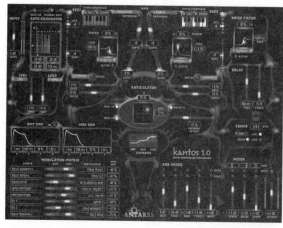

Fig. 3.18
Kantos from Antares, an audio-controlled software-based synthesizer.

Fig. 3.19 The Pro-52 software-based synthesizer from Native Instruments.

External effect processors

One reason for using an external effect processor device (external DSP) is when mixing a project in a Pro Tools system is when you run out of DSP processing power in your system. No matter how big your system is, eventually you will end up adding enough tracks, edits, and plug-ins that your system will run out of DSP chips.

If cash is no problem, you can go out and buy more DSP, or you can make use of the DSP power in the external devices that you already own.

So, instead of purchasing another software plug-in or another DSP PCI card to throw an effect or process on your mix, you might want to use a hardware based processor that does the same thing.

Another reason for using external effect processors is to give your mix a different sonic flavor. Sometimes it is just fun to be different, and to use external reverb units, delays, tube compressors, etc., on your project to create something that doesn't sound like the everyone else. See Fig. 3.20 (a), Fig. 3.20 (b), Fig. 3.20 (c), and Fig. 3.20 (d).

Fig. 3.20(a) AD2044, dual mono-stereo, pure class. An opto-compressor by Avalon Design.

Fig. 3.20(b) Orville, a 96kHz/24-bit multi-effect signal processor by Eventide.

Fig. 3.20(c) 2290 digital delay unit by t.c. electronic.

Fig. 3.20(d) The MPE 200, a dual solid-state EQ/mic preamp from Summit Audio.

Whenever you have the option, route your signals through your external effect devices using their digital ins and outs. "Keeping the signal in the digital domain" is superior to analog transfers because it adds no noise to your mix (from the electronic components inside of the unit) and avoids time lags (latency) when the audio signals go in and out of Pro Tools.

Diagram 1 illustrates the interconnection of such units to a Pro Tools system, and is worth studying.

Mixers

A Pro Tools system requires some sort of control surface that has the capability to record (with built-in mic preamps) and to monitor your sessions. Depending on your studio applications, you will need an external analog or digital mixer ranging from a small and simple 4x2 mixer, to a bigger and more complex 32x8x2 mixer.

Unless you want to use an external mixer to mix your Pro Tools project, a simple, great sounding analog line mixer such as the 16x2 line mixer from Manley (Fig. 3.21) will be more than enough to monitor the mix from your digital audio workstations.

Fig. 3.21 Manley's 16x2 line analog mixer.

If you prefer to stay in the digital domain, a wide range of digital mixers will fit your needs, such as the DDX3216 digital mixer from Behringer (Fig. 3.22), among others.

Fig. 3.22 Behringer DDX3216 digital mixer.

Speakers

Although you could use headphones at all times to listen to your Pro Tools projects, most prefer to hear their mix on speakers.

If you wish to use un-powered speakers (Fig. 3.23), you will need to purchase a power amplifier to drive them. The trick there is to match the power needs of your speakers to the power of your amplifier.

A major benefit of powered speakers (Fig. 3.24) is that they contain a perfectly matched set of built-in amp and speaker. They are not cheap, but they are mighty convenient.

Fig. 3.23 S8R two-way near-field un-powered studio monitors from SLS.

Fig. 3.24 Genelec's 1031 powered studio monitor.

Controllers

Sometimes it is nice to be able to control your Pro Tools session from outside the computer, using what is called a controller. One of these devices allows you to control most of the Pro Tools functions from a dedicated control surface, which is basically a mixer that controls your Pro Tools session. Changing any of the parameters from the control surface will change them in the Pro Tools session, and changing a parameter in Pro Tools will change it in the controller as well. Controllers are very useful for mixing because of the physical faders; the more faders the controller has, the more tracks at once you can control. Also, from a control surface you can control parameters such as pan, mute, solo, sends, automation, or even plug-ins and transport controls. There are several different kinds of controllers, offering from four to 24 faders. Some of them are expandable, like the MotorMix by CM Labs (Fig. 3.25), which allows you to add more modules to your system as your needs increase. This little unit communicates bidirectionally with the Pro Tools software via MIDI.

Fig. 3.25 CM Labs MotorMix.

Digidesign offers different control surfaces for Pro Tools which communicate with the software via Ethernet, like the ProControl and Control | 24. The Pro-Control (Fig. 3.26) offers eight motorized faders and additional Fader Expansion packs (eight faders each). The Control | 24 (Fig. 3.27) offers 24 touch-sensitive moving faders and 16 phantom-powered Class A mic/line preamps from Focusrite.

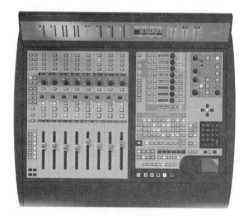

Fig. 3.26 ProControl by Digidesign.

Fig. 3.27 Control | 24 by Digidesign.

If your budget is limmited, or you do not need to have that much control over your mixes from outside the Pro Tools software, there are other good options, like the MCS-3800 (Fig. 3.28) and the CS-10, by J.L. Cooper (Fig. 3.29). Both of them communicate with Pro Tools via MIDI and give you excellent control over your Pro Tools session.

Fig. 3.28 MCS-3800.   **Fig. 3.29** CS-10 by J.L. Cooper.

Connection diagrams and explanations

Once you have purchased or borrowed all the components of your studio, the next trick is to put all these elements together.

To get you started, we have assembled some sample connection diagrams and explanations that show how this is done. Of course, these are just examples; you are not likely to have the exact system of components and processors discussed here. Hopefully, this section will give you a rough idea of how to connect up systems similar to those shown here. For example, the input and output of the audio interfaces are picked arbitrarily; you can select any input and output you desire.

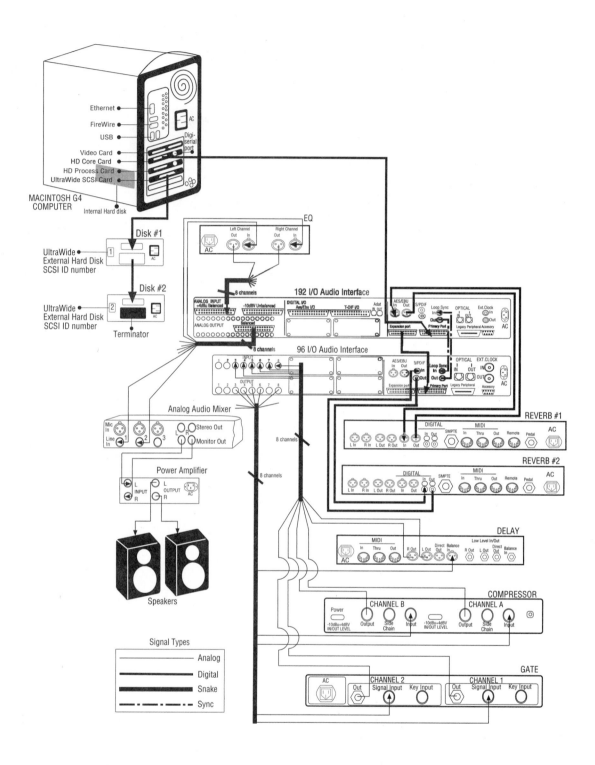

Diagram 3.1
Connecting a Pro Tools | HD 2 system.

Connecting a Pro Tools | HD 2 System

1. Connecting external SCSI hard disks to the system.

Digidesign highly recommends using a SCSI accelerator card when using Pro Tools. This should probably be the first thing that you install. In this example, we are using an Ultra Wide SCSI accelerator card instead of a FireWire external hard disk.

- Using an Ultra Wide SCSI cable, connect the Ultra Wide SCSI card from your computer to one of the SCSI ports of Ultra Wide External Hard Disk #1 (SCSI ID #1). It is better to keep the length of the SCSI cable short due to SCSI length limitations.

- Connect the other available port of Ultra Wide Hard Disk #1 to one of the SCSI ports of Ultra Wide External Hard Disk #2 (SCSI ID #2) using another SCSI cable. (If your external hard disks are stacked together or next to each other, you can probably use a short one-foot SCSI cable for this connection.)

- If this is the last disk in the chain, don't forget to terminate the last SCSI port of Ultra Wide External Hard Disk #2. When "daisy chaining" External Hard Disks together as in this example, the last unit always needs to be closed with a terminator plugged into the remaining SCSI connector.

2. Connecting the 192 I/O Audio Interface to the computer.

A 12-foot "DigiLink Interface" cable is provided when you purchase your Pro Tools|HD system. If you need a DigiLink cable other than 12 feet in length, you may purchase it from Digidesign. The available lengths are: 1.5 feet, 12 feet, 25 feet, 50 feet, and 100 feet.

- Connect the output of the "HD Core Card" (located at the back of you computer) to the "PRIMARY PORT" of the 192 I/O audio interface (located on its rear panel) using the 12-foot DigiLink cable provided.

3. Connecting a 192 I/O audio interface and 96 I/O.

- Connect the "EXPANSION PORT" of the 192 I/O audio interface, (located on the rear panel) to the "PRIMARY PORT" of the 96 I/O using the 1.5ft. "DigiLink" cable provided with your audio interfaces.

4. Connecting the LOOP SYNC.

- Connect the "LOOP SYNC OUT" of the 192 I/O audio interface to the "LOOP SYNC IN" of the 96 I/O audio interface, using the 1.5ft. BNC cable provided with your interfaces.

- Connect the "LOOP SYNC IN" of the 192 I/O audio interface to the "LOOP SYNC OUT" of the 96 I/O, using another 1.5ft. BNC cable.

5. Connecting a reverb unit to the 192 I/O audio interface using the AES/EBU digital format.

- Connect the "DIGITAL AES/EBU OUT" of reverb unit #1 to the "AES/EBU IN" of the 192 I/O ("Enclosure" section), using a 110-ohm XLR-female-to-XLR-male cable.

- Connect the "AES/EBU OUT" of the 192 I/O audio interface ("Enclosure" section) to the "DIGITAL IN" of reverb unit #1, using another 110-ohm XLR-female-to-XLR-male cable.

6. Connecting a reverb unit to the 96 I/O audio interface using the S/PDIF digital format.

- Connect the "S/PDIF OUT" of the 96 I/O audio interface ("Enclosure" section) to the "S/PDIF IN" of reverb unit #2, using a 75-ohm RCA-male-to-RCA-male cable.

- Connect the "S/PDIF IN" of the 96 I/O audio interface to the "S/PDIF OUT" of reverb unit #2, using another 75-ohm RCA-male-to-RCA-male-cable.

7. Connecting delay, compressor, and gate units to the 96 I/O Audio Interface inputs.

In this example, we are using an eight-XLR-male-to-eight-¼"-TRS-male cable snake. You should consult your manufacturer's documentation for information to select the proper snake for your units.

- Connect the "OUT L" jack on the delay unit to "ANALOG INPUT 3" on the 96 I/O audio interface. Remember, these input assignments on the 96 I/O are arbitrary.

- Connect the "OUT R" jack on the delay unit to "ANALOG INPUT 4" on the 96 I/O Audio Interface.

- Connect the "CHANNEL A" output on the compressor to "ANALOG INPUT 5" on the 96 I/O audio interface.

- Connect the "CHANNEL B" output on the compressor to "ANALOG INPUT 6" on the 96 I/O audio interface.

- Connect the "CHANNEL 1 OUT" jack on the gate to "ANALOG INPUT 7" on the 96 I/O audio interface.

- Connect the "CHANNEL 2 OUT" jack on the gate to "ANALOG INPUT 8" on the 96 I/O audio interface.

8. Connecting delay, compressor, and gate units to the 96 I/O audio interface outputs.

In this example, we are using an eight-¼"-TRS-male-to-eight-XLR-female snake. Again, you should consult your manufacturer's documentation for information to select the proper snake for your units.

- Connect the "ANALOG OUTPUT 3" of the 96 I/O audio interface to the "BALANCE IN" jack of the delay unit.

- Connect the "ANALOG OUTPUT 5" of the 96 I/O audio interface to the "CHANNEL A IN" jack of the compressor.

- Connect the "ANALOG OUTPUT 6" of the 96 I/O audio interface to the "CHANNEL B IN" jack of the compressor.

- Connect the "ANALOG OUTPUT 7" of the 96 I/O audio interface to the "CHANNEL 1 SIGNAL INPUT" jack of the gate.

- Connect the "ANALOG OUTPUT 8" of the 96 I/O audio interface to the "CHANNEL 2 SIGNAL INPUT" jack of the gate.

9. Connecting the EQ output to the 192 I/O Audio Interface input.

- Connect the "LEFT CHANNEL OUT" jack on the EQ to "INPUT #5" of the 192 I/O audio interface, using a DB25-XLR-female DigiSnake or similar cable snake.

- Connect the "RIGHT CHANNEL OUT" jack on the EQ to "INPUT #6" of the 192 I/O audio interface, using another cable of the above-mentioned DB25-XLR-female DigiSnake or similar cable snake.

10. Connecting the EQ input to the 192 I/O audio interface output.

- Connect the "LEFT CHANNEL IN" jack of the EQ to "OUTPUT #5" on the 192 I/O audio interface, using a DB25-XLR-male DigiSnake or similar cable snake.

- Connect the "RIGHT CHANNEL IN" jack of the EQ to "OUTPUT #6" on the 192 I/O audio interface, using another cable of the DB25-XLR-male DigiSnake or similar cable snake.

11. Connecting the output of the 192 I/O audio interface to the analog audio mixer.

- Connect "OUTPUT #1" on the 192 I/O audio interface to "LINE IN #1" on the analog audio mixer.

- Connect "OUTPUT #2" on the 192 I/O audio interface to "LINE IN #2" on the analog audio mixer.

12. Connecting the mixer to the power amplifier.

- Connect the "MONITOR OUT L" (for the left side of your monitor) on the analog audio mixer to the "INPUT L" of the power amplifier, using a ¼"-TRS-male-to-¼"-TRS-male cable.

- Connect the "MONITOR OUT R" (for the right side of your monitor) on the analog audio mixer to the "INPUT R" of the power amplifier using another ¼"-TRS-male-to-¼"-TRS-male cable.

13. Connecting the power amplifier to the speakers.

- Connect the "MONITOR OUT L" jack on the power amplifier to the left speaker, using a ¼"-TRS-male-to-¼"-TRS-male cable. (This is the type of cable that most speakers use. However, some speakers require other types of cables, so check your manufacturer's documentation for more information.)

- Connect the "MONITOR OUT R" jack on the power amplifier to the right speaker, using another ¼"-TRS-male-to-¼"-TRS-male cable (or the type of cable needed for your speakers).

- If your speakers are already powered (which means they already have a power amplifier built in), you do not need to connect them to an external power amplifier. In this case, you may go back to step 11 and connect the "MONITOR OUT L and R" jacks of the analog audio mixer directly to your speakers.

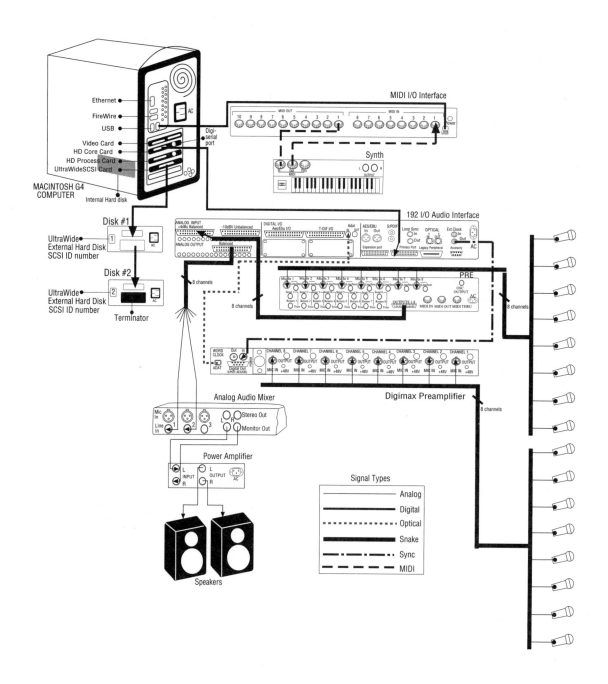

Diagram 3.2

Connecting a Pro Tools | HD 2 system to a MIDI I/O Interface, one 192 I/O, and two mic preamps

Connecting a Pro Tools | HD 2 system to a MIDI I/O interface, one 192 I/O, and two mic preamps

1. Connecting external SCSI hard disks to the system.

Make sure you have installed an Ultra Wide SCSI card in your computer.

- Connect the output of the Ultra Wide SCSI card in your computer to the "SCSI IN" port of Ultra Wide external hard disk #1 (SCSI ID #1) using a SCSI cable. It is better to keep the length of the SCSI cable short due to SCSI length limitations.

- Connect the output of Ultra Wide hard disk #1 to the "SCSI IN" port on Ultra Wide external hard disk #2 (SCSI ID #2) using another SCSI cable. (If your external hard disks are stacked together or next to each other, you can probably use a short 1ft. SCSI cable for this connection.)

- If this is the last disk in the chain, don't forget to terminate the last SCSI port of Ultra Wide External Hard Disk #2. When daisy chaining External Hard Disks together as in this example, the last unit always needs to be closed with a terminator plugged into the remaining SCSI connector.

2. Connecting the 192 I/O audio interface to the computer.

A 12-foot-long "DigiLink Interface" cable is provided when you purchase your Pro Tools|HD system. If you need a DigiLink cable other than 12 feet in length, you may purchase it from Digidesign. The available lengths are: 1.5 feet, 12 feet, 25 feet, 50 feet, and 100 feet.

- Connect the output of the "HD Core Card" (located at the back of your computer) to the "PRIMARY PORT" of the 192 I/O audio interface (located on its rear panel) using the 12-foot DigiLink cable provided.

3. Connecting the MIDI I/O interface.

- Using a USB cable, connect the MIDI I/O Interface to an available USB port on your computer (located on the back of the CPU).

4. Connecting your synthesizer to the MIDI I/O.

- Connect the "MIDI OUT 1" jack of the MIDI I/O interface into the "MIDI IN" jack of the synthesizer, using a MIDI cable.

- Connect the "MIDI OUT" jack of the synth into the "MIDI IN 1" jack of the MIDI I/O interface, using another MIDI cable.

5. Connecting the microphones to the mic preamps.

- You can connect eight microphones into a PRE (Digidesign's preamplifier), and eight more into a DigiMax (PreSonus' mic preamp) using either 16-XLR-female-to-XLR-male mic cables or two eight-XLR-female-to-XLR-male snakes.

- Connect eight microphones into "MIC IN 1 through 8" of the PRE.

- Connect eight microphones into "MIC IN 1 through 8" of the DigiMax.

6. Connecting the DigiMax to the 192 I/O audio interface.

- Connect the "ADAT OUT" jack from the DigiMax into the "ADAT IN" of the 192 I/O audio interface, using an optical cable.

- Connect the "EXT. CLOCK (256) OUT" jack from the 192 I/O into the "WORD CLOCK IN" jack of the DigiMax, using a BNC cable.

7. Connecting the PRE to the 192 I/O audio interface.

- Connect the "OUTPUTS 1–8" (DB-25 connector) of the PRE into the balanced "ANALOG INPUT" DB-25 connector of the 192 I/O, using a DB-25-to-DB-25 DigiSnake.

8. Connecting the 192 I/O to the analog audio mixer.

- Connect the "ANALOG OUTPUT #1–2" of the 192 I/O audio interface into "LINE IN #1–2" of your analog audio mixer, using a DB-25-XLR-male-to-¼"-TRS-male cable snake.

9. Connecting the mixer to the power amplifier.

- Connect the "MONITOR OUT L" jack (for the left side of your monitor) on the audio mixer to the "INPUT L" of the power amplifier, using a ¼"-TRS-male-to-¼"-TRS-male cable.

• Connect the "MONITOR OUT R" jack (for the right side of you monitor) on the Audio Mixer to the "INPUT R" of the power amplifier using another ¼"-TRS-male-to-¼"-TRS-male cable.

10. Connecting the Power Amplifier to the Speakers.

• Connect the "MONITOR OUT L" jack on the power amplifier to the left speaker, using a ¼"-TRS-male-to-XLR-male cable. (This is the type of cable that most speakers use. However, some speakers require other types of cables, so check your manufacturer's documentation for more information.)

• Connect the "MONITOR OUT R" jack on the power amplifier to the right speaker, using another ¼"-TRS-male-to-XLR-male cable (or the type of cable needed for your speakers).

• If your speakers are already powered (which means they already have a power amplifier built in), you do not need to connect them to an external power amplifier. In this case, you would connect the "MONITOR OUT L and R" jack of the audio mixer directly to your speakers.

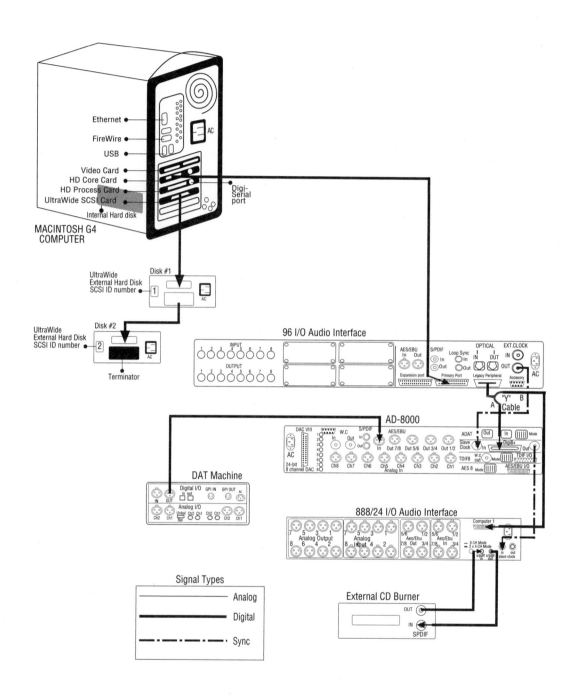

Diagram 3

Connecting a Pro Tools | HD 2 system using a 96 I/O audio interface and the "legacy" ports.

Connecting a Pro Tools | HD 2 system using a 96 I/O audio interface and the "legacy" ports.

1. Connecting external SCSI hard disks to the system.

Make sure you have installed an Ultra Wide SCSI card in your computer.

- Connect the output of the Ultra Wide SCSI card in your computer to the "SCSI IN" port of Ultra Wide external hard disk #1 (SCSI ID #1) using a SCSI cable. It is better to keep the length of the SCSI cable short due to SCSI length limitations.

- Connect the output of Ultra Wide hard disk #1 to the "SCSI IN" port on Ultra Wide external hard disk #2 (SCSI ID #2) using another SCSI cable. (If your external hard disks are stacked together or next to each other, you can probably use a short 1ft. SCSI cable for this connection.)

- If this is the last disk in the chain, don't forget to terminate the last SCSI port of Ultra Wide External Hard Disk #2. When daisy chaining External Hard Disks together as in this example, the last unit always needs to be closed with a terminator plugged into the remaining SCSI connector.

2. Connecting the 96 I/O audio interface to the computer.

A 12-foot-long "DigiLink Interface" cable is provided when you purchase your Pro Tools|HD system. If you need a DigiLink cable other than 12 feet in length, you may purchase it from Digidesign. The available lengths are: 1.5 feet, 12 feet, 25 feet, 50 feet, and 100 feet.

- Using the 12-foot long cable provided, connect the output of the "HD Core Card" located at the back of your computer to the "PRIMARY PORT" of the 96 I/O audio interface (located on the rear panel).

3. Connecting an AD-8000 to the 96 I/O audio interface.

- Synchronize the interfaces together by running a BNC cable from the "EXT.CLOCK OUT" jack on the 96 I/O audio interface to the "SLAVE CLOCK IN" of the "digi-8+" AMBUS card on the Apogee's AD-8000.

- Connect the single end of a "Y" cable to the "LEGACY PERIPHERAL" port on the 96 I/O audio interface, and connect the "A" side of the "Y" cable to the connector marked "digi-8+" on the AD-8000.

4. Connecting an 888/24 I/O audio interface to the 96 I/O.

- Using the same "Y" cable already plugged in to the "LEGACY PERIPERAL" port on the 96 I/O audio interface, connect the "B" side to "COMPUTER 1" on the 888|24 I/O audio interface.

- To complete the sync with both the 96 I/O audio interface and the AD-8000, connect a BNC cable between the "SLAVE CLOCK IN" on the 888|24 I/O audio interface and the "SLAVE CLOCK OUT" on the AD-8000.

5. Connecting the AD-8000 to a DAT Machine via AES/EBU digital format.

- Connect "DIGITAL I/O OUT" on the DAT machine to "AES/EBU IN" on the AD-8000, using a 110-ohm XLR-female-to-XLR-male cable.

6. Connecting an external CD burner to the 888|24 I/O audio interface using the S/PDIF digital format.

- Connect the "S/PDIF OUT" jack on the external CD burner to the "S/PDIF IN" on the 888|24 I/O audio interface using a 75-ohm RCA-male-to-RCA-male cable.

- Connect the "S/PDIF IN" jack on the external CD burner to the "S/PDIF OUT" on the 888|24 I/O audio interface using a 75-ohm RCA-male-to-RCA-male cable.

Pro Tools Software Windows

4

There are three main windows in Pro Tools: Edit, Mix, and Transport. A majority of the work within your sessions will occur in these three areas. It does not matter if you are using TDM or LE system configurations; the Edit, Mix and Transport windows are the same.

It's important to know and understand each element of every Pro Tools window. However, because Pro Tools is so robust, such analysis is beyond the scope of this book. What we will cover, though, will amply acquaint you with the toolset you will be using most of the time. In the event that you need to find more information about other Pro Tools windows, you can always refer to the printed or PDF file of the "Pro Tools Reference Guide" that comes with every Pro Tools system.

In this chapter we will cover the three main Pro Tools windows:

- The Edit Window

- The Mix Window

- The Transport Window

The Edit window

The Edit window is the first window you will see when you first create a new Pro Tools session. In Fig. 4.1, notice that it looks like a blank session. This is because no audio or MIDI tracks have been created yet.

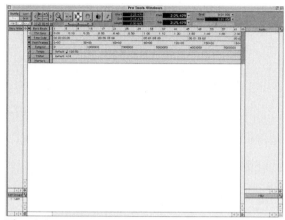

Fig. 4.1 The Edit window when you first create a new Pro Tools session.

Furthermore, if you look at the Mix window after you've created a new session, you will see an empty mixing board on the screen with no "channel strips" (input/output modules). Again, this is because you have not yet created any MIDI or audio tracks. To go to the Mix window, simply click on the "Windows" pop-up menu and select the "Show Mix" command. You can also press and hold your keyboard's "Command" key and then the "=" key (Fig. 4.2).

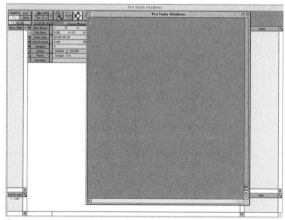

Fig. 4.2 The Mix window with no "channel strips" or faders.

Once you start creating audio and/or MIDI tracks and begin recording and editing the audio or MIDI regions, you will start to see an Edit window like the one in Fig. 4.3. In this screenshot I have identified all the elements in the Edit window. I will now explain each of them.

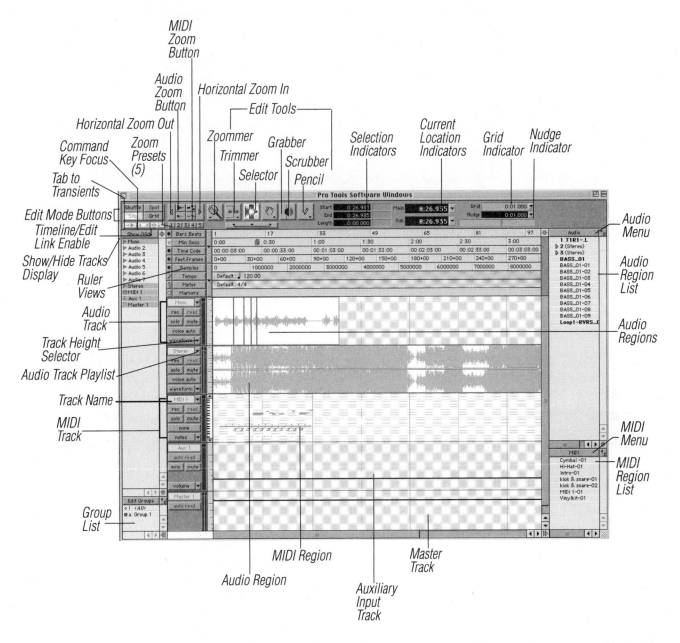

Fig. 4.3 Elements in the Edit window.

Edit Mode buttons

These four "Edit Mode" buttons—Shuffle, Slip, Spot, Grid (Fig. 4.4a and Fig. 4.4b)—are used to move audio and/or MIDI regions in different ways within or between different tracks in a Pro Tools session. Which one you should choose depends on what you want to accomplish. When using any of these modes, you will have to use the Grabber edit tool (the "little hand") to move audio or MIDI regions. You might be confused the first time you use the Edit modes, but with time and experience you will have no problems. Really—I mean it!

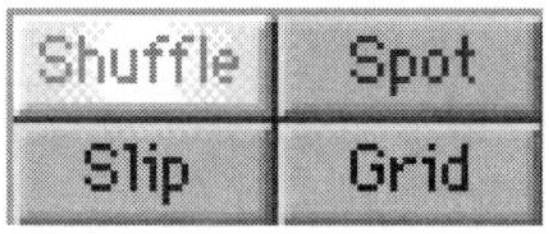

Fig. 4.4a The four Edit Mode buttons.

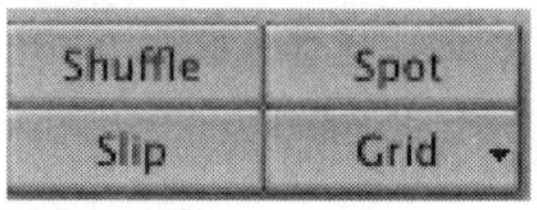

Fig. 4.4b The four Edit Mode buttons in Pro Tools 6.0.

Shuffle mode

TIP: If you are importing a region from the "Audio Regions List" to the beginning of any empty track, use the Shuffle mode, as it will snap to the beginning of the track.

When you move a region (audio or MIDI) in shuffle mode, the region will snap to the closest other region like a magnet. Shuffling flushes the beginning of the region you're moving to the next left-most region. If there are no other regions to the left, the shuffled region will align to the left-most location in the track. When you're working in this mode, it is not possible to overlap regions. You can, however, use this mode to insert regions within other regions. You can do this by first creating a separation within the region you want to make the insertion into; you then drag and drop the region you wish to insert over the newly created separation point. The right portion of the separated region will shift to the right in order to allow room for the inserted region.

SHORTCUT: You can access the Shuffle mode in different ways: a) by pressing the F1 key, b) by pressing the Option key and then "1" on the alphanumeric key (for Macintosh only), c) by continuously pressing the "~" key on your keyboard.

You will need to use the Shuffle mode to achieve the following results:

a) To make a region snap ("glue") to another one (Fig. 4.5a).

b) To insert a region inside of a specific area of another region after using the "Separate Region" command. This will automatically move the second part of the separated region to the right (Fig. 4.5b).

c) As seen in Fig. 4.5c and Fig. 4.5d, to move region B in front of region A, which will shuffle region A to the right.

Fig. 4.5a Snapping the highlighted region to the one on the left.

Fig. 4.5b After separating the region on the left into two parts, the highlighted region is inserted, sliding the right side of the separated region to the right.

Region "A"

Fig. 4.5c Selecting the B region.

Region "B"

Region "B"

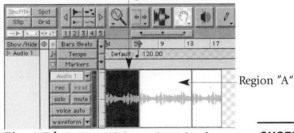

Region "A"

Fig. 4.5d Region A slides to the right after region B is inserted in front of A.

SHORTCUT: *You can access Slip mode in different ways: (a) by pressing the F3 key, (b) by pressing the Option key and then "3" on the alphanumeric keyboard (Macintosh only), or (c) by continuously pressing your keyboard's "~" key.*

Slip mode

Slip mode lets you move any region or MIDI notes freely to the left or to the right (Fig. 4.6a), or to an adjacent track (Fig. 4.6b), using the Grabber tool. By the way, you can also move a region to an adjacent track when you are in Shuffle or Grid modes. This mode also allows you to leave spaces between the regions (no audio) and to overlap one region on top of another, if so desired (Fig. 4.6c).

Selected region

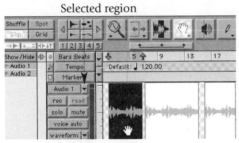

Fig. 4.6a Moving the selected region freely to the left or to the right.

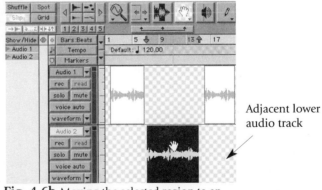

Adjacent lower audio track

Fig. 4.6b Moving the selected region to an adjacent lower audio track.

Region being overlapped

Overlapping region

Fig. 4.6c Overlapping the selected region on top of another.

Bear in mind that in Slip mode, you can accidentally overlap any region on top of another in the same track (Fig. 4.7a), and if you try to remove it by sliding it back to where it originally was without using the "Undo" command, you will delete the section of the bottom region covered by the overlapping region. This will leave a "hole" or space in between regions with no audio on the track (Fig. 4.7b).

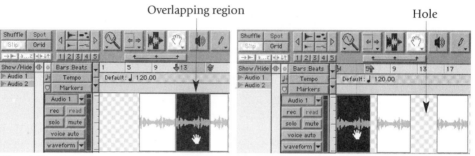

Fig. 4.7a Overlapping one region on top of another.

Fig. 4.7b Removing the overlapped region will leave a "hole" on the region of the bottom.

If this is the case, using the Trimmer tool, you can extend the regions on either side of the gap to replace the pre-gap region (Fig. 4.7c). After you have extended the region on either side of the gap to fill out the space completely, you can "heal" the separation to get the original region back—with no lines dividing the region (Fig. 4.7d).

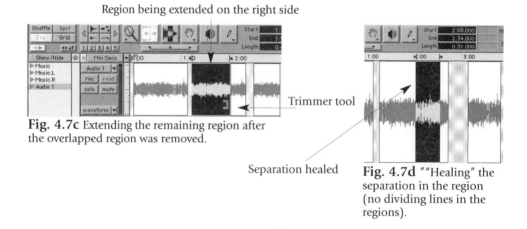

Fig. 4.7c Extending the remaining region after the overlapped region was removed.

Fig. 4.7d ""Healing" the separation in the region (no dividing lines in the regions).

You can accomplish this by highlighting the area where the division is—i.e., the line (Fig. 4.7e)—and then selecting the "Heal Separation" command located in the Edit pop-up menu (Fig. 4.7f).

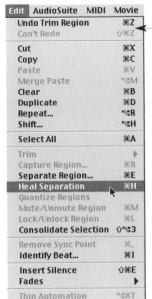

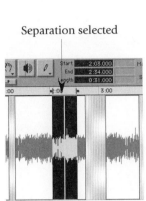

Separation selected

Fig. 4.7e Highlighting the region separation to be "healed."

Fig. 4.7f Selecting the "Heal Separation" command in the Edit menu.

Edit pop-up menu

Spot mode

Use Spot mode to place (move) regions to an exact pre-determined location in a track. The time interval the region will be moved to depends solely on the time-scale units the "Spot Dialog" box in Pro Tools is set to at the moment (Fig. 4.8). For example, you can make Pro Tools place a region to a specific setting of Bars:Beats, Mins:Secs, SMPTE time code, Feet:Frames, Samples, or a Regions/Markers location in the track. (Note that Pro Tools LE systems include only Bars:Beats, Mins:Secs, and samples.)

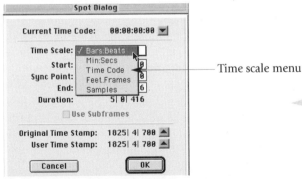

Time scale menu

Fig. 4.8 Shows the time-scale units in the Spot Dialog box.

SHORTCUT: *You can access Spot mode in different ways: (a) by pressing the F2 key, (b) by pressing the Option key and then "2" on the alphanumeric keyboard (Macintosh only), or (c) by continuously pressing your keyboard's "~" key.*

For example, as seen in Fig. 4.9a, when you click on the region in Spot mode with the Grabber tool, Pro Tools will prompt you to type the location where you want to precisely place the region. In this example, it asks for Mins:Secs because the time-scale units in the "Spot Dialog" box are set to Mins:Secs (Fig. 4.9b).

Clicking on the region
with the grabber tool

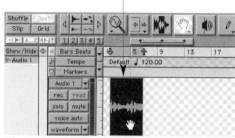

Fig. 4.9a Selecting an audio region to be
moved in Spot mode.

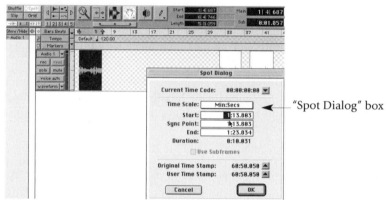

"Spot Dialog" box

Fig. 4.9b Typing the time interval (in minutes and
seconds) that you want to move the region.

In Fig. 4.9a and Fig. 4.9b, the region's original location was 01:13:803 (one minute, 13 seconds, 803 milliseconds). Since I want it to move it to the left and precisely place it at 30 seconds from the track's beginning, I typed in the "Start Time" box 00:30:000, or zero minutes, 30 seconds, zero milliseconds, and then I pressed "OK" to execute the move (Fig. 4.9c).

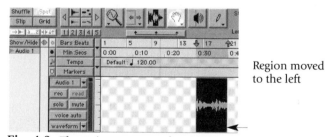

Region moved
to the left

Fig. 4.9c The region was moved to 30
seconds from the beginning of the track.

Grid mode

In Grid mode, you can move a region only within the resolution of a time grid. The time grid is set using the "Grid Indicator" window (Fig. 4.10a).

Grid Indicator

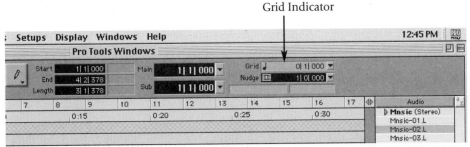

Fig. 4.10a Grid Indicator window.

Note: In Pro Tools software version 6.0, the Grid Indicator window was moved. It is now located right below the Edit tools (Fig. 4.10b).

Grid Indicator

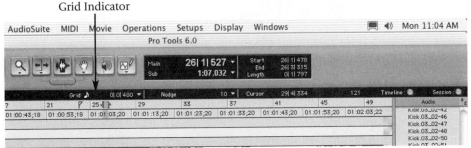

Fig. 4.10b The Grid Indicator window in Pro Tools 6.0.

SHORTCUT: *You can access Grid mode in different ways: (a) by pressing the F4 key, (b) by pressing the Option key and then "4" on the alphanumeric keyboard (Macintosh only), or (c) by continuously pressing your keyboard's "~" key.*

Use this mode to make exact moves without worrying if you're placing the region in the exact frame, sample, second, or beat you want. The region will "snap" to the nearest grid line. (This is unlike Slip mode, where you can freely move regions or MIDI notes without any time restrictions.)

In Fig. 4.11, the Grid Time Scale is set in musical terms to "Bars:Beats" and the Grid Value to "quarter-note." (This was done via the Grid Indicator window.) The region is positioned at "Bar 1|1|000," which means: bar one, beat one, zero ticks.

Grid Indicator
pop-up menu

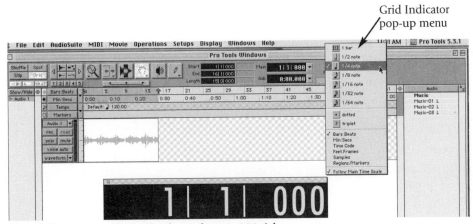

Fig. 4.11 Region positioned at bar 1, beat 1, 000 ticks.

If you wanted to move the region to bar 3:beat 2, you could just set the Edit Mode to "Grid" and use the Grabber tool to drag the region to bar 3:beat 2— that's it. Dropping the region over bar 3:beat 2 will snap the region to this starting point; you don't have to worry about placing it in this precise location. In Fig. 4.12 the region moved nine "grid lines" to the right, each grid line representing one quarter-note.

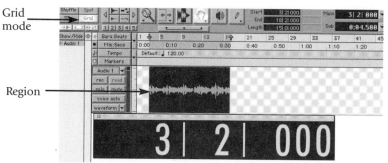

Grid mode

Region

Fig. 4.12 Region moved to bar 3:beat 2:000 ticks in Grid mode.

Of course, you can move regions using other time scales for music and post-production applications. The only thing you have to do is set the Grid Time Scale and the Grid Value in the Grid Indicator window.

Tab to Transient

Tab to Transient is a powerful function that's useful for making perfect loops. It lets you place the cursor right before an audio region's next detected transient peak. In order to navigate throughout an audio region, you will have to enable this function first by clicking on the icon located right underneath the Slip mode button (Fig. 4.13).

TIP: *Pressing the Tab key moves the cursor forward. To move the cursor backward using Tab to Transient, press the Option key and then Tab (Macintosh); for Windows systems press the Alt key and then Tab.*

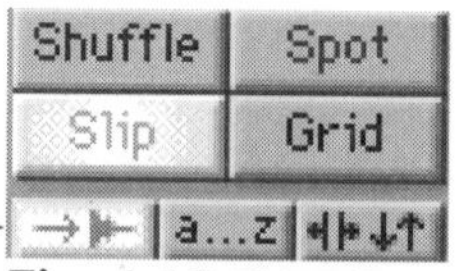

Tab to Transient ⟶

Fig. 4.13 The Tab to Transient function enabled.

Figure 4.14a shows the cursor moving from the beginning of the track to the next transient, as a result of pressing the keyboard's Tab key. Figure 4.14b shows the same waveform zoomed in to sample level: The cursor was in fact placed right before the audio region's next peak.

Tab to Transient

Cursor

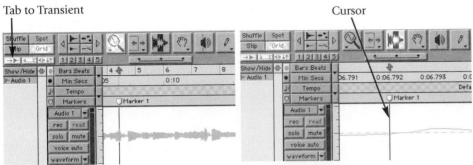

Fig. 4.14a Selecting the Tab to Transient function and pressing the Tab key to place the cursor before the next transient.

Fig. 4.14b Notice that the cursor was placed right before the next transient.

If you disable the Tab to Transient button and then press the Tab key, the cursor will be placed all the way to the end (to the right) of the region you have in your track. If you have several regions in a track, pressing the Tab key will move the cursor to the next adjacent region boundary. To move the cursor to the left from region to region, press the Option key and then Tab. Refer to Chapter 11 for more details on how to make region selections in various ways, including the Tab to Transient command.

Command Key Focus

Enabling Command Key Focus (Fig. 4.15) will allow you to use the single-key shortcuts from your alphanumeric keyboard. Before Pro Tools software version 6.0 came out, only TDM systems and not LE systems included this function. In order to access the single-key shortcuts and key commands, you have to have this function enabled.

SHORTCUT: *To enable Command Key Focus, press the Command + Option + "1" keys (Macintosh) or Control + Alt + "1" (Windows).*

Command key focus—

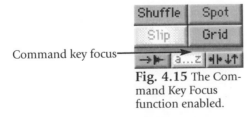

Fig. 4.15 The Command Key Focus function enabled.

Digidesign's ProTools Custom Keyboard (Fig. 4.16) provides quick visual access to all Pro Tools shortcuts and key commands. In addition to all the key commands and shortcuts being printed directly on its colored-coded keys, this alphanumeric computer keyboard has all the symbols and letters that a conventional "QWERTY" keyboard has.

Fig. 4.16
Digidesign's Pro Tools Custom Keyboard.

Timeline/Edit Link Enable

When this button is enabled (Fig. 4.17), the edit and timeline selections are linked.

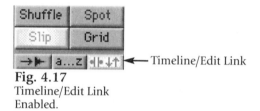

Fig. 4.17
Timeline/Edit Link
Enabled.

By disabling this function (turning the button off), you will be able to edit or audition other parts of the region or track without losing the original selection. For example, in Fig. 4.18a the region beginning at Marker 1 and ending at Marker 2 is selected. With Timeline/Edit Link Enable on, Pro Tools will play only that specific selection of the region. Additionally, if you have the Playback Loop command enabled, when you press Play, the playback will loop around that particular selection until you press Stop.

Now, disabling (button off) this function, if you place the cursor somewhere else in the region or track to start editing that specific location, playback will still start from Marker 1 and end at Marker 2 (Fig. 4.18b).

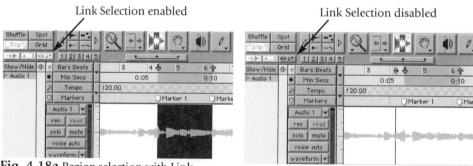

Fig. 4.18a Region selection with Link Selection enabled.

Fig. 4.18b Region selection with Link Selection disabled.

To make it more clear, suppose I want to reverse a beat of the region shown in Fig. 4.18c using the Reverse plug-in in the AudioSuite menu, but I still want to play back from the location where Marker 1 is. If I disable the Timeline/Edit Link Enable function and then press Play in the Pro Tools Transport window, the playback will start at Marker 1 and play until Marker 2. But if I want to audition how the reversed beat sounds like playing back from Marker 1, I will need to add a "post-roll" value in the Transport window to continue playing passing the Marker 2 limit and the reversed beat. Notice that in Fig. 4.18d I added (in musical terms) 1 Bar:0 Beats:000 Ticks in the Transport window's post-roll box so the playback will be extended one bar after reaching Marker 2.

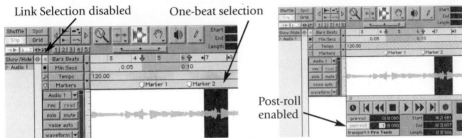

Fig. 4.18c Selecting a one-beat section of the region with Link Selection disabled.

Fig. 4.18d Reversing and playing back from the selected Marker 1 and adding a one-bar-long post-roll in the Transport window.

Show/Hide Tracks Display

In the Show/Hide Tracks Display pop-up menu (Fig. 4.19) you can show or hide selected tracks from the Edit window.

Fig. 4.19 The Show/Hide pop-up menu.

This is very useful when you have too many tracks displayed at a time (Fig. 4.20a); it can be very confusing when editing a specific track, especially if you have only one small computer monitor.

There are several options with showing or hiding tracks. You can show or hide all, few, or one of the selected tracks. (By "selected tracks" I mean tracks that are highlighted, as in Fig. 4.20b.)

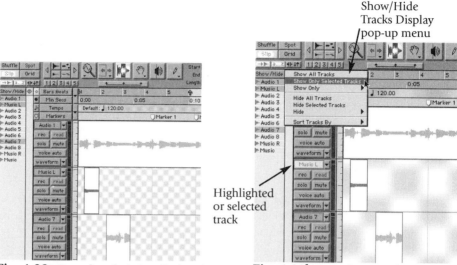

Fig. 4.20a Several tracks being displayed in the Edit window.

Fig. 4.20b Only the second track has been selected to be shown in the Edit window.

In this example I decided to show only the second track in the Edit window (Fig. 4.20c). Once I decided which track to show, I went ahead and changed the Track Height to Jumbo size (Fig. 4.20d), making it easier to edit.

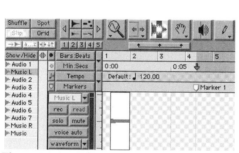

Fig. 4.20c Only the second track was selected to be shown.

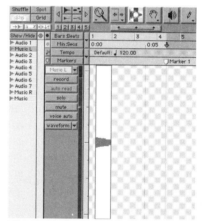

Fig. 4.20d After the second track was selected to be displayed, the Track Height was changed to Jumbo.

Ruler Views

There are two types of rulers in Pro Tools TDM and LE systems: Timebase and Conductor (Fig. 4.21a). Timebase rulers are used to provide a time reference to a region in a track, and they are also used to define Edit selections on a region and Timeline selections to set record and playback ranges in a track. The Conductor rulers indicate if there are any changes in meter and tempo in a session.

The Timebase rulers' names include: Bars:Beats, Mins:Secs, Time Code, Samples, and Feet:Frames. (Pro Tools LE systems do not include the Time Code and Feet:Frames rulers.)

The Conductor rulers' names include: Tempo, Meter, and Markers. The Markers are useful to mark specific locations in a session; for example, you can add markers to a song to identify the intro, the first verse, the bridge, etc.

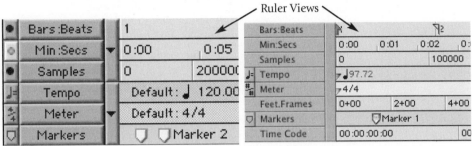

Fig. 4.21a The "Timebase" and "Conductor" rulers.

Fig. 4.21b The "Timebase" and "Conductor" rulers in Pro Tools 6.0.

Rulers can be displayed or hidden from the Ruler View Shows in the Display pop-up menu (Fig. 4.21c). They can also be displayed through the Ruler View pop-up menu located right underneath the Edit window's Zoom buttons (Fig. 4.21d).

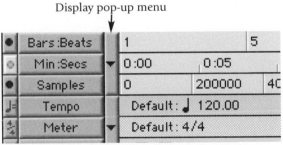

Fig. 4.21c Show/Hide rulers through the Display > Ruler View Shows in the Edit window.

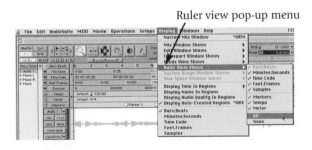

Fig. 4.21d Show/Hide rulers through the Ruler View pop-up menu.

When working in a session, you have the option to display "All" of the rulers, some of them, or "None." If you decide to hide all the rulers by selecting None in the Ruler View pop-up menu (Fig. 4.21e), the next time you open that session or create a new one, none of the rulers will be displayed (Fig. 4.21f).

Rulers View

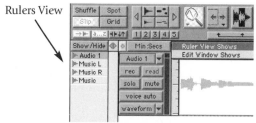

Fig. 4.21e Selecting "None" in the Ruler View pop-up menu.

Rulers View

Fig. 4.21f "None" of the rulers is displayed.

If you close a session with all the rulers displayed, the next time you open Pro Tools, all the rulers will be displayed in the Edit window (Fig. 4.21g). This is kind of a global Pro Tools function; if you hide them all, they will remain hidden in every session you open or create until you display them all again.

Rulers View

Fig. 4.21g All of the rulers are shown.

You can change the order of the rulers that are displayed—just like changing the order of the audio or MIDI tracks in the Edit or Mix window. For example, let's say you are working in a piece of music where you need to time-reference the regions in the tracks as Bars and Beats, and the Mins:Secs ruler is at the bottom of the list (nearest to the first track). Just by clicking, holding, and dragging the name of the Bars:Beats ruler, you can move it anywhere (Fig. 4.21h and Fig. 4.21i).

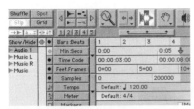 

Fig. 4.21h The Mins:Secs ruler is at the top.

Fig. 4.21i The Bars:Beats ruler is now at the bottom.

Main Time Scale

Main Time Scale is what determines the timebase units shown on the Edit window's Main Counter (Fig. 4.22a).

Fig. 4.22a Main Counter in the Edit window.

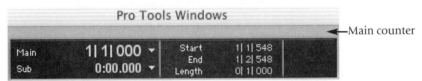

Fig. 4.22b Main Counter in the Edit window in Pro Tools 6.0.

Once you set the Main Counter Scale from the Display pop-up menu (Fig. 4.22c), the rest of the counters will display the same timebase units.

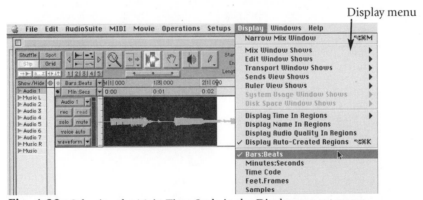

Fig. 4.22c Selecting the Main Time Scale in the Display pop-up menu.

In this case, I selected the Bars:Beats timebase units; consequently, the same units appear on the Transport's Main Counter; in the Transport window's Pre and Post amounts; in the selection of the Transport window's Start, End, and Length values (Fig. 4.22d); in the Grid and Nudge values; in the Main Counter's Start, End, and Length values (Fig. 4.22e); and in the Big Counter window (Fig. 4.22f).

Start, End, and length values

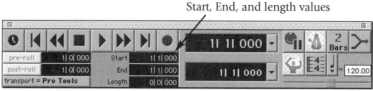

Fig. 4.22d The Transport window's Main Counter.

Start, End and length values   Grid and Nudge values

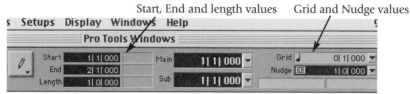

Fig. 4.22e The Grid and Nudge values and the Main Counter's Start, End, and Length values.

Fig. 4.22f The Big Counter window.

You can select only one timebase unit at a time in a session. You can set the Main Time Scale units to either Bars:Beats, Mins:Secs, Time Code (SMPTE), Feet:Frames, or Samples. (Time Code and Feet:Frames are included only in TDM systems.)

Sub Time Scale

If you need a second timing reference with different timebase units, you can assign it in the Sub Time Scale window, which is located right underneath the Main Time Scale window. For example, if you are working in musical terms (Bars:Beats) and you also want to time-reference the recording in minutes and seconds or SMPTE time code (TDM systems only), you could set the Main Time Scale counter to Bars:Beats and the Sub Time Scale counter to Mins:Secs (Fig. 4.22g).

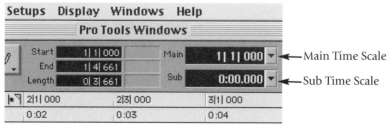

Fig. 4.22g The Main Time Scale counter is set to the timebase units Bars:Beats and the Sub Time Scale counter to Mins:Secs.

Track Height Selector

Sometimes when you are editing a region, it is very difficult to see details in the audio waveform or MIDI events. For this reason, Pro Tools gives you the option to change the track size (height).

There are six track sizes to choose from: Mini, Small, Medium, Large, Jumbo, and Extreme (Fig. 4.23a–f).

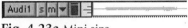

Fig. 4.23a Mini size.

Fig. 4.23b Small size.

Fig. 4.23c Medium size.

Fig. 4.23d Large size.

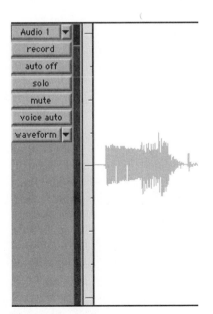

Fig. 4.23e Jumbo size.

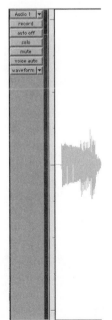

Fig. 4.23f Extreme size.

You can access the six track heights through the Track Height pop-up menu by clicking on the "down arrow" right next to the Waveform track-view selector (Fig, 4.24a). Or, click on the Amplitude Scale Area (the ruler-like bar) located just to the right of the track's level meter (Fig. 4.24b).

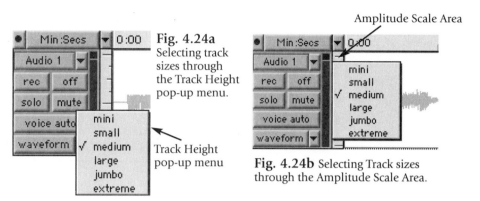

Fig. 4.24a Selecting track sizes through the Track Height pop-up menu.

Fig. 4.24b Selecting Track sizes through the Amplitude Scale Area.

Selecting the correct track size will depend on what you are doing at the moment. Maybe you have too many tracks on the screen and want to be able to see all them at once, for example. In this case, simply press and hold the Option key (Alt in Windows) and select the Mini or Small track size of any track; all the tracks will then be displayed in Mini or Small size (Fig. 4.25a–c).

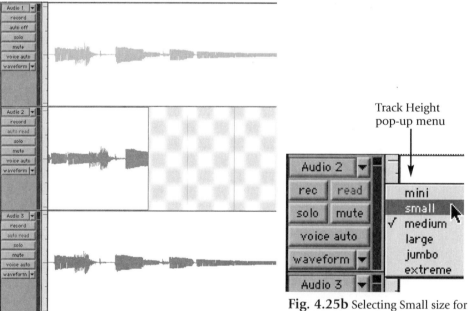

Fig. 4.25a Three of eleven audio tracks in Large size.

Fig. 4.25b Selecting Small size for all tracks at the same time using the Option key.

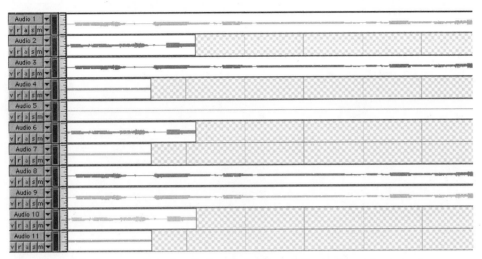

Fig. 4.25c All eleven tracks in Small size. Notice that all the tracks can be seen at once on the Edit window.

When you change the track size or height from Medium, Large, Jumbo, or Extreme to Small or Mini, some of the function buttons become hidden. For example, in Fig. 4.26a you can see that the track's name and the Rec, Read, Solo, Mute, Voice Auto, and Waveform buttons are shown in Medium size. (On LE systems, the Voice Auto button won't be displayed.) In Fig. 4.26b (Small size), the Waveform button was hidden and the Voice Auto, Rec, Read, Solo, and Mute buttons were changed from the complete name to only the initial letters. The track's name remains the same size. In Mini size only the track's name, the "S" (Solo), and the "M" (Mute) buttons are shown.

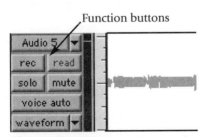

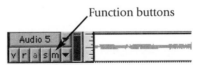

Fig. 4.26a An audio track in Medium size displaying all the function buttons with complete names.

Fig. 4.26b The track in Small size displaying only the initial letter of the function's name.

If you decide to keep all the Edit window's tracks in Mini or Small size but you want to see all the track's function buttons with complete names, you can switch to the Mix window (instead of the Edit window) to make whichever assignments you need. Regardless of the track height you select in the Edit window, the Mix window will be the default size, and you will be able to see the track's complete function buttons (Fig. 4.27). The other size of the Mix window is called Narrow Mix Window; you can select this through the Display pop-up menu.

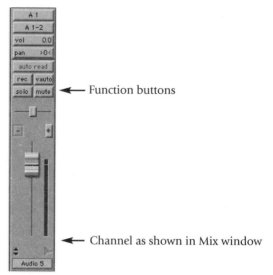

Fig. 4.27 All of the track's complete function buttons.

Track Playlist Selector

A Playlist is one or more audio or MIDI regions in a track arranged in a particular manner to be played back. A Playlist is commonly used to create a composite track or "Master Track" from several takes or passes of recorded audio or MIDI data. This technique is also known as "comping."

When you're planning to make a composite track on a TDM system, it helps to use a Playlist, because this way you won't need to sacrifice a voice every time you want to record a new audio or MIDI take. Recall from Chapter 1 that a "voice" in Pro Tools is equivalent to a track; the more tracks or voices you use in a session, the more you risk running out of tracks to record on.

With the Track Playlist Selector, you can create a "New" Playlist, "Duplicate" a Playlist, "Delete Unused" Playlists, and "Select" different Playlists in an audio or MIDI track.

You can access the Track Playlist Selector by clicking on the "down arrow" located to the immediate right of a track's name (Fig. 4.28).

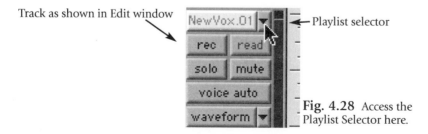

Fig. 4.28 Access the Playlist Selector here.

New Playlist

To create a new Playlist, simply click on the "down arrow." A pop-up menu will appear, prompting you to select New to create a new Playlist. In Fig. 4.28a, a region is present right underneath the pop-up menu. As soon as you select New, you will be asked to type a new name for the newly created Playlist (Fig. 4.28b). If you are recording a new take of the same audio or MIDI source, you may just want to allow Pro Tools to generate a name when you select New. This will allow you to keep track of the number of takes.

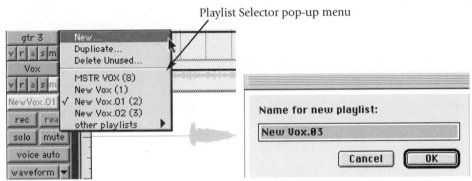

Fig. 4.28a Creating a new Playlist. **Fig. 4.28b** Renaming the Playlist.

Either type a new name for the newly created Playlist or allow Pro Tools to generate a name; then click "OK." The track that had a region on will turn blank (no audio or MIDI); this means the track is ready to record the new take (Fig. 4.28c).

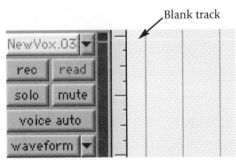

Fig. 4.28c The newly created Playlist with no audio or MIDI regions.

Duplicate a Playlist

You can duplicate a Playlist (Fig. 4.28d) if you want to experiment or practice your edits; this will keep the original Playlist or take intact. In other words, you're keeping the original take as a backup copy.

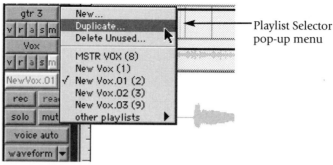

Fig. 4.28d Duplicating a Playlist.

Delete Unused Playlist

Once you are happy with the final edits you performed to create your comp or Master Track, you can delete all of the session's unused Playlists by using the Delete Unused command (Fig. 4.28e). When you command Pro Tools to delete the unused Playlists, a dialog box will appear with a list of all of the available Playlists. Select the Playlists you want to be deleted and click the Delete button (Fig. 4.28f)— all of the selected Playlists will be erased. You can select more than one Playlist at once to be deleted. If you realized you made a mistake deleting some of the Playlists, you can always Undo the commands, since you have up to 16 levels of Undo available.

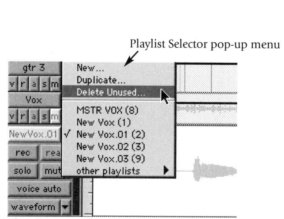

Fig. 4.28e Selecting the Delete Unused command.

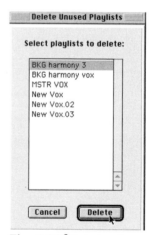

Fig. 4.28f Deleting the selected Playlist.

Selecting a Playlist

Selecting a Playlist or "other Playlist" in the same session is easy: Just choose the desired Playlist, and voila! The selected Playlist will appear on the track (Fig. 4.28g).

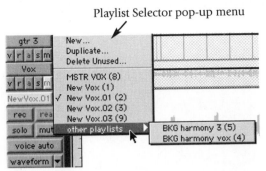

Fig. 4.28g Selecting a Playlist or "other Playlists" in a session.

Track Name

After you create a track (whether it's audio or MIDI), you can rename it. Notice I said "rename"—this is because every time you create a new track, Pro Tools gives it a default name: Audio 1, Audio 2, Audio 3, and so on (Fig. 4.29a).

Tracks as shown in the Edit window →

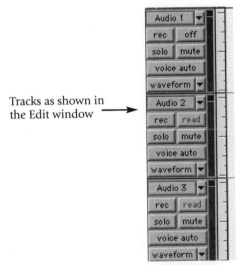

Fig. 4.29a Three audio tracks created with their default names: Audio 1, Audio 2, and Audio 3.

To rename a track, just double-click on its name section—in this case, "Audio 1." A dialog box will appear, prompting you to type a different name (Fig. 4.29b).

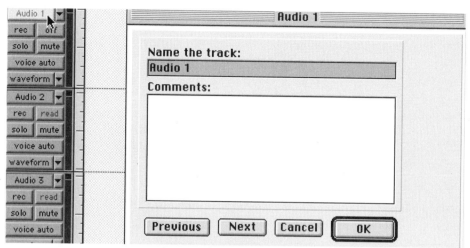

Fig. 4.29b Renaming a track.

After you've typed the new name (up to 31 characters), click "OK"; the new name ("Piano" in this example) will then appear on the track's name section (Fig. 4.29c).

TIP: I highly recommend that you rename your tracks before you record anything in them. This will prevent confusion when you search for them in the Audio Regions List. It is easier to find an audio file or region whose name makes some sense (e.g., Kick, Guitar, Piano) than it is to search through files with generic names like Audio 1 and Audio 2.

Tracks as shown in the Edit window

Fig. 4.29c Track with the new name (Piano).

Different types of tracks

There are four track types available in Pro Tools. Whether you're using a TDM or LE system, the track types are the same (Fig. 4.30a). They are:

- Audio Track
- Aux Input Track
- Master Track
- MIDI Track

New Track Dialog window

Track Type pop-up menu

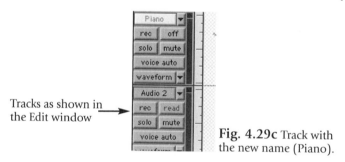

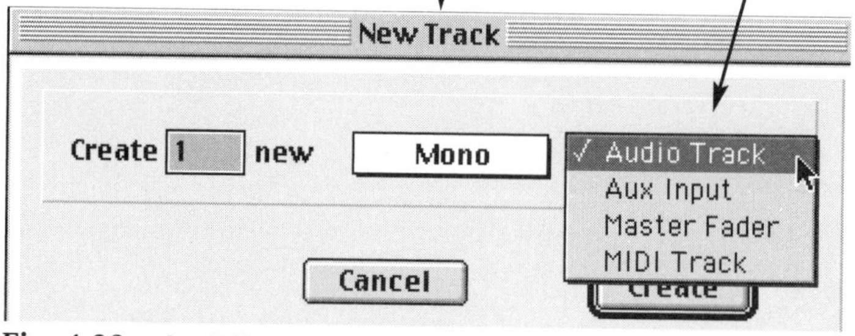

Fig. 4.30a The different types of tracks.

Audio Track

An Audio Track is one into which any sound source (a guitar, vocal, sound effect, etc.) can be recorded or imported. An audio track can be mono(phonic), stereo(phonic), or multi-channel surround. Don't confuse an Audio Track with a channel; a channel in Pro Tools is the physical connection between the audio interface and another hardware device (mixer, amplifier, etc.).

Once the sound source is on the audio track, it is displayed as a waveform (Pro Tools' default track view). This waveform is also referred as an "audio region" (Fig. 4.30b).

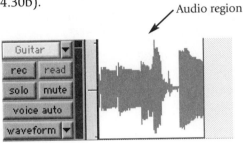
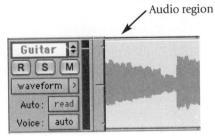

Fig. 4.30b An audio track with a waveform (audio region) displayed.

Fig. 4.30c An audio track with a waveform (audio region) displayed in Pro Tools 6.0.

An audio region can be edited and/or processed to be used in the Pro Tools session you are in at the moment, or it can be exported (bounced) and converted to any other file format supported by Pro Tools, such as SD II, AIFF, .WAV, MP3, or QuickTime.

Furthermore, an audio region can be routed internally to any destination within Pro Tools via any of the 64 buses available. It can also be routed outside Pro Tools by means of a physical audio output through an audio interface (192 I/O, 888 I/O, 1622 I/O, etc.) to any other external destination, such a hardware reverb unit, a DAT machine, an analog tape machine, etc. (Fig. 4.30d).

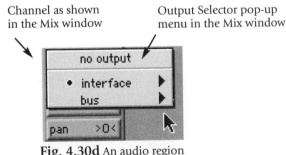

Fig. 4.30d An audio region can be routed internally within Pro Tools via an internal "bus," or externally via a physical audio output through an audio interface.

Fig. 4.30e Output selector pop-up menu in Pro Tools 6.0

Each audio track has the following controls:

- Rec
- Read (Automation Mode)
- Solo
- Mute
- Auto Voice (TDM systems only)
- Track View (Blocks, Waveform, Volume, Mute, and Pan)

Rec Button

The Rec button puts the track into Record Enable ("record ready") mode (Fig. 4.31a). Clicking (activating) this button means the audio track is ready to record the signal you want to capture, whether it be analog or digital.

TIP: To record-enable all of your session's audio tracks at the same time, press and hold the Option key (Alt in Windows) and click on any track's Rec button. All of the session's tracks will be record-enabled.

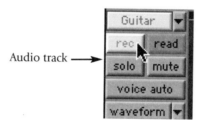

Audio track ⟶

Fig. 4.31a The Rec button enabled.

While in this mode, you will be able to check if the signal is getting into Pro Tools by looking at the level meter (just to the right of the track), and you should be able to adjust the signal recording level. Once the Rec button is activated and the recording levels satisfactory, simply click on the Transport's Record button until it is flashing, and then press the Play button to start recording.

If you want to record more than one track at once, click on the Rec button of each track you want to record onto.

Read Button

When you click on the Read button (Fig. 4.31b), all of the automation modes will be shown so that you can select the one you need to automate your session (Fig. 4.31c). Depending on the automation stage you are in, you can select Auto Write, Auto Latch, Auto Touch, Auto Read, or Auto Off. These modes can be accessed through either the Edit or Mix window.

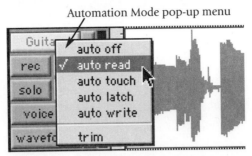

Automation Mode pop-up menu

Audio track

Fig. 4.31b The Read button.

Fig. 4.31c By clicking on the Read button, you can select the automation mode you need: Auto Read, Auto Touch, Auto Latch, Auto Write, or Trim.

Solo Button

The Solo button allows you to audition a particular track or tracks alone, as opposed to listening to all of the tracks at once. Clicking on one track's Solo button (Fig. 4.31d) automatically mutes the rest of the session's tracks. If you want to hear another track soloed along with the first one, just click on its Solo button. Pressing and holding the Option key (Alt in Windows) and then clicking on any track's Solo button will set all of the tracks to Solo.

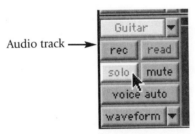

Audio track

Fig. 4.31d Selecting the Solo button.

TIP: If you want to turn off the solo function on all of a session's tracks with one click (for instance if you have so many tracks open that they cannot all be seen in the Edit or Mix window at once), just press and hold the Option key (Alt in Windows) and click on the any track's Solo button; then click again on any track's Solo button. The solos on all the tracks will be cleared.

Solo Safe Mode

You can also set a track to be in "solo safe" mode. This prevents a track from being muted when other tracks are soloed. This is useful when using Auxiliary Inputs as effect returns in a mixing situation. For example, let's say you want to Solo the snare with reverb so you can set the right amount of reverb on it. Normally, when you click on the track's Solo button, all of the other tracks are muted, right? Well, if you press and hold the Command key (Control in Windows) and then click on the Solo button of the Auxiliary Input track (in this example), every time you Solo the snare track from then on, the reverb track will be active (not muted) as well.

Mute Button

If you don't want to listen to a particular track in your session, click on that track's Mute button (Fig. 4.31e). This silences the track. You can have more than one track muted at a time. If desired, you can mute all of the session's tracks at once by clicking and holding the Option key (Alt in Windows) and then clicking on any track's Mute button.

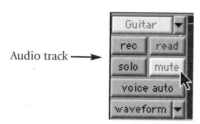

Audio track ⟶

Fig. 4.31e Enabling the Mute button.

Auto Voice Button (TDM systems only)

When in Auto Voice mode, every time you create a new audio track, Pro Tools automatically assigns a voice to that track (Fig. 4.31f). By clicking this button, you can assign a different voice number to a track (Fig. 4.31g) than the one Pro Tools automatically assigns. (Please refer back to Chapter 1 if you don't remember what a voice in Pro Tools is.)

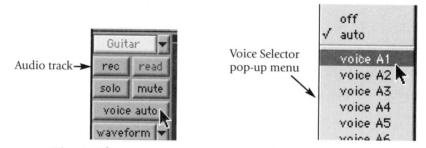

Audio track ⟶

Voice Selector pop-up menu ⟶

Fig. 4.31f Auto Voice mode.　　**Fig. 4.31g** Selecting a different voice.

Track View Selection Button

You can select the track view of an audio track any way you desire by clicking on the Waveform window (Fig. 4.31h). You can view a track by Waveform (default), by Blocks, by Volume, by Mute, or by Pan (Fig. 4.31i).

Audio track ⟶

Track view Selector pop-up menu ⟶

Fig. 4.31h The Track View Selection Window.　　**Fig. 4.31i** Selecting the track view.

- Waveform view. When you create a new audio track, it defaults to the Waveform track view (Fig. 4.32a). This means that any recorded or imported audio in the track will be displayed as waveforms with their corresponding color code, which signifies the voice assigned to the track. Only in the Waveform and Blocks view are you able to edit the audio—that is, copy, paste, capture, separate, duplicate, etc. The other views don't allow you to edit the audio.

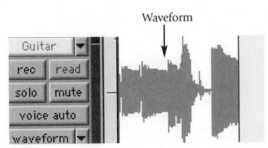

Fig. 4.32a An audio track displaying the Waveform view.

- Blocks view. If you notice that your computer slows down redrawing audio waveforms when you zoom in and out when recording, playing back, or editing, then you should use Blocks track view. As opposed to the Waveform view, the Blocks view will display only a blank rectangle with its perimeter colored the same as the voice assigned to the track (Fig. 4.32b). If you press Play, you can still hear the audio in the track, even though you don't see the waveform.

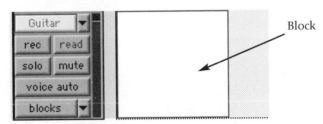

Fig. 4.32b Track displaying the Blocks view.

- Volume view. One of Pro Tools' greatest features is the ability to automate not only volume and panning but also the plug-ins' parameters as well as the send levels, among other parameters. There are two ways of automating in Pro Tools. One is the traditional way: By using the mouse or a control surface, you can make the necessary moves or adjustments on the on-screen faders, panning controls, etc. The second method involves drawing the changes in volume, muting, panning, etc., using the Grabber and/or Pencil editing tools.

One common technique for automating in Pro Tools combines the two methods. First you record all of the moves in real time using the mouse or a control surface; then, if necessary, you can edit the moves by redrawing them with the Pencil or Grabber tools. You must be in the Volume track view to be able to do this (Fig. 4.32c).

Volume

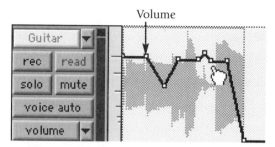

Fig. 4.32c Graphical volume automation.

- Mute view. As with the Volume track view, you can select the Mute view to automate mutes by redrawing them on the screen using the Grabber or Pencil editing tools. In a traditional mixing session usually you want to automate the muting on each track first; this is so you can clean up the unwanted noises on the tracks to get a better-sounding mix. Since you will be playing the song over and over during this process, it's an opportunity for you to learn the song and start getting ideas for your mix.

  In order to graphically automate the mutes, you must be in the Mute track view. In Fig. 4.32d, the Grabber tool is being used to create "breakpoints" to adjust the amount of muting in the track. A horizontal line over the track means the section of audio is not muted (you will hear it); conversely, a line on the bottom of the track means the particular section of audio is muted (you won't hear it).

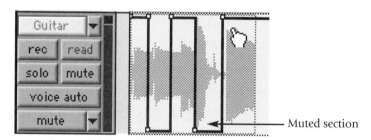

Muted section

Fig. 4.32d Graphical mute automation.

- Pan view. The Pan track view allows you to automate the panning controls graphically. In Fig. 4.32e, you can see the letter "L" on the track's upper-left side (to the right of the track's name). This means the track's left-side panning position; in the lower-left side is the letter "R" for the right panning position. You can use either the Grabber or Pencil editing tools to draw the panning controls' positions, from left to right or from right to left as well as the center position. Is a stereo track, "pan left" and "pan right" will be displayed for a selection (Fig. 4.32f). For surround mixing automation, multiple pan views will be displayed.

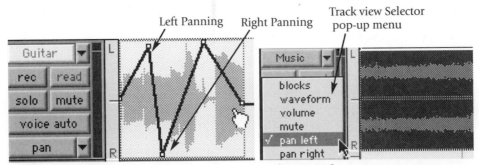

Left Panning   Right Panning   Track view Selector pop-up menu

Fig. 4.32e Graphical panning automation.

Fig. 4.32f Selection for panning automation in a stereo audio track.

Auxiliary Input Track

An Auxiliary Input track (Aux Input) can be created with the following track formats: mono(phonic), stereo(phonic), or multi-channel surround. The main difference between an audio track and an Aux Input track is that you cannot record audio onto it and you cannot assign voices to it (TDM systems only). The rest of the controls such as solo, mute, panning, automation, etc., are available in an Aux Input track (Fig. 4.33a).

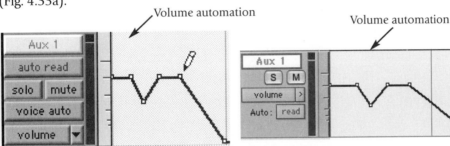

Volume automation

Volume automation

Fig. 4.33a An Auxiliary Input track with volume automation.

Fig. 4.33b An Auxiliary Input track with volume automation in Pro Tools 6.0.

Aux Input tracks are typically used for:

- effect sends or returns using plug-ins or external effect devices;
- sub-grouping tracks, meaning for instance that you can group a set of drums containing ten faders to be controlled by just one mono or stereo fader;
- monitoring external hardware devices or instruments, such as a bass guitar, a keyboard, etc.;
- assigning software-based synthesizer or sampler plug-ins as inserts.

Master Fader Track

A Master Fader track is used to control the overall output level of all your session's tracks that are routed to the main output, which defaults to Output 1 & 2 (if a stereo track). It can also be used as a sub-group track where you can assign a group of audio tracks to be controlled by just the master-track fader. This type of track can be mono, stereo, or multi-channel surround.

Because a Master Fader track controls output levels only, you cannot record audio onto it, solo it, or mute it. It also doesn't have an input selector. You can, however, assign plug-ins to it, and you can automate its volume and plug-in parameters.

A master track is displayed in the Edit window as a straight, horizontal black line. This line is the actual fader level (Mix window), which you can modify any way you desire using the Grabber or Pencil editing tools. This way you can graphically automate a Master Fader track's volume.

In Fig. 4.34a, the Grabber tool is being used to insert a new "breakpoint" to redraw the black line and create a fade-in. The "–2.4dB" on top refers to the volume level at that breakpoint. The number will appear for an instant whenever you create a new breakpoint.

TIP: If you want to see that number for a longer time period to analyze a specific breakpoint's volume level (or the level for the entire track), click and hold over the line using the Grabber or Trimmer editing tools.

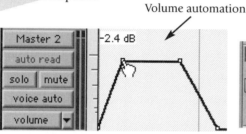
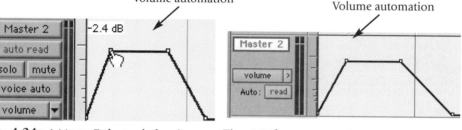

Fig. 4.34a A Master Fader track showing a fade-in and fade-out as well as the level at which the fade-in ends.

Fig. 4.34b A Master Fader track showing a fade-in and fade-out as well as the level at which the fade-in ends in Pro Tools 6.0.

MIDI Track

A MIDI Track (Fig. 4.35a) records and plays back only MIDI information, not audio signals. It stores MIDI notes, MIDI controller data, program-change information, system-exclusive data, etc.

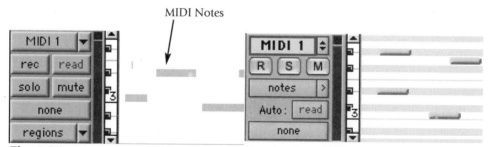

Fig. 4.35a A MIDI track containing MIDI notes.

Fig. 4.35b A MIDI track containing MIDI notes in Pro Tools 6.0.

If you were to compare a MIDI track and an audio track side by side, you'd notice they have almost the same controls, with the exception of the insert points and effect sends. Furthermore, while an audio track has a voice-assignment selector (TDM systems only), a MIDI track has a program-change selector. Also, in an audio track you can select the inputs and outputs for routing the signal internally or externally in Pro Tools; in a MIDI track, however, you can select the

MIDI channel or external MIDI device where you want to direct the MIDI information. Refer to Chapter 9 for more details on MIDI in Pro Tools.

Edit Groups List

The Edit Groups list, a column located on the Edit window's lower left side, contains all of the groups of tracks you create in your session. Why would you want to group tracks? Well, let's say you are mixing a song containing 48 tracks, and the producer would like you to solo just the drums and percussion tracks so he can listen to them without any other instruments. So what would you do? You'd group the drums and percussion tracks, of course. By grouping them, you will only have to press the Solo button on any drum or percussion track that's a member of that particular group of tracks. In other words, grouping provides a way for linking tracks and their controls, and it facilitates the editing and mixing process.

When you create a new Pro Tools session, a group named "All" is included by default and cannot be modified or deleted. Enabling (highlighting) this group by clicking on it will select every track in the session. If you don't create any groups, the Edit Groups list will be empty except for the "All" group (Fig. 4.36a). As soon as you start creating groups using the File menu's Group Selected Tracks command, the groups will begin to appear in the Edit Groups list, as seen in Fig. 4.36b.

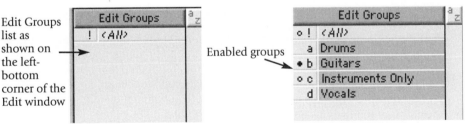

Edit Groups list as shown on the left-bottom corner of the Edit window

Enabled groups

Fig. 4.36a The Edit Groups list with no groups in it, except the "All" group created by default.

Fig. 4.36b The "Edit Groups" list with four enabled (highlighted) groups.

Every time you group a number of selected tracks, a dialog box (Fig. 4.37) will appear.

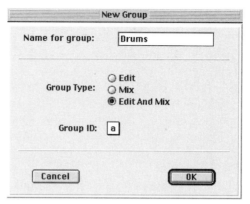

Fig. 4.37 The New Group dialog box.

- "Name for group" is where you give a name to the group. If you don't name it, it will receive a generic name such as "Group 1" or "Group 2."
- Next, select the "Group Type." This allows you to enable and disable a group through the Edit window only, through the Mix window only, or through both windows.
- Finally, select the "Group ID." You can create up to 26 different groups, from a to z. A color code will be assigned to each group. Therefore, with one glance in the Mix window, you'll be able to recognize what group a track belongs to.

As I mentioned, after you create several groups, they will appear in the Edit Groups list on both the Edit and Mix windows. While in the list, you can activate (highlight) or deactivate (no highlight) each of the groups by simply clicking on its name. You don't have to press Shift or any other key to do so.

In Fig. 4.38, notice a black dot on the left side of the Guitars group. Also notice that the track names of the members of the same group are highlighted. This is visually useful to discern which tracks belong to a specific group in the Edit and Mix windows. If you click on the left of any other group's name, the black dot will move and the names of that group's members will be highlighted.

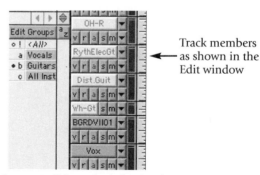

Track members as shown in the Edit window

Fig. 4.38 When you click on the left side of any group name, that group's track members are highlighted.

Zoom buttons

When editing, you may want to look at the audio or MIDI regions in greater detail by "zooming in" closer. Or maybe, you wish to see the entire waveform length of all of your project's tracks on the computer screen by "zooming out" the waveform and/or MIDI-note views without affecting the playback. To do this, use the Zoom buttons (Fig. 4.39a)—these allow you to adjust the track waveform view vertically and horizontally.

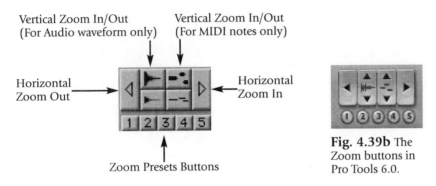

Fig. 4.39b The Zoom buttons in Pro Tools 6.0.

Fig. 4.39a The Zoom buttons.

The display's adjustments (zoom in/out) take place around the cursor or selector's center position. This will keep the location of the waveform you want to edit always in the center of your computer screen (Fig. 4.40).

Fig. 4.40 After you click once on the Zoom buttons' right arrow, the cursor will remain centered on your screen.

The Zoom buttons include:

- Horizontal Zoom Out. Clicking this button (or "left arrow") horizontally compresses the track view so you can see more of the track, albeit with less detail. This is useful when you want to see an overview of the tracks up to their entire length (Fig. 4.41a–c).

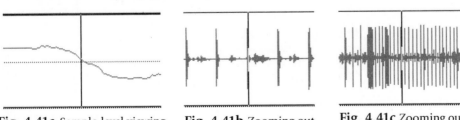

Fig. 4.41a Sample-level viewing provides the most resolution.

Fig. 4.41b Zooming out.

Fig. 4.41c Zooming out further to overview level.

SHORTCUT: *You can zoom out horizontally by pressing the Command key (Control in Windows) and using the left bracket ("[") key.*

• Horizontal Zoom In. Clicking this button (or "right arrow") horizontally expands the track view so you can get a closer look with more detail. You can zoom all the way in to "sample" level for performing extremely fine Pencil-tool edits, for example to get rid of pops and clicks in the audio (Fig. 4.42a–c).

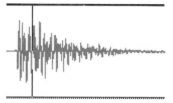

Fig. 4.42a Original view.

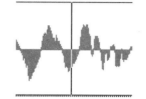

Fig. 4.42b Zooming in.

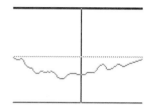

Fig. 4.42c Zooming in to sample level.

SHORTCUT: *You can zoom in horizontally by pressing the Command key (Control in Windows) and using the right bracket ("]") key.*

• Vertical Zoom In/Out (audio): Use these buttons to increase (make taller) or decrease (shorten) the height of all the audio waveform on the screen (Fig. 4.43a–c). You might do this so you can edit the audio with a more detailed view, or to see more of an overview. Remember, this is for visual purposes only; it doesn't change the audio's actual volume or amplitude.

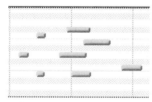

Fig. 4.43a Original view.

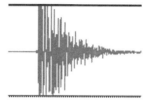

Fig. 4.43b Zooming in.

Fig. 4.43c Zooming out.

SHORTCUT: *Pressing the Command + Option keys (Control + Alt in Windows) and using the left bracket key vertically zooms out the view, making waveforms appear shorter; doing the same with the right bracket key vertically zooms in the view, making them appear taller.*

Vertical Zoom In/Out (MIDI): These two buttons perform the same function as above, but they affect all the MIDI tracks only—not the Audio, Aux Input, or Master Fader tracks (Fig. 4.44a–c).

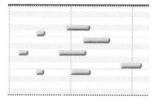

Fig. 4.44a

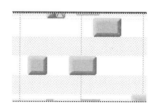

Fig. 4.44b

Fig. 4.44c

TIP: *To return to the previous zoom magnification after pressing any zoom button, press and hold the Option key (Alt in Windows) and click on any Zoom button. This will affect all audio and MIDI tracks.*

Zoom Preset buttons (1-5)

You can store and recall any zoom magnification of a waveform or MIDI track via the five Zoom Preset buttons. These are set up with factory default settings; you can cycle through them by clicking on the numbers 1 through 5.

You can also save your own zoom magnification settings. To do this:

1. Select the zoom magnification level you want by using any Zoom button or the Zoomer tool (Fig. 4.45a).

2. Next, while pressing the Command key (Control in Windows), click on one of the five numbered Zoom Preset buttons. The button will flash for a second, as if you're taking a photograph. This means the zoom magnification level has been saved. The next time you click on that specific Zoom Preset button, the zoom setting will be recalled.

Zoom buttons

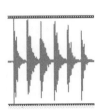

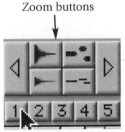

Fig. 4.45a Magnification level selected.

Fig. 4.45b Saving the zoom setting on preset on button #1.

SHORTCUT: *To recall a Zoom Preset with your computer keyboard, press and hold the Control key (Start in Windows) and type a number from 1 to 5 on your keyboard's alphanumeric section (not on the numeric keypad).*

Edit tools

Pro Tools has six Edit tools that allow you to zoom in and out, trim regions, make region selections, move regions, audition regions, and draw automation, among other functions (Fig. 4.46a).

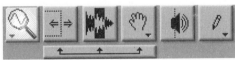 

Fig. 4.46a The Edit Tools.

Fig. 4.46b The Edit Tools in Pro Tools 6.0.

TIP: *If you have a TDM system or an LE system with Pro Tools software version 6.0, to recall a zoom preset, you can just type any number from 1 to 5 on the alphanumeric keyboard, provided you've enabled the Command Key Focus button.*

You can cycle through the Edit tools to select any of them by clicking repeatedly on your alphanumeric keyboard's "Esc" (Escape) key. You can also press and hold the Command key (Control in Windows) and click on key numbers 1, 2, 3, 4, 5, 6, or 7 to select a tool. Some of these tools have more than one mode (denoted by the "down" arrow on the tool icon); if this is the case, keep pressing repeatedly on the number key to cycle through the different tool modes.

Zoomer tool

When you select the Zoomer tool and position it on the Edit window, it turns into a miniature magnifying-glass icon with a "+" sign in it. This means that whenever you click on the region you want to zoom in, the tool will magnify it (Fig. 4.47a and Fig. 4.47b). If you keep clicking on the region, it will keep zooming in, up to sample-level view.

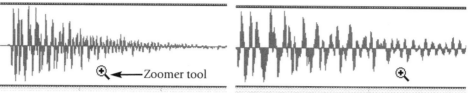

Fig. 4.47a Zooming in with one click on the region.

Fig. 4.47b Zooming in with two clicks on the region.

SHORTCUT: *To toggle between the two Zoomer tools, hold down the Command key (Control in Windows) and repeatedly click on your alphanumeric keyboard's "1" key. You can also simply use the F5 key.*

Conversely, if you press and hold the Option key (Alt in Windows), the magnifying-glass icon will have a "–" sign in it. This means that when you click on a region, the tool will zoom out or take a wider view of the region selected—or part of it—every time you click on it (Fig. 4.48a–c).

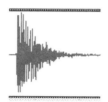

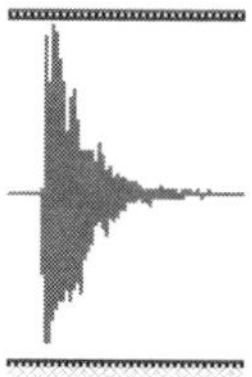

Fig. 4.48b When you press and hold the Option key, clicking once on a region zooms out the view, reducing the resolution.

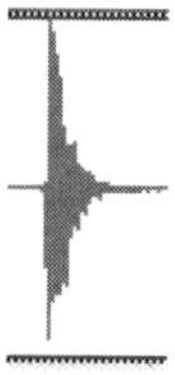

Fig. 4.48c Clicking on the region once more (while pressing the Option key) horizontally zooms out the view by one more increment.

Fig. 4.48a Original view.

You can also click and drag using the Zoomer tool over the region area you want to horizontally zoom in. This is a quicker way to magnify a specific area than just clicking over it. If you wish to zoom in this way, I suggest placing the magnifying-glass icon a little to the left of the desired area; then click and drag the Zoomer to the right, covering the specific section you want to enlarge. The Zoomer tool will be left in the place where you released the mouse button, enlarging the area you needed (Fig. 4.49a and Fig. 4.49b).

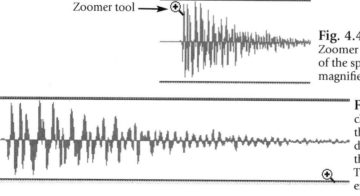

Zoomer tool ⟶

Fig. 4.49a Place the Zoomer tool to the left of the specific area to be magnified.

Fig. 4.49b After clicking and dragging the mouse over the desired area, release the mouse button. That area will be enlarged.

There are other ways to zoom in and out using the Zoomer tool:

- Press and hold the Command key (Control in Windows) while dragging the mouse over the selected area to zoom horizontally and vertically.
- To go back to the previous zoom level, press and hold the Option key (Alt in Windows) and click over the region with the Zoomer tool.
- To zoom out so that all regions are visible in the Edit window, double-click on the Zoomer tool. You can also accomplish the same thing by pressing and holding the Option key (Alt in Windows) and the letter "A."

In Fig. 4.46 (page 153), notice that the Zoomer tool has a drop-down selector (denoted by a "down" arrow). This means that the Zoomer tool has other modes. The one you see by default is "Normal Zoom," which I have been discussing above. The other is called "Single Zoom" mode. You will find this second mode in Pro Tools version 5.1.1 and higher.

Single Zoom mode is useful for when you want to zoom in within a track and quickly change the cursor to the Selector tool. First-time Pro Tools users often get frustrated when they try to zoom in once within a track and immediately try to select a section of a region without realizing they are still in the Zoomer tool. Instead of zooming in and making a selection right away, they find themselves zooming in again and again. So the next time you want to zoom in and then make a region selection, set the Zoomer tool to Single Zoom mode.

Trimmer tool

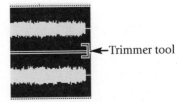

In Pro Tools, the term "trimming" refers to resizing a region to a desired length without cutting or erasing the region's trimmed portions. In other words, after you have trimmed the region's start or end point, you can always extend it back to its original length if needed.

There are certain situations when you may want to use the Trimmer tool:

- When you need to shorten or lengthen a region from the start or end point to the desired region length (Fig. 4.50a and Fig. 4.50b).

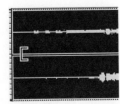

Fig. 4.50a Shortening the start of the region with the Trimmer tool.

Fig. 4.50b Lengthening the end of the region with the Trimmer tool.

- When, in graphical automation mode, you need to change (trim) a track's (or tracks') volume automation levels without affecting their relative fader values or levels, for example (Fig. 4.51a and Fig. 4.51b).

Fig. 4.51a Selecting and trimming volume automation preserves its relative values.

Fig. 4.51b Relative automation levels being lowered through trimming.

- To extend or shorten a fade-in, fade-out, or crossfade between two regions after they were done (Fig. 4.52a–c).

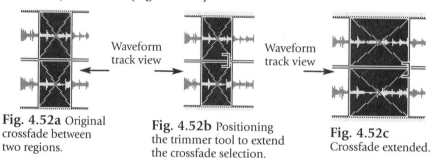

Fig. 4.52a Original crossfade between two regions.

Fig. 4.52b Positioning the trimmer tool to extend the crossfade selection.

Fig. 4.52c Crossfade extended.

The Trimmer tool and the Edit modes

While trimming a region, the shortening or lengthening of a region will be affected differently depending on the Edit mode you are in (Shuffle, Slip, Spot, or Grid). Let's look at the different situations.

TIP: *If, when trimming a region, you don't want the regions on either side to move while trimming, then "lock" those regions. You can do this by selecting the desired regions with the Grabber tool and then pressing and holding the Command key (Control in Windows) and clicking on your alphanumeric keyboard's "L" key.*

- Shuffle mode: If you shorten a region's start or end point while in Shuffle mode, the region or regions that are located after the trimmed region will move to the left—along with the trimmed region—by the exact amount of trimming you are performing. Conversely, if you are extending a region's start or end point, the other regions will move to the right. They will stay together, "glued" with each other (Fig. 4.53a–c).

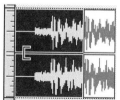 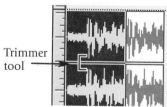 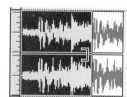

Trimmer tool

Fig. 4.53a Original region without trimming.

Fig. 4.53b The start point was shortened and the right region moved to the left.

Fig. 4.53c The end point was extended and the right region moved to the right.

• Slip mode: If you shorten or extend a region's start or end point while in Slip mode, the region or regions to the left and right of the trimmed region will not move as they do in Shuffle mode. They will stay in their respective locations, leaving a blank space on the track. This means there will be silence (no audio) for that time period. On the other hand, when you're extending a region to the left or right, you might overlap other regions if you aren't careful. This will cause the covered (overlapped) region to be muted (Fig. 4.54a–c).

TIP: *To avoid overlapping regions while trimming in Slip mode, press and hold the Control key (Alt in Windows). When you trim, you'll extend the desired region up to—but not beyond—the next region's border. Try it!*

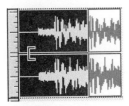

Fig. 4.54a Preparing to shorten the region's start point.

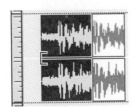

Fig. 4.54b The region was shortened according to the assigned Grid value, leaving a blank space at the beginning of the track.

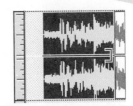

Fig. 4.54c Extending the region's end point. Notice that the right region was overlapped by the amount of the assigned Grid value.

• Grid mode: Trimming in Grid mode is similar to trimming in Slip mode: The neighboring regions won't move in either direction, and blank spaces will be left on the track(s). The only difference is that the trimming will be constrained by the grid value assigned at the time (Fig. 4.55a and Fig. 4.55b).

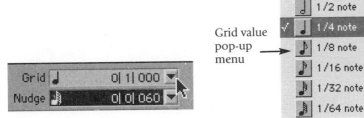

Grid value pop-up menu →

Fig. 4.55a The Grid value window.

Fig. 4.55b Selecting a Grid value of a quarter-note.

When you extend a region to the left or right in Grid mode, you might overlap other neighboring regions if you aren't careful. This will cause the covered region to be muted for the amount of time that it's overlapped (Fig. 4.56a–c).

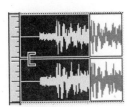

Fig. 4.56a Positioning the Trimmer tool to shorten the region's start point.

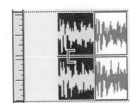

Fig. 4.56b The region was shortened, leaving a blank space on the track.

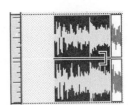

Fig. 4.56c Extending the region to the right. The adjacent region was overlapped, muting a section of the overlapped region.

- Spot mode: If you are shortening or extending a region's start or end point in Spot mode, the region or regions located after or before the region you are trimming will not move in either direction. Instead, they will be overlapped by the amount of time you typed in the Spot dialog window (Fig. 4.57a), which appears when you click on the region you are about to trim. Be aware that you can also select the Time Scale in the Spot dialog window; this can be Bars:Beats, Mins:Secs, Time Code, Samples, etc.

To trim a region while in Spot mode:

1. Position the trimmer tool on the region you need to shorten or extend (Fig. 4.57b).
2. Click on the region using the Trimmer tool. A Spot dialog window will appear on the screen, prompting you to type the length (in minutes and seconds or bars and beats) to which you want to extend or shorten the region. The time units will depend on the Time Scale you select in the Spot dialog window.
3. Once you select the length, press "OK." The region will be shortened or extended. If there is a region next to the one you are trimming, it will be overlapped if the trimming length exceeds the neighboring region's start point (Fig. 4.57c).

TIP: *Anytime you're in the Trimmer tool, you can change the tool's direction by pressing and holding the Option key (Alt in Windows).*

Fig. 4.57a The Spot dialog window set to Mins:Secs.

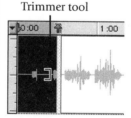

Trimmer tool

Fig. 4.57b Placing the trimmer tool to extend the region's start point to the right.

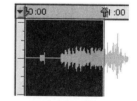

Fig. 4.57c The region was extended beyond the blank space between the regions, causing the left region to overlap the right region and muting the portion that was overlapped.

Trimming To Selection

There's a faster way to trim a region: Rather than using the Trimmer tool to trim the region's start and end points one at the time, you can select an exact length within a region and trim the start and end points with one click, if desired. This is done by using the "Trim" and the "To Selection" commands located in the Edit menu.

To Trim To Selection:

1. Select the area you desire using the Selector tool (Fig. 4.58a).

2. Go to the Edit menu and select the "Trim" command and slide the cursor to the right to select the "To Selection" option (Fig. 4.58b). You can also hold down the Command key (Control for Windows) and click on the letter "T" on your keyboard.

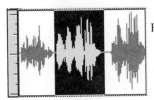 Edit menu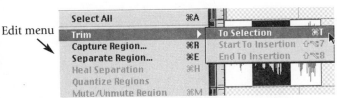

Fig. 4.58a Selecting the desired area of a region to trim the start and end points at once.

Fig. 4.58b Choosing the "Trim" and the "To Selection" command in the Edit menu.

3. Once you have chosen the "To Selection" option, release the mouse. The exact selection you made within the region will be the only section left on the track you are working on (Fig. 4.58c). In other words, the region's start and end point will be trimmed.

4. If Pro Tools is in Slip, Grid, or Spot mode at the time you release the mouse, the region's selected section will remain in the same location (Fig. 4.58c). On the other hand, if Pro Tools is in Shuffle mode, the region's selected section will snap (move) to the beginning of the track, provided no other regions are in the way (Fig. 4.58d).

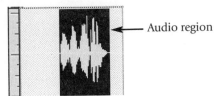 ← Audio region

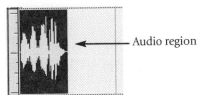 ← Audio region

Fig. 4.58c The selected trimmed region remained in the same location because Pro Tools was in Slip mode when the "Trim" and the "To selection" commands were applied.

Fig. 4.58d The selected trimmed region moved (snapped) to the beginning of the track because Pro Tools was in Shuffle mode when the "To Selection" command was applied.

TIP: You can change the direction of the Trimmer tool at any time by pressing and holding the Option key (Alt for Windows) while in the Trimmer tool.

5. If there are regions between the one you are trimming and the beginning of the track (Fig. 4.58e), the trimmed region will then snap (move) to the end point of the nearest region (Fig. 4.58f).

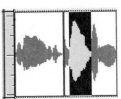

Fig. 4.58e Selecting the area to be trimmed.

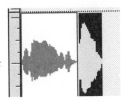

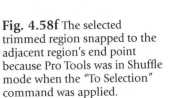 **Fig. 4.58f** The selected trimmed region snapped to the adjacent region's end point because Pro Tools was in Shuffle mode when the "To Selection" command was applied.

Trimming With "Start To Insertion" and "End To Insertion"

There are two other options in the Edit menu's "Trim" command which you can use to trim a region: "Start To Insertion" and "End To Insertion."

To trim a region using "Start To Insertion":

1. Using the Selector tool, position the cursor closer to the region's start point, up to where you want to trim it (Fig. 4.58g).

2. Go to the Edit menu, select the "Trim" command, and then slide the cursor to the right to select the "Start To Insertion" option (Fig. 4.58h). You can also hold down the Shift and Option keys (Shift and Alt in Windows) and click on your alphanumeric keyboard's "7" key.

3. After selecting the "Start To Insertion" command, the region's start point will be trimmed (Fig. 4.58i).

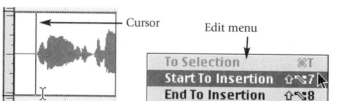
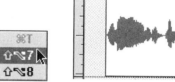

Fig. 4.58g Positioning the cursor to the desired location.

Fig. 4.58h Selecting the "Start To Insertion" command in the Edit window.

Fig. 4.58i The region's start point was trimmed.

To trim a region using "End To Insertion":

1. Using the Selector tool, position the cursor closer to the region's end point, up to where you want to trim it (Fig. 4.58j).

2. Go to the Edit menu, select the "Trim" command, and slide the cursor to the right to select the "End To Insertion" option (Fig. 4.58k). You can also hold down the Shift and Option keys (Shift and Alt in Windows) and click on your alphanumeric keyboard's "8" key.

3. After selecting the "End To Insertion" command, the region's end point will be trimmed (Fig. 4.58l).

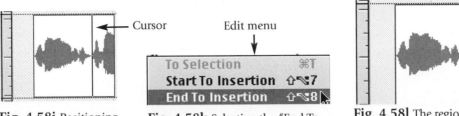

Fig. 4.58j Positioning the cursor to the desired location.

Fig. 4.58k Selecting the "End To Insertion" command in the Edit window.

Fig. 4.58l The region's end point was trimmed.

When in Slip, Spot, or Grid mode, the "Trim" > "Start To Insertion" command does the same thing regardless of the mode. The same is true of the "Trim" > "End To Insertion" command. However, these operations are not available in Shuffle mode.

Trimmer Scrub and TCE modes

When looking at the Edit toolbar, you will notice that the Trimmer tool has a drop-down selector that allows you to choose two extra trimming modes. These are the Scrub (TDM systems only) and the TCE (Time Compression/Expansion) modes.

Trimmer Scrub mode

The Scrub mode (Fig. 4.59a) allows you to listen to what you are trimming in real time—you can audition what you are shortening or extending.

To trim a region using Scrub mode, simply position the Trimmer tool where you want to begin trimming (Fig. 4.59b). Then, click and hold down the mouse and start moving the tool in either direction. In doing so, you will hear the audio as you're trimming it. Once you find the place you need to trim to, release the mouse—the trim will be completed (Fig. 4.59c).

SHORTCUT: To toggle among the three Trimmer tools , hold down the Command key (Control in Windows) and repeatedly click on your alphanumeric keyboard's "2" key. You can also simply use the F6 key.

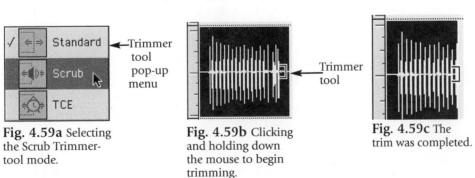

Fig. 4.59a Selecting the Scrub Trimmer-tool mode.

Fig. 4.59b Clicking and holding down the mouse to begin trimming.

Fig. 4.59c The trim was completed.

Trimmer TCE Mode

The TCE (Time Compression/Expansion) Trimmer-tool mode (Fig. 4.60a) allows you to stretch or compress a region time-wise without changing its pitch. This function has several great applications. Suppose you wrote a piece of music for a commercial and sent it to the producer—but he calls you and tells you that your music is a half-second too long for the 15-second spot. No need to panic—all you have to do is use the TCE Trimmer-tool mode and adjust the region (your music) to be exactly 15 seconds long. Pro Tools will time-compress it to the precise length, and voila! Problem solved. You wouldn't notice any pitch change in your music, but it would be a bit faster.

To trim a region using the TCE mode:

1. First, select the TCE Trimmer-tool mode (Fig. 4.60a). The Trimmer tool will look like the normal Trimmer tool, but with a small alarm clock in it.

2. Position the TCE Trimmer tool over the region you want to start trimming (Fig. 4.60b).

3. Click and hold down the mouse, and start adjusting the region to the time location you desire. You can monitor the length of your adjustment by looking at the "Length" box in the "Selection Indicators," either in the Transport window or the Edit window.

4. Once you have chosen the precise time length you want to stretch or compress the region to, release the mouse. A window will appear notifying you that the Time Compression/Expansion process is taking place. When finished, the region will be stretched or compressed to the desired time length. Play it back and listen to the difference (Fig. 4.60c).

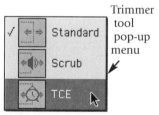

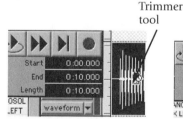

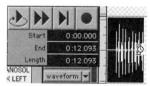

Fig. 4.60a Selecting the "TCE" Trimmer-tool mode.

Fig. 4.60b Clicking and holding down the mouse button to trim the region to the desired time length.

Fig. 4.60c The TCE process was accomplished. In this case, the region was expanded from 10 seconds to 12 seconds.

The Selector tool

The Selector tool allows you to horizontally select specific lengths of a region or multiple regions (if grouped).

To make a selection using the Selector tool:

1. Position the cursor wherever you wish to start your selection. If while making a selection the current edit mode is Shuffle, Slip, or Spot, you'll be able to freely select the section needed. If you're in Grid mode, the selection will be constrained by the Grid value assigned at the time.

2. Click and drag the mouse until you finish making your selection (Fig. 4.61a).

3. If you need to adjust your selection, I suggest zooming in until you can see the region with more detail. Then, extend or shorten the selection using the blue arrows located in the Timebase ruler (right on top of the first track in the Edit window). Just click and drag the blue arrows in the direction you need (Fig. 4.61b).

> **TIP:** *Use the blue arrows in the Timebase ruler to expand or shorten the region selection without pressing any keys. If you prefer, you can also adjust the region selection by holding down the Shift key and clicking inside the region's selection in the track, and then dragging the mouse in the necessary direction.*

> **SHORTCUT:** *To choose the Selector tool, hold down the Command key (Control in Windows) and your alphanumeric keyboard's "3" key. Or simply press the F7 key.*

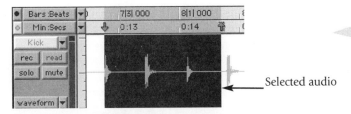

Fig. 4.61a Making a selection of a region with the Selector tool.

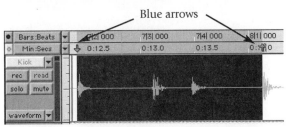

Fig. 4.61b Adjusting the region selection using the blue arrows located in the Timebase ruler.

The Time Grabber tool

Although the Time Grabber (or Grabber) tool is used mostly to move regions to a different location, you can also use it for other interesting editing applications. For example:

1. Selecting an entire region with a single click. You can do this by placing the Grabber tool over the desired region and clicking on it to select it (Fig. 4.62a and Fig. 4.62b).

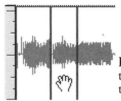

Fig. 4.62a Placing the Grabber tool over the desired region.

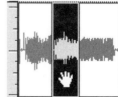

Fig. 4.62b Clicking once on the region will select it. You can then move it to a new location if desired.

2. Making a copy of a selected region. The Grabber is generally used to move regions around, but you can actually make a copy of a region just by clicking and dragging it to a new location in the track. To accomplish this:

   a. Select the Time Grabber tool and position it over the desired region (Fig. 4.63a).

   b. Press and hold down the Option key (Alt in Windows) and click the cursor over the selected region (Fig. 4.63b).

   c. Still holding down the Option key and the mouse button, drag the region to a new location in the track and release the mouse. A copy of the region will be made and placed in the new location (Fig. 4.63c).

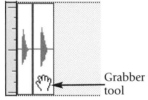

Grabber tool

Fig. 4.63a Positioning the Time Grabber tool over a region to make a copy of it.

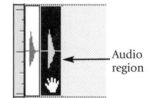

Audio region

Fig. 4.63b Pressing and holding the Option key and the cursor over the selected region.

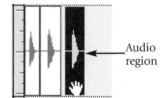

Audio region

Fig. 4.63c Dragging the region to a new location creates a copy of the region.

3. Moving audio regions within a track or between different tracks. You can also move MIDI and Conductor events with the Grabber. While moving a region with the Grabber, the tool's behavior will be different depending on the current Edit mode (Shuffle, Slip, Spot, or Grid) Pro Tools is set to:

   a. Shuffle mode: When you move a region in this mode, the region will "snap" like a magnet to the neighboring regions. This applies only if there are other regions on either or both sides of the region you are trying to move. For example, in Fig. 4.64a, the region in the middle is about to be moved to the left. In Fig. 4.64b, the region in the middle "snapped" like a magnet to the region on the left. Now, if I try to move the middle region to the right once it is snapped," I won't be able to do it, since the region is already "glued" to the one on its left. Trying to move the third region (on the far right) farther to the right isn't possible in Shuffle mode (Fig. 4.64c), because there is no other region to "glue" it to. Of course, you can always change the edit mode to Slip if you need to move the region to the right.

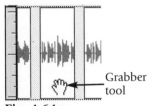

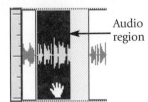

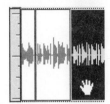

Audio region

Grabber tool

Fig. 4.64a Selecting the region in the middle.

Fig. 4.64b Moving or sliding the region to the left. Notice that the region "snapped" onto the region on the left.

Fig. 4.64c Now, the right-most region can only be moved to the left because Pro Tools is in Shuffle mode.

b. Slip mode: If you need to move a region freely in any direction and with no constraints, set Pro Tools to Slip mode. For example, let's say I have three regions in a track (Fig. 4.65a) and I need to move the middle one just a bit to the right so it will be flush with the starting point of the one on the right (Fig. 4.65b). No problem—Slip mode allows you to freely move any region any amount, in either direction. A piece of advice, though: Be careful when moving a region in this mode. If you place it right on the boundary of the region next to it (if any), you might overlap the region. The result will be muting the region underneath. In Fig. 4.65c, the region on the right was "covered" by the one in the middle. This will cause the starting point of the region on the right to be muted for that time period. Try it yourself and you will understand.

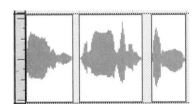

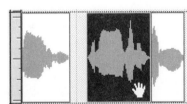

Fig. 4.65a Three audio regions.

Fig. 4.65b Moving the middle region to the starting point of the region on the right.

Overlapping region

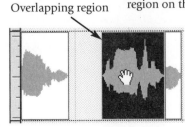

Fig. 4.65c The middle region is overlapping the one on the right, muting that region's starting point.

c. Grid mode: In Grid mode you can move or slide a region in either direction. In this way it's similar to Slip mode, except that the move will be
constrained by the Grid's current value. For example, if the Grid's current
value is set to a quarter-note, you'll be able to move the region only in
quarter-note intervals. You cannot move the region to the right or to the
left by a sixteenth-note, or by a half-second; you'd have to set the Grid
value to a sixteenth-note or to 500 milliseconds—or set Pro Tools back to
Slip mode so you can freely slide the region (Fig. 4.66a and Fig. 4.66b).

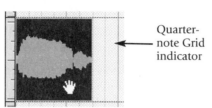 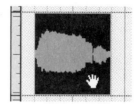

Quarter-
note Grid
indicator

Fig. 4.66a Moving the
region in quarter-note
increments. This is the
current Grid value in
this example; every
quarter-note is defined
by the vertical lines at
the end of the selected
region.

Fig. 4.66b The region
was moved to the right
by a quarter-note interval.

d. Spot mode: Let's say you need to move a region that's located at the
beginning of a track—in other words, at 0:00:000 (zero minutes, zero
seconds, zero milliseconds). The new location you need to move it to is
20:00:000 (20 minutes, zero seconds, zero milliseconds). To accomplish
this in the Slip mode, you'd have to slide the region all the way to the
right, scrolling the screen the whole way, until you got to the desired
location. This would probably take you a minute or more to position the
region exactly. Instead of going to all that trouble, move it in Spot mode:
Select Spot edit mode, position the Grabber tool over the region you need
to move (Fig. 4.67a), and click on it. A Spot dialog box will appear,
prompting you to type the new location you want to move the region to
(Fig. 4.67b). Type in 20:00:000 (for this example) and press "OK." The
region will be moved immediately to the exact location where you need
it (Fig. 4.67c). This operation takes about three seconds. Not bad, don't
you think?

Transport
window

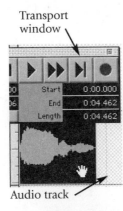

Audio track

Fig. 4.67a Positioning the Grabber over the region at the beginning of the track. Notice that the "Start" time on the Transport window is 0:00:000.

Fig. 4.67b Typing the new location where you want the region to be moved to—in this case, 20:00:000.

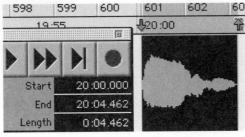

Fig. 4.67c The region has been moved to the new and exact location. Notice that the "Start" time in the Transport window is now 20 minutes, zero seconds, zero milliseconds.

4. Editing and inserting automation breakpoints. While in Volume, Pan, or Mute track view, you can edit and insert volume, panning, and muting automation breakpoints with the Grabber tool. For example, to insert and move breakpoints in the Volume track view for graphic automation, do the following: Go to the Volume track view if you are not already in it (Fig. 4.68a). With the Grabber tool, click over the black line (fader volume level) to insert breakpoints (Fig. 4.68b). To move a breakpoint—in this case, to lower the volume in the middle of the region—click and hold the mouse right on the middle breakpoint and pull it down (Fig. 4.68c).

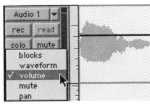

Fig. 4.68a

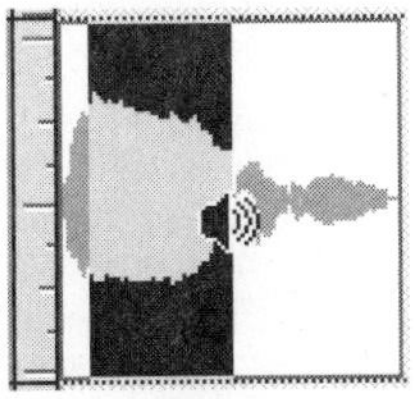

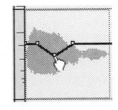

Fig. 4.68b

Fig. 4.68c

The Grabber "Separation" and "Object" modes

Similar to the Trimmer tool, the Grabber tool also has a drop-down selector that allows you to choose two other modes besides the Time Grabber mode. These are the Separation Grabber and the Object Grabber (TDM systems only).

TIP: *You can delete tempo and meter events, Markers, and automation breakpoints with the Grabber tool if you hold down the Option key (Alt in Windows) and click on each event and breakpoint with the Grabber.*

Separation Grabber

The Separation Grabber mode allows you to select an audio or MIDI region with the Selector tool and separate it out of the source region. Clicking on the selected region with the Separation Grabber tool will create a new region so you can move it to a new location in the track.

To use the Separation Grabber mode:

1. Select the Separation Grabber mode from the Grabber tool icon in the Edit window. The Grabber tool will have a miniature scissors icon in it (Fig. 4.69a).
2. Make the desired region selection using the Selector tool. This will be a portion of the source region (Fig. 4.69b).
3. Position the Separation Grabber tool over the selected area (Fig. 4.69c).
4. Click and hold the cursor on the selected region. Drag it out of the source region to a new location in the track (Fig. 4.69d).

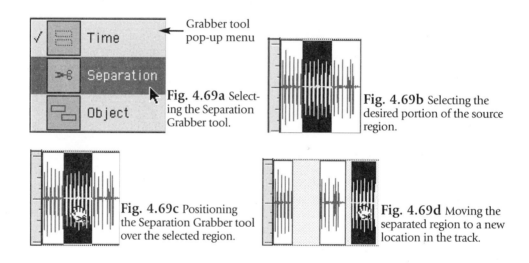

Fig. 4.69a Selecting the Separation Grabber tool.

Fig. 4.69b Selecting the desired portion of the source region.

Fig. 4.69c Positioning the Separation Grabber tool over the selected region.

Fig. 4.69d Moving the separated region to a new location in the track.

Object Grabber (TDM systems only)

The Object Grabber tool lets you select two or more audio or MIDI regions that are not located next to each other. Trying to do so with the regular Time Grabber tool would be impossible.

In Fig. 4.70a, the second region from the left was selected, and the Time Grabber is positioned to select the fourth region. After clicking on that region, you can see the third one was selected as well (Fig. 4.70b). Unfortunately, this was not what I was trying to achieve. I wanted to select only the second and fourth regions without selecting the third one.

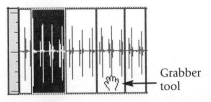

Fig. 4.70a Selecting the first region.

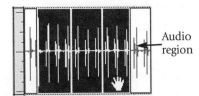

Audio region

Grabber tool

Fig. 4.70b Trying to select the fourth region without including the third one. Unfortunately, using the Time Grabber, the third region was selected as well.

SHORTCUT: *To select and toggle through the three Grabber tools, hold down the Command key (Control in Windows) and repeatedly click on your alphanumeric keyboard's "4" key. You can also simply use the F8 key.*

Here's how you could select only the second and fourth regions:

1. Select the Object Grabber mode from the Grabber tool icon in the Edit window. The Grabber tool will have a couple of horizontal bars in it (Fig. 4.7c).

2. Hold down the Shift key and click on the regions you want to select. In Fig. 4.70d I selected the second, fourth, and sixth regions with the Object Grabber tool. Notice that the regions are surrounded by thick black outlines.

3. Next, release the Shift key and click and drag the selected regions to wherever you need to move them. In Fig. 4.70e, I moved the three selected regions down to another track underneath, keeping their positions in the track. In other words, I extracted those three regions out of the source region.

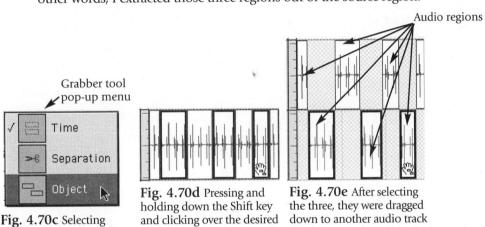

Audio regions

Grabber tool pop-up menu

Fig. 4.70c Selecting the Object Grabber tool.

Fig. 4.70d Pressing and holding down the Shift key and clicking over the desired regions to select.

Fig. 4.70e After selecting the three, they were dragged down to another audio track below.

The Scrubber tool

Before Digital Audio Workstations (DAWs) existed, the way you'd locate a specific edit spot on a reel of tape was by rocking the tape back and forth across the tape head while listening to the output, until you identified the exact location on the tape. In Pro Tools, the Scrubber tool performs the same job—but instead of rocking the tape reels back and forth, you click and drag the mouse over an audio region. An advantage you have by using Pro Tools (as opposed to any analog tape machine) is that you're not only listening to the audio while finding the right spot, you're also able to see the audio's waveform during the location process. The Scrubber tool has no effect on MIDI tracks.

Some practical applications of using the Scrubber tool:
- To audition (to listen to) an audio region in a track by clicking and dragging the mouse over the region in any direction. To achieve this:
  1. Select the Scrubber tool from the Edit Tools section in the Edit window (Fig. 4.71a). Notice that the cursor becomes a small "speaker" icon when you select the Scrubber tool.
  2. Position the Scrubber on the audio region.
  3. Click, hold down, and drag the mouse (the Scrubber) in any direction. By this point you will be able to listen to the audio region (sound) you have the Scrubber tool on (Fig. 4.71b).
- To make a region selection from one time location to another:
  1. Select the Scrubber tool.
  2. Locate and place the Scrubber at the exact spot where you wish to start your audio region selection.
  3. Hold down the Shift key.
  4. Click, hold down, and drag the mouse (while still holding down the Shift key) until you reach the end-point location of the region selection you need (Fig. 4.71c).

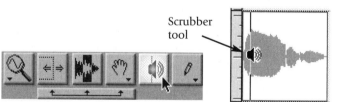
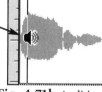
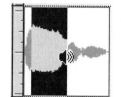

Fig. 4.71a Selecting the Scrub tool in the Edit Tools section of the Edit window.

Fig. 4.71b Auditioning an audio region in a track.

Fig. 4.71c Making a region selection and listening while making the selection.

- To separate an audio region into two regions from a specific spot:
  1. Select the Scrubber tool.
  2. Locate and place the Scrubber at the exact spot where you wish to separate the region into two.

3. Go to the Edit pop-up menu and select the "Separate Region" command, or hold down the Command key (Control in Windows) and press your keyboard's "E" key.

4. You now should see a vertical line in the source region signifying that the region has been separated (Fig. 4.71d).

- To add a "Sync Point" in a desired audio-region location after you've auditioned it:

   1. Select the Scrubber tool.

   2. Locate and place the Scrubber at the exact spot where you wish to add a Sync Point on.

   3. Go to the Edit pop-up menu and select the "Identify Sync Point" command.

   4. You will notice that a small downward-pointing triangle icon appears over the exact spot you selected (Fig. 4.71e).

TIP: The zoom level determines the resolution for the Scrubber, and the distance and speed dragged determine the speed and length for the scrubbed audio. For finer resolutions without zooming, press Command (Macintosh) or Control (Windows) while scrubbing.

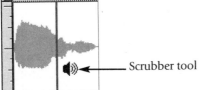

Scrubber tool

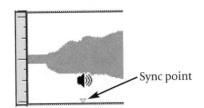

Sync point

Fig. 4.71d The audio source region separated into two regions using the Scrubber tool.

Fig. 4.71e Adding a Sync Point on a specific spot of an audio region using the Scrubber tool.

Auditioning a Stereo Audio File Using the Scrubber Tool

If you wish to audition a stereo audio file—whether this file resides on one stereo audio track or in two mono audio tracks—do the following:

1. To audition the track's left side only, place the Scrubber tool on the upper of the two mono tracks (assuming the left track is positioned above the right track). Click and drag the Scrubber to listen to that track. Depending on the direction you are dragging the Scrubber, the audio will sound accordingly. For normal playback, drag the Scrubber to the right; for reversed playback, drag the Scrubber to the left (Fig. 4.72a).

2. To audition the track's right side only, place the Scrubber tool on the lower of the two mono tracks (assuming the right track is positioned below the left track); then click and drag the Scrubber (Fig. 4.72b).

3. To audition both the left and right sides at the same time, place the Scrubber tool between both tracks (Fig. 4.72c).

SHORTCUT: To select the Scrubber tool, press F9, or press and hold the Command and the number "5" keys (Control for Windows) on the alphanumeric keyboard.

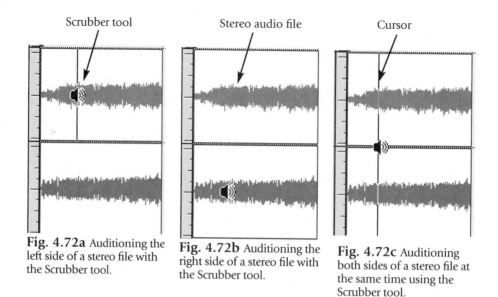

Fig. 4.72a Auditioning the left side of a stereo file with the Scrubber tool.

Fig. 4.72b Auditioning the right side of a stereo file with the Scrubber tool.

Fig. 4.72c Auditioning both sides of a stereo file at the same time using the Scrubber tool.

The Pencil tool

Unlike the Scrubber tool, the Pencil tool works on both MIDI and audio tracks. In audio, its main function is to "draw" waveform (audio) and automation changes. In MIDI, you can add MIDI note events, do MIDI velocity and pitch changes, etc. The Pencil tool's most useful applications are:

Audio applications

1. Fixing any "clicks" or "pops" that might have been generated while digitally recording in Pro Tools. One of the causes of this is the lack of good Word Clock synchronization when transferring digital audio. Bear in mind that this kind of editing is a "destructive" process—in other words, you will permanently alter the original audio information on your hard drive.

To eliminate an audio "pop" with the Pencil tool:

    a) Select the Pencil tool from the Edit Tools section in the Edit window.

    b) Zoom in to a sample-level view using the Horizontal Zoom In button to identify the problem, the "pop" (Fig. 4.73a).

    c) Position the Pencil tool over the audio track's center line (Fig. 4.73b).

    d) Click, hold, and drag (draw) a straight line with the Pencil tool; this redraws the audio waveform and fixes the problem (Fig. 4.73c).

    e) Listen to the section where you have re-drawn the audio waveform. You'll notice the "pop" is no longer there.

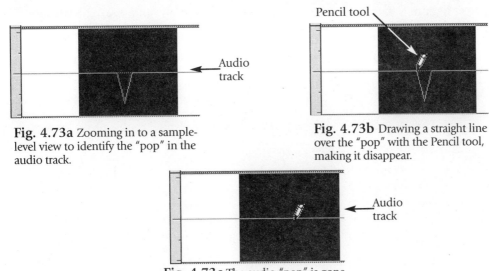

Fig. 4.73a Zooming in to a sample-level view to identify the "pop" in the audio track.

Fig. 4.73b Drawing a straight line over the "pop" with the Pencil tool, making it disappear.

Fig. 4.73c The audio "pop" is gone.

2. Creating or changing volume, panning, mute, send level, send mute, send panning, and plug-ins automation.

To "draw" volume automation:

   a) Click on the track view of the audio track you want to "draw" the automation on, and select the Volume view (Fig. 4.74a).

   b) Select the Pencil tool from the Edit Tools section in the Edit window.

   c) Place the Pencil over the black line representing the volume-level line (Fig. 4.74b).

   d) Click and hold the mouse and start drawing the volume automation as you desire (Fig. 4.74c).

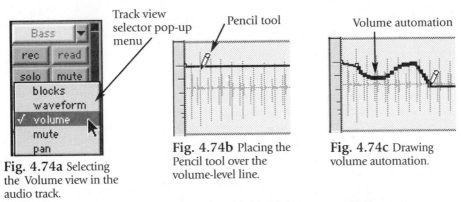

Fig. 4.74a Selecting the Volume view in the audio track.

Fig. 4.74b Placing the Pencil tool over the volume-level line.

Fig. 4.74c Drawing volume automation.

Now, if you would like to draw your automation in a more consistent and elegant manner, you can use one of the five drawing shapes available through the Pencil tool icon. Clicking and holding the Pencil tool icon will show the five different drawing shapes. They are: Freehand, Line, Triangle, Square, and Random. Let's say you would like to automate the panning of a specific sound in an audio track to go from left to right and right to left every bar for the duration of two entire bars (in musical terms). In other words, the sound should start panning from the left side ("L") gradually to the right ("R"). By the time it gets to the right side, a one-bar interval has passed. Then, starting from the right side, automatically, the sound will gradually pan to the left until another whole bar has passed.

To "draw" this automation:

(a) Select the Triangle drawing shape from the Pencil tool icon's drop-down selector (Fig. 4.75a).

(b) Select the "1 bar" Grid Value from the Grid Indicator window (Fig. 4.75b). For those still using Pro Tools Version 5.xx, this window is located in the Edit window's upper-right-hand corner (Fig. 4.75c). For Version 6.0 users, the Grid Indicator is located right underneath the Selector and Grabber tools (Fig. 4.75d).

(c) Select the Pan track view in the audio track on which you want to "draw" the panning automation (Fig. 4.75e).

(d) Position the Pencil tool in the audio track's upper-left corner.

(e) While in Grid mode, click, hold, and drag the mouse (Pencil) for a duration of two bars. You will notice that a triangle-shaped black line (the panning line) is drawn across the area from left to right (Fig. 4.75f). You can do this using other Grid Values—a quarter-note or eighth-note, for example, as well as other time scales, such as minutes and seconds.

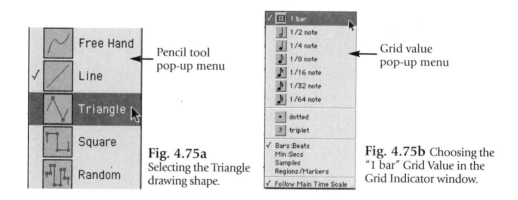

Fig. 4.75a Selecting the Triangle drawing shape.

Fig. 4.75b Choosing the "1 bar" Grid Value in the Grid Indicator window.

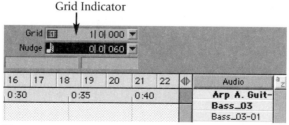

Fig. 4.75c The Grid Indicator window in Pro Tools Version 5.xx.

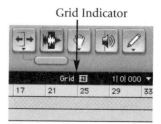

Fig. 4.75d The Grid Indicator window in Pro Tools Version 6.0.

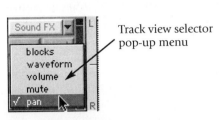

Track view selector pop-up menu

Fig. 4.75e Selecting the Pan track view.

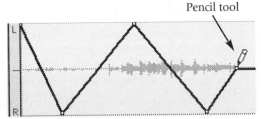

Pencil tool

Fig. 4.75f "Drawing" the panning automation using the Triangle drawing shape and the Pencil tool.

MIDI applications

1. You can add or insert MIDI notes into a newly created MIDI track, or to a MIDI track that has existing MIDI information in it.

To add or insert MIDI notes to a newly created MIDI track:

(a) Create a MIDI track from the File pop-up menu using the New Track command. You will recognize the MIDI track by the "keyboard keys" at the right side of the track view (Fig. 4.76a).

(b) Make sure the track view is set to Notes view (Fig. 4.76b).

(c) With the Pencil tool, click, hold, and drag the mouse (Pencil) to the right. You will see a MIDI note being created. If you don't release the mouse right away, you can adjust the note length as you wish (Fig. 4.76c).

TIP: If you want to delete or erase individual notes, automation breakpoints, program changes, etc., hold down the Option key (Alt in Windows); the Pencil icon will flip and become an eraser. Go ahead and try it!

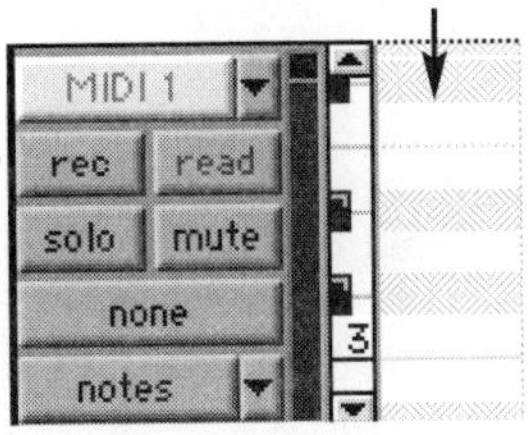

MIDI track

Track view selector pop-up menu

Pencil tool

Fig. 4.76a Creating a MIDI track.

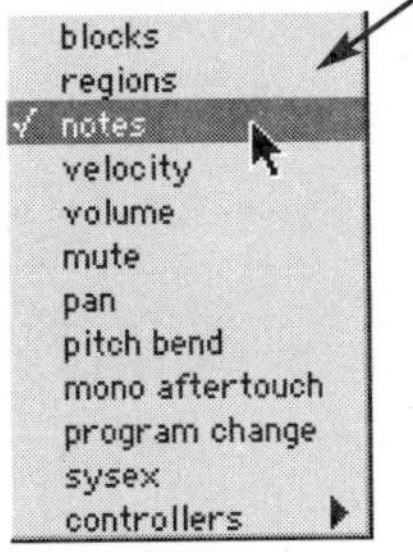

Fig. 4.76b Selecting the Notes track view.

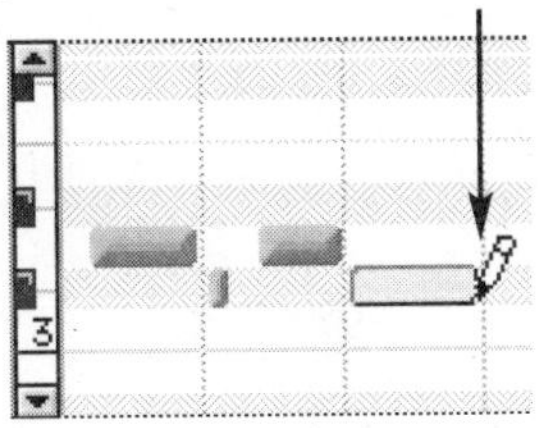

Fig. 4.76c Creating a MIDI note with the Pencil tool and adjusting its length.

2. Another MIDI Pencil tool application involves reshaping the MIDI notes' velocity, volume, and pitch data, among other parameters.

To reshape the velocity of MIDI notes already recorded in a MIDI track:

(a) Select the Pencil tool with the Freehand drawing shape (Fig. 4.77a).

(b) Make sure you've selected the Velocity track view of the MIDI track in which you want to change the velocity data (Fig. 4.77b).

(c) Once in the Velocity track view, you will see vertical lines with a diamond-like shape at the end. Each line represents the velocity value of that MIDI note (Fig. 4.77c).

SHORTCUT: To select the Pencil tool, hold down the Command key (Control in Windows). To toggle among the five Pencil shapes, hold down the Command key (Control in Windows) and repeatedly click on your alphanumeric keyboard's "6" key. Or, simply use the F10 key.

(d) Click, hold, and drag the mouse (Pencil) in any direction. You will notice that the vertical lines' heights are changed, signifying changes in the MIDI note velocities (Fig. 4.77d).

(e) Assuming that you have an external or software MIDI synthesizer, make the appropriate assignments and play back the MIDI track. You'll notice a difference between the original and reshaped MIDI note velocities.

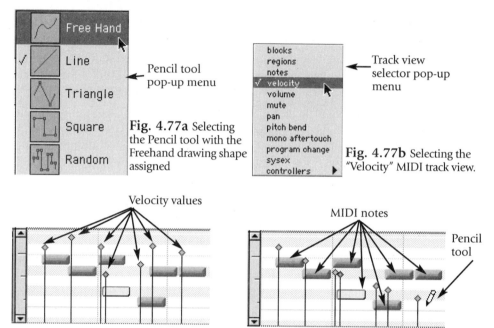

Fig. 4.77a Selecting the Pencil tool with the Freehand drawing shape assigned

Fig. 4.77b Selecting the "Velocity" MIDI track view.

Fig. 4.77c Vertical lines with a diamond like shape at the end. Each line is the velocity value of each MIDI note.

Fig. 4.77d With the Pencil tool selected as Freehand, click, hold, and drag the mouse (Pencil) to any direction and you will notice the vertical lines' height will be changed signifying the change in MIDI note velocity.

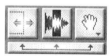

The Smart tool

In early versions of the Pro Tools software the Smart tool was not implemented. Since Digidesign added this feature, the number of times you had to switch the tools back and forth from the region you were working on to the Edit tools section was minimized. The result of switching the Edit tools back and forth was the waste of too much time. I remember in those days I used to get frustrated trying to perform a quick edit, like selecting a section of an audio region for example, without realizing I had the Trimmer tool selected, cutting the region instead of selecting it, especially if I was in the Shuffle edit mode.

Now, everything is simpler and more efficient when using the Smart tool. The Smart tool automatically switches the tool you are working with at that moment to the Selector, Grabber, and Trimmer tools depending on specific locations you move the cursor to. This tool works on audio and MIDI regions, and MIDI notes. Also, you can create fades on an audio region, and crossfades between two audio regions. Fades and crossfades cannot be performed on a MIDI region or note. As I mentioned above, the tool switching takes place depending on the position of the cursor in a region; the tools will automatically switch as follows:

TIP: To temporarily switch the Smart Tool to the Scrubber in an audio track, hold down the Control key (Start in Windows).

- If the cursor is in the upper half of the region, the Selector tool will be enabled.
- If the cursor is in the lower half of the region, the Grabber tool will be active.
- If the cursor is positioned on the beginning or end points of the region, the cursor will turn into the Trimmer tool.

Note: The above applies to the following track views: in an audio track the view should be in "waveform" or "blocks." In a MIDI track it should be in "regions" or "notes.. The "blocks" view also works, but it is useless since you cannot see the MIDI notes when in this track view.

TIP: To temporarily switch the Smart Tool to the Pencil in a MIDI track with the "notes" view assigned to it, hold down the Control key (Start in Windows).

- If working on MIDI notes, and the track view is assigned to "notes," positioning the cursor in the middle of a MIDI note, the tool changes to the Grabber. If the cursor is not over any MIDI note, it switches to the Selector tool. Furthermore, if you position the cursor at the end or beginning of a MIDI note, it turns to the Trimmer tool.
- If the cursor is positioned in the upper right hand corner or upper left side of the region, you will be able to create a fade in (left side) or a fade out (right side). In order to create a fade in or out, just click, hold, and drag the mouse—assuming that is in either upper corner—to the left or to the right and a fade will be created. The amount of the fade will be determined by how much you drag the mouse. Furthermore, the curve type of the fade can be assigned in the main pop-up menu Setups>Preferences>Editing tab> Default Fade Settings.
- Positioning the cursor in the lower half of the region, between two regions, you'll be able to create a crossfade between both regions. You can do this by clicking, holding, and dragging the mouse to either direction—left or right.

The above explanations are shown in Fig. 4.78a and Fig. 4.78b.

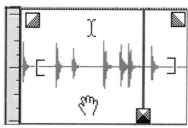

Fig. 4.78a The Smart tool shown in the different tools it converts to depending on the position of the cursor in the audio region.

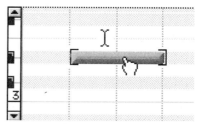

Fig. 4.78b Positioning the cursor in the middle of a MIDI note, the tool changes to the Grabber.

As you can see, the Smart tool makes it very simple for you to quickly edit in Pro Tools. If you are a newcomer to the Pro Tools world, begin using this tool—you'll be glad you did.

The Grid and Nudge Value Displays

The Grid Value Display

SHORTCUT: To choose the Smart tool you can hold down the Command key (Control in Windows) and the number "7" key on the alphanumeric keyboard. Or simply use the F6+F7 keys.

When you enable the Grid edit mode to move, trim, or quantize an audio or MIDI region, or to set and move automation "breakpoints" in intervals of say, every second, or every frame, or every quarter-note, etc., you will need to use the Grid Value Display to select the Grid time increments and units desired (i.e., the Grid Value).

To change or select a specific Grid Value:

1. Place the cursor on the down arrow icon located to the right of the Grid Value Display (Fig. 4.79a).

2. Click and hold the mouse on the arrow and a pop-up list of the Grid time increments and units will appear (Fig. 4.79b).

3. Select the Grid Value you would like to use to move, trim, or quantize an audio or MIDI region, to move automation "breakpoints," or to simply move the cursor in a specific location. In Fig. 4.79b notice the "Bars:Beats" units were selected, and the Grid time increment was set to a "1/4 note." This means that, if you are moving a region, the region will be constrained to move in "1/4 note" increments only. If you need smaller increments, then select a 1/8 note or 1/16 note values, or, simply set Pro tools in the Slip edit mode.

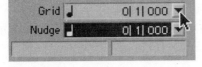

Fig. 4.79a Positioning the cursor to select the Grid Value.

Fig. 4.79b Selecting a "1/4 note" Grid time increment.

Not all the Grid Value Units included in a Pro Tools TDM system are included in a LE system. The differences are:

In TDM systems:

Bars:Beats

Min:Secs

Time Code

Feet Frames

Samples

Regions/Markers

In LE systems:

Bars:Beats

Min:Secs

Samples

Regions/Markers

The Nudge Value Display

Nudging is a very powerful technique when moving regions, adjusting selections on a region, moving MIDI notes, etc. Nudging means moving a region or selection in small increments. It is sort of like a "fine tune" adjustment technique. When nudging regions or selections, the plus ("+") and minus ("-") keys on the numeric keypad of your computer keyboard must be used. I have found out through all these years of experience working with Pro Tools that nudging is most useful when I am working in a post-production job, especially when synchronizing voice-overs or sound effects to a movie or video. Of course, by no means am I saying that it does not work great for music/MIDI production; what I am trying to say is that I nudge regions more often when working in post-production than in music production. Try it, you will be the judge.

TIP: You can define the Grid value to match the one used in the Main Time Scale by selecting the "Follow Main Time Scale" command in the pop-up time interval list (Fig. 4.79b).

The Nudge Value Display is selected in a similar manner as the Grid Value Display. To change or select a specific Nudge Value:

1. Place the cursor on the down arrow icon located to the right of the Nudge Value Display (Fig. 4.79c).

2. Click and hold the mouse on the arrow and a pop-up list of the Nudge time increments and units will appear (Fig. 4.79d).

3. Select the Nudge Value you want to use to move an audio region, to move or adjust an audio or MIDI region, to move automation "breakpoints," or to simply move the cursor to a specific location in the track. In Fig. 4.79d notice the "Min:Secs" units were selected, and the Nudge time increment was set to a "1 second." This means that if you are moving an audio region or MIDI note, they will be constrained to move in second-by-second increments. If you need smaller increments to nudge a region, like milliseconds, for example, then select a millisecond value.

Fig. 4.79c Positioning the cursor to show the Nudge Values pop-up menu.

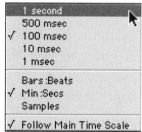

Fig. 4.79d Selecting the units to "Min:Secs" and the "1 second" Nudge time increment.

Applications using the Nudge Value Display

There are several basic and useful applications for both, audio and MIDI using the nudging technique. By the way, it does not matter what Edit mode or Edit Tool Pro Tools is in.

1) To move the cursor—not a region selection—to find a specific edit point or recording location:

a) Place the cursor in the Nudge Value Display (Fig. 4.79c).

b) Click and hold the mouse to show the Nudge Value pop-up list (Fig. 4.79d).

c) Select the Nudge Value time increments and units.

d) Referring to Fig. 4.79e, the cursor is positioned on the first "line"—to the right of the beginning of the track. In this particular example, the units were assigned to "Bars:Beats" and a "1/4 note" as the increment value. In this case, the Grid Value was set to "Bars:Beats" and to "1/4 note"

increments as well. Continuing with our example, pressing once the "+"
key in the numeric keypad, the cursor will move the equivalent of a "1/4
note" value to the right—"one line" away from the beginning of the track
(Fig. 4.79f). Pressing the "+" key two more times, the cursor will be
moved two more quarter-note values to the right (Fig. 4.79g and Fig.
4.79h). Assuming that the beginning of the track in this example is set to
be at Bar#1:Beat #1, then the fourth line you see on any of the screen
shots below is equivalent to the start of Bar #2. This means in this case,
I moved the cursor from Bar #1:Beat #2 to Beat #1 of Bar #2. Of course,
you can also move the cursor to the left using the "-" key by any increment and time units you desire.

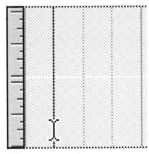

Fig. 4.79e The cursor is positioned
at Bar #1:Beat #2, assuming that the
session's "Start Time" is set to Bar
#1:Beat #1, and the increment value
is set to a quarte-note.

Fig. 4.79f The cursor was
moved to the right a quarter-
note value to Bar #1:Beat #2.

Fig. 4.79g The cursor was moved
to the right another quarter-note
value to Bar #1:Beat #3.

Fig. 4.79h The cursor was moved
to the right again another quarter-
note value to Bar #2:Beat #1.

2) To move an audio or MIDI region, or MIDI notes, in a predetermined time
increment:

a) Select the needed Nudge Value time increment and units as mentioned
above.

b) Using the Grabber edit tool, click on the audio/MIDI region or MIDI note
you wish to move to select it (Fig. 4.80a).

c) Referring to Fig. 4.80b, by pressing the "-" key once, the selection (audio region) was moved a sixteenth-note value to the left. I had set the Nudge increment value to a "1/16 note." The Units were set to "Bars:Beats."

d) In Fig. 4.80c, you notice the audio region moved by two sixteenth-notes to the right by pressing the "+" key. Each Grid line represents an eighth-note.

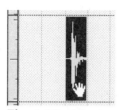 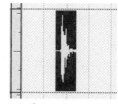 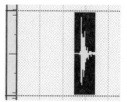

Fig. 4.80a Selecting an audio region.   **Fig. 4.80b** Region moved a sixteenth-note value to the left.   **Fig. 4.80c** Region moved two sixteenth-note value to the right.

e) You can also move MIDI regions applying the same process as if it were an audio region as mentioned above (Fig. 4.80d and Fig. 4.80e).

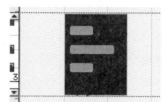   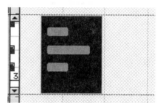

Fig. 4.80d Selecting a MIDI region.   **Fig. 4.80e** Region moved a sixteenth-note value to the left.

f) By the same token, if you need to move a single MIDI note on either direction, follow these steps:

- Set the MIDI track you are working with to "notes" track view.
- Select the Grabber tool and click on the MIDI note you need to move. (Fig. 4.80f) Notice the hand icon becomes a finger icon.
- Press the "+" key to move the MIDI note to the right.
- In Fig. 4.80g, the MIDI note at the bottom, was moved performing the last three steps, but in this case the "-" key on the numeric keypad was pressed once, moving the note to the left. It will be more obvious if you refer to Fig. 4.80d, since you can see all the three MIDI notes are aligned in the MIDI track.

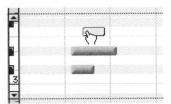

Fig. 4.80f Clicking on the MIDI note with the grabber tool.

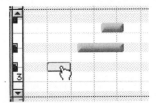

Fig. 4.80g The MIDI note in the bottom, was moved to the left.

3) To move a region selection—not the audio region—by a predetermined time increment to find a "perfect" loop:

f) Select the desired Nudge Value time increments and units as mentioned above.

g) Make the desired region selection (Fig. 4.80h).

h) Referring to Fig. 4.80i, by pressing the "+" key, the selection (not the actual audio region) was moved half a second to the right since the nudge time increment value was set to "500msec" and the units to "Min:Secs."

i) In Fig. 4.80j, again, the selection moved another 500 milliseconds to the right by pressing the "+" key. Notice the actual audio regions remained in the same place. This means that if you are looking to find a "perfect" loop on the audio region, all you need to do is to find the right spot in the already predetermined selection.

j) In Fig. 4.80k, by pressing the "-" key, this time the selection moved back (to the left) a half a second.

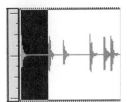

Fig. 4.80h A half a second selection was made.

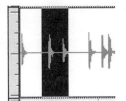

Fig. 4.80i The selection was moved 500 milliseconds to the right pressing the "+" key.

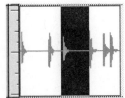

Fig. 4.80j The selection was moved another 500 milliseconds to the right pressing the "+" key once more.

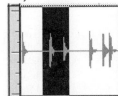

Fig. 4.80k This time, the selection moved to the left 500 milliseconds by pressing the "-" key on the numeric keypad.

SHORTCUT: *To highlight the Main Location Indicator, press Equal (=) on the numeric keypad. Press period (.) to navigate the different time fields in an indicator, and press Enter to go to the new location.*

4) To extend the start or end points of a selection using the Option (Alt), Command (Control) keys in conjunction with the "+" and "-" keys on the numeric keypad:

a) Select the Nudge Value time increments and units as mentioned above.

b) Make the desired region selection (Fig. 4.80m).

c) Hold down the Option (Alt) key and press the "-" key and notice the start point of the selection will move to the left. In the example in Fig. 4.80m, the Nudge and Grid values were set to Bars:Beats and time increments of "1 bar." This means the start point of the selection moved to the left two bars, since I pressed the "-" twice.

d) In Fig. 4.80n, I pressed the "+" key three times (three bars) while holding down the Option (Alt) key. Notice this time the start point of the selection moved a total of three bars to the right, shrinking the selection.

e) In Fig. 4.80o, the end point of the selection moved to the right four bars by pressing the "+" four times while holding down the Command (Control) key.

f) Finally, Fig. 4.80 p shows the selection got smaller by holding down the Command key and pressing the "-" key four times.

Fig. 4.80l An audio region selection.

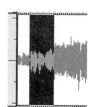

Fig. 4.80m The start point of the selection moved to the left by pressing and holding the Option (Alt) key and the "-" key on the numeric keypad.

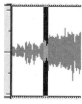

Fig. 4.80n The start point of the selection moved to the right by pressing and holding the Option (Alt) key and the "+" key on the numeric keypad.

Fig. 4.80o The end point of the selection moved to the right by pressing and holding the Command (Control) keys and clicking on the "+" key on the numeric keypad.

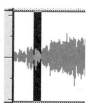

Fig. 4.80p The end point of the selection moved to the left by pressing and holding the Command (Control) key and clicking on the "-" key on the numeric keypad.

The Audio Regions List

Whenever you record a sound (musical instruments, vocals, sound effects, etc.) into Pro Tools, import an audio file from another Pro Tools session, import a sound (music or sound effects) from an audio CD, or import an audio file from a CD-ROM, these recordings/files are placed in the Audio Regions List. The list is located at the right hand side of the Edit window (Fig. 4.81a).

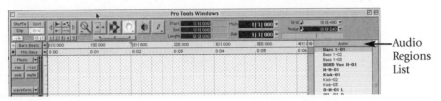

Fig. 4.81a The Audio Regions List in the edit window.

From this list you can click and drag any audio file or audio region into a stereo or mono audio track in the Edit window.

Fig. 4.81b Clicking and dragging a mono audio file into a mono audio track in Shuffle mode.

Since Pro Tools is a "non-destructive" system, edits you perform on an audio file (sound) in the edit window will not affect the original sound or file (i.e., they won't be permanently altered), and a copy of the original file will be generated and added to the Audio Regions List. If you notice in Fig. 4.81c, there are two letter types in the instrument names. Some are in "bold" type and others in "plain" type. A bold type file name means the file is the original recording of the sound in your session. They are known as "Audio Files" or "Whole Files." By any means, *don't erase it*! If you do, then you will permanently lose your original recording and will never be able to get it back unless you record it again in your session, and you know how expensive and time consuming that could be.

The "plain" type file names are known as "Audio Regions." An audio region is an extract or derivative of an audio file (original recording), which is generated when an edit is made to an audio file. They can be created automatically by Pro Tools or by the user when performing edits to the original recording. Audio regions are not stored as separate files in the hard disk, but rather, they are stored as "region definitions" within a Pro Tools session file. Audio regions can also be dragged into audio tracks in the Edit window from the Audio Regions List to be played back or edited, just the same way as an audio file.

Fig. 4.81c Audio Regions List showing audio regions.

The MIDI Regions List

The MIDI Regions List contains the file names of all your MIDI recordings, as well as the names of the edits you perform on the original MIDI tracks recorded. This list is located on the right hand side of the Edit window, right underneath the Audio Regions List (Fig. 4.82a).

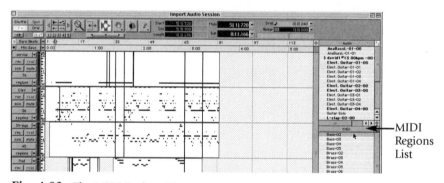

Fig. 4.82a The MIDI Regions List.

Unlike the Audio Regions List, the file names in the MIDI Regions List are only in "plain" type letters (Fig. 4.82b). In other words, you cannot easily differentiate between an original MIDI recording and an edited MIDI region just by looking at the type (bold or plain) of letters. Instead, you will have to look closely at the regions' name numbers. For example, referring to Fig. 4.82b I recorded three different MIDI tracks, Bass, Drums, and Piano. Notice the original MIDI files are in plain type letters. Also, notice there is a number (-01) following the name of the instrument. The "01" means that the MIDI file is the original recording. Now, take a look at Fig. 4.82c. After editing the original MIDI recordings, a new MIDI region with the name of the instrument followed by the numbers "02" and "03" was created. This means that every instrument was edited twice.

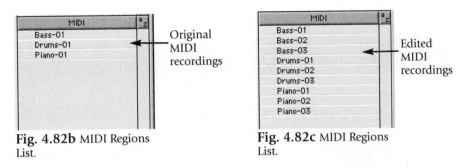

Fig. 4.82b MIDI Regions List.

Fig. 4.82c MIDI Regions List.

The MIDI regions are imported to a MIDI track from the MIDI Regions List in the same manner an audio region is imported to an audio track in the Edit window, i.e., just by clicking and dragging the MIDI file/region to the desired track (Fig. 4.82d).

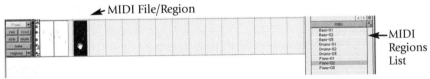

Fig. 4.82d Dragging a MIDI file/region to a MIDI track in the Edit window.

Hiding and Showing the Audio/MIDI Regions Lists

There are times where you need to hide or show the Audio/MIDI Regions List; it all depends on which task are you doing at the time. For example, let's say I had finished editing a song I am about to mix. Personally when I mix, I like to see nothing but the audio waveform (sound) in the Edit window. For some reason the lists ("Show/Hide Tracks List" and "Audio Regions List") on the extreme left and right of the Edit window distract me. So what I do is to hide them by clicking on the double arrow icon on the lower side of each extreme of the Edit window.

To hide the Audio/MIDI Regions List, simply position the cursor on the double arrow icon located on the lower right hand side of the Edit window (Fig. 4.82e).

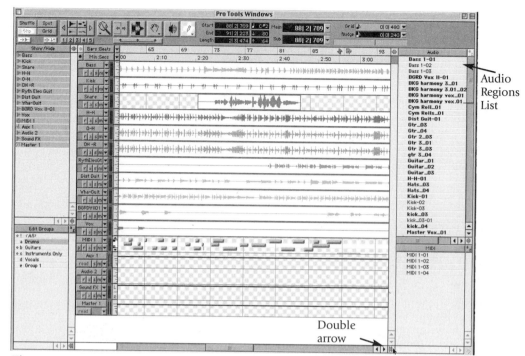

Fig. 4.82e Positioning the cursor on the double arrow icon located on the lower right hand side of the Edit window.

Next, click once on the double arrow icon and you will notice the list will disappear (become hidden) from the Edit window (Fig. 4.82f).

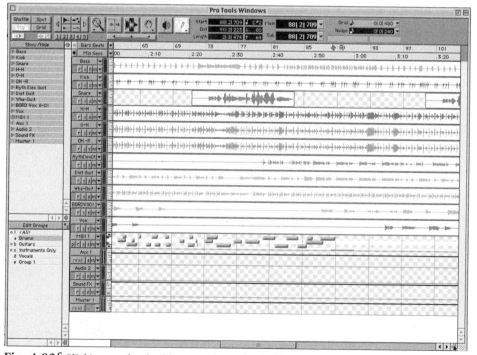

Fig. 4.82f Clicking on the double arrow icon, the Audio/MIDI Regions List will be hidden.

The Mix Window

As I mentioned at the beginning of this long, but important chapter, there are three main windows in Pro Tools in which the majority of the work within your sessions will occur. Up to now, I discussed pretty much all the elements included in the Edit window. Now it's the Mix window's turn (Fig. 4.83a).

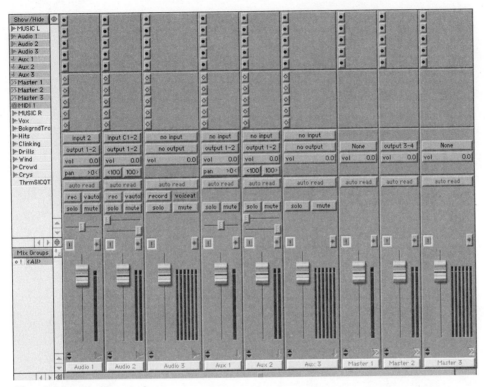

Fig. 4.83a The Mix window.

Throughout the last twenty years as a recording/mixing engineer, I became accustomed to recording and mixing utilizing hardware mixing boards and external signal processors, with physical faders, push buttons, and rotary knobs. I liked it! Then, Pro Tools came along, and just like all my peers at the time, I was hesitant to use a computer to record and mix an entire project. It wasn't until 1992 when I convinced myself to use nothing but Pro Tools as my recording and mixing system, and I am so glad that Pro Tools became the industry standard.

One of the main reasons I started using this incredible digital audio workstation for all my projects is that the Mix window looks and functions just like any hardware mixing board. I can process and route any signal anywhere I need, and control Pro Tools' virtual faders with any control surface available specifically for Pro Tools such as: ProControl, Control|24, MotorMix, the HUI, the MiniDesk, etc.

Different types of tracks ("Channel Strips")

When working with Pro Tools, you can create four different types of tracks: Audio tracks, Aux Input tracks, Master Fader tracks, MIDI tracks, and multi-channel tracks for surround sound. Each of these tracks possesses its own function, as I discussed earlier in this chapter. Furthermore, any of these types of tracks can be created in mono, stereo, or multi-channel, except MIDI tracks, of course.

Regardless of the track type, it can be displayed in both the Mix and Edit windows. When is displayed in the Mix window, it is referred as a "Channel Strip"; therefore, an audio track will be considered as an "Audio Channel Strip" (Fig. 4.83b–e).

Fig. 4.83b
Audio Channel
Strip.

Fig. 4.83c
Aux Input
Channel Strip.

Fig. 4.83d
Master Fader
Channel Strip.

Fig. 4.83e
MIDI Channel
Strip.

While in the Mix window view, you can identify each type of track by looking at the "Track Type Selector" or icon. This icon is located on the lower right hand side of each Channel Strip, right above the track name box. Fig. 4.83f shows the different types of tracks in Pro Tools. They can be created in several formats: mono, stereo, or multi-channel for surround sound.

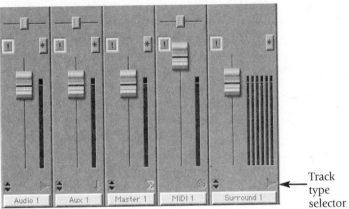

Track type selector

Fig. 4.83f The Mix window showing the four types of tracks or "Channel Strips" in Pro Tools: Audio track (in mono), Aux Input track (in mono), Master Fader track (in mono), MIDI track, and a multi-channel Audio track.

Differences among the types of tracks

The following chart summarizes the types of tracks available in Pro Tools. Their controls, their formats, their icons, and their functions:

Track Type	Identifiable Icon	Track Format	Track Control Buttons	Signal Routing Paths	Function
Audio		• Mono • Stereo • Multichannel	• Automation • Record enable • Voice assignment • Solo • Mute • Pan slide • Output window • Group assignment • Volume fader	• Digital/analog inputs and outputs • Sends • Inserts	• Record audio • Signal routing
Aux Input		• Mono • Stereo • Multichannel	• Automation • Solo • Mute • Pan slide • Output window • Group assignment • Volume fader	• Digital/analog inputs and outputs • Sends • Inserts	• Monitoring audio • Signal routing
Master Fader		• Mono • Stereo • Multichannel	• Automation • Record enable • Output window • Group assignment • Volume fader	• Digital/analog inputs and outputs • Inserts	• Monitoring audio • Signal routing
MIDI		• Mono	• Automation • Record enable • Solo • Mute • Pan slide • Output window • Group assignment • Volume fader	• MIDI inputs and outputs	• Record MIDI • Data routing

Table 1 Differences among the types of tracks.

Displaying a track in the Mix and Edit windows

When a new track is created in a session, the track is available to you in both the Mix and Edit windows. Referring to the audio track in Fig. 4.84a and Fig. 4.84b, notice—in this particular section of the Mix window—the same track controls appear in both windows. In these examples, the Mix window is displaying: the input and output selector, the volume value, the panning value, the automation modes, the record enable button ("rec"), the voice assignment (for TDM systems only), the "solo" button, the "mute" button, and the panning slider. In Fig. 4.84b, the same track is shown in the Edit window. You can observe the control buttons are the same, except the track name and the track view assignment is showing in a "normal" view of an audio track in the Edit window.

SHORTCUT: *You can toggle between the Mix and Edit windows by pressing and holding down the Command key (Control for Windows) and the "=" key on your alphanumeric keyboard, not the numeric keypad.*

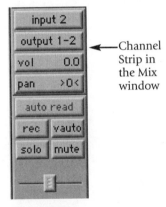

← Channel Strip in the Mix window

Fig. 4.84a
The middle section of an audio "Channel Strip" in the Mix.

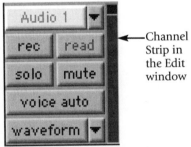

← Channel Strip in the Edit window

Fig. 4.84b The same audio track in the Edit window. Notice both windows contain the same controls (rec, read, solo, mute, and voice assignment).

Different tracks contain different controls

Depending on the type of tracks you may have in your session, the "Channel Strip" (the track) will have different controls and buttons in the Mix window. For example, observe in Fig. 4.85 the Aux Input and Master Fader tracks don't have a "rec" button, i.e., the record enable button, which means that you cannot record audio on any of those tracks. You can use them for signal routing and monitoring purposes, however.

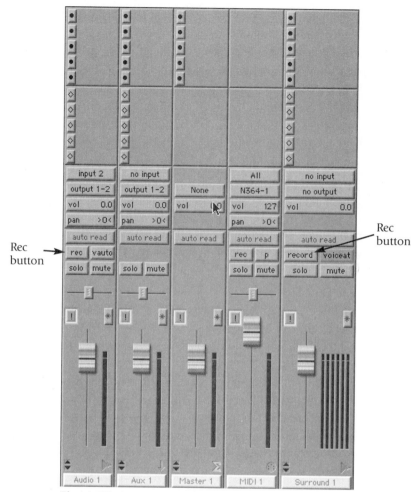

Fig. 4.85 The Aux Input and Master tracks don't have the "rec" button; therefore, you cannot record audio on them.

Displaying the Mix window controls in the Edit window

In case you only have one computer monitor in your studio, and you are tired of going back and forth from the Mix to the Edit window and vice-versa, you'll be glad to know that you may have access to all the Mix window controls (faders, panning sliders, inputs and output assignments, sends, inserts, MIDI channels), output window, and the track "comments" box, in the Edit window.

To display all Mix window controls in the Edit window, follow these steps:

    a) Click on the "Display" pop-up menu.

    b) Select the "Edit Window Shows" command.

c) While still holding down the mouse, slide the cursor to the right and select the "All" option (Fig. 4.86a).

d) Release the mouse and you will notice all the Mix window controls ("Channel Strip" controls) are now displayed in the Edit window (Fig. 4.86b).

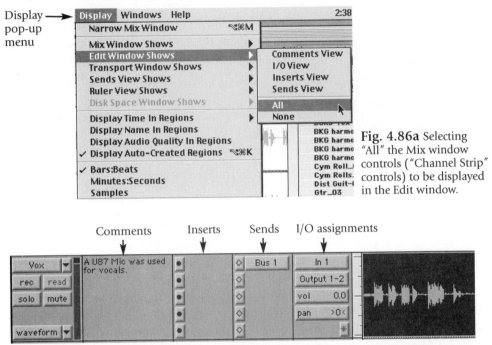

Fig. 4.86a Selecting "All" the Mix window controls ("Channel Strip" controls) to be displayed in the Edit window.

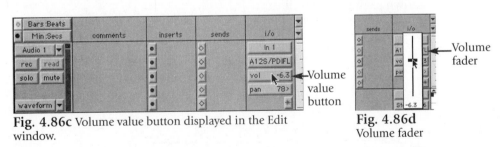

Fig. 4.86b The "Channel Strip" controls displayed in the Edit window.

You can access the volume fader while in the Edit window by clicking and holding the mouse over the "vol" value button (Fig. 4.86c and Fig. 4.86d).

Fig. 4.86c Volume value button displayed in the Edit window.

Fig. 4.86d Volume fader

You can access the panning slider while in the Edit window by clicking and holding the mouse over the "pan" value button (Fig. 4.86e and Fig. 4.86f).

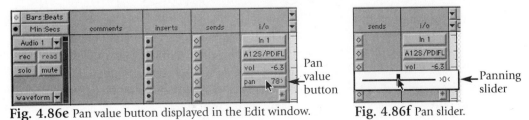

Fig. 4.86e Pan value button displayed in the Edit window.

Fig. 4.86f Pan slider.

Understanding the signal flow in a mixing board

When you connect a microphone (mic) or a musical instrument (electric guitar, electric bass, a synthesizer, etc.) to a mixing board (mixer), you usually have to adjust the signal level, push some buttons, and turn some knobs to send the signal either outside or within the mixer. You might even want to insert an external signal processor such a compressor or equalizer (EQ) to affect the signal (sound).

When someone is new in the audio world, at the beginning, he/she pushes buttons and adjusts knobs without even knowing why they are doing it. We do it (I say "we" because I used to be in that situation twenty years ago) because someone tells us to do so. For this reason, I would like to share in a non-technical and a very simplistic manner how the signal travels inside a mixer after a microphone or instrument is connected into it. Of course, every mixing board is designed differently, so what I am explaining in this chapter's section is a very basic concept of a typical input section in a mixer. I did not base this explanation on any mixing board in particular.

Referring to Diagram 4.1, let's say we want to record a vocal track. Obviously, the first thing we need to do is to connect a microphone (Mic) [1] into the mixer. Usually this connector is labeled in the mixer's rear panel as "MIC INPUT." Once the mic is connected, we need to assign—in the mixer—the Mic/Line selector switch [2] to the Mic position. Since the signal level coming out of a microphone is very small, we need to increase its level using the mixer's microphone preamplifier or "PreAmp," sometimes labeled Trimmer or Gain [3]. Adjusting the mic input level too high, we may get a distorted signal. To visually monitor a high level signal, we can keep an eye on the red light or LED most mixers have. This LED is known as the "Peak Indicator" [4].

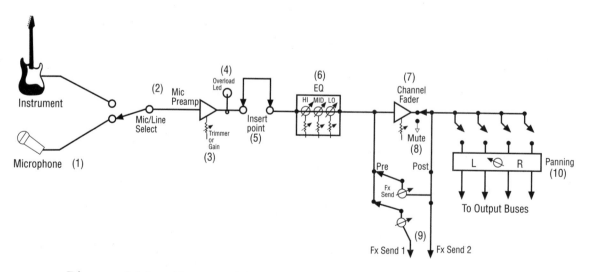

Diagram 4.1 Input/Output module signal flow.

Channel Insert Point

Once we had obtained a good signal level from the mic, if we desire, we can connect an external compressor, an EQ, a delay unit, or any other external signal processor to affect only our mic signal through a "channel insert point" [5]. Notice I said "only" the one mic input channel, and not a group of other input signals. Well, this is because each input channel module has its own insert point and whatever you connect in it, it will only affect that particular input signal—in our case, the microphone signal or vocal.

A channel insert point is just a simple input/output connector, which sends or routes the signal to elsewhere outside the mixer and back again to continue through the input channel path. The insert jack is usually located on top or on the rear panel of the mixer, near the Mic, Line, or Direct Out jacks (Fig. 4.87).

Fig. 4.87 The Insert jack is usually located on the rear panel or top of the mixer.

An "effects loop" or "stereo-to-dual-mono" adapter is typically used in a channel insert point jack. This adapter that looks like a "Y" adapter, contains one ¼" stereo plug (TRS=Tip, Ring, Sleeve) and two ¼" mono plugs (TS=Tip, Sleeve) as seen in Diagram 4.2. The Tip is usually assigned to be the output path (effects send) towards the input jack of the external device. The Ring will be connected to the output jack of the external device (effects return), sending the signal back to the mixer's main signal path by means of the "effects loop" adapter. Depending upon the mixing board design, an channel insert point can be placed before or after the mixer's EQ section (Diagram 4.3).

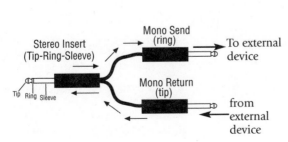

Diagram 4.2 An Effects Loop adapter for channel Insert points.

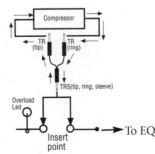

Diagram 4.3 The channel insert point is placed before the EQ section.

EQ section

Proceeding with our discussion about the signal path of an input channel module of a mixer, the next section is the EQ section [6 in Diagram 4.1]. This section is used to change the tone of the voice in the microphone we wish to record, for example. Since we are recording the signal, I recommend not recording the vocal with the EQ on; just use a good mic that will best capture the female or male vocal's tone.

Fader section

The next stage of the signal flow is the "fader" section [7 in Diagram 4.4]. The fader is the master volume control of the input signal—in this case the mic signal—leaving the input module to another section of the mixer, or outside the mixer.

Right after the fader's output, there is the "mute" button [8], which mutes (silences) or prevents the signal from going out of the input module.

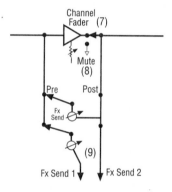

Diagram 4.4 The fader control, the mute on/off button, and two aux sends with pre-fader and post-fader selection.

Aux sends

Referring still to Diagram 4.4, underneath the fader, notice a pair of "Auxiliary Sends" controls [9]. The auxiliary sends are used to provide mixes for headphone cuing (the headphone mix sent to the musicians who are in the studio room recording), and for effects sends to external signal processors. A mixer can have from two to six aux effects sends.

A typical application using effects sends—besides for headphone cuing—is the following: Suppose you have a 16-channel mixing board and you are mixing a song. Also, suppose you only have one external reverb unit to add to the vocal track, the snare, and the stereo piano tracks. How are you going to send all those signals? You guessed it, through auxiliary sends or "effects sends." Since a mixer can have up to six effects sends on each input channel module or channel strip, you can send out, in our example, the vocal, snare, and stereo piano tracks individually with an "Aux Send." The amount of "dry" signal (original sound) you want to send out to the external reverb unit can be controlled by the master aux send levels (Fig. 4.88).

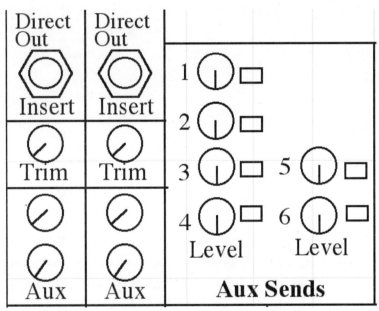

Fig. 4.88 Two of the six aux sends in the input channel module. Also, notice the six master send levels in the master section of the mixer.

Pre or Post Fader?

An aux send input can be selected before the fader (Pre) or after the fader (Post). This means if you set the aux send to the pre-fader position (Fig. 4.89), the signal you are sending out to the reverb unit—in our example—won't be affected by the fader. In other words, if you lower the fader level all the way down, the signal will still be sent to the reverb unit through the aux send and controlled by the aux send level. On the other hand, if you set the aux send to the post-fader position (Fig. 4.90), whatever changes you make on the fader, will affect the aux send. Which means that if you lower the fader all the way down, no signal will go to the reverb unit, even if the aux send levels are turned up.

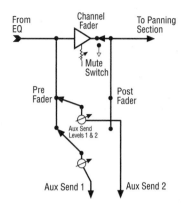

Fig. 4.89 Pre-fader.

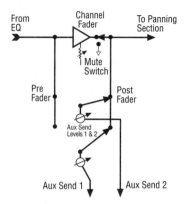

Fig. 4.90 Post-fader.

Panning and bus section

The next stage the signal goes to after the fader or volume control is the panning section [10 in Diagram 4.1]. With the panning controls, you can route the signal to the left (L) or to the right (R) of the stereo image. Also, you can route the signal to any of the mixer's "buses." A "bus" is a mixing circuit or network that combines the output of two or more channels. Each input channel module contains a bus selector section which allows the signal of the input module be routed to one or more buses. Depending on the complexity of a mixer, there can be from two to 64 buses. In Diagram 4.6, notice that this particular mixer has eight buses which can route any signal you assign to it.

At times, you will see push switches along the input channel faders on a mixer (Fig. 4.91). These switches are known as "bus assignment switches" which depending on the pan position in the module, will route the signal on any of the eight buses in the mixer (Diagram 4.6). For example, referring to Fig. 4.91, if you press switch #1 you are assigning the input signal to bus 1 & 2. Turning the pan knob to the right, the signal will be routed to bus #2, turning the pan control to the left, the signal will be sent to bus #1. If you keep the pan control in the center as shown in Fig. 4.91, then the signal will be sent to both buses, bus 1 and bus 2.

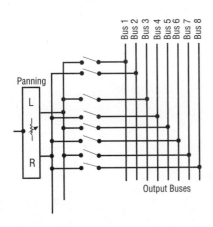

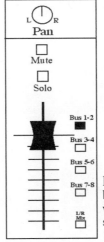

Diagram 4.6 Panning and output bus assignment section.

Fig. 4.91 A mixing board fader section with bus assignments switches. Notice "Bus 1-2" are selected.

Comparing a Pro Tools Channel Strip and an input/output mixing board module

Now that I have explained the signal flow of an input/output channel module on a "hardware" mixing board (Fig. 4.92a), I'd like to compare it with a Pro Tools audio channel strip (Fig. 4.92b).

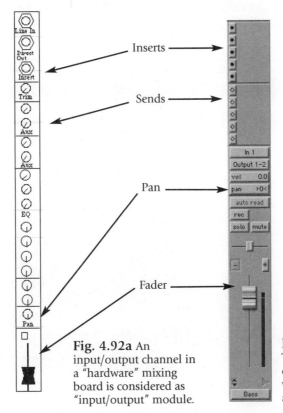

Fig. 4.92a An input/output channel in a "hardware" mixing board is considered as "input/output" module.

Fig. 4.92b In Pro Tools, an audio track displayed in the Mix window is known as a "Channel Strip".

Inserts

Starting from the top section of a Pro Tools audio channel strip, there are five "Insert" points on each track you create in a Pro Tools session. Remember what an Insert point is used for? Right, to add any external signal processor device (compressors, gates, delays, EQs, reverb units, etc.) to the main input audio signal stream.

Fig. 4.93a
Insert points in a
Pro Tools audio
channel strip.
Notice there are
five of them.

Fig. 4.93b
Insert point in an
input/output
channel module
in "hardware"
mixer. Notice
there is only one.

You have the choice in a Pro Tools audio Channel Strip to insert an external (hardware) signal processor through the "i/o" option (Fig. 4.94a), or an internal one by means of a plug-in. A plug-in is basically a software signal processor that is loaded into a DSP chip of a Pro Tools TDM system. In a Pro Tools LE system, the host computer's processing capabilities do the job. So for instance, let's "insert" a software compressor (plug-in) in a Pro Tools audio Channel Strip:

    a) First, click and hold the mouse on the first insert point in the audio channel strip (Fig. 4.94a).

    b) Slide down the mouse and select either a TDM plug-in or a RTAS plug-in (Fig. 4.94b).

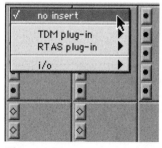

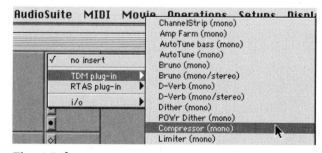

Fig. 4.94a Insert point in Pro Tools.

Fig. 4.94b Selecting a TDM plug-in.

c) Release the mouse and a plug-in window will appear on your computer screen. In this case, it will be the window of a compressor with all its parameters (Fig. 4.94c). If you take a look at Fig. 4.94d, you will be able to see and have an idea of how the signal flows when you insert a processor in an insert point in either Pro Tools or in a "hardware" mixer. A hardware compressor is inserted in a hardware mixer.

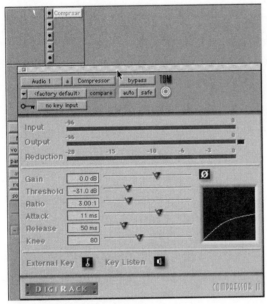

Fig. 4.94c Plug-in window.

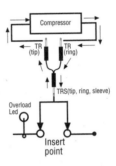

Fig. 4.94d Signal flow when inserting a processor in an Insert point.

Sends

The next row down in a Pro Tools audio Channel Strip are the "Sends." In our discussion earlier on the input/output channel module, I said that most hardware mixer contain from two to six aux sends (Fig. 4.95a). Well, in Pro Tools there are five, and you can identify them by the "diamond" icon in the left (Fig. 4.95b). These "Sends" can be used to route headphone mixes (up to five) to the musicians who are recording in the studio room. Also, the signal in the audio Channel Strip can be sent out through one (if mono) or two—if it is a stereo signal—of the "sends" in the audio Channel Strip In turn, the sent signal can be returned back to Pro Tools through an Aux Input channel strip (track) to listen to it back with the effect on it, like a reverb, for example. In other words, to listen to a "wet" signal (processed signal) coming back from the external processor.

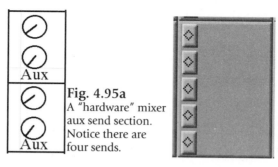

Fig. 4.95a
A "hardware" mixer aux send section. Notice there are four sends.

Fig. 4.95b The five Sends a Pro Tools has on each Channel Strip.

To send out a signal in an audio track in Pro Tools to an external signal processor like an external reverb, for example:

a) First, click and hold the mouse on the first Send in the audio Channel Strip (Fig. 4.95c).

b) Slide down the mouse and select "interface" (Fig. 4.95d).

c) Slide the mouse to the right and select the output number in which you want to send the audio track's signal out to the external reverb (Fig. 4.95d). If your track is a stereo track, then you can select output 1-2 (stereo), for example; conversely, if your audio track is in mono, then you can only select the output your external device is connected to, "output #1", for example.

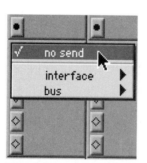

Fig. 4.95c Send in Pro Tools.

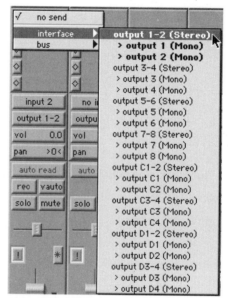

Fig. 4.95d Selecting an output.

As I mentioned just a couple seconds ago, if you send the signal out of Pro Tools, then you must bring it back. You can do this by means of a mono or stereo Aux Input track, depending on whether you need to "return" the processed signal back in mono or stereo. To accomplish this, do the following:

a) Create a mono or stereo Aux Input track from the "New Track" command in the File pop-up menu (Fig. 4.95e).

b) Position the mouse (cursor) in the input selection box of the Aux Input track (Fig. 4.95f).

c) Select the input that corresponds to the connection from the external device to the Pro Tools audio interface. In this case it is "In 1-2" (Fig. 4.95g).

Fig. 4.95e Creating an Aux Input track.

Fig. 4.95f Input selection box.

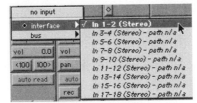

Fig. 4.95g Selecting an input.

Going back to Fig, 4.95c, you can select either "interface" or "bus." This is because when you want to send audio outside Pro Tools—to an external device—you need to use the "interface" option. Now, if you want to route the signal internally in Pro Tools, i.e., not going out of Pro Tools, then use the "bus" option.

Remember what a "bus" was from our earlier discussion? Just in case, a "bus" is a mixing circuit or network that combines the output of two or more channels. This means you can send—talking in music production terms—more than one instrument to a signal processor (maybe a reverb) through a mono or stereo "bus." Again, why am I using a "bus" in this case? Because the audio signals are staying inside Pro Tools; I am not sending it to an external reverb unit. Instead, I am using a software reverb (plug-in).

Let's do a practical mixing example: Let's suppose I am mixing a song and I would like add a reverb effect to the vocal, snare, and acoustic guitar tracks. But I just want to use one reverb plug-in. Well, no problem—what you need to do is the following:

a) Assign a "bus" on each track you want to send the reverb plug-in to. You do this by placing the cursor on any "Send" selection button and pick a mono or stereo bus. In this case, I have chosen "Bus 9-10 (Stereo)". See Fig. 4.96a.

b) After making the bus assignment on each instrument you want to send to a reverb plug-in, create a stereo Aux Input track and assign its input to "Bus 9-10" (stereo). See Fig. 4.96b.

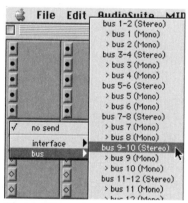

Fig. 4.96a Assigning a send to a stereo bus.

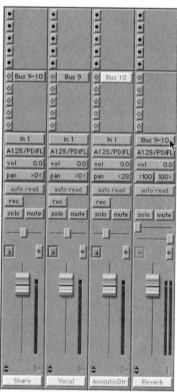

Fig. 4.96b Mix window showing audio and Aux Input tracks.

c) Place the cursor on the first insert box of the stereo Aux Input track you created above, and assign a stereo reverb plug-in. In this case I am selecting the "D-Verb (stereo)" (Fig. 4.96c). Of course, if you have other reverb plug-ins, by all means use them.

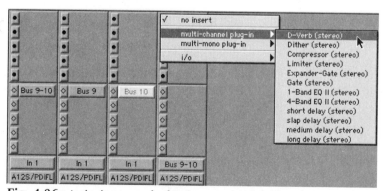

Fig. 4.96c Assigning a reverb plug-in to an Aux Input track.

d) Next, you will see the "D-Verb" plug-in appearing on your computer
screen. Notice a "fader" window showing as well in Fig. 4.96d. This fader
is known as the "send level control." Each time you assign a send to any
interface output or internal bus, this fader appears. It is the equivalent of
an Aux Send level control in a "hardware" mixer. Not bringing this fader
up, no signal will be sent to the Aux Input track from any assigned audio
source track, consequently, you won't be able to hear any reverb effect
when playing back your session.

Still referring to Fig. 4.96d, since the fader is up and the send assignment
box of the "Acoustic Guitar" track is highlighted, the send level control is
on the screen, corresponding to the guitar track, therefore, you can see in
the screen shot that the Aux Input track is receiving signal. By the way, in
this example I am selecting a "D-Verb (stereo)" plug-in as my reverb effect
(Fig. 4.96c), and of course, if you have other reverb plug-ins, by all means
use them to practice.

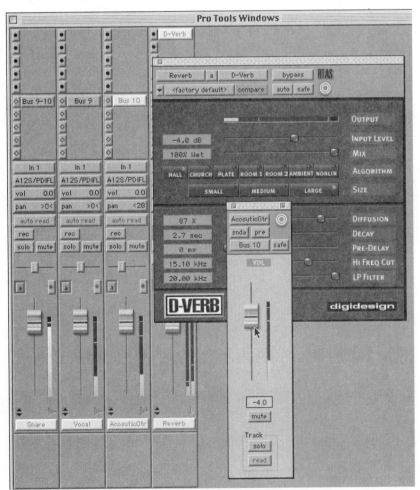

Fig. 4.96d A reverb plug-in is assigned to a stereo Aux Input track and is
receiving signal from all three audio tracks assigned to Bus 9-10.

Input Selector

The input selector allows you to assign or route any input signal coming externally from an audio interface or through an internal Bus in Pro Tools to an audio or Aux Input track. In the case of selecting Buses, if a Bus is already assigned to another track, Pro Tools will display it in bold type (Fig. 4.97). The number of inputs or buses that can be assigned depends on the I/O Setup configuration window located in the Setups pop-up menu (Fig. 4.97b).

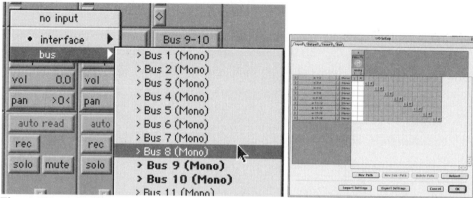

Fig. 4.97a Assigning Bus 8 in a track's Input selector. Notice Bus 9 and Bus 10 are already assigned to another track since they are in bold type.

Fig. 4.97b I/O Setup configuration window.

Output Selector

The output selector lets you assign or route a track to any audio output or internal bus. The number of outputs available to be selected is determined by the I/O Setup configuration.

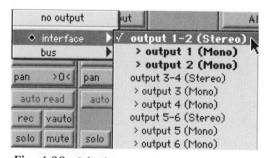

Fig. 4.98a Selecting an output.

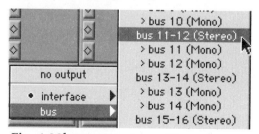

Fig. 4.98b Selecting a internal Bus.

The Output window

The Output window is just another way of viewing a Channel Strip. It contains all the controls shown in the regular Mix window view including the name of the track, the main output, the output selector pop-up menu, fader, panning buttons, volume value, and mute, solo, and automation mode buttons. In addition it contains an automation "safe" button, a stereo "link" (for stereo tracks) and an "inverse" selector.

To display the Output window, just click on the asterisk icon ("*") located right underneath the panning slider on the right hand side (Fig. 4.99a). As soon as you click on the "*" the output window will appear on the screen. Depending on the track's format (mono, stereo, or multi-channel) the output window will be different (Fig. 4.99b and Fig. 4.99c).

Fig. 4.99a
Clicking the "*"
to display the
output window.

Fig. 4.99b A
mono output
window.

Fig. 4.99c A
stereo output
window.

Group ID Indicator

In Pro Tools you can create up to 26 different track groups (a to z). You also can create nested groups as well, i.e., a group within a group. The Group ID Indicator allows you to identify how many groups a particular track belongs to. To access the Group ID Indicator window, click on the small box icon containing the group's letter ID as shown in Fig. 4.100a.

To find out if a particular track belongs to more than one group, simply click on the Group ID Indicator selector and choose the group you want to view the tracks belonging to the group you selected. For example, in Fig. 4.100b notice the Acoustic Guitar track belongs not only to the group named "All Tracks" (f), but also to the "Drums (a)" group.

Fig. 4.100a
Accessing the
Group ID
Indicator.

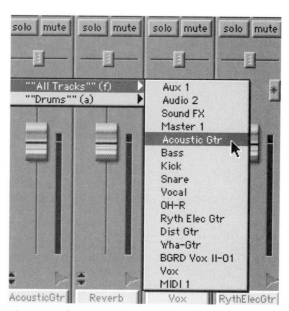

Fig. 4.100b Viewing the groups a track belongs to.

Mix Window Track Controls

You can have access to the Mix Window Track Controls (Fig. 4.101) from the Edit window as well. They perform exactly the same functions in both windows. You can refer to their functions in the Audio Track section description earlier in this chapter.

Fig. 4.101 The Mix
window track controls.

Volume and Pan values

These buttons show the Volume and Pan values, which are determined by the Volume fader and the Pan slider.

Fig. 4.102 The Volume and Pan values.

Comments section

This section is where you can write your comments for each track, so you will not forget any important details of the recording process.

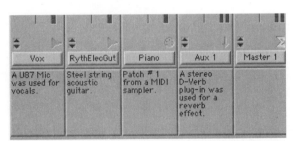

Fig. 4.103 The Comments section showing in the Mix window.

The Transport window

The Transport window (Fig. 4.104) is where all the controls for playing back, recording, stop, etc., are located.

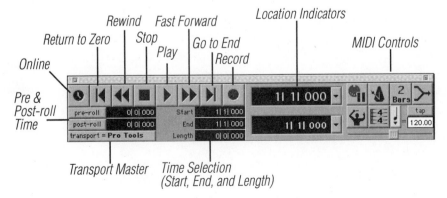

Fig. 4.104 The Transport window.

Online

This button puts Pro Tools online, which means that when time code from an external source is received, playback and recording will start.

Return to Zero

The Return to Zero button takes the selector to the beginning of the session.

Rewind

This button rewinds from the current position. If you click repeatedly, you can rewind incrementally (1 sec, 1 frame, 1 bar, or 1 foot).

Stop

To stop playback or recording, press the Stop button.

Play

The Play button starts playback or recording, if the Record button was enabled first.

Fast Forward

This button fast forwards from the current position. If you click repeatedly, you can fast forward incrementally (1 sec, 1 frame, 1 bar, or 1 foot).

Go to End

The Go to End button places the selector at the end of the session.

Record

The Record button prepares Pro Tools to record. There are four types of recording modes: Non-Destructive, Destructive, Loop Record, and Quick Punch. To know more about these recording modes refer to chapter 7.

Pre & Post-roll

Enter here the amount of time, frames, bars, foot, or samples (depending on the Main Time scale selection) you want Pro Tools to play before and/or after the timeline selection. When these buttons are enabled, they become highlighted. You can enable either one or both of them at the same time just by clicking on them.

Start, End, and Length

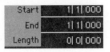

These fields display the beginning, the end, and the length of the playback or recording. You can enter any of these fields by clicking on them.

Transport window views

Sometimes you will see the Transport window as the one showing in Fig. 4.105a, where some of the controls are not visible.

Click here to expand the view

Fig. 4.105a The Transport window showing only the main controls.

You can expand this view by clicking on the little square located at the top right corner of the Transport window and you will be able to see the Pre and Post-roll buttons and the start, end, and length fields, as shown in Fig. 4.105b.

Fig. 4.105b The Transport window showing the main controls, Pre and Post-roll buttons, and the Start, End, and Length fields.

If you want to show all the controls in the Transport window, go to the 'Display' pop-up menu, select "Transport Window Shows" and then make sure that all the options have a check mark, as shown in Fig. 4.105c.

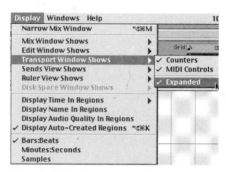

Fig. 4.105c The "Display" pop-up menu

Once this is done, your Transport window will show all the controls and will look like Fig. 4.105d.

Fig. 4.105d The Transport window showing all the controls.

CHAPTER FIVE

Most Frequently Used Menus

Since I have been teaching Pro Tools in the last ten years to hundreds of musicians, engineers, producers, and newcomers to to the Pro Tools world, I have noticed—regardless of their experience—they are still not clear on basic concepts and applications for some of the most basic menu selections in Pro Tools. For this reason, I decided to include in this chapter what I call "the most frequently used menu selections" in Pro Tools. This does not mean the menu selections I won't mention in this chapter are less important; on the contrary, some are extremely useful for more advanced editing tasks. For now, I just would like to keep it simple and emphasize the menus that most users, especially beginners, will be using when recording, editing, and mixing with Pro Tools. Furthermore, you will also notice that menus I don't mention in this particular chapter are mentioned in more detail throughout the book.

If you think the menu selections I am about to discuss are too basic for you, please, by all means, consult the Pro Tools Reference manuals, either printed or the PDF files already included in the software.

Having mentioned the above, in this chapter you will:

- Learn the functions and applications of some of the menus.

- Learn to use shortcuts or keystrokes to access specific menus.

- Use menus in a creative way.

The File Menu

New Session

When starting a new project, whether in music, post production, or MIDI, the first thing you have to do is to launch Pro Tools—if it is not already open—selecting the "New Session" command from the "File" pop-up menu in Pro Tools (Fig. 5.1).

Shortcut: *To create a New Session, press and hold the Command (⌘) key and then press the letter "N" on your computer keyboard.*

File	Edit	AudioSuite	MIDI	Movi
New Session...				⌘N
Open Session...				⌘O
Close Session				⇧⌘W
Save Session				⌘S
Save Session As...				
Save Session Copy In...				
Revert to Saved...				
Bounce to Disk...				
New Track...				⇧⌘N
Group Selected Tracks...				⌘G
Duplicate Selected Tracks				⇧⌥D
Split Selected Tracks Into Mono				
Make Selected Tracks Active				
Delete Selected Tracks				
Import Audio to Track...				
Import MIDI to Track...				
Export MIDI...				
Export Session As Text...				
Import Tracks...				
Get Info...				
Quit				⌘Q

Fig. 5.1 "File" pop-up menu.

You will see a dialog box appear, asking you to type your session parameters such as sample rate, bit depth, type of file format, name of the session, etc. (Fig. 5.2). Refer to Chapter 6 for more details about the session parameters.

As soon as you type a name to the New Session, you will be prompted or asked to save the session. It is important that you know where your New Session will reside. Generally you want to save it in the external hard drive of your system, if you have one; otherwise, save it in the internal hard disk or volume.

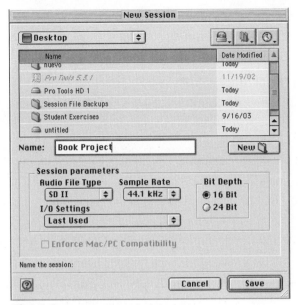

Fig. 5.2 New Session window.

Once you save your session in your computer's hard drive, a new folder is automatically created, which will contain two folders and one "tape" icon (Fig. 5.3).

Fig. 5.3
New Session's Folder.

The tape icon is actually your Session, where all your recorded and edited tracks reside (Fig. 5.4). In other words, it is your working area, and the window that you see in Fig. 5.4 is known as the "Edit window."

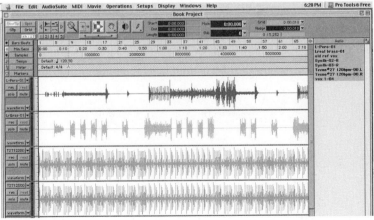

Fig. 5.4
Edit window.

One of the two folders created is automatically named Audio Files. This folder contains all the recorded audio you did during your recording session. By recorded audio I mean instruments, vocals, music already mixed, sound effects, etc. Also, all the regions "Exported As Files…" (refer to Chapter 8 for more info) will be saved in this folder if you direct them to the Audio Files folder. See Fig. 5.5.

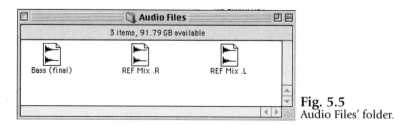

Fig. 5.5
Audio Files' folder.

The other folder is the Fade Files folder. In this folder, any fade ins, fade outs, and crossfades you create in your session are stored. See Fig. 5.6.

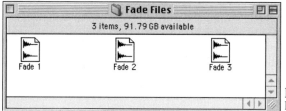

Fig. 5.6
Fade Files' Folder.

Open Session

Let's say that you were asked to mix a Session that somebody else recorded in Pro Tools. In order to start working on it, you need to open it using the "Open Session" command. See Fig. 5.7.

Shortcut: To Open a Session, press and hold the Command (⌘) key and then press the letter "O" on your computer keyboard.

Fig. 5.7 Selecting the "Open Session" command.

After selecting the Open Session command, what you need to do next is to look for the Session in the hard drive or volume that session was stored in. In this case, referring to Fig. 5.8, the Session named "Book Project" is stored in the external drive in a folder called "Pro Tools Sessions."

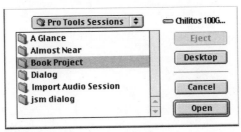

Fig. 5.8 Open Session window.

If I double-click on "Book Project" or I simply press "Open" on the dialog box while the folder is highlighted, I will be able to see the Session I want to open. You can see in Fig. 5.9 the "tape" icon named "Book Project."

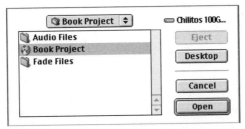

Fig. 5.9 Selecting the session file to be opened.

By selecting it and double-clicking on it, or simply pressing the "Open" button, I'll be able to see the Edit window of the Session I need to work on, in this case the "Book Project" Session (Fig. 5.10).

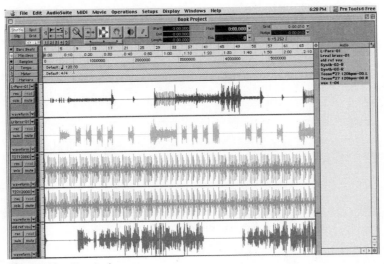

Fig. 5.10 Edit window.

Close Session

The "Close Session" command is pretty much self-explanatory. After you have finished working on a Session, you can just select the "Close Session" command in the File menu, and that is it (Fig. 5.11).

Shortcut: To Close a Session, press and hold the Command (⌘) key and then press the letter "W" on your computer keyboard.

Fig. 5.11 Selecting the "Close Session" command.

If you had not saved the Session when you selected the "Close Session" command, a dialog box will appear giving you three different options: to "Don't Save" the Session, to "Cancel" closing the Session, or to "Save" the Session as seen in Fig. 5.12. If you decide not to save it, simply press "Don't Save" and either open another Session or just "Quit" Pro Tools to exit the program.

Tip: Digidesign recommends reducing the "Cache Size" of your Macintosh computer to 512k. This is to speed up any session saves and "bounce to disk" functions. To do this, you can go to the "Control Panel" folder located inside of your "System Folder" folder. You can also access it through the "Apple" menu (on your upper left corner of your computer screen). Once in the Control Panel folder, select the "Memory" file and change the "Cache Size" to 512k.

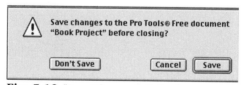

Fig. 5.12 "Save Changes" dialog box.

Save Session

Sometimes, we concentrate so much when we are either recording, editing, mixing, or mastering that we forget to continuously save our work. If you are one of these people, I suggest you should, at least, enable the "AutoSave" function in the "Preferences" command located in the "Setups" pop-up menu. For more details on how to enable the AutoSave function, refer to Chapter 6.

Saving is a very easy process. It should be done frequently. It ensures that all the changes made to a Session are stored properly in the hard drive (Fig. 5.13).

Shortcut: To Save a Session, press and hold the Command (⌘) key and then press the letter "S" on your computer keyboard.

Fig. 5.13 Selecting the "Save Session" command.

Save Session As

"Save Session As" means making a copy of the Session you are editing at the time and giving it a new name. For example, let's say you come into the studio in the morning to start working on a Session you were working on the night before. Also, let's say you liked what you did, but you would like to experiment with a couple of things. Before you make any changes to your Session, you should do a "Save Session As" (Fig. 5.14) to make a copy of your "original" Session. This way, whatever changes you make won't affect what you already had. Once you use the "Save Session As" command and give it a different name, the "original" Session automatically closes and the newly saved copy appears on your computer screen.

Fig. 5.14 Selecting the "Save Session As…" command.

When you use the "Save Session As" command, you will see a dialog box prompting you to give a new name to the Session. In this case (Fig. 5.15), I am renaming it as "Book Project II."

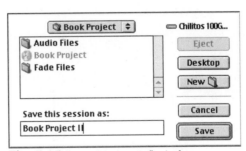

Fig. 5.15 "Save Session As" window.

If you don't change the name, Pro Tools will ask you if you want to replace the old Session (the "original" one) for the new copy (Fig. 5.16). If you click on "Replace," you will lose the "original" Session, which I would not advise you to do unless you are certain. Again, to avoid this type of catastrophe, and depending on what software version of Pro Tools you have (from version 5.1 and higher), you should enable the "AutoSave" function (Refer to Chapter 6). You will be glad you did.

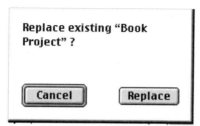

Fig. 5.16 "Replace Session" dialog box.

Revert to Saved

If you are editing a Session, and after an hour you realize that you don't like any of the changes you made to it and want to go back to the version you first started with and have not saved that Session since the time you first opened it, you still have the opportunity to go back to the non-edited version by selecting the "Revert to Saved" command. See Fig. 5.17.

Fig. 5.17 Selecting the "Revert to Save..." command.

Group Selected Tracks

This command is extremely useful when editing and mixing. To group one or more tracks, they must be "selected" first; by that I mean, highlight their names. To "select" a number of tracks to be grouped, click on the name of one track first, then hold down the Shift key on your keyboard and click on the names of the other tracks you want to group. Once all the tracks you want to group are highlighted, choose "Group Selected Tracks" from the File pop-up menu (Fig. 5.18).

Shortcut: *To Group Selected Tracks, ress and hold the Command (⌘) key and then press the letter "G" on your computer keyboard.*

Fig. 5.18 Selecting the "Group Selected Tracks..." command.

A new Group dialog box (Fig. 5.19) will appear. This box will ask you to provide a Group Name, a Group Type (Edit, Mix, or Edit & Mix), and a Group ID.

Fig. 5.19 "New Group" dialog box.

If the group's name in the "Edit Groups" list is highlighted with a purplish color, it
means the group is enabled. If the name is white or clear, it means the group has
been disabled, and the tracks are no longer grouped. This is very useful when you
need to edit one track at the time once they are already grouped (Fig. 5.20).

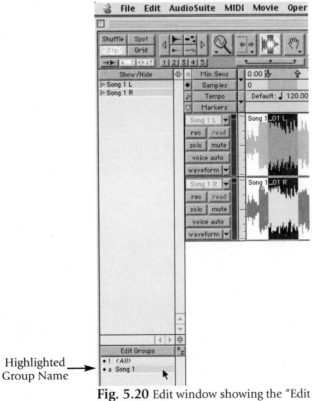

Highlighted
Group Name

Fig. 5.20 Edit window showing the "Edit
Groups" list.

Delete Selected Tracks

Sometimes we create more tracks (audio, MIDI, etc.) than what we need in a Session, and that is when "Delete Selected Tracks" comes in handy: to delete all the unnecessary tracks. To "erase" those tracks from your Session, you need to highlight them first (Fig. 5.21).

Fig. 5.21 Selected (highlighted) track.

Then select the "Delete Selected Tracks" option from the File pop-up menu (Fig. 5.22).

Fig. 5.22 Selecting the "Delete Selected Tracks…" command.

In the case where you have any audio or MIDI information in the track at the time you select the Delete command, a dialog window will appear warning that you are about to delete active regions (Fig. 5.23).

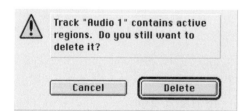

Fig. 5.23 A dialog box appears when selecting "delete tracks" and the tracks contain active regions.

If you are sure you want to delete those active regions, then go ahead and delete them. Don't worry, you will still have those audio/MIDI regions available in the Audio and MIDI Regions Lists.

Quit

The "Quit" command is used when you are ready to stop working and turn Pro Tools off. For example, after you have finished working long hours on a Session, you can just select the "Quit" command in the File pop-up menu to leave the program. Don't confuse it with the "Close Session" command (Fig. 5.24). If you have not saved your Session before you select the "Quit" command, Pro Tools will ask you to do so.

Shortcut: *To Quit, press and hold the Command (⌘) key and then press the letter "Q" on your computer keyboard.*

Fig. 5.24 Selecting the "Quit" command.

The Edit Menu

Undo / Redo

Shortcut: *To Undo, press and hold the Command (⌘) key and then press the letter "Z" on your computer keyboard.*

Pro Tools allows you to "Undo" and "Redo" almost any performed edit operation. If you are working on any Pro Tools software version below 6.0, you have up to 16 Undo's. These Undoes and Redoes may "save your life" when recording, editing, and/or mixing. They will allow you to return to the last 16 undoable and redoable editing states. If you upgraded to Pro Tools 6.0 or higher, you can now enjoy a total of 32 undoable operations.

To Undo the last action, choose the "Undo" command from the Edit pop-up menu (Fig. 5. 25a). To Redo an operation, select "Redo" from the Edit pop-up menu (Fig. 5.25b).

Shortcut: *To Redo, press and hold the Command (⌘) key, the Shift key and then press the letter "Z" on your computer keyboard.*

Edit	AudioSuite	MIDI	Movie	Operati
Undo Cut				⌘Z
Can't Redo				⇧⌘Z
Cut				⌘X
Copy				⌘C
Paste				⌘U
Repeat Paste To Fill Selection				⌥⌘U
Merge Paste				⌥⌘M
Clear				⌘B
Duplicate				⌘D

Fig. 5.25a Selecting the "Undo Cut" command in the Edit menu.

Edit	AudioSuite	MIDI	Movie	Operati
Can't Undo				⌘Z
Redo Cut				⇧⌘Z
Cut				⌘X
Copy				⌘C
Paste				⌘U
Repeat Paste To Fill Selection				⌥⌘U
Merge Paste				⌥⌘M
Clear				⌘B
Duplicate				⌘D

Fig. 5.25b Selecting the "Redo Cut" command in the Edit menu.

Copy

Perhaps the "Copy" command is the most used command in Pro Tools. Whatever you Copy, it remains copied in memory so you can "Paste" it afterwards anywhere you desire.

For example, select a section of a region you wish to copy (Fig. 5.26a); then choose the "Copy" command from the Edit pop-up menu (Fig. 5.26b).

Shortcut: *To Copy, press and hold the Command (⌘) key and then press the letter "C" on your computer keyboard.*

Fig. 5.26a Selecting a region.

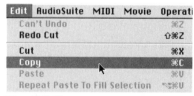

Fig. 5.26b Selecting the "Copy" command in the Edit menu.

Paste

After making a "Copy" of a section of a region, if desired, you must Paste it somewhere. To Paste the region selection, position the cursor (by this time you must have the Selector tool assigned) wherever you want to Paste the selection in (Fig. 5.27a). Next, select the "Paste" command from the Edit pop-up menu (Fig. 5.27b). When you release the mouse after selecting "Paste," you will see the selection previously copied appearing in the location where you have the cursor pointing (Fig. 5.27c).

Shortcut: *Press and hold the Command (⌘) key and then press the letter "V" on your computer keyboard.*

Fig. 5.27a Positioning the cursor.

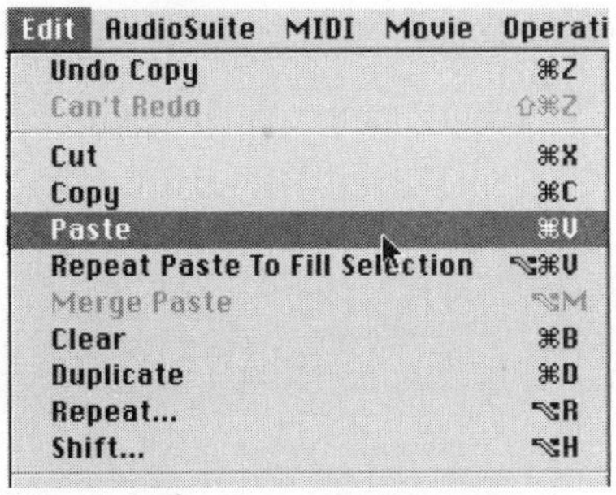

Fig. 5.27b Choosing the "Paste" command from the Edit menu.

Fig. 5.27c Pasting the section of the audio region copied.

Duplicate

Use the "Duplicate" command when you want to duplicate a selected region (audio or MIDI) only once. If you want to duplicate it more than once, keep selecting this command as many times as you desire.

To Duplicate a region, first select the entire region of part of it (Fig. 5.28a), Then, choose "Duplicate" from the Edit pop-up menu (Fig. 5.28b). The new duplicated region will appear right next to the region previously selected (Fig. 5.28c).

Shortcut: To Duplicate, press and hold the Command (⌘) key and then press the letter "D" on your computer keyboard.

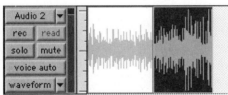

Fig. 5.28a Region selected.

Fig. 5.28b Selecting the "Duplicate" command in the Edit menu.

New duplicated region

Fig. 5.28c Region duplicated.

Repeat

Similar to Duplicate, the "Repeat" command allows you to repeat a region as many times as you need at once by entering the number of repeats. With "Duplicate" you can only do one repeat at the time.

To "Repeat" a region "x" amount of times: a) select the audio or MIDI region you wish to repeat (Fig. 5.29a); b) choose the "Repeat" command from the Edit pop-up menu (Fig. 5.29b). A dialog box will prompt you to enter the number of

Shortcut: To Repeat, press and hold the Shift key and then press the letter "R" on your computer keyboard.

times you want the region to be repeated, as shown in Fig. 5.29c; c) click on "OK." The region will be repeated by the number of times you entered, and they will appear right next to the region previously selected (Fig. 5.29d).

Fig. 5.29a Region selected.

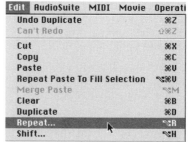

Fig. 5.29b Selecting the "Repeat" command in the Edit menu.

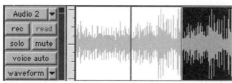

Fig. 5.29c Repeat dialog box.

Fig. 5.29d New repeated region.

Select All

The "Select All" command allows you to select all the audio and MIDI regions in your tracks at once. To select all the tracks—including their regions—choose "Select All" from the Edit pop-up menu (Fig. 5.30a). All the tracks and regions in your session will be highlighted as shown in Fig. 5.30b.

Shortcut: *To Select All, press and hold the Command (⌘) key and then press the letter "A" on your computer keyboard.*

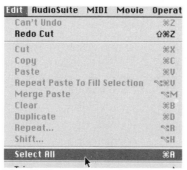

Fig. 5.30a Choosing the "Select All" command.

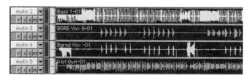

Fig. 5.30b All the tracks and regions in the session were selected.

Capture Region

The "Capture Region" command is useful for when you need to create a new region with its own name, out of a "source" or "original" file. For example, let's say you are a drummer and you want to create your own CD-ROM of drum loops to either sell or for personal use. No problem, just select a two-bar loop, Capture it and name it, and that is it! You then will be able to Export (refer to Chapter 8 for more details) captured regions as audio files and in whatever file format you wish, and then burn them onto a CD-audio or CD-ROM.

To capture a region:

a) Select a section of an audio file or region (Fig. 5.31a).

b) Choose "Capture Region" from the Edit pop-up menu (Fig. 5.31b).

c) A dialog box will appear prompting you to name the new region, as shown in Fig. 5.31c.

d) Name it and click "OK." The new audio region will appear highlighted on your Audio or MIDI Regions List (Fig. 5.31d).

Shortcut: To Capture a region, press and hold the Command (⌘) key and then press the letter "R" on your computer keyboard.

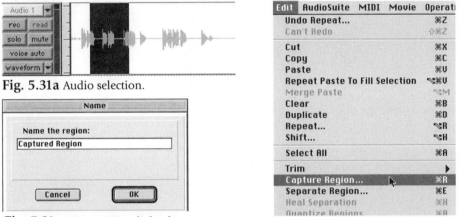

Fig. 5.31a Audio selection.

Fig. 5.31c Name region dialog box.

Fig. 5.31b Selecting the "Capture Region" command in the Edit menu.

Fig. 5.31d New captured region on the Audio Region List.

Audio Region List

New region

Separate Region

The "Separate Region" command is similar to Capture Region, with the exception that "Separate Region" will insert a new region name within the region you are separating it from; consequently, a new audio or MIDI region will be created and listed in the Audio or MIDI Regions Lists.

One common application for separating regions is, for example, when you need to insert a region in the middle of another region. If you don't make a region separation, there is no way you will be able to insert a particular region between the start and end points of another region. By the way, if you need to insert a region within another one, don't forget to set the Edit mode into "Shuffle" mode.

To separate a region:

a) Select a section of an audio file or region (Fig. 5.32a).

b) Choose "Separate Region" from the Edit pop-up menu (Fig. 5.32b).

c) A dialog box will appear prompting you to name the new region, as shown in Fig. 5.32c.

d) Name it and click "OK." The new audio region will appear highlighted on your Audio or MIDI Regions List (Fig. 5.32d).

Shortcut: *To Separate a region, press and hold the Command (⌘) key and then press the letter "E" on your computer keyboard.*

Fig. 5.32a Audio selection.

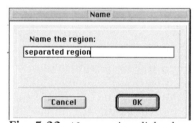

Fig. 5.32c Name region dialog box.

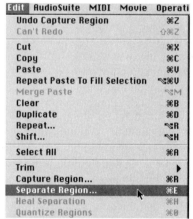

Fig. 5.32b Selecting the "Separate Region" command in the Edit menu.

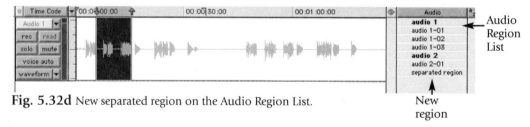

Fig. 5.32d New separated region on the Audio Region List.

Audio Region List

New region

Heal Separation

Shortcut: *To Heal a Separations, press and hold the Command (⌘) key and then press the letter "H" on your computer keyboard.*

After you have separated an audio or MIDI region, leaving a "line" marking the separation, you can get rid of that line with the "Heal Separation" command. If you are trying to heal a separation, and notice you cannot select the "Heal Separation" command, this means that for some reason you edited (trimmed or cut) the separated region and won't be able to heal the separation, i.e., not all the separated region segments are in their original adjacent locations.

To heal a separation:

a) Select the section where the line(s) are on the separated region (Fig. 5.33a).

b) Choose "Heal Separation" from the Edit pop-up menu (Fig. 5.33b).

c) After selecting the command, the "line(s)" on the separated regions will disappear, meaning the separation is no longer there (Fig. 5.33c).

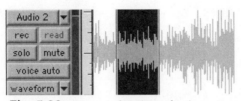

Fig. 5.33a Separated region selection.

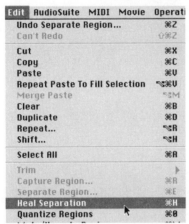

Fig. 5.33b Selecting the "Heal Separation" command.

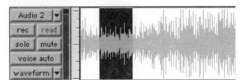

Fig. 5.33c Healed selection.

Mute/Unmute a region

This Edit command mutes only individual audio or MIDI regions within a track, instead of the entire track. When you mute a region using the "Mute/Unmute Region" command, you will notice the muted regions will appear dimmed in the track. This means that you won't be able to listen to them when you press the play button.

To mute a region using the Mute/Unmute Region command:

a) Select an audio or MIDI region, or a section of it. If you decide to mute only a section of a region, you must first separate it using the "Separate Region" command and then select it using the Grabber tool (Fig. 5.34a).

b) Choose "Mute/Unmute Region" from the Edit pop-up menu (Fig. 5.34b).

c) You will notice the muted regions will appear dimmed, meaning they are muted and won't be heard when the playback button is pressed (Fig. 5.34c).

Shortcut: *To Mute or Unmute a region, press and hold the Command (⌘) key and then press the letter "M" on your computer keyboard.*

Fig. 5.34a Region selected.

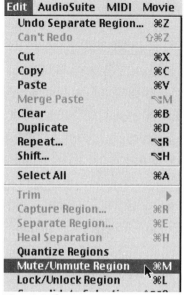

Fig. 5.34c Muted region.

Fig. 5.34b Selecting the "Mute/Unmute Region"
command in the Edit menu.

If you need to unmute regions already muted, you can do so by using the
Mute/Unmute Region command as well. To achieve this, do the following:

a) Select the Grabber tool and position it on the muted region (Fig. 5.35a).

b) Select the muted region by clicking on it once using the Grabber tool
(Fig. 5.35b).

c) Choose the "Mute/Unmute Region" command from the Edit pop-up
menu. Select the muted region by clicking on it once using the Grabber tool
(Fig. 5.35c).

d) After selecting the command, you will notice the muted region is now
unmuted. Select the muted region by clicking on it once using the Grabber
tool (Fig. 5.35d).

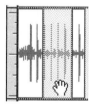
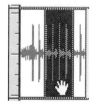

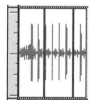

Fig. 5.35a
Positioning the
Grabber on the
muted region.

Fig. 5.35b
Selecting the
muted region.

Fig. 5.35c Selecting the
"Mute/Unmute Region"
command in the Edit
menu.

Fig. 5.35d
Unmuted
region.

Lock/Unlock Region

Whether you are working on a music production or audio for a video post-production project, it will be a good idea to "Lock" (secure in place) your audio or MIDI regions. If you "Lock" your regions once you know their final location, you won't run into the problem of "region shifting" every time you trim or delete a region, especially if Pro Tools is set in the "Shuffle" edit mode. For example, in Fig. 5.36a, an audio region is selected to be deleted (erased) from the track. Pro Tools at this time is set in "Shuffle" edit mode. In Fig. 5.36b, notice the selected region (second region from the left) was deleted and the third region shifted to the left. Now, in Fig. 5.36c, notice the second region is selected again to be deleted and the third regions is "Locked" (small padlock showing). In Fig. 5.36d, the second region was deleted, just like in Fig. 5.36b, but this time since the third region was "Locked," it did not shifted (moved) to the left.

Shortcut: To Lock or Unlock a region, press and hold the Command (⌘) key and then press the letter "L" on your computer keyboard.

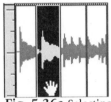

Fig. 5.36a Selecting a region to be deleted.

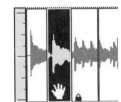

Fig. 5.36b The region shifted to the left.

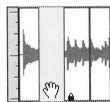

Fig. 5.36c Selecting a region to be deleted.

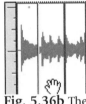

Fig. 5.36d The region did not shift to the left.

To "Lock" a region using the Lock/Unlock Region command:

a) Select the Grabber tool and position it on a region (Fig. 5.37a).

b) Click once on the region to be "Locked" (Fig. 6.37b).

c) Choose "Lock/Unlock Region" from the Edit pop-up menu (Fig. 5.37c).

d) You will notice a small padlock appearing on the lower left hand side of the region, meaning the region won't be able to be moved or be deleted (Fig. 5.37d).

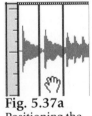

Fig. 5.37a Positioning the Grabber on a region.

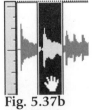

Fig. 5.37b Selecting the region.

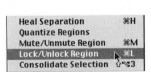

Heal Separation	⌘H
Quantize Regions	
Mute/Unmute Region	⌘M
Lock/Unlock Region	⌘L
Consolidate Selection	⇧⌥3

Fig. 5.37c Selecting the "Lock/Unlock Region" command in the Edit menu.

Fig. 5.37d The region is locked.

If you need to unlock regions already locked, you can do so by using the "Lock/Unlock Region" command as well. To achieve this, do the following:

a) Select the Grabber tool and position it on the Locked region (Fig. 5.38a).

b) Select the Locked region by clicking on it once using the Grabber tool (Fig. 5.38b).

c) Choose the "Lock/Unlock Region" command from the Edit pop-up menu (Fig. 5.38c).

d) After selecting the command, you will notice the small padlock on the lower left of the region will disappear (Fig. 5.38d).

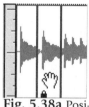
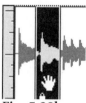
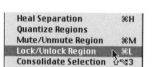

Fig. 5.38a Positioning the grabber on a region.

Fig. 5.38b Selecting the region.

Fig. 5.38c Selecting the "Lock/Unlock Region" command in the Edit menu.

Fig. 5.38d Region unlocked.

Consolidate Selection

The "Consolidate Selection" command is a way to create a new region—in the Edit window—and a new Audio File which will be stored in the "Audio Files" folder of your session, out of multiple regions in an audio or MIDI track. In other words, all the vertical lines which divide a region into small ones will disappear (Fig. 5.39a and Fig. 5.39b).

Shortcut: To Consolidate a Selection, press and hold the Control key, the Shift key and then press the number "3" on your computer keyboard.

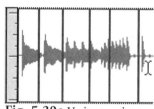
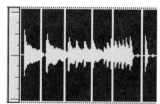

Fig. 5.39a Various regions in a track.

Fig. 5.39b Selecting all the regions in a track.

Fig. 5.39c Regions consolidated.

A good example for consolidating a selection would be "fixing" a snare drum track in a song. Let's say the drummer missed hitting the snare on time in two places during the solo section of a song. Let's fix the problem and consolidate the fix:

a) Assuming that Pro Tools is in the Grid edit mode and the Grabber tool is chosen, select the region you need to move—in this case to the left—to the next Grid line (Fig. 5.40a).

b) Using the Grabber tool, move the first region to the left, to where the closest Grid line is (Fig. 5.40b).

c) Using the Grabber tool, move the second region to the left, to the nearest Grid line (Fig. 5.40c).

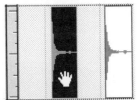

Fig. 5.40a Selecting a region.

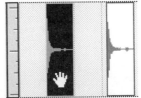

Fig. 5.40b Moving the region to the left.

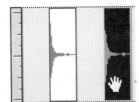

Fig. 5.40c Moving the region to the left.

d) Once you moved both regions to where they're supposed to go, select both regions and extend it all the way to the beginning of the track. To extend the selection to the left (beginning of the track), hold down the Shift key on your keyboard and use the Selector tool and move it to the left (Fig. 5.40d).

e) Go to the Edit pop-up menu and choose the "Consolidate Selection" command (Fig. 5.40e).

f) When you release the mouse after selecting the "Consolidate Selection" command, you will see a momentary window that will read "Calculating Overview For… (name of the file being consolidated)". Then, you will notice the newly created region (Fig. 5.40f) in the Edit window and the newly created Audio File in the "Audio Regions List."

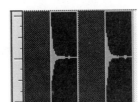

Fig. 5.40d Selecting all regions.

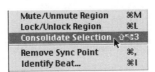

Fig. 5.40e Selecting the "Consolidate Selection" command in the Edit menu.

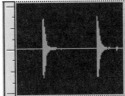

Fig. 5.40f Selection consolidated.

Identify Sync Point

When you need to move or align a specific point within a region (not Start or End point of a region, but somewhere in between) to a particular location in the session, you should use the "Identify Sync Point" command. A Spot mode/Grabber tool or a Grid mode/Grabber tool combination is used to align a "Sync Point" to a specific SMPTE time code, minutes/seconds, or bars/beats location.

This command is very useful, especially when placing sound effects or music to an exact frame location in a post-production job. For example, suppose you need to align a sound effect to a particular spot in a music passage (Fig. 5.41a). Let's follow the process step-by-step:

a) First, make sure Pro Tools is in the Slip edit mode, the Selector tool, and the Main counter is reading Time Code (SMPTE) or Min:Secs.

Shortcut: To Identify a Sync Point, press and hold the Command (⌘) key and then press the letter "," on your computer keyboard.

235

b) Position the cursor using the Selector tool right on the place you want to align the sound effect to. Find out its time location by reading the Main counter. In my case it reads 0.00.620, which means zero minutes:zero seconds:620 milliseconds (Fig. 5.41b).

c) Once you find the time destination of the sound effect you are about to move or align, position the Selector tool right on the exact location you want to insert a Sync Point—in this case, on the sound effect (fig. 5.41c).

Fig. 5.41a Two tracks showing audio content.

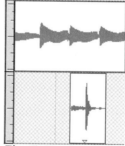

Fig. 5.41b Positioning the cursor and reading the counter.

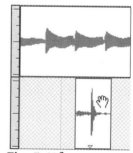

Fig. 5.41c Positioning the cursor to insert a Sync Point.

d) Go to the Edit pop-up menu and select the "Identify Sync Point" command (Fig. 5.41d).

e) After selecting the command, you will notice a small triangle pointing down right on the spot you had positioned the Selector tool (Fig. 5.41e). This means you inserted a Sync Point in the region.

f) Next, select the Spot edit mode and the Grabber tool and place it on the region you inserted the Sync Point—in this case, the sound effect (Fig. 5.41f).

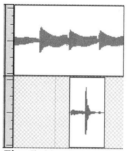

Fig. 5.41d Selecting the "Identify Sync Point" command in the Edit menu.

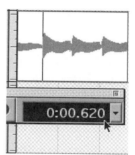

Fig. 5.41e Sync Point inserted.

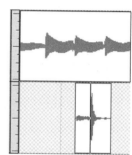

Fig. 5.41f Clicking on the region in Spot mode.

g) Click on the mouse and you will see what is called the "Spot Dialog" window. Notice the Sync Point box the first number is highlighted. This means it is asking you to type the time location number to where you want the sound effect to go—in this case, to 0.00.620 (Fig. 5.41g).

h) Once you typed the time destination number and clicked on "OK," you will see the Sync Point of the region or sound effect moved and aligned exactly to the time location you wanted to go (Fig. 5.41h).

i) You can see in Fig. 5.41i, I placed the Selector tool on the upper region (music passage) where the I wanted the sound effect to go to, to visually indicate that that specific place is aligned with the Sync Point in the lower region.

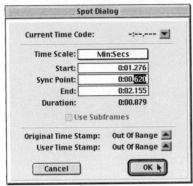

Fig. 5.41g Spot Dialog box.

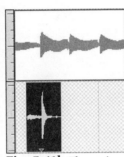

Fig. 5.41h The region was moved to the time location inserted.

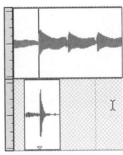

Fig. 5.41i The Sync Point and the selector aligned.

Identify Beat

The "Identify Beat" command is commonly used to analyze and calculate the tempo of a region selection based on the specified meter. I find it most useful to get the exact tempo of a particular song imported into a new Pro Tools session, for example. Also, I have noticed that DJs are taking more advantage of the use of this command to do dance remixes.

As I mentioned just a second ago, I frequently use this command to calculate the tempo of a song when I import it from an audio CD or DAT machine, for example, into a newly created Pro Tools session. As you may know, every time you create a new Session in Pro Tools, the default tempo is 120.00 beats per minute or BPM, which may not be the real tempo of the song you imported. You can see the tempo in the expanded section of the Transport window (Fig. 5.42a). If you don't see this part of the Transport window, go to the Display pop-up menu, select the "Transport Window Shows" command, and slide the cursor to the right to select the "Expanded" option (Fig. 5.42b).

Shortcut: To Identify Beat, press and hold the Command (⌘) key and then press the letter "I" on your computer keyboard.

Fig. 5.42a Transport window.

Fig. 5.42b Display pop-up menu.

To find the tempo of a song or piece of music using the "Identify Beat" command, do the following:

    a) For simplicity, select a two-bar perfect loop of the song you want to find the tempo from. It is very important to be very precise in selecting the loop. Notice in Fig. 5.42c the expanded section of the Transport window reads "120.00," which means 120.00 BPM. This is not the real tempo of the song.

    b) Once you think you've captured a perfect two-bar loop, go to the Edit window and select the "Identify Beat" command (Fig. 5.42d).

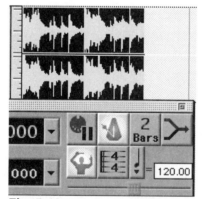

Fig. 5.42c Two-bar loop selected and tempo showing in the Transport window.

Fig. 5.42d Edit pop-up menu.

    c) A dialog box will appear prompting you to type the Start and End locations. Now, the loop starts at the beginning of the track, which means that the Start location is 1|1|000. The time signature in this case is 4/4. Of course if you have a song that has a time signature of 3/4, then you should enter the right signature. The End location should be 3|1|000, since it is a two-bar loop (Fig. 5.42e).

d) When you click on the "OK" button, you will see the tempo window in the Transport window change to the real tempo of the song, in this case 108.84 BPM (Fig. 5.42f).

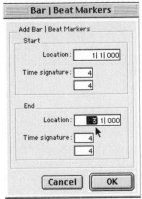

Fig. 5.42e Bar/Beat Markers dialog box.

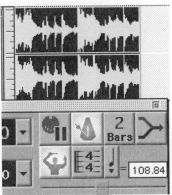

Fig. 5.42f The tempo showing in the Transport window has changed.

Fades

A Fade is a way to gradually increase (fade-in) or decrease (fade-out) the volume of a sound (Fig. 5.43a and Fig. 5.43b). A crossfade is a gradual sound dissolve from one audio source to another. In Pro Tools terms, a crossfade is lowering the volume of one audio region to a zero level (fade-out) and at the same time, increasing the volume (fade-in) of an adjacent audio region from zero to its maximum level (Fig. 5.43c).

Shortcut: To create a Fade, press and hold the Command (⌘) key and then press the letter "F" on your computer keyboard.

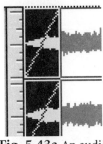

Fig. 5.43a An audio region fading in.

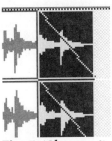

Fig. 5.43b An audio region fading out.

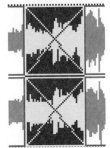

Fig. 5.43c A crossfade between two audio regions.

In Pro Tools you can create "Fade ins," "Fade outs," and "Crossfades" by means of the "Fades" command (Fig. 5.43d) in the Edit pop-up menu. This command will be active only if you have made a selection in an audio region, either, to create a fade-in, fade-out, or a crossfade. Otherwise, this command will be grayed-out.

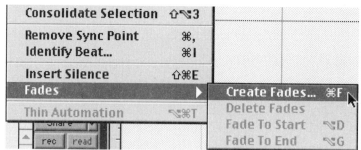

Consolidate Selection	⇧⌥3		
Remove Sync Point	⌘,		
Identify Beat...	⌘I		
Insert Silence	⇧⌘E		
Fades	▶	**Create Fades...**	⌘F
Thin Automation	⌥⌘T	Delete Fades	
		Fade To Start	⌥D
rec read		Fade To End	⌥G

Fig. 5.43d The "Fades" command in the Edit pop-up menu.

To create a Fade-in:

a) First, select the beginning of an audio region (Fig. 5.44a).

b) You must touch the beginning of the track to be able to create a Fade-in; otherwise, you won't be able even to select the "Fades" command (Fig. 5.44b).

c) Once you have selected the beginning of the audio region, all the way to the left, go to the Edit pop-up menu and choose the "Fades" command (Fig. 5.43d).

d) As soon you release the mouse after you have selected the "Fades" command, a window will appear showing you the types of curves you may want the fade-in to be (Fig. 5.44d). In this window, you can experiment and audition the way the type of curve you have selected sounds like. To audition it just click on the "small speaker" icon located on the upper left hand side of the "Fades" window.

e) When you have decided on the curve and other parameters you want, click the "OK" button. You will see the Fade-in appearing at the beginning of the track or region (Fig. 5.44c).

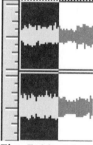

Fig. 5.44a Selecting the beginning of an audio region.

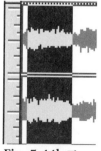

Fig. 5.44b The selection doesn't touch the beginning of the track.

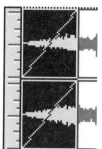

Fig. 5.44c Fade-in showing at the beginning of the track or region.

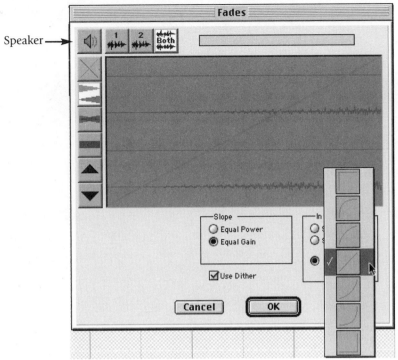

Speaker →

Fig. 5.44d Fades window.

To create a Fade-out:

a) Select a section at the end of an audio region (Fig. 5.45a).

b) The selection must pass the end of the audio region to be able to create a Fade-out; otherwise, you won't be able to even select the "Fades" command (Fig. 5.45b).

c) Once you have selected the end of the audio region, all the way to the right passing the end of it, go to the Edit pop-up menu and choose the "Fades" command (Fig. 5.43d).

d) As soon you release the mouse after you have selected the "Fades" command, a window will appear showing you the types of curves you may want the fade-out to be (Fig. 5.45d). In this window, you can experiment and audition the way the type of curve you have selected sounds like. To audition it just click on the "small speaker" icon located on the upper left hand side of the "Fades" window.

e) When you have decided on the curve and other parameters you want, click the "OK" button. You will see the fade-out appearing at the end of the audio region (Fig. 5.45c).

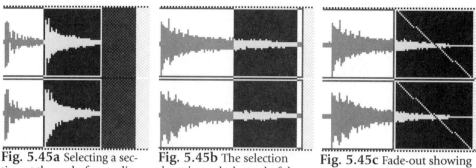

Fig. 5.45a Selecting a section at the end of an audio region.

Fig. 5.45b The selection doesn't touch the end of the track.

Fig. 5.45c Fade-out showing at the end of the track or region.

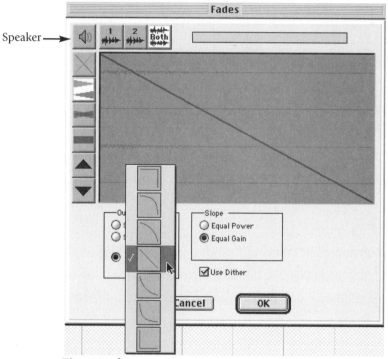

Speaker ——→

Fig. 5.45d Fades window.

To create a Crossfade:

    a) In order to create a Crossfade, you need to have two audio regions placed next to each other. They should be touching each other. To make sure they are touching, use the Grabber tool and the Shuffle mode to move the audio region on the right side of the two (Fig. 5.46a).

    b) Make a selection that includes both audio regions. The selection must pass the boundary line as it shows in Fig. 5.46b.

    c) Once you have made the selection between both audio regions, go to the Edit pop-up menu and choose the "Fades" command (Fig. 5.43d).

    d) As soon you release the mouse after you have selected the "Fades" command, a window will appear showing you the types of curves you may want the crossfade to be (Fig. 5.46d). In this window, you can experiment and audition the way the type of curve you have selected sounds like. To audition it just click on the "small speaker" icon located on the upper left hand side of the "Fades" window.

e) When you have decided on the curve and other parameters you want, click the "OK" button. You will see the crossfade appearing between both audio regions (Fig. 5.46c).

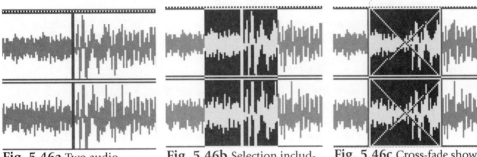

Fig. 5.46a Two audio regions placed next to each other.

Fig. 5.46b Selection including both audio regions.

Fig. 5.46c Cross-fade showing between both audio regions.

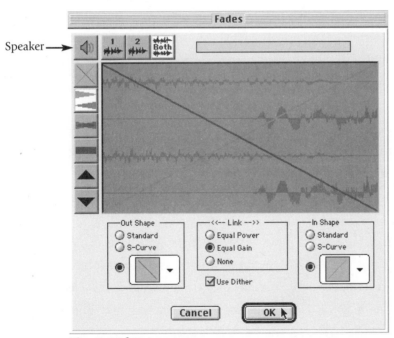

Fig. 5.46d Fades window.

AudioSuite Menu

This menu allows you to select any AudioSuite plug-ins available in your Pro Tools system and "process" the selected audio region. When I say "available in your system" I mean that you may not have some plug-ins that your friend might have, for example. The reason is that when you purchase a Pro Tools LE system, for example, you get some free AudioSuite plug-ins developed by Digidesign. If you want more, you must purchase them from third party developers. Some of the AudioSuite plug-ins you get when you purchase a Pro Tools LE system such as the Mbox, for example, are: "Normalize"; "Gain"; "Compressor"; "1 Band EQ II"; "4 Band EQ II"; "Reverse," "Short," "Medium," and "Long" delays; and "Time Compression Expansion,"among others.

The plug-ins in this menu are file-based only and they are "destructive." Also, they are "non-real time" plug-ins. This means that first you have to audition or "preview" the plug-in in the audio regions selection you made, and if you like it, you must "process" it in order for the effect to be added in the audio region selection. If you don't change the default in the AudioSuite plug-in window when you "process" an audio region, a new audio file will be created and stored on your hard drive and shown in the "Audio Regions List" bin. On the other hand, if you select the "overwrite the files" option in the AudioSuite plug-in window, the original audio file on your hard drive, will be destroyed or permanently altered, so be careful.

To show the process of adding an effect to an audio region selection using an AudioSuite plug-in, let's suppose we want to reverse the sound of a snare drum roll:

a) First, we need to select the snare roll audio region using the Selector or Grabber tool (Fig. 5.47a).

b) Next, go to the AudioSuite pop-up menu and choose the "Reverse" plug-in (Fig. 5.47b).

c) As soon you release the mouse to select the plug-in, a rectangular window will be displayed (Fig. 5.47c). In this window you can make selections of its parameters. For example, you can "preview" or audition the effect before you commit to it. If you decide to do so, click on the "preview" button and you will start to listen to the sound with the effect.

Fig. 5.47a Audio region selected.

Fig. 5.47b AudioSuite pop-up menu.

Fig. 5.47c Plug-in window.

d) Once you've listened to the sound with the effect, if you liked it, click on the "process" button. Depending of how large is the audio region or file you are processing, and how fast your computer is, it might take an instant or a few seconds (Fig, 5.47d).

e) When finishing processing the audio region or audio file, you will see the region being reversed, since in our example, the goal was to reverse the sound of a snare drum roll (Fig. 5.47e).

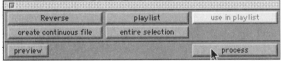

Fig. 5.47d Plug-in window.

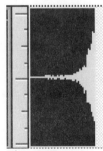

Fig. 5.47e Processed audio region.

The Movie Menu

Import Movie

Whether you are working on a Pro Tools TDM or LE system, both can import QuickTime movies. This feature allows you to do audio for video post-production projects such as home movies, music videos, video commercials, and film.

In early Pro Tools software versions, you were not able to work with SMPTE Time Code in an LE system. Now you can purchase the "DV ToolKit" option for Pro Tools LE from Digidesign and be able to read Time Code as well as opening OMF or AAF file formats from applications such as Avid's Xpress DV on either Mac OS X or Windows XP.

To import a QuickTime movie into a Pro Tools session:

a) First, create a new Session or open an existing one on your hard drive and go to the Movie pop-up menu and select the "Import Movie" command (Fig. 5.48a). Pro Tools will prompt you to look for the movie you are trying to import. In other words, you have to find the folder the movie is stored in.

b) Once you find the movie and import it, a movie track will be created for you with the QuickTime movie on the track (Fig. 5.48b). You will also notice a floating window appearing on your screen; this window is called the "Movie Window." When you press the Play button, you will be able to see the movie playing back along with the audio, if any. The created movie track behaves almost the same as a Pro Tools audio or MIDI track in that you can move the movie region with the Grabber or other editing tools. One thing you cannot perform on a movie track is editing. In other words, you cannot trim the movie track or capture frames like an audio or MIDI track. For that, you will have to purchase a video editing software such as Final Cut Pro or iMovie among others.

Fig. 5.48a Movie pop-up menu.

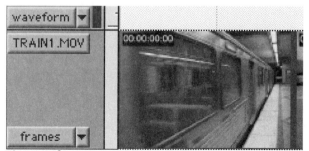

Fig. 5.48b Movie track with a QuickTime movie on it.

Import Audio From Current Movie

Let's say you were hired to incorporate sound effects into a video commercial. Suppose the music was already recorded into a QuickTime movie file when it was captured. How do you import the music track from the QuickTime movie commercial into Pro Tools? You guessed it, through the "Import Audio From Current Movie" command in the Movie pop-up menu.

To import audio from a QuickTime movie that is already in the Session:

a) Choose the "Import Audio From Current Movie" command from the Movie pop-up menu (Fig. 5.49a). A "Track Import Window" will appear showing the audio track(s) associated with the QuickTime movie.

b) Select the track(s) you want to import and click the "OK" button (Fig. 5.49b). In this case, it is the music track.

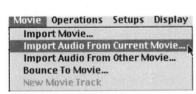

Fig. 5.49a Selecting the "Import Audio from Current Movie" command in the Movie menu.

Fig. 5.49b Track Import window.

c) Select the folder in your session you want the imported audio track to be directed. Obviously, you should direct the audio track to the Audio Files folder located in your Session (Fig. 5.79c). After clicking on the "Select Audio Files" button, a window reading "processing audio" will appear indicating the audio track is being converted to the session's sample rate and bit resolution.

d) For each imported file, a new region will appear in the Audio Region List (Fig. 5.49d).

Fig. 5.49c Choosing a destination.

Fig. 5.49d Audio Regions List.

e) Once the imported audio file (music track) is in the Audio Regions List, create an audio track in stereo since the music is in stereo. Then click and drag the file in the track. Make sure you are in the Shuffle edit mode when you drag the audio file in the track so it will start playing in synchronization with the movie track; otherwise it will be out of sync (Fig. 5.49e).

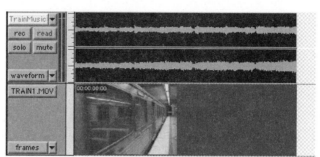

Fig. 5.49e Edit window showing an audio and a movie track.

Import Audio From Other Movie

If you need to import sounds from other QuickTime movies in your computer, use this Movie command. Also, this command is used to import audio from an audio CD inside your computer's CD-ROM. Refer to Chapter 8 and follow the steps to import audio from an audio CD without using other software.

Movie Online

By selecting the "Movie Online" command from the Movie pop-up menu (Fig. 5.50a) the QuickTime movie will play along with the audio in your session. If you do not select this option, your movie will not play along with the rest of the audio tracks. Notice in Fig. 5.50b, the cursor in the audio track is almost at the end and the movie track is still at the beginning of the track, as you can see in Fig. 5.49e where the cursor is at the beginning of the audio track as well as the movie track.

Shortcut: To select Movie Online, press and hold the Command (⌘) key, the Shift key and then press the letter "J" on your computer keyboard.

Fig. 5.50a Selecting the "Movie Online" command in the Movie menu.

Fig. 5.50b Edit window showing an audio and a movie track.

Show Movie Window

I know this command is not part of the Movie pop-up menu, but I just thought I'd mention this command at this time. Many of you have been in the situation where you cannot find the movie window when working with QuickTime movies in Pro Tools. Whether you purposely hid it or it disappeared by accident, you can find it under the "Windows" pop-up menu. Select the "Show Movie Window" command or hold down the Command key (Control in Windows) and press the number "9" on the numeric keypad of your computer's keyboard (Fig. 5.51).

Shortcut: To Show Movie Window, press and hold the Command (⌘) key and then press the number "9" on your computer keyboard.

Windows Help	
Show Mix	⌘=
Hide Edit	⌘W
Show MIDI Event List	⌥=
Show Tempo/Meter	
Show MIDI Operations	
Show MIDI Track Offsets	
1–9 on numeric keypad only	
Show Transport	⌘1
Show Session Setup	⌘2
Show Big Counter	⌘3
Show Automation Enable	⌘4
Show Memory Locations	⌘5
Show Movie Window	⌘9
Show Strip Silence	⌘U
Show System Usage	
Show Disk Space	

Fig. 5.51 Windows pop-up menu.

The Operations Menu

Loop Playback

There are some times when you need to listen to the same audio or MIDI section over and over again, maybe because you are trying to capture the perfect loop to insert it in or remove it from a song, or maybe because you are producing your own CD of drum loops—if you are a drummer—for example. Whatever the reason, in order to listen to that audio section back and forth, you need to enable the "Loop Playback" command. This command is located in the "Operations" pop-up menu.

Shortcut: *Press and hold the Command (⌘) key, the Shif key and then press the letter "L" on your computer keyboard.*

To play back an audio or MIDI loop:

a) Select a section of an audio or MIDI region using the Selector tool (Fig. 5.52a).

b) Go to the Operations pop-up menu and choose the "Loop Playback" command (Fig. 5.52b).

c) If you have the Transport window displayed at the time, you will notice a circle around the Play button (Fig. 5.52c).

d) Last thing is to press Play on the Transport window or press the spacebar on your computer keyboard.

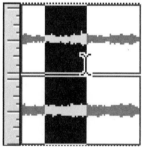

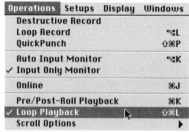

Fig. 5.52a Selecting a section of an audio region.

Fig. 5.52b Operations pop-up menu.

Fig. 5.52c Transport window with the Loop Playback button showing.

Scroll Options

I have noticed some Pro Tools users manually scrolling the computer screen to follow the cursor when playing back a session. Sometimes they don't realize they zoom in too much and cannot follow the cursor. Well, if that happens to you, just go to the Operations pop-up menu and enable the "Page Scroll During Playback" option (Fig. 5.53). Although, there are times you don't want the screen to follow the cursor; if that is the case, then select the "No Auto-Scrolling" option in the same menu command.

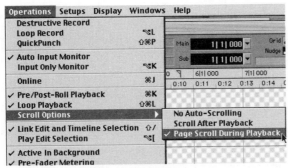

Fig. 5.53 Operations pop-up menu.

The Setups Menu

Hardware Setup

The "Hardware Setup" command in the "Setups" pop-up menu (Fig. 5.54a) is perhaps the most used command when working with Pro Tools.

Fig. 5.54a Selecting the "Scroll Options" command in the Operations menu.

Whether you have a Pro Tools HD, Mix, or LE series, this is the menu command where you will be making all your assignments regarding which audio interfaces you are going to be using for TDM systems, selecting "Clock" sources, whether you will be recording analog or digital audio sources, selecting which digital transfer format you wish to use such as AES/EBU, S/PDIF, Lightpipe for ADATs, T-DIF, etc. (for HD systems only). See Fig. 5.54b and Fig. 5.54c. Please refer to Chapter 6 for more details on these types of assignments.

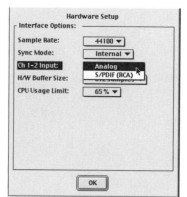

Fig. 5.54b Hardware Setup window.

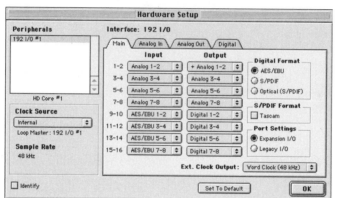

Fig. 5.54c Hardware Setup window.

Peripherals

If you are going to be using any type of optional equipment in your Pro Tools setup, the "Peripherals" command (Fig. 5.55a) is the place where you need to go to assign them. For example, let's say that you purchased a MIDI controller for your Digi 001 or HD system. Well, you will need to click on the "MIDI Controllers" tab (Fig. 5.55b) to assign the controller you acquired. This could be a MotorMix from CmLabs, a HUI from Mackie, a CS10 from JL Cooper, etc. On the other hand, if you purchased a Control|24 or a ProControl from Digidesign, then you would have to select the "Ethernet Controllers" tab in order to assign this type of surface controller. Furthermore, if you are going to be using some type of synchronizer or time code converter, you need to click on the "Synchronization" tab of the "Peripherals" command to make the selection.

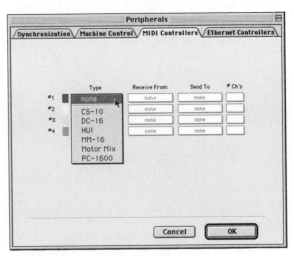

Fig. 5.55a Setups pop-up menu.

Fig. 5.55b Peripherals window.

I/O Setup

The "I/O Setup" command (Fig. 5.56a) allows you to define which physical inputs and outputs of your audio interface the signals will be routed to and from Pro Tools. Are they going to be sent on analog or digital outputs? Are they coming into Pro Tools through the analog or digital inputs? The I/O Setup window (Fig. 5.56b and Fig. 5.56c) is like a "patchbay" in a recording studio. You can create and customize signal path definitions. These signal paths can be renamed, remapped, deleted, de-activated, and activated. You can even save your own I/O Setup configurations as "I/O Settings" files and recall them at any time when you need them.

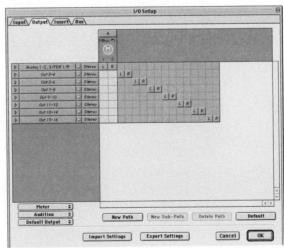

Fig. 5.56a Setups pop-up menu.

Fig. 5.56b I/O Setup window.

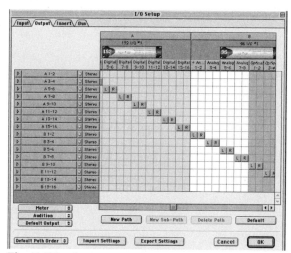

Fig. 5.56c I/O Setup window.

This window will also allow you to customize the names of the inputs, outputs, inserts, and buses of your Mix window for easy use and understanding. For example, if your analog outputs 1 and 2 are always connected to your speaker monitors, you can rename those outputs to always read "Speakers" in the Mix window (Fig. 5.56d and Fig. 5.56e).

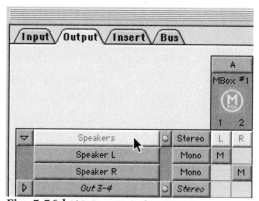

Fig. 5.56d I/O Setup window.

Fig. 5.56e Mix window.

By the same token, let's say that you have a small home studio and you are using an Mbox LE system. Let's also suppose you do voice-overs for radio commercials and you always have a U87 microphone connected to input 1 in your Mbox and an SM57 mic to input 2. If this is the case, then rename input 1 to be U87 and input 2 to be SM57 (Fig. 5.56f). This way, every time you create a new Session or open an existing one, you will always know which input the U87 is connected, so you will be able to assign it right away without thinking (Fig. 5.56g).

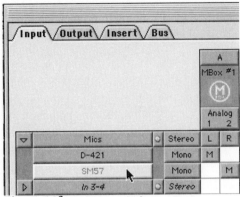

Fig. 5.56f I/O Setup window.

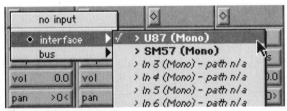

Fig. 5.56g Mix window.

The Display and Windows Menus

The Display menu commands basically control the display of Pro Tools windows, tracks, and track data. Throughout the book I describe most of commands you will mostly use, with the exception of the following, which I am about to describe.

Narrow Mix Window

When you are working on a big Pro Tools session where there are too many tracks to display all of them in the Mix window, then is when you need to use the "Narrow Mix Window" command (Fig. 5.57a). Notice in Fig. 5.57b only five channel strips are displayed in the Mix window. Selecting the "Narrow Mix Window" command, without enlarging the Mix window, you can see that nine channel strips are displayed now. In other words, this command makes the tracks in the Mix window narrow.

Fig. 5.57a Display pop-up menu.

Fig. 5.57b Mix window.

Fig. 5.57c Narrow Mix window.

Display Time in Regions

When editing, there are times when you need to see audio regions with no numbers or letters in the way (Fig. 5.58a). But then again, you may want to keep track of the length of the audio regions by just looking at them in the Edit window. You can do this by selecting the "Display Time in Regions" command in the Display pop-up menu. You have four options in this command (Fig. 5.58b):

    1) to not display any numbers on the audio region by selecting the "None" option,

    2) to select the "Current Time" of the audio region,

    3) to select the "Original Time Stamp" on the region, i.e., to display in what minute and seconds or bar and beats the region was originally recorded,

    4) to select the "User Time Stamp."

Once you have selected any of the four options in the "Display Time in Regions" command, you will see the numbers appearing on the audio region (Fig. 5.58c).

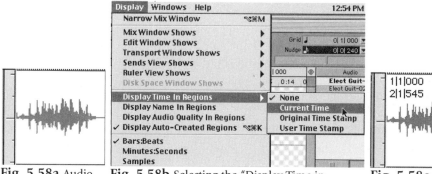

Fig. 5.58a Audio region.

Fig. 5.58b Selecting the "Display Time in Regions" command in the Display menu.

Fig. 5.58c Audio region showing the selected options.

Display Name in Regions

Another useful command from the Display pop-up menu is "Display Name in Regions" (Fig. 5.59a). If you like to see the names of the audio regions right on them (Fig. 5.59b), use this command. Although, sometimes it is hard to edit small and short regions when you are showing the names on the regions (Fig. 5.59c), so you may not want to use this command, since it will take too much space for the name and not enough for the actual audio region.

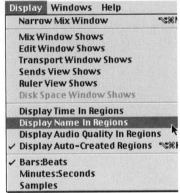

Fig. 5.59a Selecting the "Display Name in Regions" command in the Display menu.

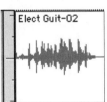

Fig. 5.59b Audio region showing the name on it.

Fig. 5.59c Audio region showing the name on it.

CHAPTER SIX

Recording Audio Files

The previous chapters have introduced you to the three main windows (Edit, Mix, and Transport) in Pro Tools, as well as some of the most frequently used menus. In this chapter you will learn how to:

- Launch Pro Tools

- Create a New Session

- Determine where your New Session will be saved

- Name a New Session

- Name audio tracks

- Set your input format (analog or digital)

- Assign track inputs

- Assign track outputs

- Record audio tracks

- Play back audio tracks

- Group audio tracks

- Save a Session

- AutoSave, and

- Other options

Conventions

In order to successfully follow the step-by-step exercises throughout this chapter, you will need to conform to the following conventions:

I. View the items on your computer screen as icons. To do this, click on the "View" pop-up menu in your computer's standard menu (Fig. 6.1).

Fig. 6.1 Macintosh computer standard menu.

In the View Menu, select the option called "as Icons" (Fig. 6.2).

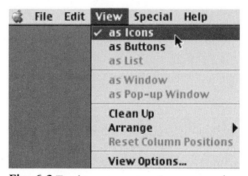

Fig. 6.2 To view your computer screen as icons.

If your icons are too big, you can change them to a smaller size. Go to the View Menu and select "View Options" (Fig. 6.3).

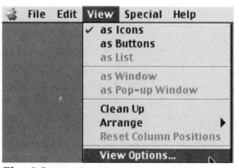

Fig. 6.3. To select the icon size options.

The View Options Window will appear, and you can set the "Icon Size" to small (Fig. 6.4).

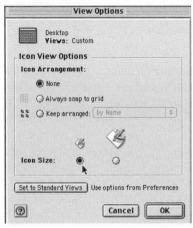

Fig. 6.4 To select the icon size in your computer screen.

II. Whenever you encounter "Pro Tools X.XX" anywhere in this book, the "X.XX" means the version of Pro Tools that you are currently running. So, for you, it might mean Pro Tools Version 3.2, 4.0, 4.2, 5.0, 5.1, 5.1.1, 5.2, 5.3, or 6.0 or higher.

Launching Pro Tools

Launching Pro Tools is a simple process. First, find the Pro Tools application icon. It is located in the "Digidesign" folder of your computer's start-up hard disk. The start-up hard disk is usually the internal hard drive (main drive) of your computer (although it is possible to use an external drive to boot up your system).

In case you are new to the computer world, Fig. 6.5 shows you an example of a two-drive computer system.

Fig. 6.5 Example of a computer system with both internal and external hard drives.

In this scenario, a "Start-up Hard Disk" icon appears in the upper right hand corner of the computer's desktop (for a Macintosh). This icon represents the drive where your computer programs are usually stored. The icon below it, labeled "External Hard Drive," represents a second drive, where your music files can be saved.

To open your hard disk, double-click the "Start-Up Hard Disk" icon. When you "open" a hard disk, you will see a window that displays the contents of this hard disk. Each icon in this window represents a program—or another folder containing more icons to choose from.

Locate and double click the folder icon named "Digidesign."

This folder was created when the Pro Tools software was first installed in your computer (Fig. 6.6).

Fig. 6.6 The Digidesign folder contains the Pro Tools software.

Inside the "Digidesign" folder, open the Pro Tools folder and then look for the Pro Tools application icon. In this case, you would be selecting the icon labeled Pro Tools 5.3.1 (Fig. 6.7). Double-click the Pro Tools icon to launch (open) Pro Tools.

Pro Tools software icon

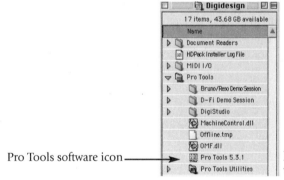

Fig. 6.7 Inside the Pro Tools folder.

When Pro Tools starts up, your screen will fill up with the Pro Tools logo. This display is meant to let you know that the system is starting up, but it takes some time to load Digidesign's operating system, the DAE (Digidesign Audio Engine), and the plug-ins' software, and to initialize any control surfaces (Pro Control, Control | 24, MotorMix, etc.) that are attached to your system.

The amount of time that it takes Pro Tools to open will depend upon the speed of your CPU, and upon the number of plug-ins and AudioSuites that you have on your hard drive (refer to Chapter 10 for more details).

The next thing you will see on your computer screen is the main Pro Tools menu (Fig. 6.8). When this menu appears, it means that Pro Tools is opened and ready to create a new session.

Fig. 6.8 Pro Tools software main menu.

This is not the only way to open Pro Tools, just the most direct. You will find a number of other ways to open Pro Tools in a section named "Other Options" located at the end of this chapter.

Creating a New Session

Once you have started Pro Tools, you can begin the recording session. When you see the main Pro Tools menu, select "New Session" from the File menu (Fig. 6.9).

Fig. 6.9 Creating a new Pro Tools Session.

TIP: You can also create a New Session with a shortcut in your computer's keyboard by pressing and holding the Command (⌘) key and pressing the letter "N" on your keyboard (for a PC: Ctrl N).

Depending upon which version of Pro Tools you are running, you will see one of the following "New Session" dialog boxes. See Fig. 6.10 (a) and (b).

"New Session" dialog window

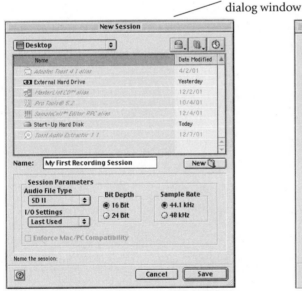

Fig. 6.10(a) This "New Session" dialog box is from a TDM MIX-series system, and allows you to select a sample frequency only up to 48kHz.

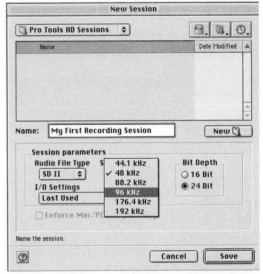

Fig. 6.10(b) This "New Session" dialog box is from a TDM HD-series system, and allows you to select a sample frequency from 44.1kHz to up to 192kHz.

In this New Session window, you need to choose what Sample Rate, Bit Depth, and Audio File format you wish to use for this project. The Sample Rate choices for TDM MIX-series systems are: 44.1kHz or 48kHz. The Sample Rate choices for TDM HD-series systems are: 44.1kHz, 48kHz, 88.2kHz, 96kHz, 176.4kHz, and 192kHz. Both the MIX-series and HD-series systems offer Bit Depths of 16 or 24 bits.

The Audio File Formats that are typically chosen are: SDII (Pro Tools), AIFF (Macintosh), or .WAV (PC). Base your choice of Sample Rate, Bit Depth, and File Formats upon how you intend to deliver your final product. Are you going to deliver the project on a DVD (96kHz/24 bits), a 2" analog tape, a DAT (48kHz/24 or 16 bits), or an audio CD (44.1kHz/16 bits)? Although it is possible to perform conversions later, it is always easier to match your Session to the final medium.

This decision process is similar to the one you have to make when formatting an S-VHS (ADAT) or Hi-8mm (DA-88) tape before you start recording. For example, let's say that you have a final stereo mix of your latest single on a DAT tape (or audio CD) that needs to be edited. Let's also say that the DAT tape (or audio CD) was recorded at 44.1kHz and 16 bits (standard for CDs). This means you want to set the "Session Parameters" in the New Session dialog box to the Sample Rate of 44.1kHz, the Bit Depth to 16 bits, and the Audio File Format to SD II (Sound Designer II), just as it shows in Fig. 6.10 (a). Normally, leave the I/O Settings pop-up menu on the factory default setting of "Last Used," unless you need a different I/O setup for a specific project.

You should not enable the "Enforce Mac/PC Compatibility" or "Enforce PC/Mac Compatibility" option if you are going to use Japanese or non-ASCII characters to name tracks and regions, or type track comments.

If you use Japanese or non-ASCII characters in a Session, and if you use the "Save Session Copy In" command to save the Session in a different software version, all non-ASCII characters will be lost when you save the Session.

TIP: Bear in mind that higher bit rates and higher sample rates take more memory and more storage.

Creating a 24-bit Session takes about 50% more hard drive space than a 16-bit Session, and a 192kHz session takes four times more hard drive space than a 44.1kHz Session.

Determining where your New Session will be saved

Once you have set the parameters of your Session, you must determine where your New Session will be saved.

To begin this process, select "Desktop" on the upper left pop-up menu (click the down arrow and select "Desktop") in the "New Session" window (Fig. 6.11).

Current Directory ──→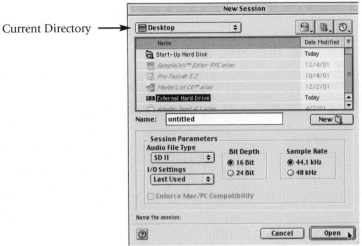

Fig. 6.11 Selecting the folder your Session will be saved in.

When you select "Desktop," you will see the available hard drives and *Aliases* on your computer's desktop.

From this point, you can select the external drive—if you have one available—to save your new Pro Tools Session. Digidesign strongly recommends the use of a separate drive for better results.

If you do not have an external hard drive, you will only see the internal drive icon (which, in our example, is called the Start-Up Hard Disk).

To select the target drive, either double click on the drive icon, or click once on the icon to select it, and then click on "Open" to save the Session to that drive.

Naming a New Session

Whenever you create a New Session, the "Name" box seen in Fig. 6.11 will read "untitled." When you type in a name for your Session, Pro Tools will prompt you to "Save" it (Fig. 6.12).

Before you click on "Save," double check that the Session's parameters are the ones you want, and that you are saving the Session to the right hard drive. For our example, let's name this Session "My First Recording Session."

After you type in the Session name, click on "Save" to initiate the storage of your Session in the location that you have chosen to save it (Fig. 6.12).

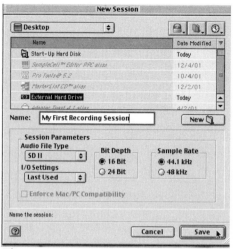

Fig. 6.12 Saving your New Session.

After you press "Save" on the New Session dialog box, your screen will fill up with an empty Pro Tools Edit window. This window will display some control buttons, but it will not show any tracks—because you have not created any yet (Fig. 6.13).

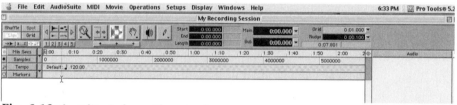

Fig. 6.13 The Edit window with no tracks.

When you pressed "Save," Pro Tools created a new folder with the name of the Session you specified (in this case "My First Recording Session"). If you look inside this newly created folder, you will see a "tape" icon—which is your actual Pro Tools Session file—and two other folders, named "Audio Files" and "Fade Files" (Fig. 6.14).

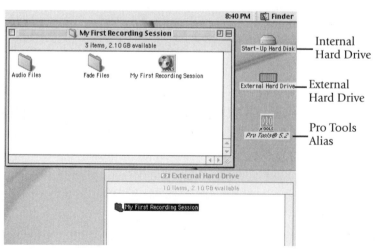

Fig. 6.14 Folders created when starting with a new Pro Tools Session.

Note: The Session file contains all the elements that you see on your computer screen when you open a Session. The "Audio Files" folder is where all your audio recordings and imported / converted audio files are stored. The "Fade Files" folder is where all the fades generated by Pro Tools reside.

If you want to see these files and folders right now, you can do it by "hiding" the Edit window for a moment. Click and hold the Pro Tools icon that is located on the upper right hand corner of your computer's screen, and select "Hide Pro Tools X.XX."

Look in the hard drive where you saved your work and you will see a folder with the name of your newly created Session. Double-click on the folder "My First Recording Session" (assuming that you are following this exercise step-by-step). You will see a "tape" icon, which is your Session file, as well as the other two folders named Audio Files and Fade Files.

To reiterate, you do not have to create these folders. They are automatically created by Pro Tools when you save a New Session (Fig. 6.14). If you enabled the AutoSave option, you will also notice a third folder called "Session File Backups." (We will discuss the AutoSave feature later on in this chapter.)

To return to Pro Tools, go the upper right hand corner where it says "Finder," place the cursor on "Finder," and click and hold the button down. A pop-up window will appear offering the selection of "Pro Tools X.XX." Select Pro Tools, and you will return to the Edit window.

Advice: Pay close attention to where you save your Session. Preferably, you should save it on an external hard drive. Digidesign strongly recommends that you save your audio files on an external hard drive. If you don't have one—and want to get one—refer to Chapter 3 for some suggestions and requirements, or check Digidesign's web site at www.digidesign.com for compatibility. Don't just pick any drive. Choose one that has been tested and recommended by Digidesign.

If you have successfully returned to the Pro Tools Session, you are looking at a screen with no tracks (because you have not created any yet), a palette of editing tools, icons representing the editing modes (Shuffle, Slip, Spot, and Grid), some counters, the Audio and MIDI Region Lists, the Show/Hide list, and the Edit Group list, as shown in Fig. 6.13 to the left.

Creating audio tracks

Let's get started by creating two new mono audio tracks, one for the left channel of the DAT machine (or CD player), and another one for the right.

To create audio tracks, click on the File menu, and select "New Track" as seen in Fig. 6.15 below.

TIP: *You can also create a new track by using a computer keyboard shortcut. On your Mac, hold the "Shift" and Command (⌘) keys down, and press the letter "N" on your keyboard.*

Fig. 6.15 Creating a new audio track.

After you select "New Track" on the File menu, you will see a New Track dialog box (Fig. 6.16).

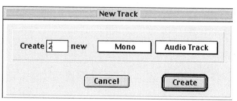

Fig. 6.16 Selecting the number and type of audio tracks.

To create two new mono audio tracks, type the number "2" to create two new tracks, select the "Mono" track format for the tracks, then select "Audio Track" for the track type. The other options for track formats which you may use in the future are: Stereo, LCR, Quad, LCRS, 5.0, 5.1, 6.0, 6.1, 7.0, and 7.1 (Fig. 6.17).

TIP: *There are keyboard shortcuts for selecting audio formats. On a Mac, hold the Command (⌘) key down, and click the left and right arrow keys. On a PC, CTRL+left and CTRL+right arrows.*

There are also keyboard shortcuts for selecting track types. On a Mac, hold the Command (⌘) key down, and click the up and down arrow keys. On a PC, CTRL+ up arrow and CTRL+ right arrow.

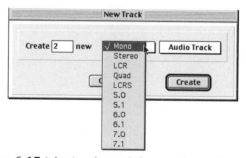

Fig. 6.17 Selecting the track format of an audio track.

The other options for track types you may use in the future are: Aux Input (mono or stereo), Master Fader (mono or stereo), and MIDI Track (Fig. 6.18).

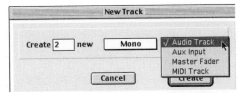

Fig. 6.18 Selecting the track type of an audio track.

We could also have created one stereo track for our example, but let's keep the two mono tracks for now. We will discuss the reason for this choice later on in this chapter.

In order to select any other track format or track type in the New Track dialog box, click on the currently displayed choice and scroll down until you find the format or type you want.

On the other hand, if you want a new track to appear at the end of all the tracks in a Session, just be sure that no track names in the Session are selected before you create the new track. The newly created track will appear as the last track in the Session.

After you press the "Create" button, the Edit window will contain two new audio tracks named "Audio 1" and "Audio 2." These tracks will be highlighted (selected) with white background, as shown in Fig. 6.19.

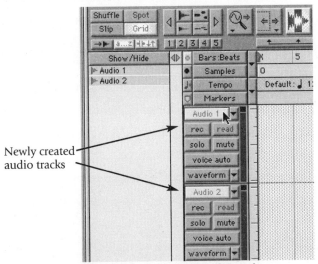

Fig. 6.19 Highlighted audio tracks.

As you add more audio tracks, the system automatically assigns them the next available track number. If you were to create another two tracks, their names would be "Audio 3" and "Audio 4." The next track would be "Audio 5," and so on, up to a limit of 128/256 tracks that can be created in a MIX/HD TDM system.

Creating 128 or more tracks does not mean that you can play back all of them at once. The number of tracks you can play back simultaneously depends upon the number of voices available in your TDM system. For example, with a Pro Tools HD 1 system, you can play back up to 96 audio tracks at the same time. With a Pro Tools MIX or MIXplus system, you can play back up to 64 tracks, while a Pro Tools HD2 and HD3 system allow you up to 128.

Pro Tools LE systems (Digi 001, Digi 002, or Mbox) do not support "voice" assignments, but now they can play back 32 tracks simultaneously. Although they offer fewer tracks than the larger systems, the LE systems are often sufficient for a home studio. When you need more than 32 tracks, you will have to upgrade to a Pro Tools TDM MIX or a TDM HD-series system (HD1, HD 2, or HD 3).

Continuing with our example, now that we have added two tracks to our Session, we need to name them. Actually, we need to rename them, since Pro Tools automatically generated the name "Audio" for each newly created audio track and numbered them in sequence.

I cannot emphasize enough how important it is to name your tracks before you start recording. You must do this for the sake of organization. If you don't rename the tracks before recording, all you will see on your "Audio Regions List" is a bunch of names that will look like: "Audio 01-01-00," "Audio 02-01-00," "Audio 03-01-00," and so on.

If you don't name your tracks, your audio takes quickly become unidentifiable. It is very frustrating to not know what the #@$% tracks are, especially if you are in a high-pressure session where "time is money." Nothing feels worse than accidentally erasing an important audio or MIDI file!

If you carefully name your tracks, Pro Tools will assist you in identifying your takes by automatically adding a sequential number to each audio region (following the track's name). For example, if you named your vocal track "Vox" before you started recording, the first recording on this vocal track would be given a name like "Vox-01-00" in your audio regions list.

The "01" in this naming convention means the take number. The second pair of digits means the 'region' number, which is generated automatically whenever you make certain edits to the audio file. If you use the same track to record another vocal track (take 2), the name that will appear next on the Audio Regions List is "Vox-02-00," which means "Vox-take two-region zero."

Naming audio tracks

To rename a newly created audio track in Pro Tools, position the cursor over one of the track names (Fig. 6.20), which in our example are labeled "Audio 1 and Audio 2." The name of the newly created tracks will be highlighted with a white background and blue letters. Position the cursor on "Audio 1," and double-click. A dialog box will appear that prompts you to give the track a new name, as shown in Fig. 6.20.

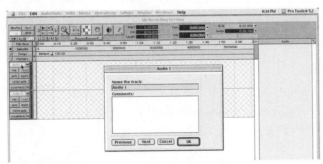

Fig. 6.20 Dialog box to rename your audio tracks.

TIP: To enter a carriage return in the Comments text box, press and hold the "Shift" and click on the "Return" key on your computer's keyboard. (For PC: shift+enter)

In addition to renaming the track, this dialog box allows you to write down notes about this track in a "Comments" window. You can use this to record important information about the track, such as the name of the instrument used on the track, the name of the vocalist, or the name of the patch or program you are using in your synthesizer for a MIDI track, etc.

After renaming track 1, you can press the "Next" button (Fig. 6.20) to go to the next track name dialog box, in this case, to "Audio 2." If you need to go back to a previous track, you can press "Previous" to go back. When you have finished renaming tracks, press "OK" to execute the function. You can also rename your tracks via the Mix window (Channel Strip) by double-clicking on the track's name. The process of renaming MIDI, Auxiliary Inputs, and Master Tracks is the same as renaming an audio track.

TIP: You can use keyboard shortcuts for going the "Next" or "Previous" track. On a Mac, press and hold the Command (⌘) key down and use the Up/Down arrows. (For PC: CTRL+ up arrow and CTRL+ down arrow).

For our example, let's rename track 1 (which Pro Tools labeled Audio 1) to Song 1 L, and rename track 2 (which Pro Tools labeled Audio 2), to Song 1 R.

Setting your input format (analog or digital)

In our example, we said that our source was a DAT machine (or a CD player). This gives us the choice of recording analog or digitally. Since your mix was recorded in a digital medium, I would suggest that you transfer it digitally. When you make a transfer in analog format, you add the risk of not setting up the right recording levels, and of adding unwanted noise by going through the electronic components of your analog mixing board's preamplifier.

So, let's learn how to set up Pro Tools to record digitally. First, you need to find out what digital format the DAT machine (or CD player) is able to handle. The typical options are AES/EBU (which uses XLR connectors), S/PDIF (which uses RCA connectors), or fiber optic (which uses Toslink-type connectors).

Let's assume that your DAT machine (or CD player) can handle more than one format, and we decide to use AES/EBU. On the Pro Tools side, we will also need an AES/EBU connector. This connection is available on Digidesign's 192 I/O, 96 I/O, 888 I/O (16 or 24 bits), and ADAT Bridge (16 or 24 bits), and on Apogee Electronics' AD-8000 I/O and Trak2 I/O.

We would have had to choose the S/PDIF format if your Pro Tools I/O did not have an AES/EBU connector. This would be the case if you were using Digidesign's 882 I/O (16 or 20 bits), 1622 I/O (20 bits), Digi 001, Mbox, or Digi 002. These units would force you to use the S/PDIF digital format, since they only have the RCA connectors in and out.

To choose the digital transfer method for your interface, click and hold the "Setups" menu in Pro Tools. As soon as the pop-up window appears, select "Hardware Setup" (Fig. 6.21).

Fig. 6.21 Selecting the digital transfer format.

Depending on your audio interface, you will see one of the following windows: Fig. 6.22a 888 I/O, Fig. 6.22b Digi 001, Fig. 6.22c 96 I/O, Fig. 6.22d 192 I/O, Fig. 6.22e 1622 I/O, Fig. 6.22f ADAT Bridge, Fig. 6.22g 882 I/O, and Fig. 6.22h Mbox.

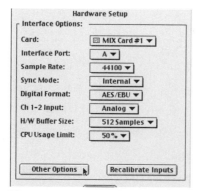

Fig. 6.22a For an 888 I/O.

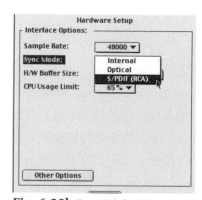

Fig. 6.22b For a Digi 001.

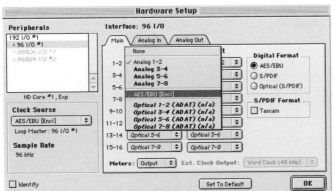

Fig. 6.22c
For a 96 I/O.

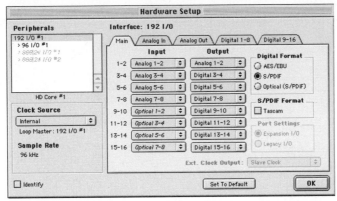

Fig. 6.22d
For a 192 I/O.

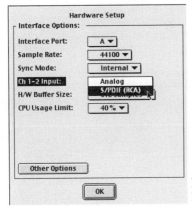

Fig. 6.22e
For a 1622 I/O.

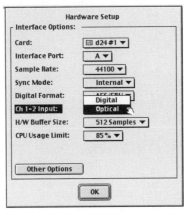

Fig. 6.22f
For an
ADAT Bridge.

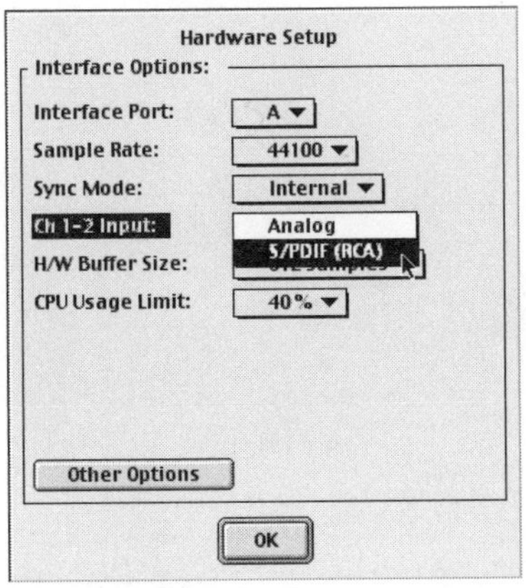

Fig. 6.22g For
an 882 I/O.

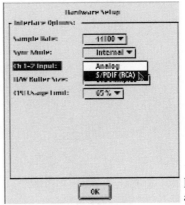

Fig. 6.22h For
an Mbox.

When you see this dialog box on the computer screen, select the digital input format (from the digital and analog choices displayed). If you are using the 888 I/O (16 or 24 bits), then click on "Other Options" and select which inputs you want to be digital (Fig. 6.23a).

After you have selected the desired inputs to "Digital," press "Done." This will take you back to the prior dialog box ("Hardware Setup") where you need to press "OK" to execute the input assignment.

If you have an 888 I/O connected to a 96 I/O or to a 192 I/O through their "legacy" ports, you will need to select ">888/24 I/O #1" (Fig. 6.23b) to be able to select an analog or digital input on the 888/24 I/O audio interface. Notice that these inputs can only be selected in pairs. Once you are in the Mix or Edit windows, you will be able to select inputs individually, as you need them (for stereo or mono inputs).

TIP: *Remember, if you are using a Pro Tools HD system with a 192 or 96 I/O, you can only connect a 24 bit (not a 16 bit) 888 I/O audio interface through the "legacy" port of the 96 and 192 I/Os.*

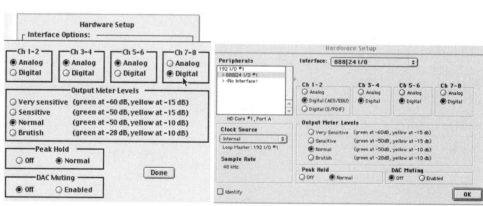

Fig. 6.23a Digital/analog input and output selection window when using an 888 I/O.

Fig. 6.23b Digital/analog input and output selection window when using an 888 I/O through the "legacy" port of a 192 I/O.

Input assignments

After assigning the input format to digital, we need to go to the Mix window to assign the hardware inputs of the two tracks that we created earlier. To display the Mix window, position the cursor on the "Windows" menu and select "Show Mix" (Fig. 6.24).

SHORTCUT: *You can use a keyboard shortcut for displaying the Mix window. On a Mac, press and hold the Command (⌘) and hit the "=" key on your keyboard.*

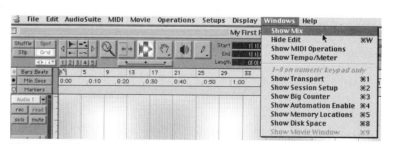

Fig. 6.24 Selecting the Mix window.

Let's assign input 1 for the left channel and input 2 for the right channel, using each track's "Input Selector." Remember, we will be digitally transferring two tracks at the same time.

As soon as you have assigned the inputs, pan the tracks. Pan track Audio 1 to the left, and pan track Audio 2 to the right. This will fully separate the tracks, and will avoid any clipping or distortion in your monitoring system when listening to playback. See Fig. 6.25.

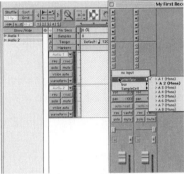

Fig. 6.25 Input assignments through the Mix window.

Note: On some Digidesign interfaces, only channels 1 and 2 (Ch 1-2) can be set to digital input. These include the 882 I/O, the Digi 001, the MBox, the Digi 002, the ADAT Bridge, and the 1622 I/O.

If you are using an interface such as the 888 I/O, you could assign any pair of inputs (i.e., Ch 3-4, Ch 5-6, or Ch 7-8) to be digital sources.

When you create eight tracks at one time, using only one audio interface (eight ins and outs), the Inputs will default automatically to Input 1 thru Input 8. This means that track 1 will automatically be assigned to input 1, track 2 to input 2, and so on.

After the first eight tracks, all subsequent tracks will automatically be assigned to input 1. So track 9 will be assigned back to input 1, and track 10 will also be assigned to Input 1 (Fig 6.26).

TIP: Whenever you are trying to record and don't see any signal coming in, check your input assignments to make sure your system is pointed to the correct audio source. If that appears to be correct, but you still don't see signal, make sure that both systems are set to the same format (both must be either analog or digital).

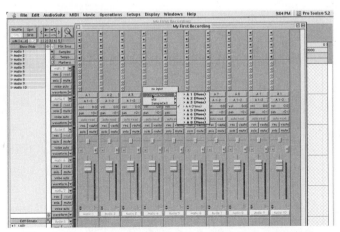

Fig. 6.26 Input reassignment after the eighth audio track.

Output assignments

When you create new tracks—audio, auxiliary, or Master Fader—their output default hardware assignments are always "Output 1-2." You may reroute them to a different output at any time.

If the destination of your output is to a digital device, such as a DAT machine, the data stream will get to the DAT machine just by connecting any digital output (AES/EBU) from your 888 I/O or 192 and 96 I/O to the DAT's digital input. This will be the case even if the input selector (in the "Hardware Setups") is set to analog.

If you are using S/PDIF, the connection from your audio interface to the DAT machine should be from output 1 and 2 only, since no output other than 1 and 2 can be assigned to S/PDIF. Output is continuously active on both AES/EBU and S/PDIF jacks. See Fig. 6.27.

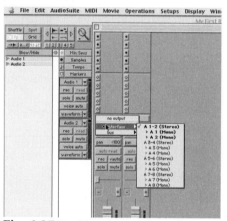

Fig. 6.27 Track's output assignment.

Whenever you create a stereo track, the inputs will be assigned in pairs, and the panning buttons will pan "Left and Right" automatically (Fig. 6.28). Using mono tracks, you must manually pan them as desired.

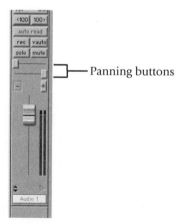

Fig. 6.28 Panning of a stereo audio track.

Recording audio tracks

Once you have made the proper input and output assignments, you are ready to
start recording. Recording is usually done with the Mix window on the computer
screen, so that you can see the recording levels entering Pro Tools. This window
looks just like a real mixing board, with panning and volume controls. Recording
can also be done in the Edit window, if you so desire.

TIP: *If you have a 24-track
Session or more, and you
wish to display as many tracks
as possible on your computer
screen, you could reduce the
track's size. If you desire to do
so, click on the "Display"
pop-up menu, and then select
"Narrow Mix Window" (or
Press and hold the Option
and Command keys and the
letter "M").*

There is a "Record Enable" push button on each track, labeled "rec"
(Fig. 6.29). This button puts selected tracks in a record-ready mode. You can see
this button on both the Edit and Mix window. Click the "rec" button on each
track you wish to record.

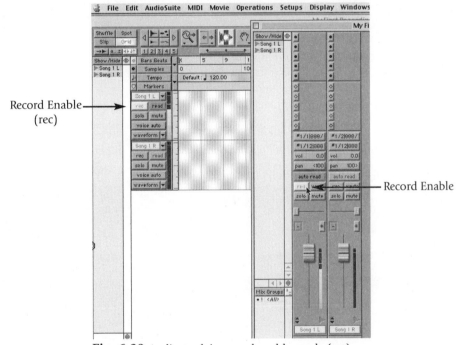

Record Enable
(rec)

Record Enable

Fig. 6.29 Audio track in record enable mode (rec).

When you click on the "rec" button in a specific track, it will turn red, meaning that you have just "record enabled" or "armed" the track. Notice the "rec"
button turned red on both the Edit window and the Mix window.

In record mode, the faders act as monitor levels, and not as recording levels.
To increase the recording level, you will normally want to adjust the output of
the external preamplifier, mixer, or instrument connected to this input. Some of
the Digidesign audio interfaces will allow you to adjust recording levels within
the Pro Tools software (the 1622 I/O and the Digi 001).

To check your audio source, press the "Play" button on your DAT machine (or
CD player) so you can see and listen to your sound source.

If you see movement in the Pro Tools level meters, it means that audio is being read by Pro Tools (Fig. 6.30).

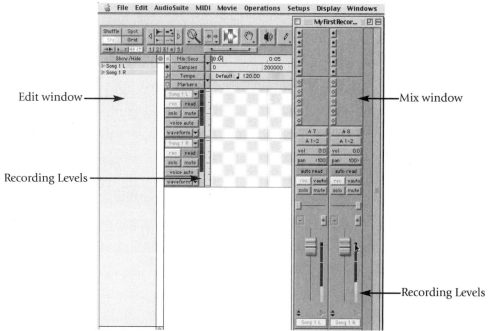

Edit window

Mix window

Recording Levels

Recording Levels

Fig. 6.30 Meters showing the input recording levels in the Edit and Mix windows.

When we record digitally, levels do not have to be set, as we would otherwise have to do in an analog setting. All the digital bits (0's and 1's) are transferred from one device to another without conversion. This type of transfer adds no noise whatsoever to the original signal. That is why we prefer digital transfers whenever possible.

Of course, if the original signal is ugly, the copy will be perfect, and just as ugly. As they say in the computer world: "garbage in, garbage out."

Once you have verified that Pro Tools is reading your audio, press "Stop" on your DAT machine (or CD player), go to the "Windows" menu, and select "Show Transport" (Fig. 6.31).

Shortcut: *You can use a keyboard shortcut to "Show the Transport" keys. On a Mac, press and hold the Command key (⌘) and then hit "1" on the numeric keypad of your computer's keyboard. Don't try to use the number "1" located over the letters on your keyboard—it won't work (Fig. 6.31).*

Windows	Help	
Hide Mix		⌘W
Show Edit		⌘=
Show MIDI Event List		⌥=
Show Tempo/Meter		
Show MIDI Operations		
Show MIDI Track Offsets		
1–9 on numeric keypad only		
Show Transport		⌘1
Show Session Setup		⌘2
Show Big Counter		⌘3
Show Automation Enable		⌘4
Show Memory Locations		⌘5
Show Machine Track Arm		⌘6
Show Universe		⌘7
Show Beat Detective		⌘8
Show Movie Window		⌘9

Fig. 6.31 Selecting the Transport window.

Before pressing "Record," press the "Return to Zero" button on the Transport window. This will return to the beginning of the Session (Fig. 6.32). You can also do this by simply pressing the "return" key on the computer's keyboard. A "time stamp" will be set from the moment you start recording. Returning to zero will ensure that the recording will start from the beginning of the track.

Return to zero

Fig. 6.32 The Return to Zero button in the Transport window.

When you press the "Record" button in the Transport window (Fig. 6.33), you will notice that it will begin to flash. Next, press "Play" on the Pro Tools transport window, and right away press "Play" on the DAT machine (or CD player). This way, you will avoid the risk of missing the beginning of the sound source, since you might experience a very short delay getting into the recording mode right after you press "Play" in the Transport window.

This delay can be caused by how fast your computer system reacts to the recording function, or it can be caused when recording a large number of tracks.

It is also possible to begin the recording process by hitting the "F12" key. You can also enable the "3" key on your numeric keypad to perform this function. (The Numeric Keypad Mode in the "Preferences" menu must be set to "Transport.")

Shortcut: *There are a number of keyboard shortcuts to begin the recording process (see Other Options at the end of this chapter). To start recording: Press and hold the Command key (⌘) and hit the spacebar. (For a PC: hit Ctrl + Spacebar.)*

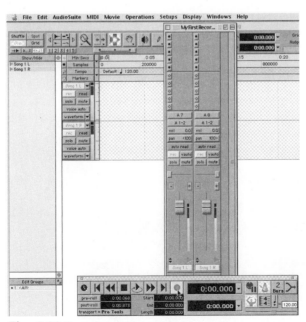

Fig. 6.33 Record stand-by mode.

As soon as the track is done, you will want to stop the DAT machine (or CD player) and press the "Stop" button on Pro Tools' Transport window (or simply tap the spacebar on your keyboard). Don't forget to hit the "Stop" button, or you will continue to record silence or noise, wasting valuable hard disk storage, especially if you are recording with a sample rate of 192kHz.

On the Edit window, you will see the audio (the song) that has been recorded in both tracks (Fig. 6.34a).

Once your recorded audio is written onto the hard drive, you should be able to see both tracks ("Song 1 L" and "Song 1 R") in the "Audio Regions List" (Fig. 6.34b).

If the Numeric Keypad Mode in the "Preferences" menu has been set to Transport, you can also stop the transport by hitting the zero key on the numeric keypad.

Shortcut: *You can use a keyboard shortcut to stop the transport. On either the Mac or PC, click once on the spacebar of the keyboard while in playback or record mode.*

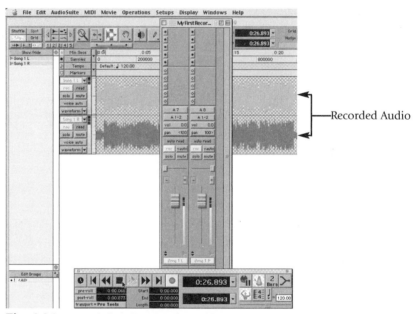

Fig. 6.34a Recorded audio in audio tracks.

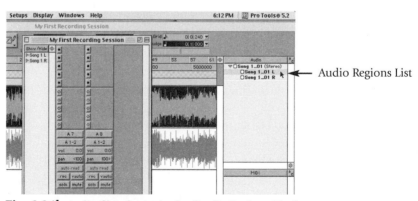

Fig. 6.34b Audio files shown in the "Audio Regions List."

Once you have finished recording your audio, disable the record function on a track by tapping its "rec" button. You can also disable all "rec" buttons at once by pressing and holding down the "Option" key and clicking on the "rec" button of any track (Fig. 6.35).

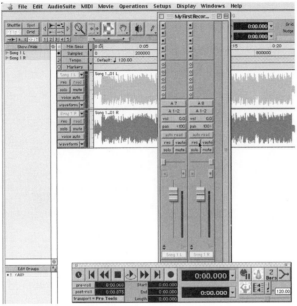

Fig. 6.35 Disabling the record enable button (rec).

TIP: This "Option" key trick can be used to globally enable or disable a number of functions on all the tracks in your Session. By pressing and holding the "Option" key, and any other function such as the "Rec," "Solo," or "Mute" buttons, you can enable or disable globally all the tracks in your session at once. (For PC: ALT + applicable function.)

Playing back audio tracks

To listen to your recorded tracks, click on the "Play" button in the Transport window. This places you immediately into playback mode.

In this mode, the faders on the Mix window act as playback level controls, so that you can do a mix of all the tracks in your session. Make sure that your audio system is set up correctly so you can listen to your recording.

Don't forget to "Return to Zero" to start playing back from the beginning of the track(s). And, once you finish listening to your recording, press the "Stop" button in the Transport window, or Pro Tools will continue to play the sound of silence indefinitely.

If the Numeric Keypad Mode in the "Preferences" menu has been set to "Transport," you can also start or stop the transport by hitting the zero key on the numeric keypad.

Shortcut: The keyboard shortcut to start playing back a track is the same as the shortcut for stopping the playback. On either the Mac or PC, click once on the spacebar of the keyboard.

Grouping audio tracks

The goal of this recording exercise is to record a song that was already mixed, but which needed to be edited. To edit two mono tracks at the same time, we need to "group" them.

To group tracks, we first need to select the tracks by clicking on their names. The tracks in our example are named "Song 1 L" and "Song 1 R." Click on "Song 1 L" first. You should see the name highlighted (white background with blue letters); then press and hold the Shift key and click on the second track's name ("Song 1 R").

Once both tracks are highlighted, go to the File menu in Pro Tools and select "Group Selected Tracks" (Fig. 6.36).

Shortcut: You can use a keyboard shortcut to group selected tracks. On the Mac press and hold the Command key (⌘) and then hit the letter "G" (for PC: Ctrl + G).

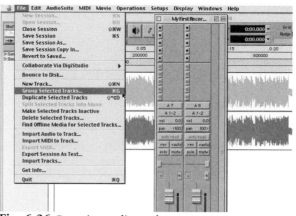

Fig. 6.36 Grouping audio tracks.

A "New Group" dialog box will appear. This box will ask you to provide a Group Name, a Group Type (Edit, Mix, or Edit & Mix), and a Group ID. When you have finished these entries, click on the "OK" button, as shown below (Fig. 6.37).

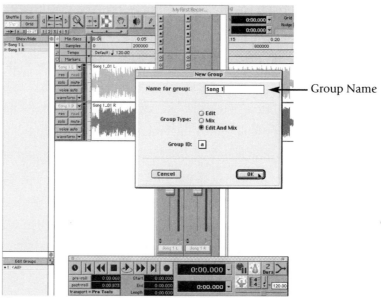

Fig. 6.37 The "New Group" window.

If the group's name in the Edit Group list is highlighted with a purplish color, it means that the group is enabled. If the name is white or clear, it means that the group has been disabled, and that the tracks are no longer grouped. This is very useful when you need to edit one track at a time once they are grouped. See Fig. 6.38.

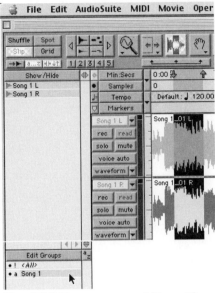

Fig. 6.38 The group named "Song 1" enabled (highlighted).

One reason that we chose to record our stereo Session as two mono tracks was to illustrate this grouping concept. If a stereo track had been used for this example, we would not have been able to group these tracks, as stereo tracks are grouped by default (see additional grouping options at the end of this chapter).

Saving a Session

The importance of saving your work at regular intervals cannot be over-emphasized. Computers freeze up, hardware hangs up, and ugly things can happen. By regularly saving, you will record all the work that you have performed up to that moment. If your system does go down, you will only lose the work done since your last save.

To save your Session, click on the File pop-up menu, and select the "Save Session" option (Fig. 6.39).

Shortcut: You can use a keyboard shortcut to save your Session. On the Mac press and hold the Command key (⌘) and then hit the letter "S."

Fig. 6.39 Saving a Session.

AutoSave option

Forgetting to save a Session can have catastrophic results. And it is easy to forget when you are concentrating so much on the processes of recording, editing, or mixing. Knowing how important regular saving is, Digidesign has added an AutoSave Option on all systems released since Pro Tools version 5.1.

The settings for AutoSave allow you to specify the time interval between auto backups, and how many backups you want to maintain. For example, you might specify an auto backup be performed every eight minutes, and that you retain the last ten backups.

To set the AutoSave option, go to the "Setups" pop-up menu and select "Preferences" (Fig. 6.40).

Fig. 6.40 Selecting Preferences.

When you see the Pro Tools Preferences screen (Fig. 6.41), select the "Operation" tab. On the dialog box that appears there, you will see a section named "AutoSave," and underneath it, a check box called "Enable Session File Auto Backup."

If you check this box (by clicking it), Pro Tools will automatically save the Session you are working on in the background. If you desire, you may change the time interval between each "AutoSave," where it says "Backup every 5 minutes." You may also change the number of copies or backups you want to keep, where it says, "Keep 10 most recent backups," as shown in Fig. 6.41 and Fig. 6.42 below.

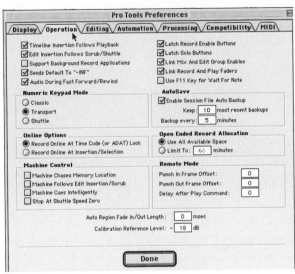

Fig. 6.41 Selecting the AutoSave option.

Fig. 6.42 Number of backups kept.

With the AutoSave option enabled, you won't notice that Pro Tools is making backups of your project in the background while you are working. You will only know how many backups Pro Tools has made when you take a look at the Session File Backups folder on your hard drive (Fig. 6.43).

For example, we named the Session in this chapter's exercise "My First Recording Session." If you open the folder with that name, you will see the Session's "tape" icon, an Audio Files folder, a Fade Files folder, and a Session File Backups folder (Fig. 6.43). This is where your Session file backups will be located, if you enabled the AutoSave option.

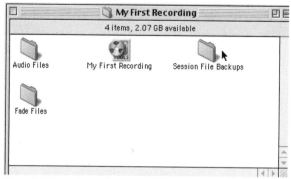

Fig. 6.43 Session File Backups folder.

It is important to note that the AutoSave function will not affect the session you currently have on the screen. By that I mean, you can still choose to "Revert to Saved," and Pro Tools will discard any changes that you made since the last time you saved the session, or since you first opened it.

In other words, Pro Tools makes copies of all your changes in the background, but leaves the version on your screen intact until you decide to save it yourself.

Other Options

Option #1

Opening the Pro Tools Software

You can also launch Pro Tools by means of an "alias" icon on your computer's desktop. You can create an alias by selecting the Pro Tools application icon inside of the Digidesign > Pro Tools folder, as shown below (Fig. 6.44). Choose it by clicking once, not twice.

Fig. 6.44 Selecting the Pro Tools application to create an alias.

When the icon changes color or texture, go to the standard File menu of your computer and select "Make Alias." Alternatively, you can simply press and hold the Command (⌘) key and then press the letter "M" on the computer's keyboard (Fig. 6.45).

Fig. 6.45 Creating an alias.

If you have done this correctly, you should see a "ghost" copy of the Pro Tools icon that reads "Pro Tools X.XX alias" (Fig. 6.46).

Fig. 6.46 Pro Tools alias created.

To place your Pro Tools alias on your computer's desktop as shown in Fig. 6. 47, you can click on the icon named *"Pro Tools 5.2 alias"* to select it, hold it, and drag it out of the "Digidesign" folder, and position it right underneath the external hard drive icon.

A Pro Tools alias allows you to launch Pro Tools by double-clicking on the alias icon, instead of digging down into the "Digidesign" folder every time you want to start Pro Tools.

Fig. 6.47 Dragging the alias icon to the computer's desktop.

A third way to launch Pro Tools is through the "Apple Menu" on your computer's main menu (for Mac OS 9.X.X systems only).

You can add Pro Tools to your "Apple Menu" by dragging the Pro Tools 5.2 alias icon you just created directly into the "Apple Menu Items" folder. This folder is located inside of the System Folder in your computer's start-up hard drive as shown below (Fig. 6.48).

Pro Tools alias ——→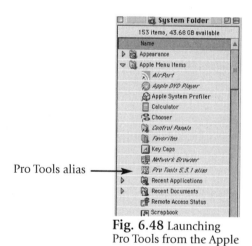

Fig. 6.48 Launching Pro Tools from the Apple menu.

Option #2

Track's input/output assignments

If you don't want to switch back and forth between the Mix and Edit windows, you can make track assignments directly from the Edit window. Some Pro Tools users like to record, mix, and edit using only the Edit window. This is a likely scenario when they don't have the luxury of two computer monitors in their system. If you are one of these users, you can show all or part of the Mix window default functions in the Edit window. Such functions include volume changes (fader moves), track input/output assignments, track panning, etc.

To display all the Mix window default functions on the Edit window, select "Edit Window Shows" in the "Display" pop-up menu, and then select the "All" option (Fig. 6.49). If you wish to show only some of these functions, you also have the option of selecting just those functions that you want to see. The only down side of displaying all the functions at once in the Edit window is that you won't have enough space on your computer screen to work on your edits, especially if you have a 15" flat-screen monitor.

Personally, I prefer to use the Mix window for these types of assignments. When you have two monitors in your system, none of this is an issue. Just assign the Edit window to one screen, and the Mix window to the other.

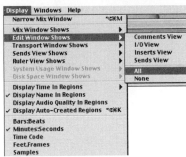

Fig. 6.49 Displaying the I/Os in the Edit window.

Option #3

Record Pause Mode

To avoid delays when you start recording a track, you can set Pro Tools in "Record Pause Mode." You can set this mode by pressing and holding down the "Control" and "Command" (⌘) keys simultaneously and then the "spacebar" of your keyboard.

In this mode, the "Play" and "Record" buttons in the Pro Tools Transport window will flash, meaning that Pro Tools is in "Record Pause" mode. To start recording, simply press "Play" on the Transport window or your computer's keyboard spacebar (Fig. 6.50).

Fig. 6.50 Record Pause Mode.

Option #4

Grouping audio tracks

Another way to create a group is by means of the "Edit Groups" list.
This list is on the lower left hand side of the Edit window. If you click on the shaded area where it says "Edit Groups," a pop-up menu will appear. One of the selections is "New Group." When you select "New Group," a dialog box will prompt you to give a name to the group, as shown in Fig. 6.51.

Fig. 6.51 Creating a new group through the "Edit Groups" list.

In this example, I named the group "Song 1." If you look at Fig. 6.52, you can see the name of this new group in the "Edit Groups" list. You might also note that the audio regions in both tracks are now selected or highlighted, meaning that these tracks are now grouped.

If you now move a fader on one of these tracks, the fader on the other track will follow.

Edit Groups List ───▶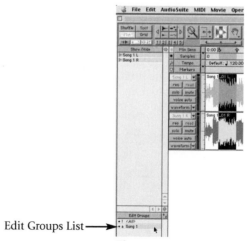

Fig. 6.52 Grouped tracks.

Congratulations! You have just learned how to record digital audio from an external sound source to Pro Tools. Recording an analog source is nearly identical to the process we have just completed. After making the right connections, the only differences are that you must assign the recording format to "Analog," and adjust your recording levels with an external preamplifier or mixer. Again, if you are using the Digi 001 or the 1622 I/O, you can use the internal preamps of these I/O boxes, and will not require external preamps.

CHAPTER SEVEN

Other Audio Recording Modes

This chapter focuses on different methods for audio recording in Pro Tools, in which you will learn:

- The difference between an audio file and an audio region

- What is a non-destructive recording

- How to do a destructive recording

- How to Loop Record

- How to perform a QuickPunch recording

The difference between an audio file and an audio region

It is very important that you understand the differences between an "audio file" and an "audio region." For this reason, I will cover the differences in a few paragraphs and screen shots to make this concept clear to you.

Every time you press the record button in the Pro Tools Transport window, the recorded audio appears in the Edit window in two different ways. One appears as a visual representation (waveform) of the recorded sound in an audio track. The other appears in the "Audio Regions List" (located on the right hand side of the Edit window), with only the name of the file, as seen in Fig. 7.1. In Pro Tools, the original recorded sound is known as an "audio file," but some Pro Tools users have other names for it. Some call it "original recording," "whole file," "parent file," and "source file," among other names.

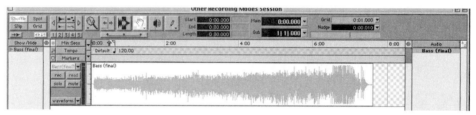

Fig. 7.1 The two ways an audio file is shown in the Edit window after it has been recorded: as a visual representation (waveform) and as a file name (bold type letters).

Once you make an edit to the audio file, whether you trim it, separate it, capture it, etc., you will notice—in the Audio Regions List—that a new file name is created (Fig. 7.2). This file is known as "audio region," which is a derivative of the original audio file (recorded sound).

One way to recognize the difference between an audio file and an audio region is that the name of an audio file appears in the audio regions list in bold-type letters and an audio region does not.

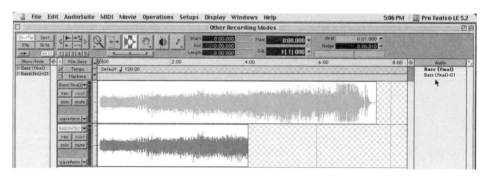

Fig. 7.2 Comparison between an audio file and an audio region.

As mentioned in Chapter 6, it is very important to name your audio tracks before you record any sound (instrument, vocal, sound effect). If you name your tracks before recording, the recorded sound will appear in the Audio Regions List with its respective name (Fig. 7.3). This way you will be able to keep track and organize all your audio files and audio regions so you won't erase any of them by accident, which could be catastrophic.

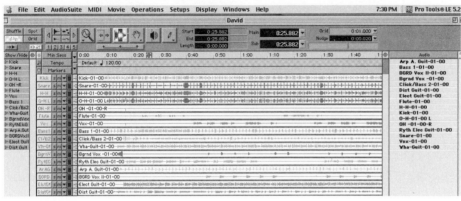

Fig. 7.3 This Audio Regions List only contains "audio files" (bold-type letters).

In Fig. 7.4, notice the increased number of audio regions created in the audio regions list after doing some editing on this particular Session.

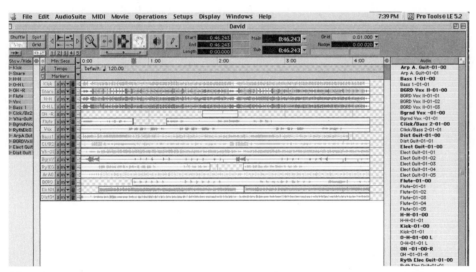

Fig. 7.4 An Audio Regions List containing both audio files (bold-type letters) and audio regions (not in bold type letters).

In order to "clean up" or get rid of all the audio regions not needed after you finished editing your session, you can make a selection of all the unused audio regions to be "removed" from the session. Be careful not to delete your original audio files, because once you delete them, either purposely or by accident, that is it. They will be erased forever. For this reason, you should select the "Unused Regions Except Whole Files" command in the "Audio" pop-up menu (Fig. 7.5).

This command selects only the audio regions that are not in the Edit window. I strongly advise you to always double-check whatever files you are deleting or removing from your session.

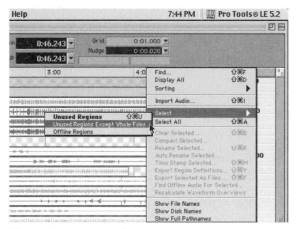

Fig. 7.5 Selecting the "Unused Regions Except Whole Files" command in the "Audio" pop-up menu.

Once you have selected the audio regions you no longer need in your Session, they will be highlighted. Notice in Fig. 7.6, the highlighted or selected files are not in bold-type letters. This means that, indeed, they are only audio regions and not audio files (original recordings); unless you purposely want to erase them, you can select them as well.

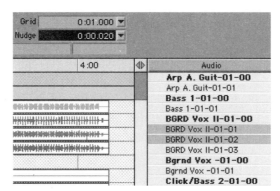

Fig. 7.6 Audio regions not used (highlighted) in the Edit window.

After you select the files you want deleted or removed from your Session for the sake of organization, you need to select the "Clear Selected" command in the "Audio" pop-up menu (Fig. 7.7).

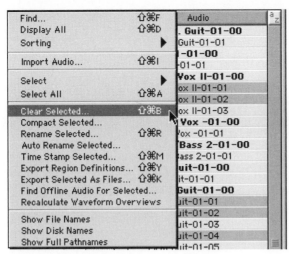

Fig. 7.7 The "Clear Selected" command.

This command will either remove or delete the selected files. You will notice in Fig. 7.8 the "Delete" option is not active. This means that the files you have selected to be removed off the session are audio regions. If you selected audio files (original recordings), then Pro Tools would ask you if you want to permanently "Delete" the audio files you selected from your hard drive. If so, press the "Delete" button. In this example, there are only audio regions selected. Consequently, Pro Tools will only prompt you to "Remove" them from the Session and not permanently "Delete" them from the hard drive.

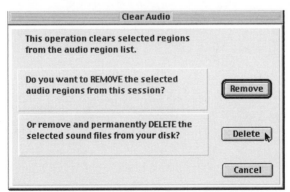

Fig. 7.8 "Remove" or "Delete" the unused audio regions.

After you press the "Remove" or "Delete" button, the Audio Regions List of your Session will clear up (Fig. 7.9) and be less cluttered and easier to read.

Fig. 7.9 Compare to Fig. 7.6 and notice that two audio regions were removed from the session.

Once you start working in Pro Tools and start wondering where all those file names are coming from and how you can get rid of them, you will better understand their functions.

What is a non-destructive recording?

In Chapter 6, I showed you the complete process of a basic two-track digital audio recording from beginning to end. The recording mode we were in was the "Non-Destructive" mode. In this mode, every time you record any type of audio (music, dialog, sound effects, etc.) over an existing one in a record-enabled (rec) audio track, a new audio file is created and stored on your hard drive. In other words, while the existing audio will look like as if it had been erased (Fig. 7.10), it remains intact on your hard drive and a new audio file has been created. The newly created file takes visual preference over the existing one in the Edit window up to the time you stop the recording (Fig. 7.10).

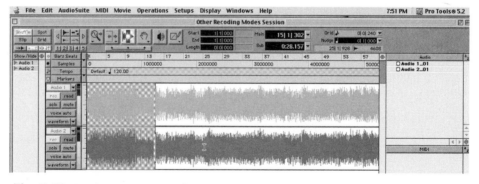

Fig. 7.10 Visual representation of an non-destructive recording.

After every new non-destructive recording, you can select both the "new" and the "old" audio file from the Audio Regions List located on the upper right hand side of the Edit window, as shown in Fig. 7.11.

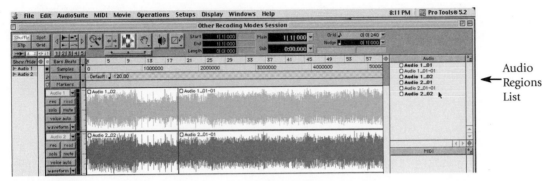

Audio Regions List

Fig. 7.11 "New" and "old" audio files in the Audio Regions List.

Before you push the record button, you need to set the recording range. One way is to type start and end points, either in the Transport window or in the "Selection Indicators" of the edit window (Fig. 7.12).

By the way, you will know that you are in a non-destructive recording mode if you see the recording button in the Transport window with no letters or a circle for "Loop recording" in it, as seen in Fig. 7.12a.

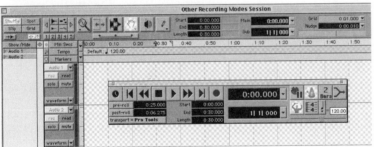

Fig. 7.12 Setting the recording range in the Transport window and "Selection Indicators."

Fig. 7.12a
Non-destructive recording mode.

Another way to set the recording time range is to drag the "Playback Markers" (up/down arrows) located in the Time Line's ruler, as shown in Fig. 7.13. Notice that when tracks are record-enabled (in rec mode), the Playback Markers turn red. If no tracks are record-enabled (playback mode), the Playback Markers stay blue.

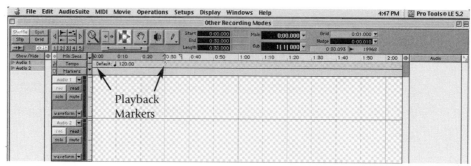

Fig. 7.13 Setting the recording range using the "Playback Markers."

Furthermore, if you don't know how long you are going to record, then you don't need to set any recording range; simply start recording and stop it whenever you have finished. I think it is more useful to set a range when you are doing punch in and outs, as we will see later on in this chapter.

If you are not sure what recording mode you want to be in when tracking (recording), and you have enough memory space on your hard drive, I recommend staying in the non-destructive recording mode, unless it is necessary to change to a different one.

Shortcut: To Cancel Recording: You can use a keyboard shortcut to cancel the recording process, and store no audio on the hard drive. On a Mac, press and hold the Command key (⌘) and hit the "." (period) key on your computer keyboard (For PC – Control + ".")

You can always "undo" the recording you just did if you thought the take was not good, just by selecting the "Undo" command in the Edit menu. This removes the take from your hard drive and deletes the region from the track.

How to do a destructive recording

As I mentioned before, Pro Tools is a non-destructive digital audio workstation. This means whatever edits (delete, copy, paste, duplicate, etc.) you perform to an audio file in the Edit window, it won't affect the original recording.

Shortcut : If you are unhappy with a recording, you can always "Undo" the take. Go to the Edit pop-up menu in Pro Tools and select "Undo Audio Recording," or simply press and hold the Command key (⌘) and hit the letter "Z".

There are two ways of destructing (erase digital data) audio files in Pro Tools. One way is to highlight an audio file or region in an audio track, or to click (select) on a file's name in the Audio Regions List, and then select the "Clear Selected" command (Shortcut: Shift + Command + B)—located in the "Audio" pop-up menu (Fig. 7.14)—then press the "Delete" button in the appearing dialog box as shown in Fig. 7.15. This command will erase the audio file from the hard drive forever.

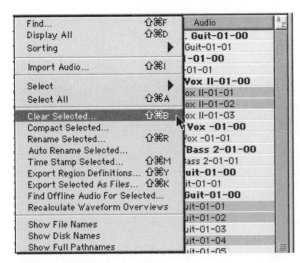

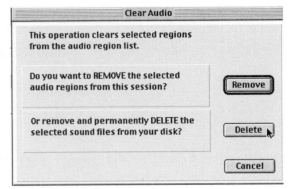

Fig. 7.14 Selecting the "Clear Selected" command to delete audio files.

Fig. 7.15 Deleting audio files.

The other way to erase audio files is through the "Destructive Record" command located in the "Operations" menu in Pro Tools (Fig. 7.16). You will know if you are in the Destructive Record mode if the letter "D" appears in the record button of the Transport window (assuming the Transport window is active in the Edit window). See Fig. 7.17.

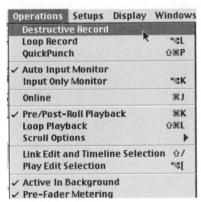

Fig. 7.16 Selecting "Destructive Record" mode.

Fig. 7.17 Visual representation of the "Destructive Record" mode in the Transport window.

Be careful when using the Destructive Record mode, since it will permanently erase from the hard drive the existing information (audio file) in a particular audio track you are recording in. In other words, if you have an existing vocal track in an audio track named "Vox" for example, and you record-enable (rec) that track and don't change the name of that audio track to something else, the existing vocal track will be erased (assuming Pro Tools is in Destructive Record

301

mode). Even worse, you cannot cancel record in this mode, unlike the other recording modes. This is the same situation as if you were recording on a tape machine and accidentally press the record-enable button and start erasing the tape. That, my friend, could get you fired from the job. So please, be careful!

When do you want to be in the "Destructive Record" mode? Well, one of the main reasons is that you are running out of hard disk space. Unlike non-destructive recording, this time you will see the new audio replacing the existing one in a particular audio track.

How to Loop Record

Let's say that you need to record a guitar solo after the basic tracks have been recorded. To avoid losing the guitar player's spontaneity by stopping and playing back the track every time he/she makes a mistake in his/her performance, you want to use the "Loop Record" mode.

For loop recording, first you need to enable the Loop Record mode. For this, go to the "Operations" pop-up menu and select the "Loop Record" command (Fig. 7.18).

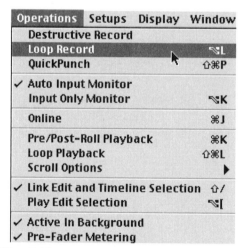

Fig. 7.18 Selecting the "Loop Record" command.

You will know if you are in this mode if you see a circle on the record button of the Transport window (Fig. 7.19).

Fig. 7.19 The "Loop Record" mode in the Transport window.

Once in the Loop Record mode, you need to select the specific range (number of bars or seconds) in the song where the guitar solo (or any other instrument, including vocals) is going to be recorded. You can do this by a simple click and drag with the "Selector" editing tool to the range you need for the solo (Fig. 7.20).

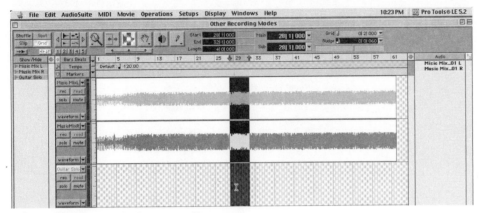

Fig. 7.20 Selecting the loop recording range.

TIP: For loop recording, the Edit and Timeline selections must be linked.

Sometimes, you find yourself in a high-pressure recording session, where you don't have the luxury to take the time to create and rename a track every time you record a different take of the same instrument. So if a high paid bass player walks into the session, and you don't know how many takes he or she will end up doing because the producer wants to experiment, if you don't know the other techniques for audio recording that Pro Tools offer, you better be prepared—not only by creating and renaming new tracks ahead of time, but also you need to assign their hardware inputs and outputs. If you don't, you will end up with a list of the same instrument.

Once you have selected the loop, record enable the track and press the play button to begin the Loop Recording process.

How to QuickPunch Record

Let's say now that you need to record a specific little part, a couple of notes, for example, and you want to do it "on-the-fly" because you do not want to disturb the artist by making him/her play the whole section again. Here is when you would use the "QuickPunch Record" mode. QuickPunch lets you punch in and out on record-enabled audio tracks during playback by clicking the Record button in the Transport window.

QuickPunch switches to monitor as soon as you punch-out, and all QuickPunch recording is nondestructive.

To enable the QuickPunch Record, select the "QuickPunch" command from the "Operations" pop-up menu (Fig. 7.21).

Fig. 7.21 Selecting the "QuickPunch" command.

You will know if you are in this mode if you see a "p" on the record button of the Transport window (Fig. 7.22).

Fig. 7.22 Showing the "QuickPunch" mode in the transport window.

Record enable the track you want to QuickPunch record in and start playing back (Fig. 7.23). Notice that the Record button flashes.

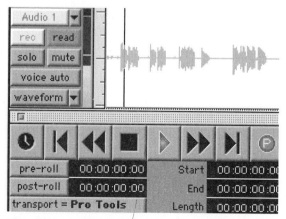

Fig. 7.23 Track record enabled and playing back in QuickPunch mode.

Whenever you want to punch-in, press the Record button and Pro Tools will create a region with the new recorded material until you press the Record button again to punch-out (Fig. 7.24a and Fig. 7.24b).

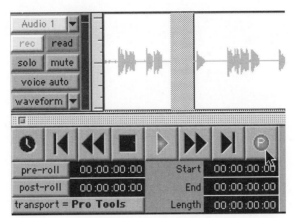

Fig. 7.24a Punching-in in QuickPunch mode.

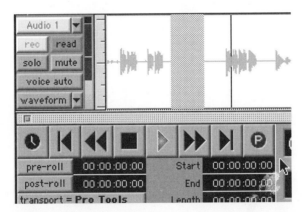

Fig. 7.24b Punching-out in QuickPunch mode.

You can perform up to 100 punches during a single pass. These new region(s) will show up in your Audio Regions List.

CHAPTER EIGHT

Importing and Exporting Audio

One of the most useful tools offered by Pro Tools is the ability to import a wide variety of digital audio file formats. Pro Tools can import a file from the same Pro Tools Session, another Session, from the same or a different hard drive (volume), even from another program or application written by other manufacturers. Not only can you import audio files and/or regions from other sessions, but you can also import entire Pro Tools' tracks. This means you can copy entire audio regions (sounds and waveforms), including such information as audio levels (volume), panning (left and right), and plug-in settings (effects processors: reverbs, delays, compression, etc.).

In this chapter you will learn how to:

- Import audio files or audio regions (through the "File" menu)

- Import audio files or audio regions (through the "Audio" menu)

- Convert and import audio files and audio regions

- Import audio from an audio CD

- Import audio tracks from different sessions

- Batch import audio files

- Export audio files and audio regions

How to import audio files or audio regions and automatically create their own tracks with their respective names (through the "File" menu)

Whenever you record sound in Pro Tools (such as a human voice, a flute, an electric guitar, etc.), your analog sound source is converted into digital bits (0's and 1's), in order to be stored in digital form on your computer's hard drive.

There are many digital audio file formats in existence. The format that you use will depend upon the type of computer system you use and the digital audio software application that you choose. For example, Pro Tools Mix TDM Systems utilize an audio file format known as Sound Designer II (SDII), the Macintosh creates AIFF (Audio Interchange File Format) files, and a PC generates .WAV (PC Wave) files. All three can be used in the same Session at the same time. Pro Tools High Definition (HD) Systems use AIFF and .WAV formats only whenever you create sessions with any sample rate higher than 48kHz.

In addition to being able to import audio files into Pro Tools, you can also export them to a wide range of file formats. For example, if you have an SDII audio file, you can convert it to a QuickTime or MP3 format either by using the "Bounce to Disk..." function or the "Export Selected As Files..." command located in the "Audio" pop-up menu in the Audio Region List. The file formats that Pro Tools can import and export are: .WAV (PC Wave), AIFF (Audio Interchange File Format), MPEG-1 Layer 3 (MP3), QuickTime, Real Audio, Sound Designer II (SDII), and Sound Resource. See Fig. 8.1.

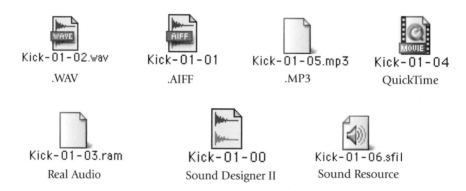

Fig. 8.1 Different types of file formats.

The ability to import audio and region files from one session to another means you don't have to waste time and hard disk storage to re-record sound or instrument tracks. Importing audio will allow you to collaborate with others, regardless of the hard disk recording system they use, or where they are located. Pro Tools will facilitate your collaboration with other artists and studios whether next door or on another continent. You can share files via regular mail or FedEx (sending files on a hard drive, CD-ROM, DVD-ROM, a Zip, or a Jaz cartridges), through an Internet service such as Digidesign's DigiProNet (Digidesign Production Network), or as attachments via e-mail (MP3, QuickTime, Real Audio, etc.). No matter how they are moved, you can import, export, and share files whenever you have the need.

You can learn how to import audio by using the sample Session file that is located on the CD-ROM in the back of this book. Two talented musicians have sent us a stereo drum loop and a guitar section recorded in a Pro Tools file format (SDII), and we will add these tracks to a song we are working on.

First, open the session called "Import Audio Session" by double-clicking on the tape icon (Fig. 8.2). If you forgot how to open Pro Tools, refer to Chapter 6.

Fig. 8.2 Import Audio Session's Folder.

You should see the following window on your computer screen (Fig. 8.3):

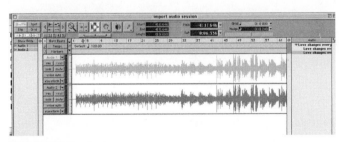

Fig. 8.3 Edit window.

Go to the "File" pop-up menu and select the "Import Audio to Track…" option (Fig. 8.4).

Fig. 8.4 "File" pop-up menu.

The following dialog box will appear on your computer screen (Fig. 8.5):

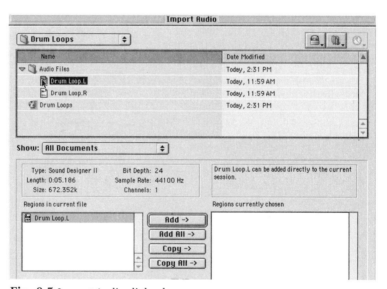

Fig. 8.5 Import Audio dialog box.

This dialog box lists all the audio files and regions available to be imported from one Pro Tools Session to another, including the ability to import audio from within the Session you are currently working on. Also, this dialog box provides you with information about your Session's settings, such as sample rate, bit depth, the file's duration in time, its size in kilobytes, and its format. Furthermore, this window will also notify you if the file or region you want to import is at a different sample rate, bit depth, or file format than your session, and offers you the option of converting it to the current Session's settings.

Two sliders and Stop and Play buttons are also provided in this dialog box. These controls allow you to audition and select from the list of files on the screen. You can click on any file, click on the "Play" push button, and adjust the volume slider (vertical) to listen to the clip. If you want to advance further in the file for playback, then move the horizontal slider. When you are finished, you can click on the "Stop" push button to stop playback.

After selecting the "Import Audio File to Track..." option, we need to search for the audio that we want to import. In this example, we first want to import a stereo drum loop audio file that a musician friend has sent us to use in the song. He has told us that the name of the Session is "Drum Loops," so we need to select that Session name on the "Current Folder" pop-up menu. Fig. 8.6 displays two different icons. One is called "Audio Files," and the other (which looks like a tape reel) is the actual Session icon. On the right hand side, you can see the date and time that these files were last modified.

If you click on the arrow that is on the left side of the "Audio Files" folder, you will see all of the audio files in the "Drum Loops" Session. In this case, we only have two, one called "Drum_01.L," and the other "Drum_01.R." Since this file is a stereo audio file, the letters ".L" and ".R" were added automatically by Pro Tools.

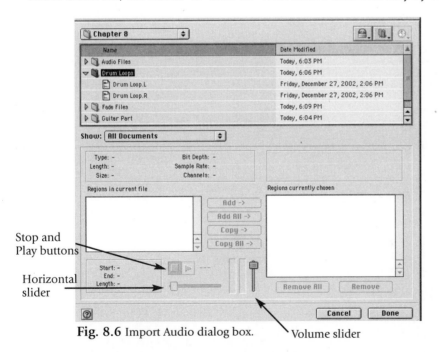

Fig. 8.6 Import Audio dialog box.

When you first open the Import Audio dialog box (Fig. 8.6), no files will have been selected in the two empty white boxes at the bottom. These two boxes contain a list of "Regions in current file" (on the left side), and a list of "Regions currently chosen" (on the right). Click on the audio file named "Drum_01 .L" (Fig. 8.7), and that file name will appear on the "Regions in current file" list.

Between the two lists is a column of four prompt buttons. They become active when you select a file to be imported. The first button permits you to "Add" one file at the time to the list to be imported (Fig. 8.7). The second button allows you to "Add All," if you want to import all the audio files at once. When you press either button, the file(s) will appear on the right side in the list called "Regions currently chosen." If you decide not to import one or all of the files you have selected, you can remove them from the list by pressing the "Remove" or "Remove All" prompt buttons.

TIP: *You can also double–click on the audio files you want to import into your session.*

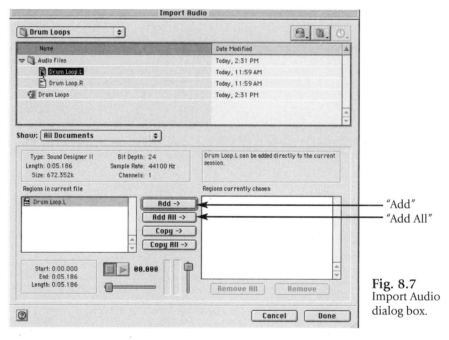

Fig. 8.7
Import Audio
dialog box.

In order to get both sides of the stereo drum file, select both drum loop audio files (.L and .R), as shown in Fig. 8.8.

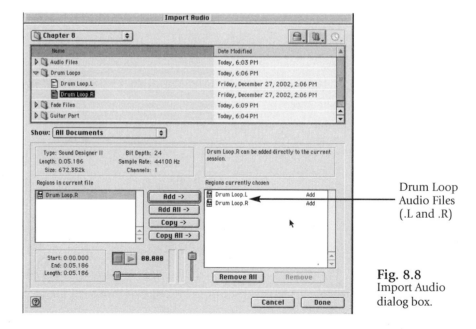

Drum Loop
Audio Files
(.L and .R)

Fig. 8.8
Import Audio
dialog box.

When both files appear on the right-hand-side box, press the "Done" button to execute the audio file import option (Fig. 8.9). You can press the "Cancel" button at any time to discontinue.

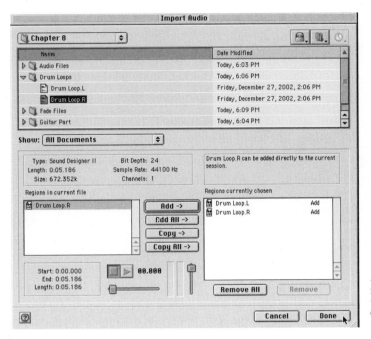

Fig. 8.9
Import Audio dialog box.

When you click "Done," a dialog box will appear asking you where you would like to place the audio file(s). Obviously, you want them to go to the Audio Files folder of the Session that you are currently working on. Pro Tools automatically points to the current Session's folder, so all you have to do is press the "Choose" button to send these files to the Audio Files folder of our Session (named "Import Audio Session" in Fig. 8.10). You can also send audio to any other Session's Audio Files folder by clicking and holding on the "Current Folder" pop-up list, and selecting the Audio Files folder you want to place the audio. You can even send audio to a new, separate folder by clicking on the "New Folder" option located underneath the "Choose a destination folder" line.

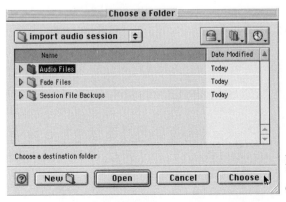

Fig. 8.10
"Choose a Folder" dialog box.

Once the drum loops have been imported into "Import Audio Session," the new drum loop tracks will appear in the Tracks Window, properly named, along with the rest of the instruments of the song (Fig. 8.11). Spot the drum loop to bar 22|1|064.

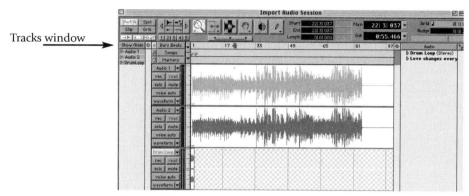

Tracks window →

Fig. 8.11 Edit window.

If the tempo of our drum loop sample matches the tempo of the song, and if the loop feels right, all we need to do is to "repeat" the loop several times until it covers the length of the song. If the loop does not have the same tempo, but it fits with the beat of the song, we could use the "Time Compression/Expansion" function in the AudioSuite pop-up menu to make the tempo of the loop match the tempo of the song. Read Chapter 12 for a step-by-step exercise on this. Select the loop samples (using the Grabber tool) by tapping on both (while holding the Shift key down) and use the "Repeat" command under the "Edit" pop-up menu. See Fig. 8.12. (We studied the "Repeat" command—and other types of editing techniques—in more detail in Chapter 5.)

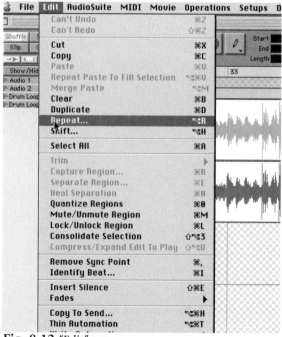

Fig. 8.12 "Edit" pop-up menu.

When you select the "Repeat" option, a dialog box will appear and ask how many times you want to repeat the drum loop. For now, type in 25 times, which is enough to cover the entire song (Fig. 8.13). Repeating the loop now does not mean you will have to use it throughout the song. You will be able to add and drop drum loops when you begin mixing.

Fig. 8.13 Repeat dialog box.

Tap the "OK" button in the "Repeat" dialog box, and the loop will be repeated 25 times in the "Drum Loop" tracks in the Edit window. See Fig. 8.14.

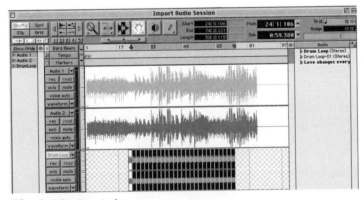

Fig. 8.14 Edit window.

Now that we have imported our drum loop, we need to import the guitar section sent to us by our other musician friend, but we will import this track using the "Audio" pop-up menu.

Importing audio files or audio regions (through the "Audio" menu)

When an audio or region file gets imported through the "Audio" menu, as shown in Fig. 8.15, the name of the file appears on the Audio Region List only. This method does not automatically create a new track like the "File" menu method. This can be very useful when you don't want to add unnecessary audio tracks, and will allow you to place the audio file or region (the guitar section in this example) anywhere you wish.

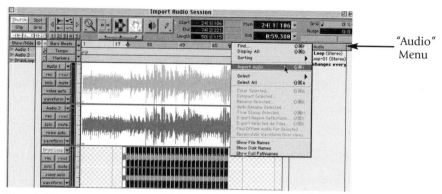

"Audio" Menu

Fig. 8.15 Edit window.

When you select the "Import Audio" option on the "Audio" menu, the same Import Audio dialog window that we saw in the last example will appear (Fig. 8.16).

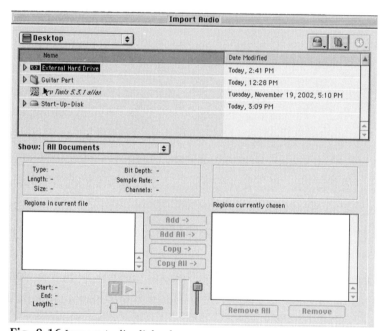

Fig. 8.16 Import Audio dialog box.

In our case, we will select the lead guitar_03-02 audio file from the "Guitar Parts" session that our second musician friend sent us (Fig. 8.17). After selecting the guitar part audio file in the "Audio Files" folder of the "Guitar Parts" session, press the "Done" button to execute importing the file. To double-check that it is the right audio file we need, let's audition the file by pressing the play button that is located right under the "Regions in current file" box. If you need it to be louder, you would have to slide the vertical fader up, which is to the right of the stop and play buttons.

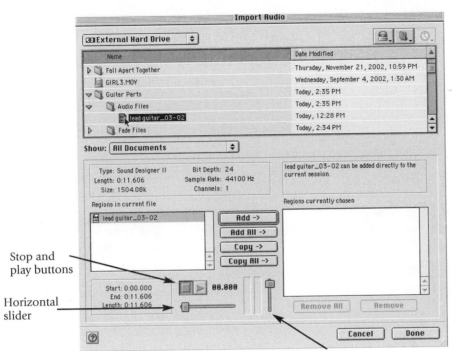

Stop and play buttons

Horizontal slider

Fig. 8.17 "Import Audio" dialog box.   Volume slider

TIP: *A shortcut for importing audio files through the "Audio Region" menu, is pressing and holding down the "Shift" and "⌘" (Command) keys, and then pressing on the letter "I" of your computer keyboard.*

Again, a dialog box will appear asking you where to save the "lead guitar" file, and by pressing "Choose" the file will be stored in the right folder since Pro Tools automatically points to the current session audio files folder (Fig. 8.18).

Fig. 8.18 "Choose a Folder" dialog box.

Once you have the "lead guitar" audio file imported in the song's Session, you will have to place it manually in the proper location. You can do that by clicking and holding the file in the Audio Region List and dragging it to the right place in the Session. Let's say we need to place it at bar 15 (Fig. 8.19). Notice the current editing mode is "Grid" so you can place the region exactly at bar 22|1|064.

Grid mode→

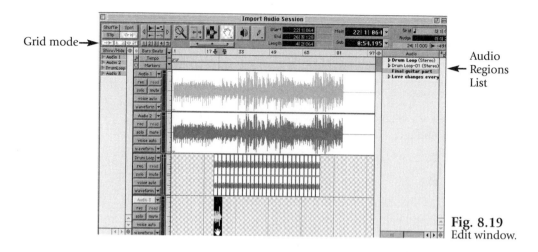

Audio
Regions
List

Fig. 8.19
Edit window.

After you positioned the guitar part to bar 22|1|064, play the song from the
beginning by pressing the "Return" key and pressing the spacebar of your
computer keyboard. Feel free to make changes including the track levels.
In other words, mix it and have fun.

How to convert and import audio files and audio regions

The process of importing audio files that have different file formats, sampling
rates, and bit depths to an existing Pro Tools Session is pretty much the same as
discussed earlier. The only thing you have to do is read the different warning
messages that Pro Tools gives you if you want to proceed with the process—in
other words, if you agree or disagree to convert the audio file's format.

Different warning messages will appear for different cases (Fig. 8.20a—d). For
example, if you create a new Pro Tools Session set to generate a Sound Designer
II audio file format, its sample rate will be at 44.1kHz and the bit depth 16 bits.
The following messages will appear if you are:

a) Trying to import a 24-bit audio file into as 16-bit session:

Message: "<file name> must be converted to be used because it has a
different bit depth than the current session."

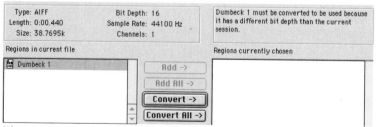

Fig. 8.20a Warning message: "different bit depth."

b) Trying to import a stereo file into the Session: Message: "<file name> must be converted to be used because it is not a mono file."

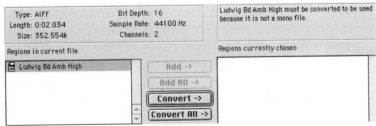

Fig. 8.20b Warning message: "is not a mono file."

c) Trying to import an audio file that is not a Sound Designer II file (AIFF, .WAV, QuickTime, MP3, etc.): Message: "<file name> can be added directly to the current Session, or it can be converted to the Session's audio file type."

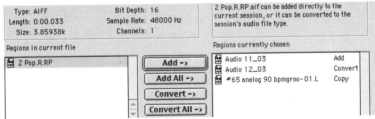

Fig. 8.20c Warning message: "can be added or converted."

d) Trying to import an audio file that is the same format type as the current Session's file type: Message: "<file name> can be added directly to the current session."

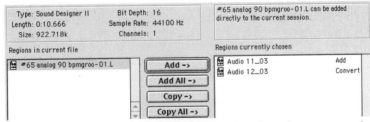

Fig. 8.20d Warning message: "Can be added directly to the current session."

Whichever the case, you can see in Fig. 8.20(a–d) that Pro Tools prompts you to either "Convert," "Add," or "Copy" the file into the Session you are currently working on. Notice that the files to be imported are added to the "Regions currently chosen" list.

Once you decide to import the file(s), and after you click on the prompts "Done" and "Choose," you should be able to see the following window, as the file is being converted. Depending on what menu you selected to import the file(s), either the "File" or "Audio" pop-up menus, the file will be placed in the Session with its own track, or simply on the Audio Region List, respectively. See Fig. 8.21.

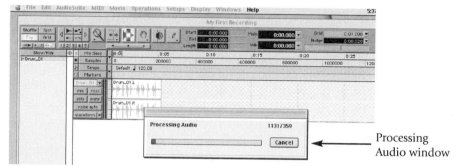

Processing Audio window

Fig. 8.21 Edit window.

How to import audio from an audio CD

Another easy and efficient way to import audio (whether it is music or sound effects) without adding noise is by means of the "Import Audio from Other Movie" menu in Pro Tools.

You don't need any other type of software (if you own Pro Tools) to import audio from any audio CD. The way you do this is by placing an audio CD in your computer's CD-ROM reader. Once the CD icon appears on your computer's desktop (Fig. 8.22), double-click on it.

Fig. 8.22 Desktop.

After you double-click on the "Audio CD" icon, you should see the following window (Fig. 8.23). This window shows the number of tracks or songs available in the audio CD you put in your computer's CD-ROM. In Fig. 8.23, you can see that this particular audio CD contains 12 songs.

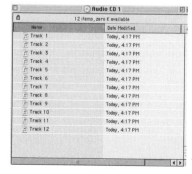

Fig. 8.23
Audio CD window.

If you double-click on any track's icon, the computer's internal audio CD player controls will appear. With these controls, you can play back and stop a track or song, you can fast forward or rewind a track, or you can select any track you wish (Fig. 8.24). By the way, the sound from the audio CD tracks will come out from the computer's internal speaker.

Note: If you cannot hear any sound out of your computer, go to the "Control Panels" in the "Apple" menu and select "Sound" (Fig. 8.24a).

Fig. 8.24 CD player controls.

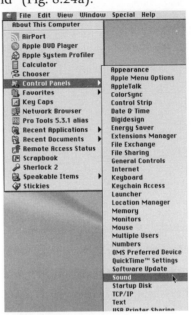

Fig. 8.24a "Control Panels" pop-up menu.

You will see the following window (Fig 8.24b). Make sure the "Mute" check box is not checked, and/or the volume slider is not all the way to the left (off).

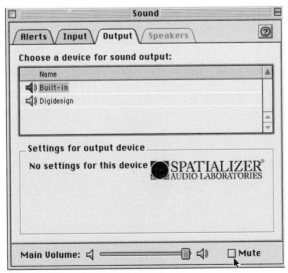

Fig. 8.24b Sound Control Panel.

After you audition the song or audio track you want to import, go to the "Movie" menu in Pro Tools and select the "Import Audio From Other Movie..." option (Fig. 8.25).

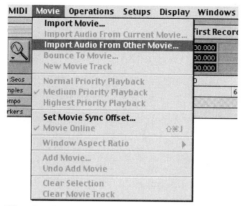

Fig. 8.25 "Movie" menu.

Pro Tools will prompt you to look for the source the audio will be imported from, in this case the audio CD. If you look at Fig. 8.26, the current folder is "Desktop," which means that the computer is showing you what is on the desktop. Notice in Fig. 8.26, the desktop contains the "Audio CD 1," which is the audio CD you put in your computer. Also, notice that the internal and external hard drives are shown as well.

Fig. 8.26 "Import Audio From Other Movie" dialog box.

Next, click on the "Audio CD 1" icon and press "Open"; you should see a list of all the tracks or songs that this particular audio CD contains (Fig. 8.27).

Fig. 8.27 "Import Audio From Other Movie" dialog box.

Once you decide which song or track to import, you need to press the "Convert" button to execute the import process. Pro Tools will then prompt you to give a name to the newly converted audio file as shown in Fig. 8.28.

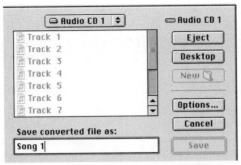

Fig. 8.28 "Save converted file as" dialog box.

After giving the new file a name ("Song 1"), it needs to be saved in the Audio Files Folder you are currently working on (Fig. 8.29a). If you don't want the entire track in the audio CD, but maybe only 30 seconds' worth, then click on "Options" (Fig. 8.29b). You can set other parameters besides the track's length in "Options" as well (Fig. 8.29c). Otherwise, once you save the new file ("Song 1"), you will see it has been directed to be stored in the "External Hard Drive" (Fig. 8.29a).

Right after you give it a name ("Song 1" in this case), you need to save the new file in the Audio Files folder of the Pro Tools Session you are currently working on.

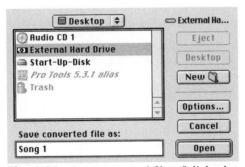

Fig. 8.29a "Save converted file as" dialog box.

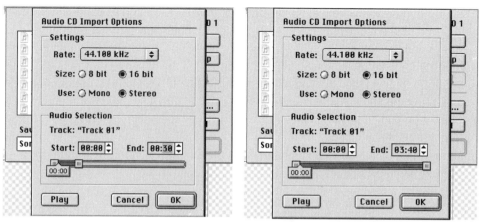

Fig. 8.29b Audio CD Import Options.   Fig. 8.29c Audio CD Import Options.

If you click on "Open," you will find the Session's Audio Files folder where you need to store the imported audio file (Song 1). See Fig. 8.30.

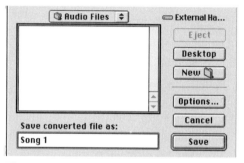

Fig. 8.30 Session's Audio Files folder.

When you press the "Save" button, you'll get the next dialog box (Fig. 8.31), which asks you to "Select Tracks to Import."

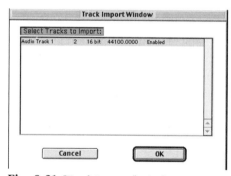

Fig. 8.31 "Track Import" window.

Once you click "OK," another dialog box will prompt you to "Choose destination folder on a valid audio drive." Since you already set the file to be directed to the Audio Files folder of your currently open Session, which resides in the external hard drive, just by clicking on "Select 'Audio Files'" in Fig. 8.32 below, the track or "Song 1" will be saved and imported into the current Pro Tools Session.

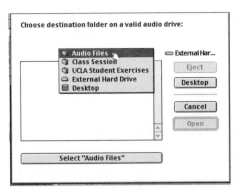

Fig. 8.32 "Choose destination folder on a valid audio drive.

Right after you click on "Select 'Audio Files'," you'll notice a window appearing on you computer screen that will read "Processing Audio" (Fig. 8.33).

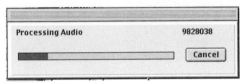

Fig. 8.33 "Processing Audio" window.

As soon as it finishes processing the audio, the newly imported audio file ("Song 1") will appear on the Audio Region List as a stereo file named "Song 1 T1R1-(Stereo)" since it was extracted from an audio CD (Fig. 8.34). Pro Tools splits the stereo file when importing it, you can see in Fig. 8.34 that the file was split as "Song 1 T1R1-.L" and "Song 1 T1R1-.R." In other words, it automatically assigns the left and right channel of the stereo file.

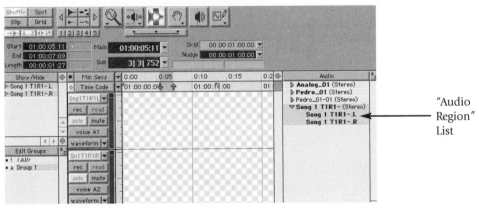

Fig. 8.34 Edit window.

Once you have the file on the Audio Region List, create either a stereo audio track or two mono audio tracks and name them "Song 1 L" and "Song 1 R." Please refer to Chapter 6 if you don't remember how to create a new audio track and how to name it. Next, click, hold, and drag "Song 1 T1R1-(Stereo)" from the Audio Region List and place it on the audio tracks you have created. Place them using the Shuffle edit mode so the region will snap to the beginning of the track (Fig. 8.35).

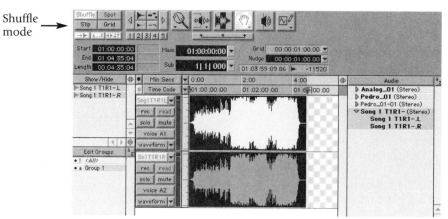

Shuffle mode →

Fig. 8.35 Edit window.

Press and hold the "Command" (⌘) key and then press "=" on your computer keyboard you should be able to see the Mix window. In this window you'll notice you now have two Channel Strips or mixer modules, one for the left channel and another for the right one (Fig. 8.36). Also, you can lower and raise the volume control (fader) when you play the track back.

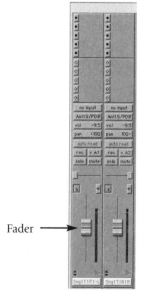

Fader →

Fig. 8.36
Channel Strips or mixer modules.

How to import audio tracks from different Sessions

Another great option that Pro Tools offers is the "Import Tracks..." command (you must have Pro Tools software version 5.1 or higher for this option). You can import audio tracks, Master Fader tracks, Auxiliary Input tracks, and MIDI tracks from other Sessions to the one you are currently working on. There are many situations where you want to import an entire track. For example, let's say that you are collaborating on a song project with a friend who has a Pro Tools system that is compatible with yours. And let's say he or she has already recorded, edited, and processed (used plug-ins) some of the tracks in his/her studio. Instead of just importing the audio files, which you will then have to place in the right position (time-wise) in the song and, if he or she used some plug-ins, you would still have to assign them in the Session, including their settings, you can just import the entire track or tracks, which will include all the settings I mentioned above. You can even import tracks from Sessions that were created in old Pro Tools software versions, from 3.2 and later on Macintosh, and on PC, from software version 4.2.5 or later.

Now, let's say that you and your friend never discussed what sample rate or bit depth or file type you were going to use in your sessions. Not a problem. You can convert the sample rate, bit depth, and file format while importing the tracks to your Session. Isn't that great!

Let's go through the process of importing an audio track. First, go to the File menu in Pro Tools (assuming that your Session is already open), and select the "Import Tracks..." command. (Fig. 8.37).

Fig. 8.37
File pop-up menu.

Pro Tools will prompt you to select the Session you want to import the tracks from (source Session). Look for the Session through the current folder pop-up menu. Remember, you need to select the Session (tape icon), not the Audio Files folder like we had to do when importing audio files. See Fig. 8.38.

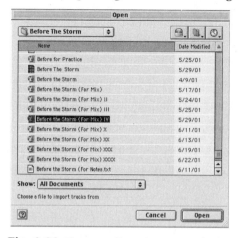

Fig. 8.38 Choose a file to import tracks from.

Once you find the Session you are looking for, a dialog box will appear on your computer screen like the one in Fig. 8.39. In this dialog box, you can see all the information about that particular Session in the "Source Properties" section. In other words, you can find out what sample rate, bit depth, file type, type of Session, the Session's start time, and in what type of Pro Tools system (TDM/Non-TDM) the Session was created in, including the software version.

If the source Session was created with a sample rate of 48kHz and 16 bits of resolution, and your Session is at 44.1kHz and 24 bits, you will have to check the "Apply SRC" check box in the "sample rate conversion options" section, and assign the sample rate required by your Session (Fig. 8.39).

Furthermore, you can also set the time to where the imported track will be placed in your Session. Be aware that if you are using a TDM system, the time code values displayed in Fig. 8.39 will be in hours:minutes:seconds:frames (SMPTE), and if you are using a Digi 001, the time code will be displayed in minutes:seconds. You can specify the track start time by: a) maintaining the absolute time code value, b) maintaining the relative time code value, and c) assigning the time code value where you desire.

Let's say for example that you want to maintain the relative time code value when you import a track, and that the Session which you are importing the track from (source Session) starts at 00:00:00:00 (zero), and the track you want to import starts at 00:01:00:00 (one minute). If your Session starts at 01:00:00:00 (one hour), then the imported track will be placed in your current Session at 01:01:00:00 (one hour:one minute:zero seconds:zero frames).

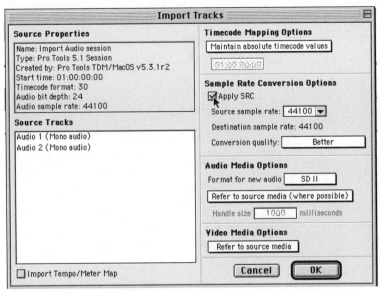

Fig. 8.39 Import Tracks window.

Once you have selected the settings, click on the "OK" button (Fig. 8.40).

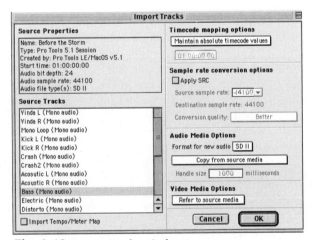

Fig. 8.40 Import Tracks window.

Next you should see the following window, where Pro Tools is letting you know that it is locating the audio files at the moment (Fig. 8.41).

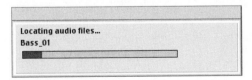

Fig. 8.41 "Locating audio files" window.

Right after, you will be prompted to select the folder where you want the track's audio file to reside. Generally you want to just press the "Choose" button, since Pro Tools automatically selects the folder where you should save the audio file (Fig. 8.42).

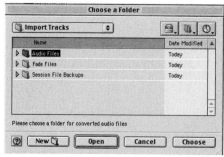

Fig. 8.42 "Choose a Folder" window.

As soon as you press "Choose," you'll notice the next window lets you know that it is processing the file (Fig. 8.43).

Fig. 8.43 "Processing" window.

If your Session has a different disk allocation than the source Session, you'll get the message shown in Fig. 8.44. Either click on "Check Disk Allocation" or "No" to continue.

Fig. 8.44 "Check Disk Allocation" dialog box.

By this time you should be able to see the audio file you have just imported in the Audio Region List of the Edit window. You can also see the track and the region (audio file) placed at the right location in the song (Fig. 8.45).

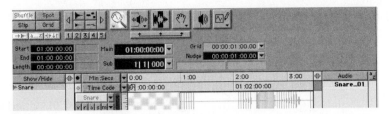

Fig. 8.45 Edit window.

If you go to the Mix window by pressing and holding the Command (⌘) and the "=" keys on your computer keyboard, you can see the track just imported as a Channel Strip (Fig. 8.46). Notice this particular track had a plug-in already assigned. This shows you when you import any type of track, all the settings and plug-ins applied to them are also imported.

Plug-In ⟶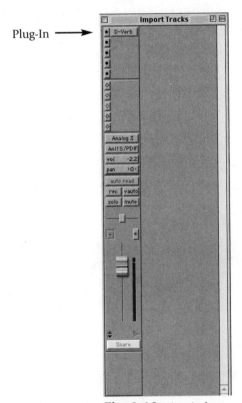

Fig. 8.46 Mix window.

Batch Import audio files to an opened Pro Tools Session

Let us say you are working on a movie, and you need to import more than 100 sound effects files for the project. The sound effects have been provided to you by your client, but come in a number of different file formats such as: SDII, AIFF, .WAV, and QT.

Of course, you could import one file at a time. As we have seen above, Pro Tools is able to read the most commonly used digital audio file formats, detect different sample rates, and convert file formats automatically. But doing this one file at a time would be really tedious.

Instead of asking Pro Tools to convert individual files, you can provide Pro Tools with a list of files that need to be converted, and Pro Tools does the rest. This "Batch Import Audio Files" feature of Pro Tools can save a great deal of time on larger projects.

The first step in the Batch Import process is to copy all the audio files (or sound effects) onto your hard drive (either internal or external). When you have all the effects in one location, select all the audio files that you want to import, and drag them to the Pro Tools alias on your computer desktop.

TIP: You can toggle between different open applications by holding down the "Command" (⌘) key and pressing "Tab" on your computer keyboard.

That's it! After the conversions are completed, the audio files will appear on the Audio Region List of your opened Pro Tools Session.

Let's do this one step at a time. First, you have to create a new Session, or open the Session you want to work on (Fig. 8.47).

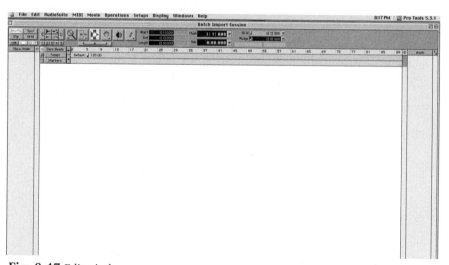

Fig. 8.47 Edit window.

Second, you have to temporarily hide the Pro Tools Session in order to see the files that need to be imported. To do this, go to the upper right hand side of your computer's desktop and select the Finder (Fig. 8.48).

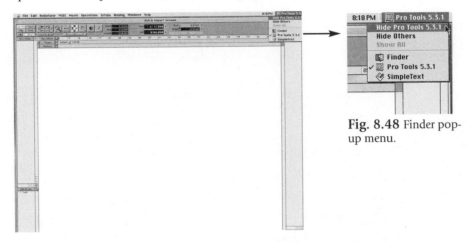

Fig. 8.48 Finder pop-up menu.

Now you can see the folder containing the audio files you have stored on your hard drive, and you can select them for Batch Import. Just go to one corner of the window, and holding the mouse down, drag an outline around the files (Fig. 8.49). This makes the icons turn dark, indicating that they have been selected.

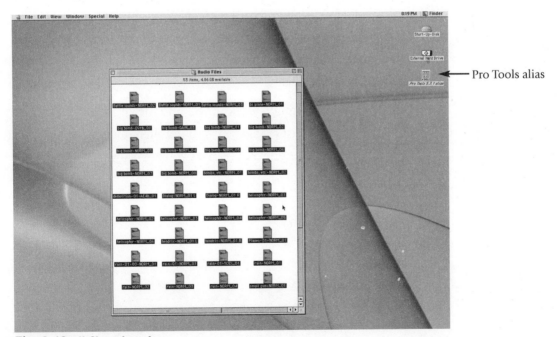

Fig. 8.49 All files selected.

After the icons turn dark, place the arrow on one of these icons, press and hold the mouse down, and drag the group of icons to the Pro Tools alias on your computer's desktop (Fig. 8.50). Or, even easier, you can just double-click on one of the selected files to Batch Import them.

Fig. 8.50 Desktop.

You will notice that after you drag the files into the alias, the Pro Tools session will reappear on your computer screen, and you will see the files being loaded (and converted, if necessary) into the Audio Region List of your Session (Fig. 8.51).

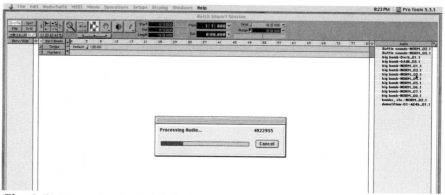

Fig. 8.51 "Processing Audio" dialog box.

Once the conversions are completed, you will find the entire list of effects in your Session's Audio Region List (Fig. 8.52). You can then drag individual sounds from the list and place them on the audio tracks you are using for sound effects.

Fig. 8.52 Edit window.

The Batch Import process is another example of how Digidesign engineers have created a superior working environment for end users. In this case, Pro Tools has reduced a series of highly complex and tedious technical processes to a simple routine. What this means for you is less time spent on drudgery, and more time for creativity.

Exporting audio files and audio regions

In the same way you can import audio files in Pro Tools, you can export them. The ability to export audio and region files from one session to another means you don't have to waste time and hard disk storage to re-record sound or instrument tracks. There are three main ways to export audio in Pro Tools: Bounce to Disk, record to tracks, and export as files.

Bounce to Disk

The Bounce to Disk option is really helpful to create a final mixdown of your Session, including all the edits, automation, and plug-ins, or to master any output or path bus directly to disk, since any available output or bus path can be selected as the bounce source. This command writes your Session, or selection, as a new audio file and does not take any voices. There are some things you should know before starting the process. It is important to have in mind that when you bounce to disk, the bounced mix will include all the Audible Tracks (which means that if a track is muted, it will not appear in the bounce; and if a track or region is soloed, that track or region will be the only element bounced to disk), Automation, Inserts and Sends, and Time Stamp Information (so you can drag it back to a Session and place it at the same location as the original material). If you make a selection in your Session and then apply the Bounce to Disk command, the bounced mix will be the length of the selection. If no selection is made, the bounced mix will be the length of the longest audible track in the session. During the Bounce to Disk process, you will be able to hear the bounce in real time, but you cannot adjust any controls during the bounce.

To Bounce to Disk, select the tracks or regions you want to bounce. If you want the whole session to be bounced, do not select anything. Choose "Bounce to Disk" from the File pop-up menu (Fig. 8.53).

Fig. 8.53 File pop-up menu.

Once you apply the command, a dialog window will appear giving you different options (Fig. 8.54).

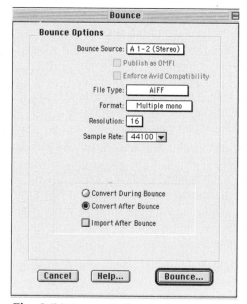

Fig. 8.54 Bounce dialog window.

Select the Bounce Source (if, for example, all the tracks' outputs are routed to Analog 1 and 2, select that option to bounce all the tracks), File Type (SDII, Wav, Aiff, Real Audio, MPEG 3, QuickTime, or Sound Resource), Format (mono, multiple mono, and stereo interleaved), Resolution (8, 16 or 24 bits, depending on the final use of the bounce; for example, if you are planning on burning an audio CD, you should choose 16-bit because is the standard bit resolution for Compact Disc) and Sample Rate (again if you are planning on burning an audio CD, you should choose 44.1kHz because is the standard sample rate for Compact Disc). It is important to keep in mind that Bounce to Disk does not apply dither. To dither a bounce file, you should insert one of the included Digidesign dither plug-ins, or another dithering plug-in, on a Master Fader assigned to the bounce source path.

You have three options right below the ones we just talked about. The Use Squeezer option performs 8-bit conversion of simple files (voice overs) using a propietary algorithm, optimizing the dynamics of the audio by using compression. In the Convert During or After Bounce option, choosing After will offer the highest level of plug-in automation accuracy possible, while choosing During will be faster, but at the expense of plug-in automation playback accuracy. And finally, you have the option of automatically importing the newly bounced files into the Audio Regions List so you can place them in tracks by selecting the Import Into Session After Bounce option.

Once you have selected your options, just click on Bounce. A new dialog window will appear asking you to choose where to save the bounced files, as shown in Fig. 8.55.

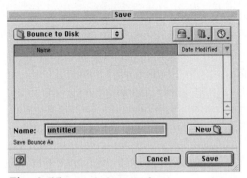

Fig. 8.55 Save dialog window.

Click on the "Save" button, and the next thing that will appear is another dialog box on your Session showing you the time remaining for the bouncing process (Fig. 8.56).

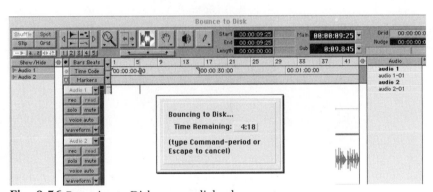

Fig. 8.56 Bouncing to Disk process dialog box.

After the process is completed, your bounced files will be in the folder where you saved them before. Now you can open a new Session and import those files if you want to hear them, or drag them into your current Session from the Audio Regions List if you chose "Import Into Session After Bounce," or just burn a CD with your mix!

Recording to Tracks

Choose this option whenever you want to record a submix to new audio tracks in the same Session. This option will take tracks, voices, and bus paths, but unlike the Bounce to Disk command, you can adjust all the controls while the process takes place. You would record to tracks, for example, when you have three tracks with background vocals and you want to free up some voices. Then you could record the three of them to a new track and have them mixed together.

To Record to Tracks, apply all the plug-ins or external processors you want to your tracks, as shown in Fig. 8.57, and do not forget to set the panning of each track if you are recording in stereo.

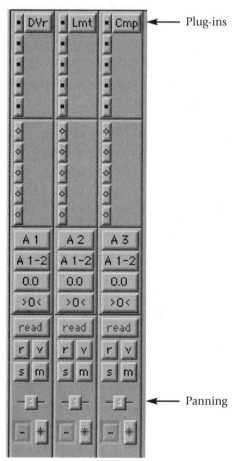

Fig. 8.57 Three tracks showing in the Mix window.

Set the outputs of the tracks you want to record to a bus path (Fig. 8.58a and Fig. 8.58b).

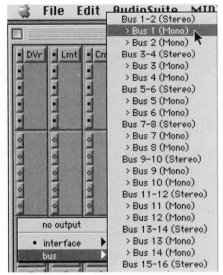

Fig. 8.58a Assigning the outputs to a bus path.

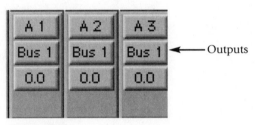

Fig. 8.58b Output assignments to Bus 1.

Create a new track (Fig. 8.59), which is going to be the destination track for all three tracks we are recording.

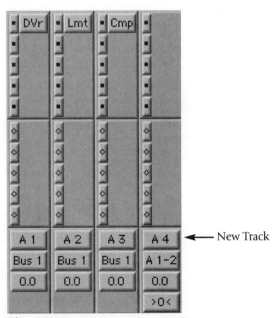

Fig. 8.59 Four tracks showing in the Mix window.

The input assignment of the new track must be the same as the bus path to which you are recording, and the output should be your main output (Fig. 8.60a and Fig. 8.60b).

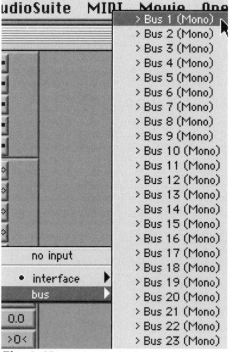

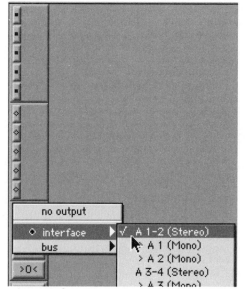

Fig. 8.60a Assigning the input of the new track.

Fig. 8.60b Assigning the output of the new track.

Now, the outputs of the tracks you want to record should match the input of the new track, as shown in Fig. 8.61.

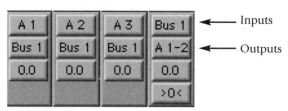

Fig. 8.61 Input/Output assignments.

Once all the assignments are done, you can make a selection of the audio you want to record or not select anything at all, in which case the recording will begin from the location of the playback cursor and will not stop until you hit the spacebar or the Stop button from the Transport window. If you do make a selection, make sure to include time at the end of it for reverb tails, delays, etc.

Record-enable the new track and click Record on the Transport window, as shown in Fig. 8.62.

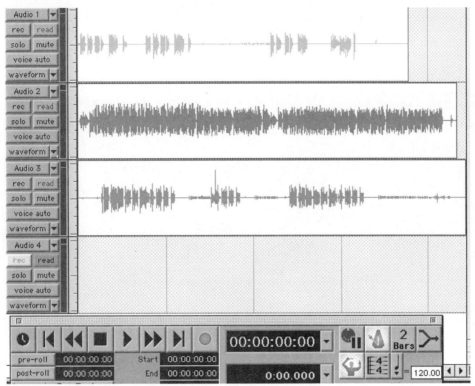

Fig. 8.62 Track ready to record.

Click Play in the Transport window to start recording. While the recording process takes place, you can tweak knobs and adjust parameters and controls. All the changes will be recorded in the new track(s), as shown in Fig. 8.63.

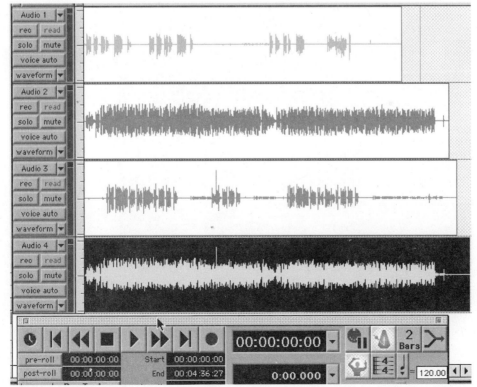

Fig. 8.63 New recorded audio.

Export as Files

This command is useful when you have done some edits to an audio file and the final result shows as a region in your Audio Regions List. In this case, if you want to import that particular region into another Session, you will not be able to find it, unless you export it as a file.

What this option does is convert your regions into whole audio files so you can export, import, bounce, or whatever you want to do with them.

If you wan to export a region as a file, select the region(s) from your Audio Regions List, as shown in Fig. 8.64.

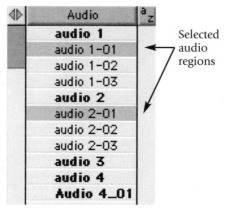

Selected audio regions

Fig. 8.64 Audio Regions List.

From the Audio pop-up menu, select the "Export Selected As Files" option (Fig. 8.65).

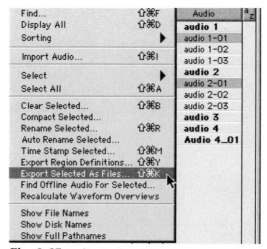

Fig. 8.65 Audio Regions List pop-up menu.

A new dialog window (Fig. 8.66) will appear asking you to choose the options for the export. As with the Bounce to Disk command, you have different options to choose from.

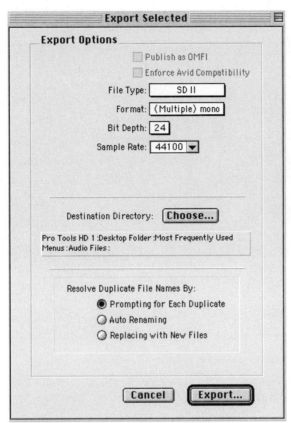

Fig. 8.66 Export Options dialog window.

Select the File Type (SDII, Wav, Aiff, Real Audio, MPEG 3, QuickTime, or Sound Resource), Format (multiple mono or stereo), Bit Depth (8, 16, or 24 bits), and Sample Rate. By pressing the button labeled "Choose" you can select the destination of your files. Check if you want Pro Tools to prompt you for each duplicate, to Auto Rename, or Replace the regions being exported with the new files in your current Pro Tools Session. Click the "Export" button.

CHAPTER NINE

MIDI

9

If you are a Pro Tools user, at one point, you may have to use MIDI synthesizers, software synthesizers and samplers, MIDI control surfaces, effects processors controlled via MIDI, MIDI samplers, synchronizers to read and generate MIDI Time Code (MTC), etc., and you need to know about this protocol implemented since 1983. For this reason, I am including this chapter in the book, especially for people who still have problems understanding the basic MIDI concepts. I will briefly explain its functionality and connections, as well as how to implement it in a Pro Tools LE or TDM system.

In this chapter you will learn:

- What is MIDI?

- What are some MIDI applications?

- The MIDI ports.

- Basic MIDI connections.

- Why do you need a MIDI interface?

- MIDI track controls

- Recording a MIDI track

- MIDI controls in the Transport Window

- MIDI connections using a TDM or a LE system.

- MIDI messages.

- The MIDI cable.

- The MIDI channels.

- Working with MIDI in Pro Tools.

- The MIDI track.

- Creating a MIDI track.

- Editing MIDI.

- How to configure OMS in Pro Tools.

What is MIDI?

MIDI stands for "Musical Instrument Digital Interface," which means a digital interconnection between MIDI electronic instruments and other MIDI devices. These MIDI electronic instruments and devices refer to MIDI synthesizers, MIDI sequencers, MIDI drum machines and modules, MIDI guitar synthesizers, samplers, audio signal processors controlled by MIDI, control surfaces, and computers, among others. All these MIDI instruments and devices are interconnected by means of a cable known as a "MIDI cable," which includes a 5-pin DIN (Deutsch Industry Norm) connector on each side. A MIDI cable is connected on the rear panel of a MIDI instrument. A MIDI instrument transmits and receives digital data via MIDI (0's and 1's) and not audio (sound).

MIDI allows you to record digital information (data) using a MIDI sequencer and play it back, generating the sound you have selected on your MIDI instrument such a synthesizer, sampler, or drum module. This means you can record your musical performances as MIDI information using a piano sound, and in turn, play it back with a guitar sound, for example. You can also record rhythms so a drum module can play it back, bass lines, and MIDI continuous controller information to control the amount of effect on an instrument using an audio signal processor such a reverb unit, for example.

MIDI instruments communicate via MIDI messages. For example a "Note On" message results from the action of pressing a key on your MIDI keyboard. This action is converted into numbers (0's and 1's) and transmitted in groups of bytes (1 byte = 8 bits) through a MIDI Out port on your "master" synthesizer and received by another synthesizer "slave." In turn, the receiving synthesizer—the "slave"—interprets those numbers received and converts them into sounds.

MIDI messages

MIDI transmits and receives MIDI messages or commands, include:
- Note On—pressing a key on your keyboard,
- Note Off—releasing a key after being pressed,
- Velocity—how hard you pressed a key,
- Pitch Bend—altering the pitch of a sound,
- Program Change—changing the sound or preset,
- After Touch—applying pressure to a key after being pressed to modify it, and
- Control Change—using a controller rather than a key to modify the sound of

a note. A controller can be the mod wheel and the pitch bend lever of your MIDI keyboard, a footswitch, a volume pedal, etc.

What are some MIDI applications?

MIDI can be used for a good number of applications; with some MIDI knowledge and imagination, you can do almost anything you desire. The most common applications of MIDI are:

- Playing several synthesizers of different brands using only one MIDI keyboard controller to create sounds you can only imagine, including majestic orchestral sounds, special sound effects, complex drum and percussion sounds, etc.

- In live performances, MIDI helps to diminish the number of keyboards on stage. Also, if a keyboardist is playing a piano sound on the synthesizer, for instance, and in the middle of the song he needs to play a Hammond organ sound, instead of running to another keyboard on the stage that contains the organ sound, he could just send a MIDI "Program Change" command to the receiving MIDI keyboard and play the organ with the keyboard he is playing at the moment. In other words, he could change the sound of the keyboard via remote control through his MIDI keyboard.

- MIDI can control the quantity of an effect (reverb, echo, chorus, flanging, etc.) through the synthesizer's keys or continuous controllers like the modulation wheel and pitch bend levers.

- MIDI can also be used for generating MIDI Time Code (MTC) to synchronize MIDI sequencers, drum machines, analog and digital tape machines, computers, etc.

- Another useful application of MIDI is to speed up the process of transcribing a recorded music composition to music notation. You can achieve this using a software MIDI sequencer on a computer.

The MIDI cable

As I mentioned above, MIDI instruments and other devices are interconnected via a MIDI cable (Fig. 9.1a). This 5-pin DIN cable uses only three pins to transmit and receive MIDI data. In order to avoid digital signal degradation during data transmission and reception, the MIDI cable must be limited to a length of 50 feet (50 meters). This cable length was established by the International MIDI Association (IMA). If you need to use longer cables, you can purchase electronic devices that will solve this problem.

Fig. 9.1a MIDI cable.

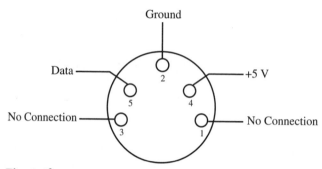

Fig. 9.1b MIDI cable pin assignment.

Pin # 1 is not connected.

Pin # 2 is connected to ground.

Pin # 3 is not connected.

Pin # 4 is connected to +5 volts.

Pin # 5 is the pin that transmits and receives the MIDI messages.

MIDI ports

A MIDI cable is connected to a MIDI port on the rear panel of a MIDI instrument or device. Most MIDI devices have three MIDI ports: MIDI IN, MIDI OUT, and MIDI THRU (Fig. 9.2). I did not say all of them because some MIDI devices only have a MIDI IN and a MIDI OUT/THRU combined.

MIDI port functions

- The MIDI OUT port transmits the MIDI messages to another MIDI device; this could be to a synthesizer, a drum machine, a MIDI sequencer, a MIDI lighting system, etc.
- The MIDI IN port receives the digital information transmitted by the MIDI OUT port of another MIDI device.
- The MIDI THRU port is not the same as a MIDI OUT port; instead, it retransmits the exact MIDI data coming in the MIDI IN port of the same receiving device. See Diagram 9.1 on page 351.

Fig. 9.2 MIDI IN, MIDI OUT, and MIDI THRU ports.

MIDI channels

As I mentioned earlier, MIDI devices communicate via MIDI "messages." These MIDI messages are sent and received by means of a MIDI cable through 16 channels known as "MIDI channels." These channels are not physical channels commonly found on an audio mixer. They are software channels that carry the MIDI information and they can be routed to any MIDI device that needs it.

You may be asking yourself, "But why do I need that many MIDI channels?" Well, the answer is very simple: The more MIDI channels you have available, the more MIDI devices you can control by using only one MIDI keyboard, MIDI hardware sequencer, or MIDI software sequencer in a computer, for example.

The concept of MIDI channels is very easy to understand with the following analogy: Think of your TV, which receives many TV channels at the same time, which means different TV shows coming from different TV stations through just one cable. Your TV is always receiving the different TV shows or programs 24 hours a day, seven days a week. For example, if you want to watch one particular TV show, you have to select the channel on which the show is being transmitted. For instance, let's say the 6 o'clock news is being transmitted on channel 2, the football game on channel 4, and a reality show on channel 8. If you wish to watch the football game, you just have to select channel 4 to be able to watch it, right?

This concept works similarly when using MIDI channels. You have to select the MIDI channel a sound is transmitted on to be able to listen to it. For example, referring to Diagram 9.1, let's suppose synth "A" has an internal sequencer and a song has been programmed in it. In this scenario, synth "A" is considered a "master" keyboard and synth "B" and "C" the "slave" keyboards. Let's also suppose that synth "A" was programmed to play and send the piano part on MIDI channel 2, the bass part on MIDI channel 4, and a flute part on MIDI channel 8. If I want to listen to the song using all three synths, then I need to make the sound and MIDI channel assignments on each synth. So when synth "A" starts playing its internal sequencer, it will start transmitting the MIDI data through the three MIDI channels I mentioned, 2, 4, and 8. If I want synth "A" to play the piano sound, I have to assign it to produce a piano sound and to send MIDI channel 2. If I want synth "B" to play the bass sound, I have to assign it to a bass sound and to receive MIDI channel 4, and if I want synth "C" to play the flute sound, I have to assign it to a flute sound and to receive MIDI channel 8. Think of the master synth "A" as the cable company that is transmitting all channels at the same time, and the slave synths ("B" and "C") as the TV receivers.

Basic MIDI connection

There are several ways to interconnect MIDI devices. It is important you understand what a master and slave keyboard means in the MIDI domain. Notice in Diagram 9.1 that synth "A" is acting as the master controller or keyboard and synths "B" and "C" as the slaves. This means that every time the user press a key on the master keyboard (synth "A"), MIDI data is generated and transmitted through its MIDI OUT port. The slave keyboards (synths "B" and "C") will receive and convert this data into continuous voltage, and in turn, into sounds or musical notes that can be heard. This type of connection is called daisy-chaining because the synthesizers are connected in series.

Also notice in Diagram 9.1, since synth "A" is the master keyboard, its MIDI OUT port is connected to the MIDI IN port of synth "B" (slave). At the same time, notice the MIDI THRU port of synth "B" is connected to the MIDI IN port of synth "C." This means that whatever MIDI information synth "B" receives from synth "A", the third synth ("C"), will receive the same information that synth "B" receives in its MIDI IN port. This is because the MIDI THRU port sends out a replica of the information received in the MIDI IN port of any device.

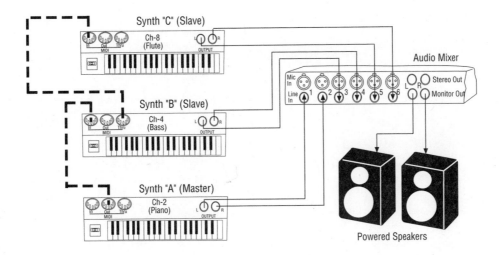

Diagram 9.1 Daisy-chain MIDI connection.

Working with MIDI in Pro Tools

Now that I briefly covered the basic concepts of MIDI, I will discuss how to implement it in Pro Tools.

Pro Tools not only allows you to record, import, edit, and mix audio, it also allows you to record, import, edit, and mix MIDI data by means of its built-in MIDI sequencer. Pro Tools deals with MIDI in a similar manner as it does audio. Instead of creating audio tracks, you must create MIDI tracks to record and import MIDI.

Why do you need a MIDI interface?

If you are going to use a hardware MIDI synthesizer or sound module, you must use a MIDI interface to establish a communication between Pro Tools and your external MIDI devices. There are several types of MIDI interfaces with several inputs and outputs. Depending of your needs, you can purchase from a simple one-MIDI In, one-MIDI Out (1x1) interface to a 10x10 interface with ten MIDI Ins and Outs. Furthermore, if you are still using an old computer to work with MIDI, then you have to have a MIDI interface with a serial connector and plug it into the modem or printer port of your computer. If you are using a new computer model, you can buy a USB MIDI interface and connect it into a USB port available in your computer. If you don't have any USB ports available, then you might have to purchase a

USB hub, which has several USB ports available. You can see how to connect a MIDI interface in your Pro Tools system in Diagrams 9.2–9.6 later in this chapter.

The MIDI track

When you create a MIDI track in Pro Tools, you can view it in both the Edit and Mix windows (Fig. 9.3a and Fig. 9.3b), just like audio tracks. Regardless of whether you are viewing a MIDI track from the Edit or Mix window, you will see the same controls in both windows. If you cannot not see the input and output selectors and the MIDI volume and MIDI panning controls through the Edit window, then you have to assign Pro Tools to show all the MIDI Channel Strip controls you want in the Edit window. You can achieve this by selecting the "Edit Window Shows" command in the Display pop-up menu.

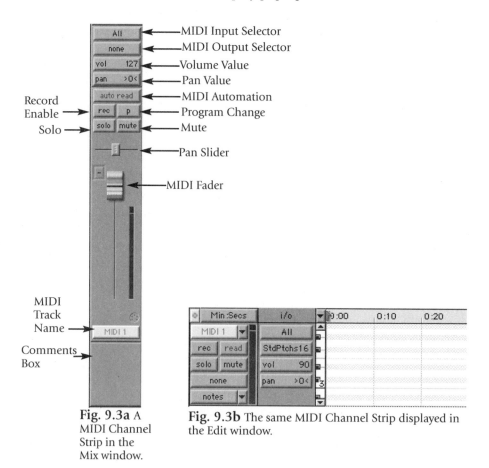

Fig. 9.3a A MIDI Channel Strip in the Mix window.

Fig. 9.3b The same MIDI Channel Strip displayed in the Edit window.

MIDI track name and comments box

Each time a MIDI track is created, Pro Tools gives it a default name such as "MIDI 1." If you create a second track, it will automatically be named "MIDI 2," and so forth. Well, you can rename a MIDI track to a more logical and practical name. Let's say you are recording a MIDI piano track, so you might rename the track "Piano." To change the name of a MIDI track, double-click on the track's name box and rename it (Fig. 9.3c). Furthermore, the "Comments" box located below the name's track allows you to type any comments you have about the track. For example, if I am using a Korg Trinity synthesizer and I have assigned it to play Program #1 of the Trinity, I can type all that information in the Comments dialog box (Fig. 9.3c).

Fig. 9.3c Renaming a MIDI track and writing comments.

MIDI track controls

The volume control and volume indicator

With the volume control or fader you can control the volume of a MIDI track from 0 to 127 (Fig. 9.4a). You can see the volume value in the box located right underneath the MIDI Output Selector in the MIDI Channel Strip (Fig. 9.3a). The volume indicator shows the MIDI volume of the MIDI data recorded in the track (Fig. 9.4a), not the audio volume. You can manually edit the volume through the "Show MIDI Event List" command in the Windows pop-up menu (Fig. 9.4b). You can also edit this information using the Pencil tool and setting the MIDI track view to "volume" (Fig. 9.4c and Fig. 9.4d).

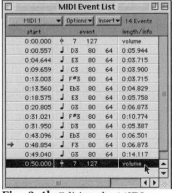

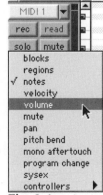

Fig. 9.4a The volume control and indicator in a MIDI track.

Fig. 9.4b Editing the MIDI volume through the MIDI Event List.

Fig. 9.4c Selecting the MIDI volume track view in a MIDI track.

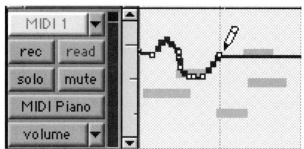

Fig. 9.4d Editing MIDI volume in the volume track view using the Pencil tool.

The pan control and value

This control or slider (Fig. 9.5a) and value indicator (Fig. 9.5b) are similar to an audio track pan control and value indicator, but instead of showing and controlling the audio panning, it controls the MIDI information recorded in the MIDI track from hard left (<64) to hard right (63>).

Fig. 9.5a The MIDI Pan Slider.

Fig. 9.5b The MIDI panning and volume values.

The automation, record enable, program change, solo, and mute controls

With the exception of the program change button, the automation, record enable, solo and mute controls (Fig. 9.6) function exactly as they do on an audio track:

Fig. 9.6 The MIDI track controls.

Automation: This button allows you to select the various automation modes when ready to mix your session. The modes are:
- "auto off"—disables the recorded MIDI automation on the track.
- "auto read"—play back the recorded MIDI automation.

- "auto touch"—updates the recorded MIDI automation while a fader or control button is touched or moved with the computer mouse or controller. When the fader or control button is released, automation will stop and the fader or button will return to its previously automated position in the "auto write" mode.
- "auto latch"—is similar to the "auto touch" mode: It updates the previously recorded automation as soon as you move or touch a fader or control button. The difference is that in "auto latch" when you release the fader or mouse, it continues writing automation until you stop the playback. Furthermore, the fader or button does not return to its previously automated position when the mouse or control is released; it stays in the position where you left it when you stopped the playback.
- "auto write"—records MIDI automation.

Record enable: Push this button when you are going to record MIDI information on a track. It also allows you to check if you are receiving MIDI information from your MIDI devices and to set MIDI recording levels. This button does not start the recording; you would have to click on the Record and Play buttons on the Transport window, or simply hold down the Command key (Control in Windows) and the spacebar on your computer keyboard.

Solo: When you click on this button in a MIDI track, the rest of the tracks will be muted or silenced so you can audition the soloed track by itself. You can solo more than one track at a time.

Mute: This button mutes or silences the output of the MIDI track you muted. You can mute more than one track at a time.

Program change: You can select any "program" or sound on your MIDI synthesizer or sound module from Pro Tools by means of the program change MIDI command.

To do a program change from Pro Tools to your MIDI synthesizer:
a) Assuming that all your MIDI setup is properly connected, click on the "Program Change" button ("p") on the MIDI track (Fig. 9.7a).
b) A window will appear showing all the program numbers or names of the synthesizer you are using (Fig. 9.7b).
c) Select a program number or name. In this case I have selected a MIDI Piano sound of Korg's Trinity MIDI keyboard (Fig. 9.7c).

Fig. 9.7a Accessing the program change window on a MIDI track.

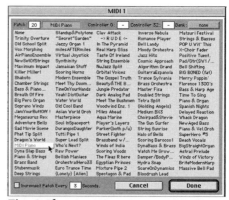

Fig. 9.7b Selecting a new sound in the program change window.

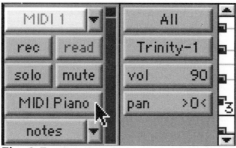

Fig. 9.7c The selected new sound (MIDI Piano) shown on the MIDI track.

The MIDI Input Selector

The MIDI Input Selector pop-up menu allows you to choose which MIDI device and MIDI channel you will be listening to when you are ready to record MIDI into Pro Tools (Fig. 9.8a).

Note: You must first configure the "OMS (Open Music System) MIDI Setup" in Pro Tools for Pro Tools version 5.3 or earlier. If you are using Pro Tools 6.0 or later, then you have to configure what is call now the AMS (Audio MIDI System) in order to select the MIDI device and MIDI channel you wish to use to record. If you want a MIDI track to listen to "All" MIDI channels on all devices (Fig. 9.8b), you also have the option. Be aware that when you assign more than one input MIDI channel to a MIDI track, all the recorded MIDI signals will be combined into that particular MIDI track.

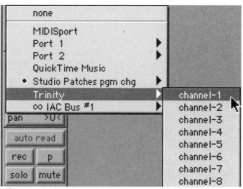

Fig. 9.8a Selecting a MIDI device and MIDI channel in a MIDI track.

Fig. 9.8b Setting a MIDI track to "All" to listen to all MIDI channels on all MIDI devices.

The MIDI output selector

Once you have recorded MIDI data on a MIDI track, you can play it back. But first, you must select an output MIDI channel in the track (Fig. 9.9a). Assigning several outputs on a MIDI track, all the MIDI data recorded in that track will be sent to all assigned MIDI channels.

Fig. 9.9a Selecting a MIDI output for playing back recorded MIDI data in a MIDI track.

Creating a MIDI track

A MIDI track, as I mentioned before, is very similar to an audio track, but instead of recording audio, it records MIDI data. Also, a MIDI track is created in the same manner as an audio track. To create a MIDI track:

  a) Go to the File pop-up manu and select the "New Track" command (Fig. 9.10a).
  b) A dialog box will prompt you to choose the track's type. Select "MIDI Track" and release the mouse (Fig. 9.10b).

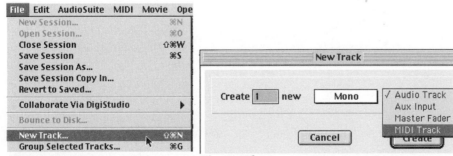

Fig. 9.10a Selecting the "New Track" command.

Fig. 9.10b The New Track dialog box.

  c) Click on "Create" (Fig. 9.10c). Notice there is no track format, i.e., mono, stereo, 5.1, etc. This is because it is a MIDI track.

d) An empty MIDI track will appear on your screen (Fig. 9.10d).

Fig. 9.10c Creating a MIDI track. **Fig. 9.10d** The newly created MIDI track.

Recording MIDI

Recording MIDI information is very similar to recording audio. By this I mean, you need to assign the proper inputs and outputs, record-enable the track (the "rec" button), set the recording levels, and press the Record and Play button in the Transport window.

Once you have set your "OMS Studio Setup" (for software versions 5.3.1 or earlier) or "AMS Setup" (for Pro Tools version 6.0 and higher)—explained ahead—and have made the proper recording settings, then you are ready to record MIDI.

To record MIDI:

a) Assuming all your connections and the recording settings are done, go to the Windows pop-up menu and select the "Show Transport" command and press the Record button once. You will notice the Record button (the red button will start flashing, indicating Pro Tools is ready to record.

b) Position the cursor in the "Play" button and click on it. By doing this, you have asked Pro Tools to start recording (Fig. 9.11a).

Fig. 9.11a Clicking on the Play button to initiate the recording process.

c) Once Pro Tools starts recording, you can start playing your MIDI keyboards, MIDI drums, guitar synthesizer, etc., to enter the MIDI information you want. When you finish playing your MIDI device, press the Stop button in the Transport window. You will see the MIDI information displayed in the MIDI track you just recorded (Fig. 9.11b).

d) If you take a look on the right hand side of the Edit window, you will see the "MIDI Regions List" containing a MIDI file with the name of the track you recorded. This file has all the MIDI information you recorded from your MIDI device and can be imported and edited any way you desire (Fig. 9.11c).

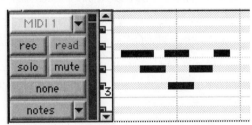

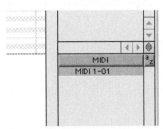

Fig. 9.11b MIDI data recorded in a MIDI track.

Fig. 9.11c The MIDI file generated in the MIDI Regions List.

Editing MIDI

When you have MIDI information in the Edit window, you can display it and edit it any way you desire through the MIDI track view selector (Fig. 9.12a). You can move notes around, trim them, draw them (which is a good thing in case you do not know how to play), you can draw the volume, the velocity (Fig. 9.12b), the panning (Fig. 9.12c), change, erase or add MIDI events, quantize, change the tempo, meter, or duration of a note, or even transpose them. The possibilities of working with MIDI are endless!

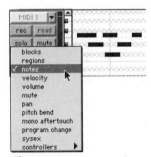

Fig. 9.12a Selecting the MIDI track to view its MIDI information as notes.

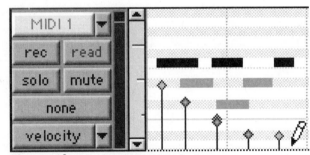

Fig. 9.12b Drawing the MIDI velocity information in a MIDI track.

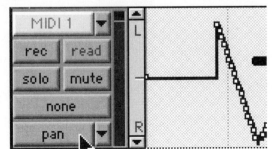

Fig. 9.12c Drawing the panning data in a MIDI track.

MIDI controls in the Transport window

If you display the Transport window and what you see is a short version of it (Fig. 9.13a), don't worry, what you need to do is to do is to go to the Display pop-up menu and select the "Transport Window Shows" command (Fig. 9.13b). In this menu you can select to display all the Transport window's sections such as: the counters, the MIDI controls, and the expanded version of it (Fig. 9.13c). Selecting the "MIDI Controls" option, you will be able to generate a click, to merge MIDI information, to tap a tempo, etc. Fig. 9.13d shows these MIDI controls which I will discuss next.

Fig. 9.13a Short version of the Transport window.

Fig. 9.13b Selecting all the sections of the Transport window.

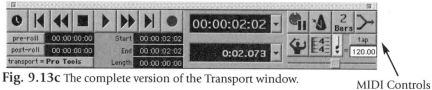

Fig. 9.13c The complete version of the Transport window.

MIDI Controls

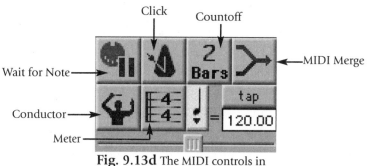

Fig. 9.13d The MIDI controls in the Transport window.

The "Wait for Note" button

Enabling this MIDI control button, Pro Tools won't start recording until it receives a MIDI event from you. What that means is that Pro Tools will wait for you to press a key on your MIDI keyboard or hit a drum on your MIDI drums to initiate the recording process. This is very useful when you are alone trying to record your music as your hands are too busy playing the MIDI keyboard, MIDI guitar, or MIDI drums to press the Record button to start recording.

The "Click" button

When you have the need to generate a "click" (metronome) for yourself or the musicians that are about to record, enable this button. You have the option to listen to the metronome or click "during play and record" mode, or "only during record" mode, or "only during countoff" mode. By double-clicking on the "click" button using the mouse, the "Click/Countoff Options" window will appear. In this window you can specify the settings for the click and the countoff (Fig. 9.14).

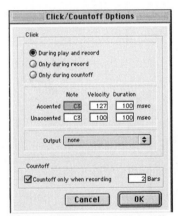

Fig. 9.14 The Click/Countoff Options window.

There are several ways to generate a click in Pro Tools:
- Using external MIDI devices,
- using an internal software synthesizer plug-in such as "Virus" , and
- using the "click" plug-in available now in Pro Tools version 6.0.

To generate a click using a external MIDI devices like a synthesizer or drum module, for example (assuming you already have configured your OMS Studio Setup, that your MIDI connections are properly done, and that you have the Transport window showing on your computer screen), do the following:

a) Double click on the "click" button of the Transport window, or go to the MIDI pop-up menu and select the "Click Options" command (Fig. 9.15a). The "Click/Countoff Options" window should appear (Fig. 9.15b).

b) Select the MIDI output in which the click will be sent through. When you click on the "Output" option, if your MIDI connections and OMS Studio Setup are configured, then you will see among the options your MIDI interface, or MIDI device or devices you have created during your OMS Studio Setup. In this example I have selected MIDI "channel-1" from my Korg's Trinity Plus MIDI keyboard I created during the OMS Studio Setup (Fig. 9.15c). This means the Trinity Plus will receive the MIDI events from Pro Tools through MIDI channel 1 (out of the 16 channels MIDI provides), and generate the click's audio through its audio outputs. You can listen to the click if you have your keyboard or sound generator connected to your speakers.

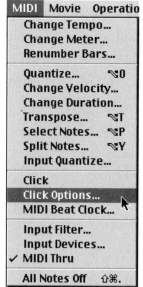

Fig. 9.15a Selecting the Click Options command.

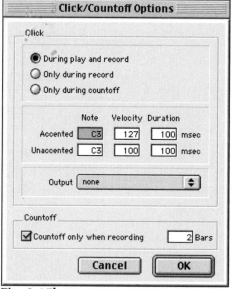

Fig. 9.15b The Click/Countoff Options window.

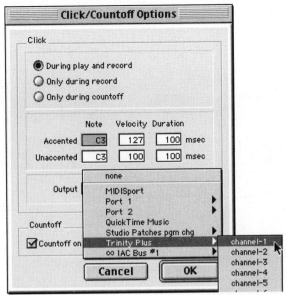

Fig. 9.15c Selecting the "output" MIDI channel on the Click/Countoff Options window.

c) Once you successfully listen to the click through your speakers, if you don't like the sound generated, i.e., maybe you assigned a cowbell sound and you want to listen to a wood block sound, you can change it remotely through the "Accented" and "Unaccented" note boxes in the "Click/Countoff Options" window (Fig. 9.15d). Just highlight the box, then press the key that has the sound you want the click to be on your MIDI keyboard, and you will notice the note will change to the key you press on the keyboard.

d) Click "OK" when the click output assignment is done. You will notice the Click/Countoff Options window will disappear. Click on the Play button to test if Pro Tools is generating a click. If you cannot hear the click after you press the Play button, check on the Transport window that the "Click" button is on or enabled (Fig. 9.15e). If you still cannot listen to the click, then check your audio and MIDI connections.

e) If you do hear the click, you will notice the click's tempo will be the tempo of the Session. You can change the tempo by turning the "Conductor" button off and moving the horizontal slider (Fig. 9.15f) which becomes active as soon as you disable the "Conductor" button.

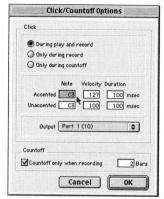

Fig. 9.15d Remotely changing the click's note for playback.

Fig. 9.15e Enabling the "Click" button.

Fig. 9.15f Changing the tempo of the Session.

To generate a click using an internal software synthesizer plug-in such as "Virus," do the following:

a) Create a mono Aux Input track and click on the first insert point of the Aux Input track (Fig. 9.16a).

b) Select a "virtual" synthesizer plug-in if available in your Pro Tools system. In this example I am selecting "Virus" (Fig. 9.16b).

c) Once you see the plug-in window (in this case the "Virus") on the screen, choose the sound you desire to be generated as the click. You can select a different sound if you click on the "<factory default>" pop-up menu in the plug-in (Fig. 9.16c).

Fig. 9.16a Placing the cursor on the first insert point of an Aux Input track.

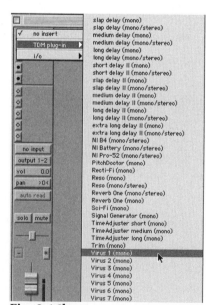

Fig. 9.16b Selecting a software synthesizer plug-in ("Virus").

Fig. 9.16c The plug-in window.

d) Next, double-click on the click button of the Transport window, or go to the MIDI pop-up menu and select the "Click Options" command (see Fig. 9.15a above). The "Click/Countoff Options" window should appear (see Fig. 9.15b above).

e) Select the MIDI output in which the click will be sent through. When you click on the "Output" option, if your MIDI connections and the OMS Studio Setup (AMS Setup if using Pro Tools 6.0 or higher) is configured, then you will see among the output choices your MIDI interface, your external MIDI devices, and whatever software synthesizers you have assigned in an Aux Input track or tracks. In this example I have selected the "Virus" virtual synth, since I assigned it on my Aux Input track (Fig. 9.16d). This means the "Virus" will receive the MIDI events generated by Pro Tools' metronome or click.

f) Click "OK" when the click output assignment is done. You will notice the "Click/Countoff Options" window will disappear. Click on the Play button to test if Pro Tools is generating a click. You will see, on the Aux Input track you assigned the virtual synth to, its volume indicator showing the click's level (Fig. 9.16e).

g) If you cannot hear the click after you press the Play button, check on the Transport window that the Click button is on or enabled (Fig. 9.16f). If you still cannot hear the click, but you can see signal going in the Aux Input track, then check your Aux Input track's output assignment and make sure it is assigned to the correct output where your speakers are connected.

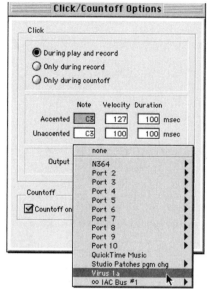

Fig. 9.16d Selecting the software synthesizer to generate the click's sound.

Fig. 9.16e The click volume level shown on an Aux Input track.

Fig. 9.16f Enabling the Click button.

Generating a click using the "click" plug-in available now in Pro Tools version 6.0 is a much simpler process. Obviously, you must have Mac OS X and Pro Tools 6.0 or higher installed in your computer in order to do the following:

a) Create a mono Aux Input track and click on the first insert point of the Aux Input track.

b) Select the "click" plug-in from the list of plug-ins in your system (Fig. 9.17a).

c) The "click" plug-in window will appear on your screen (Fig. 9.17b).

d) You can select a different sound if you click on the plug-in's "<factory default>" pop-up menu. In this example, I have selected the "Cowbell 1" sound (Fig. 9.17c).

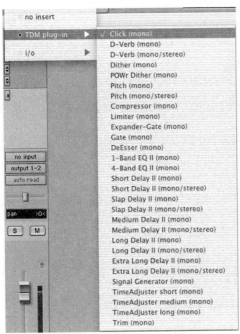

Fig. 9.17b The click's plug-in window.

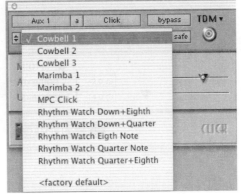

Fig. 9.17a Selecting the "click" plug-in on an Aux Input track.

Fig. 9.17c Selecting the click sound on the plug-in's "<factory default>" pop-up menu.

e) If the Click button (metronome icon) in the Transport window is on (Fig. 9.17d), press the Play button (Fig. 9.17e) to test if the click sound is being generated.

f) If the click is playing, you will see on the Aux Input track you assigned the click plug-in, its volume indicator showing the click's level (Fig. 9.17f).

g) If you still cannot hear the click, but you can see signal going in the Aux Input track, then check your Aux Input track's output assignment and make sure it is assigned to the correct output where your speakers are connected.

Fig. 9.17d The Click button enabled.

Fig. 9.17e Pressing the Play button in the Transport window.

Fig. 9.17f The click's volume level on the Aux Input track.

The "Countoff" button

If you double-click on the "Countoff" button, or or go to the MIDI pop-up menu and select the "Click Options" command, the "Click/Countoff Options" window will appear (Fig. 9.18a). In this window, you can specify the number of bars or measures Pro Tools will count off before starting recording or playing back. For example, if you type "4" in the bars dialog box (Fig. 9.18a), then a number "4" will be displayed on the "Countoff" button (Fig. 9.18b). This means that Pro Tools will count four bars before it starts recording or playing back.

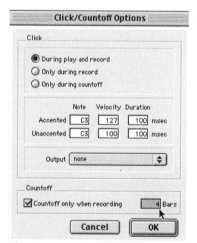

Fig. 9.18a The Click/Countoff Options window after double-clicking on the Countoff button.

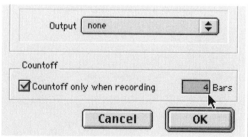

Fig. 9.18b After typing 4 bars for countoff.

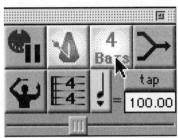

Fig. 9.18c. The four bars are displayed on the "Countoff" button.

The "MIDI Merge" button

Suppose you want to record a drum rhythm on a MIDI track using your external MIDI keyboard. Also, let's suppose you have to record the kick and snare rhythm in one pass because you don't have an extra hand to play and record the hi-hat part. Well, if you don't turn the "MIDI Merge" button on when you are trying to add the hi-hat part on a second pass using the same MIDI track, you will erase the kick and snare MIDI data you have recorded in the first pass. In other words, when the "MIDI Merge" button is on, the recording of new MIDI information merges with the existing information in a MIDI track. If this button is off, the recording of new MIDI data replaces the existing data in the MIDI track.

The "Conductor" button

When the "Conductor" button is on (Fig. 9.19a), Pro Tools uses the tempo defined in the tempo ruler (Fig. 9.19b). If you turn the Conductor button off, Pro Tools switches to the "manual" tempo mode and ignores the tempo track. Once in the manual tempo mode, you can move the tempo slider control (Fig. 9.19c) and change the Session to the tempo you desire. Notice in Fig. 9.19c, a "tap" button appears right above the BPM (beats per minute) number when in the manual tempo mode. The "tap" button allows you to calculate a sort of "ball park" tempo of the song or piece of music you have in your Session at the time. This is in the case if you don't know the real Session's tempo. To use the "tap" button, simply click four times on it with the mouse and the BPM number will appear in the tempo box (Fig. 9.19d). The Session tempo then will be changed to the number you came out with when you tapped the button four times.

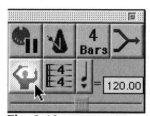

Fig. 9.19a Turning the Conductor button on.

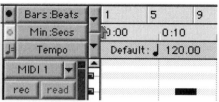

Fig. 9.19b The tempo (120.00) on the tempo ruler.

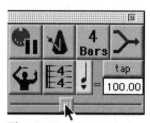

Fig. 9.19c Moving the tempo slider to 100.00 BPM.

Fig. 9.19d Tapping the "tap" button to calculate the Session's real tempo.

The "Meter" button

The "Meter" button displays the Session's current meter based on the play location. To change the meter:

a) Double-click the Meter button to open the "Tempo/Meter Change" window, or go to the MIDI pop-up menu and select the "Change Meter" command (Fig. 9.20a).

b) Type the new meter where it says "Meter" and then click on "Apply" (Fig. 9.20b).

c) Once the meter is changed, you can see the new meter through the "Meter" button in the Transport window (Fig. 9.20c).

Fig. 9.20a Selecting the "Change Meter" command.

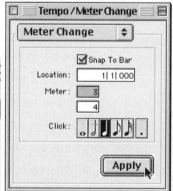

Fig. 9.20b Changing the meter of the Session to 3/4.

Fig. 9.20c The new meter is displayed on the Meter button.

The "Tempo" button

Whatever the tempo the Pro Tools session you are currently working on is in, the "Tempo" button will display it. In other words, it shows the Session's current tempo based on the play location. When you create a new Session, the default tempo is 120.00 BPM. You can change this tempo by turning the Conductor button off. This means that Pro Tools goes into the manual tempo mode, which is when you can change it. You can even tap in a tempo, either by tapping on the "tap" button or a MIDI controller.

How to configure OMS in Pro Tools

As I mentioned earlier in this chapter, if you are going to work with MIDI in Pro Tools, you must configure your OMS or Open Music System first (for Macintosh only). The OMS is an application which can be accessed through the Pro Tools software. This application used by Pro Tools to be able to recognize any MIDI devices (MIDI interfaces, instruments, peripherals, etc.) that are connected to your system setup so you can select any of them to playback and record MIDI using Pro Tools' built-in MIDI sequencer.

The OMS configuration process is not difficult at all, even though it seems like it. If you follow the next step-by-step instructions, you will successfully be able to configure it. I will first explain the process for Pro Tools version 5.xx or lower for those who still are using Mac OS 9.x.x, and then, for those using 6.0 or higher on Mac OSX.

To configure OMS for Pro Tools 5.xx or lower:
a) When you launch Pro Tools for the first time, automatically the OMS application will ask you to create a "new studio setup". If you cancel this request because you don't have any MIDI devices connected in your Pro Tools system at the moment, then you can create it at a later time. If this is the case, select the "OMS MIDI Setup" command in the Setups pop-up menu (Fig. 9.21a). A dialog window will appear prompting you to either create a "New Easy Setup"; to "Edit Custom Setup" in case you want to reconfigure an existing one; to generate an "Error Log"; or simply to click on "OK" if you decide not to go ahead with the process.
b) If you want to create a new setup, then click on the "New Easy Setup" option (Fig. 9.21b).
c) Another dialog window will appear asking you to select the serial port you have your MIDI devices connected to. Make the selection if you are using

an old-model Macintosh computer. If your computer has a USB port, then don't select anything on either of the two checkboxes; just click on "Search" (Fig. 9.21c).

Fig. 9.21a Selecting the "OMS MIDI Setup" command.

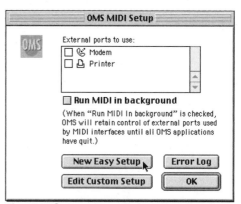

Fig. 9.21b Creating a "New Easy Setup."

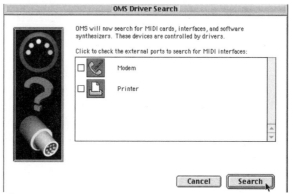

Fig. 9.21c Searching for any devices connected in your computer.

d) By this time, OMS will search for and display any detected MIDI devices installed on your computer such as MIDI interfaces, OMS drivers, and MIDI cards, but not external MIDI devices. If the list seems incorrect, click on the "Troubleshoot" button to find out why a device that should be on the list is missing. If you want to add any drivers manually, then click on "Customize" or "cancel" to abort the OMS setup. If everything looks good on the list, click "OK" (Fig. 9.21d).

e) A new dialog window displaying a representation of your studio will appear. Notice in Fig. 9.21e two MIDI ports were displayed in this OMS Studio Setup example. In this case, a Midiman "MIDI Sport 2x2" USB MIDI interface is connected to the computer; therefore it shows "Port 1" and "Port 2". The keyboard icon with the question mark on it means that OMS detected non-recognizable external MIDI devices connected to these ports, i.e., synthesizers, samplers, drum machines, etc. Returning to Fig. 9.21e, notice both ports are checked because they will be used to connect external MIDI devices to playback and record MIDI in Pro Tools. Once you have checked all the ports you will be using in your MIDI interface setup and to leave the OMS MIDI Device Setup window, click on the "OK" button (Fig. 9.21e).

f) Now you need to define all the MIDI devices in your OMS Studio Setup, so go to the Setups pop-up menu and select the "OMS Studio Setup..." command (Fig. 9.21f).

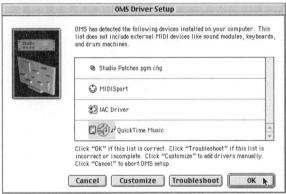

Fig. 9.21d The detected MIDI devices such as MIDI interfaces, OMS drivers, and MIDI cards.

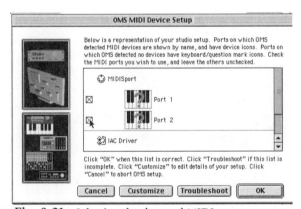

Fig. 9.21e Selecting the detected MIDI ports you are going to be using from your MIDI interface.

Fig. 9.21f Choosing the "OMS Studio Setup" command to configure your studio.

g) A new window, the "Auto Setup" window will appear showing you all the MIDI ports that were found. In this example, since the MIDI Sport 2x2 has only two MIDI inputs and two MIDI outputs, only two ports are shown (Fig. 9.21g).

h) To define a new MIDI device for your setup, go to the Studio pop-up menu and select the "New Device" command (Fig. 9.21h). A dialog window called "MIDI Device Info." will show prompting you to select the manufacture and model of your external MIDI device in your setup.

i) Click on the "Manuf" pop-up selector (Fig. 9.21i).

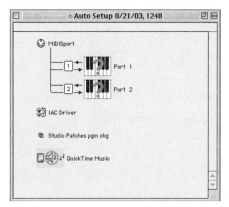

Fig. 9.21g The Auto Setup window to configure your studio.

Fig. 9.21h Adding a new device in your studio configuration.

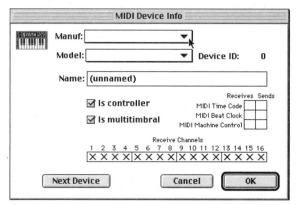

Fig. 9.21i Placing the cursor to select the manufacturer of the device just added in your studio configuration.

j) Select the name of the company that manufactured your MIDI device. In the example I have selected "Korg" (Fig. 9.21j).

k) Now click on "Model" and select the MIDI device you have. In the example, I have selected the "01/W pro X" from Korg (Fig. 9.21k). If the name of your device is not on the model list, then select "other" and enter the name of your device in the "Name" dialog box.

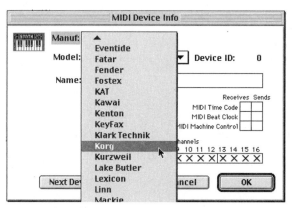

Fig. 9.21j Selecting the device's manufacturer.

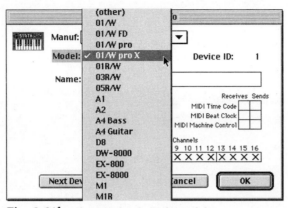

Fig. 9.21k Selecting the device's model.

l) Make the appropriate settings for your device; i.e., if you will be recording MIDI in Pro Tools from your MIDI device, which means it has a keyboard or some type of triggering device, then check the "Is controller" checkbox (Fig. 9.21l). If your MIDI device can receive multiple MIDI channels at the time, check the "Is multitimbral" box. Also, you need to select the receiving channels for your device. Finally, if your device can send and/or receive MIDI Time Code (MTC), MIDI Beat Clock, and MIDI Machine Control commands, make the appropriate selections. Consult your device's instruction manuals if you are not sure of the settings for your MIDI machine.

m) Once you have defined all your MIDI devices in your setup and click on "OK," the "Auto Setup" window will now show all MIDI-device icons you just added connected to the MIDI interface's ports you will be using (Fig. 9.21m).

n) Finally, assign on a MIDI track the input and output MIDI channels you wish to use to record and playback MIDI data in and from Pro Tools (Fig. 9.21n).

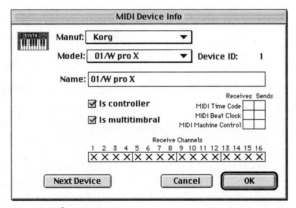

Fig. 9.21l Making the proper setting assignments for the device just added.

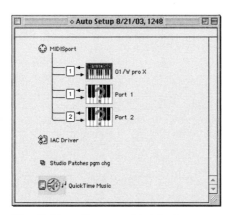

Fig. 9.21m The new added device connected to a MIDI port after selecting its manufacturer and model.

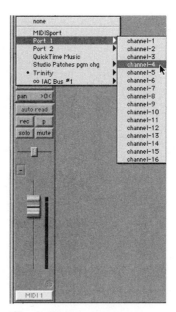

Fig. 9.21n Selecting the MIDI channel output in the MIDI track using "Port 1."

The OMS configuration process in Pro Tools 6.0 or higher is very similar to the one in Pro Tools version 5.x.x or lower. Since Pro Tools 6.0 uses the Mac OSX operating system, the windows look different. For this reason, instead of the Setups pop-up menu showing the commands "OMS MIDI Setup" and "OMS Studio Setup," now it shows it as "Edit MIDI Studio Setup." When you access this command, a window named "Audio MIDI Setup" or AMS will be displayed on your screen. This window allows you to set up your audio and MIDI devices in your system. Through this window, you can change the "View Icon Size," configure your MIDI studio ("Configuration"), "Add Device," "Remove Device," "Show Info," "Rescan MIDI," and "Clear Cables," among other things.

To configure the OMS version for Pro Tools 6.0 or higher, follow these steps:
a) Select "Edit MIDI Studio Setup" located in the Setups pop-up menu (Fig. 9.22a).
b) A window named "Audio MIDI Setup" or AMS will be displayed on your screen (Fig. 9.22b). If a USB MIDI interface is already connected to your computer, its icon will appear in the AMS window (Fig. 9.22b); otherwise, you can click on "Rescan MIDI."

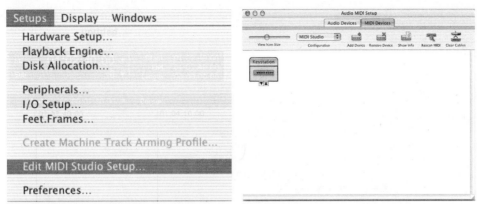

Fig. 9.22a Selecting "Edit MIDI Studio Setup" to configure your studio setup.

Fig. 9.22b The AMS window showing a detected MIDI interface.

c) To create a new MIDI studio configuration, click on the "Configuration" pop-up menu and select "New Configuration…" (Fig. 9.22c). If you want to edit an existing one, then select the "Edit Configuration…" command.

d) Define your MIDI devices by clicking on the "Add Device" button (Fig. 9.22d).

e) An icon representing your external MIDI device will appear in the AMS window (Fig. 9.22e).

Fig. 9.22c Selecting the "New Configuration" command in Pro Tools 6.0 or higher.

Fig. 9.22d Clicking on the "Add device" button.

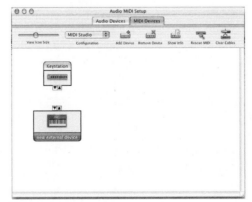

Fig. 9.22e The added device's icon appears in the AMS window.

f) To define a device, double-click on the device's icon or click on the "Show Info" button (Fig. 9.22f).

g) Assign the manufacturer and model of your device (Fig. 9.22g).

Fig. 9.22f Clicking on the "Show Info" button to assign the device's manufacturer and model.

Fig. 9.22g Selecting the device's manufacturer and model.

h) Make the appropriate settings such as which MIDI channels your device will transmit and receive MIDI data to and from Pro Tools, does it generate and/or read "clock" information, its SysEx information, etc. (Fig. 9.22h).

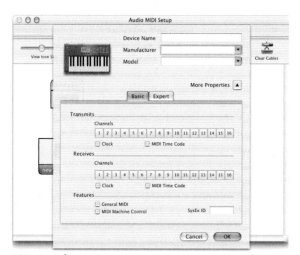

Fig. 9.22h Making the device's proper assignments, such as which MIDI channels will transmit and receive MIDI data to and from Pro Tools.

i) After defining all the external devices in your system, click and hold the mouse on the "up arrow" of the MIDI interface icon and drag it to the "up arrow" of your defined MIDI device. If more than one device, do it to all of them. You will see a "cable" appearing simulating the MIDI In connection between both the MIDI interface and your MIDI device (Fig. 9.22i).

j) Now, click and hold the mouse on the "down arrow" of the MIDI interface icon and drag it to the "down arrow" of your defined MIDI device. If more than one device, do it to all of them. You will see a "cable" appearing

simulating the MIDI Out connection between both the MIDI interface and
your MIDI device (Fig. 9.22j).

k) If for any reason you want to disconnect a device from one end, you can
just click on the "Clear Cables" button in the AMS window (Fig. 9.22k)

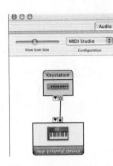

Fig. 9.22i Making
the MIDI In "cable"
connection between
the MIDI interface
and the MIDI
device.

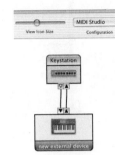

Fig. 9.22j Making
the MIDI Out
"cable" connection
between the MIDI
interface and the
MIDI device.

Fig. 9.22k The
"Clear Cables" button
delete any connec-
tions if needed.

MIDI connections using a Pro Tools TDM or LE system

Depending on your MIDI application needs with your Pro Tools system, there are
many different ways to connect your particular system. Over the next few pages I
will show you some examples of how to connect your MIDI devices to your Pro
Tools TDM or LE system. This may not be your exact situation, but you can study
them and get ideas of how to apply them to your own Pro Tools setup.

Diagram 9.2 shows two different configurations using an Mbox. The one on
top is using a USB MIDI interface to record and playback MIDI in Pro Tools. The
diagram on the bottom half of the page uses a USB MIDI controller keyboard
such as Midiman's Oxygen 8. This controller acts as a MIDI interface, since it has
one built-in. Recording MIDI with one of these keyboards is no problem. If you
want to playback the MIDI data you recorded with this keyboard controller, you
will have to connect a MIDI sound module or a MIDI synthesizer to be able to
listen to the MIDI data. This is because MIDI controllers like the one in the diagram don't generate sound.

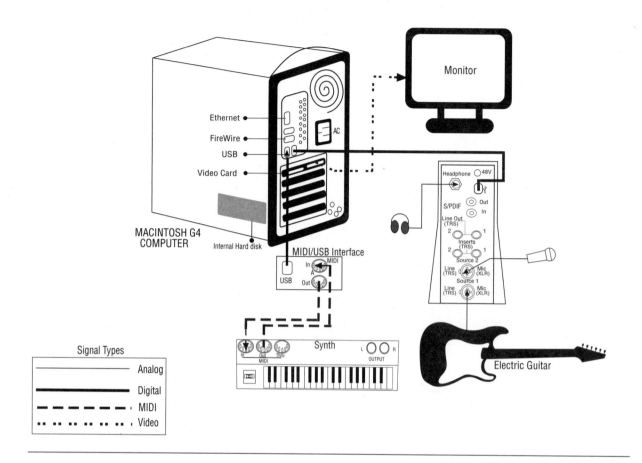

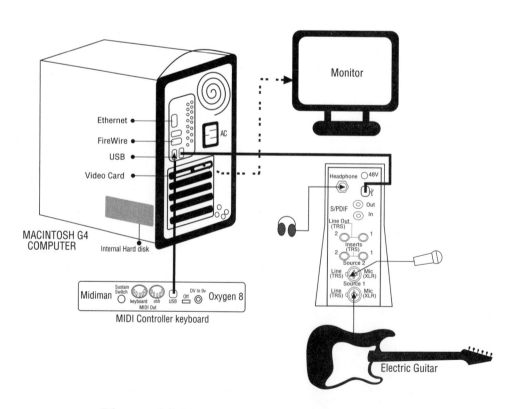

Diagram 9.2 Two MIDI Setups with the Mbox.

Explanation of the hardware MIDI connections using an Mbox

Connections:

1. Connecting the Mbox to the computer.
   - Using a USB cable, connect the USB port on the Mbox to an available USB port on your computer.

2. Connecting a microphone to the Mbox.
   - Using a XLR-male-to-XLR-female cable, connect the XLR-male connector of the microphone cable to "SOURCE 2" MIC (XLR) input.

3. Connecting a guitar to the Mbox.
   - Using a ¼"-male-to-¼"-male cable, connect an electric guitar to "SOURCE 1" LINE (TRS) input.

4. Connecting headphones to the Mbox.
   - Connect the ¼" TRS connector of the headphones to the "HEADPHONE" jack on the Mbox's rear panel. You can also use headphones with ⅛" male connectors by inserting them in the Mbox's frontpanel ⅛" headphone jack.

5. Connecting a USB MIDI interface to the computer.
   - Using a USB cable, connect the MIDI interface's USB port to any available USB connector on the back of the computer.

6. Connecting the MIDI interface to a MIDI synthesizer (top diagram only).
   - Using a MIDI cable, connect the MIDI IN jack on the MIDI interface to the MIDI OUT on the MIDI synthesizer.
   - Using a second MIDI cable, connect the MIDI OUT jack on the MIDI interface to the MIDI IN jack on the MIDI synthesizer.

7. Connecting a MIDI controller to the computer (bottom diagram only).
   - Using a USB cable, connect the USB port on the MIDI controller (an Oxygen 8 for example) to an available USB port on your computer.

Software Setup

Assuming all the connections are correctly done, follow these steps to configure your MIDI devices and to be able to record and play MIDI information in a Pro Tools LE Session using your Mbox.

- Create a new Pro Tools Session.
- Create a MIDI track.

- If you are working with Pro Tools version 5.x.x, you will need to configure your OMS studio setup. First make sure Pro Tools is recognizing your MIDI interface. To do so, go to the Setups pop-up menu and select the "OMS MIDI Setup" command. Create a "New Easy Setup" and follow all the instructions until you see your MIDI interface being recognized by Pro Tools. Now configure your OMS studio setup to define all your external MIDI devices by going to the Setups pop-up menu and selecting the "OMS Studio setup…" command. Follow the instructions and define all your MIDI devices.

- If you are working in Pro Tools 6.0 or higher, go to Setups > Edit MIDI Studio Setup. A new window with two tabs will appear on your screen. Make sure the "MIDI Devices" tab is selected.

  - Click on "Add Device."

  - Double-click on the newly added device icon on your screen.

  - Select the "Manufacturer" and "Model" of your devices.

  - Click on "More Properties," make sure you are on the "Basic" tab, and select the channels you want to use to transmit and receive MIDI data from and to Pro Tools LE.

  - Go to the Mix window and assign the appropriate MIDI inputs and outputs with their respective MIDI channels on a MIDI track or tracks. Don't forget to make the respective MIDI-channel assignments on your external MIDI devices as well.

  - Record-enable the MIDI track (press the "rec" button), and press the Record button and then Play button in the Transport window.

- Once the recording starts, play on the MIDI synthesizer or MIDI controller's keys to enter the MIDI data into Pro Tools.

- When you finish recording, you will notice the data recorded in the MIDI track.

- Click on the Play button of the Transport window to playback the MIDI information you recorded in Pro Tools. If all your connections and MIDI assignments are correct, you should be able to hear sound coming out of your synthesizer or MIDI sound module.

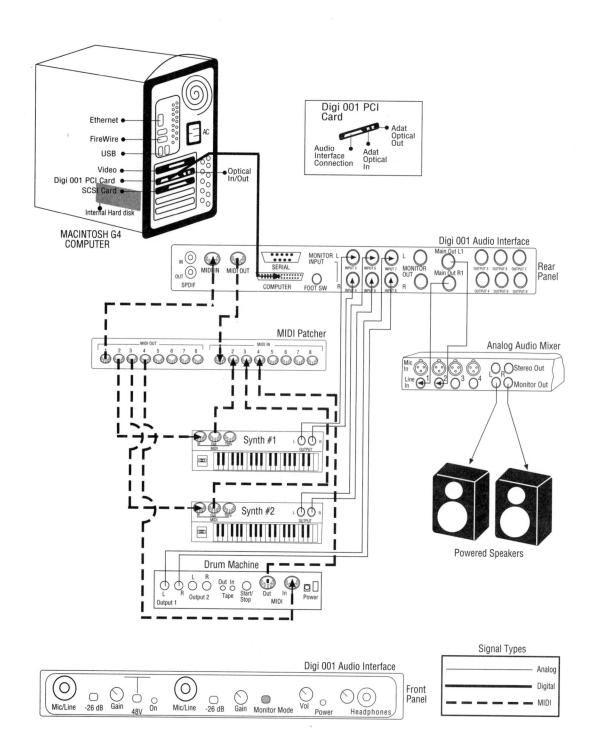

Diagram 9.3 A MIDI setup with the Digi 001.

Explanation of the hardware MIDI connections using a Digi 001

Diagram 9.3 shows a MIDI connection using the Digi 001, a MIDI patcher, two synthesizers, a drum machine, and a small analog mixer for monitoring more than one output signal.

Connections:

1. Connecting the Digi 001 audio interface to the computer.
   - Plug the Digi 001 interface cable to the connector labeled "COMPUTER" on the rear panel of the Digi 001 audio interface. Connect the other end of the interface cable to the Digi 001 PCI Card located inside of the computer (see Diagram 9.3).

2. Connecting the Digi 001 audio interface to the MIDI patcher.
   - Using a MIDI cable, connect the MIDI output 1 of the MIDI patcher to the MIDI input port of the Digi 001 audio interface.
   - Using a second MIDI cable, connect the MIDI output of the Digi 001 audio interface to the MIDI input 1 of the MIDI patcher.

3. Connecting the MIDI patcher outputs to the synthesizers and drum machine MIDI inputs. Using six MIDI cables, make the following connections:
   - MIDI OUT #2 of the MIDI patcher to the MIDI input of synth #1.
   - MIDI OUT #3 of the MIDI patcher to the MIDI input of synth #2.
   - MIDI OUT #4 of the MIDI patcher to the MIDI input of the drum machine.
   - MIDI OUT of synth #1 to MIDI IN #2 of the MIDI patcher.
   - MIDI OUT of synth #2 to MIDI IN #3 of the MIDI patcher.
   - MIDI OUT of the drum machine to the MIDI IN #4 of the MIDI patcher.

4. Connecting the synths and drum machine audio outputs to the Digi 001 audio interface. Using six ¼"-TRS-male-to-male cables, make the following connections:
   - "OUTPUT L" of synth #1 to "LINE IN 4" of the Digi 001 audio interface.
   - "OUTPUT R" of synth #1 to "LINE IN 3" of the Digi 001 audio interface.
   - "OUTPUT L" of synth #2 to "LINE IN 6" of the Digi 001 audio interface.
   - "OUTPUT R" of synth #2 to "LINE IN 5" of the Digi 001 audio interface.

- "OUTPUT L" of synth #2 to "LINE IN 6" of the Digi 001 audio interface.
- "OUTPUT L" of the drum machine to "LINE IN 8" of the Digi 001 audio interface.
- "OUTPUT R" of the drum machine to "LINE IN 7" of the Digi 001 audio interface.

5. Connecting the Digi 001 audio interface to an analog audio mixer for monitoring and submixing.
   - Using a ¼"-TRS-male-to-¼"-TRS-male cable, connect the "MAIN OUT R1" of the Digi 001 audio interface to "LINE IN 1" of the audio mixer.
   - Using another ¼"-TRS-male-to-¼"-TRS-male, connect the "MAIN OUT L1" of the Digi 001 audio interface to "LINE IN 2" of the audio mixer.

6. Connecting the speakers to the analog audio mixer for monitoring and submixing.
   - Connect the "MONITOR OUT L" of the audio mixer to the left speaker, using a ¼"-TRS-male to whatever type of connector your speaker has.
   - Connect the "MONITOR OUT R" on the audio mixer to the right speaker, using a ¼"-TRS-male to whatever type of connector your speaker has.

Note: Generally, speakers use XLR or ¼" connectors, but it would be a good idea to consult the speaker's documentation for detailed information.

Software Setup

Assuming all the connections are correctly done, follow these steps to configure your MIDI devices and to be able to record and play MIDI information in a Pro Tools LE Session using your Digi 001.
- Create a new Pro Tools Session.
- Create a MIDI track.

- If you are working with Pro Tools version 5.x.x, you will need to configure your OMS studio setup. First make sure Pro Tools is recognizing your MIDI interface, in this case, the Digi 001. To do this, go to the Setups pop-up menu and select the "OMS MIDI Setup" command. Create a "New Easy Setup" and follow all the instructions until you see your MIDI interface being recognized by Pro Tools. Now configure your OMS studio setup to define all your external MIDI devices by going to the Setups pop-up menu and selecting the "OMS Studio setup…" command. Follow the instructions and define all your MIDI devices.

- If you are working in Pro Tools 6.0 or higher, go to Setups > Edit MIDI Studio Setup. A new window with two tabs will appear on your screen. Make sure the "MIDI Devices" tab is selected.

  - Click on "Add Device."

  - Double-click on the newly added device icon on your screen.

  - Select the "Manufacturer" and "Model" of your devices.

  - Click on "More Properties," make sure you are on the "Basic" tab, and select the channels you want to use to transmit and receive MIDI data from and to Pro Tools LE.

  - Go to the Mix window and assign the appropriate MIDI inputs and outputs with their respective MIDI channels on a MIDI track or tracks. Don't forget to make the respective MIDI channel assignments on your external MIDI devices as well.

  - Record-enable the MIDI track (press the "rec" button), and press the Record button and then Play button in the Transport window.
  - Once the recording starts, play on the MIDI synthesizer or MIDI controller's keys to enter the MIDI data into Pro Tools.

  - When you finish recording, you will notice the data recorded in the MIDI track.

  - Click on the Play button of the Transport window to playback the MIDI information you recorded in Pro Tools. If all your connections and MIDI assignments are correct, you should be able to hear sound coming out of your synthesizer or MIDI sound module.

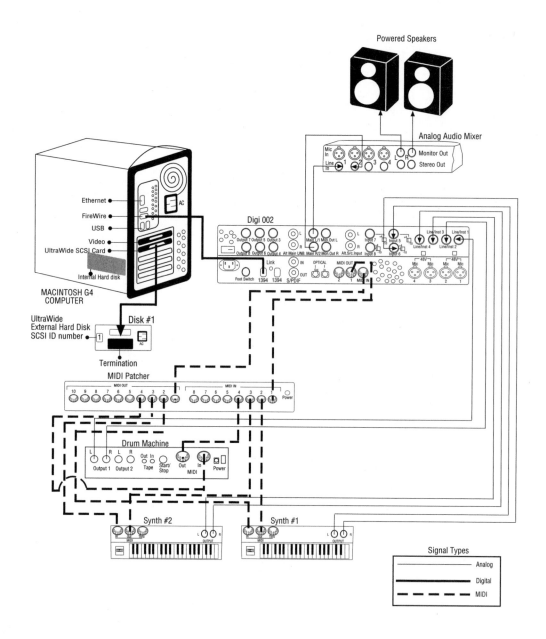

Diagram 9.4 A MIDI setup with the Digi 002.

Explanation of the hardware MIDI connections using a Digi 002

Diagram 9.4 shows a MIDI connection similar the previous one, except this time a Digi 002 is used. In case you are not using a MIDI patcher or patchbay, you can make the synths and drum machine MIDI connections in a daisy-chain manner (see Diagram 9.1 above) and using the MIDI in and two MIDI outs from the Digi 002.

Connections:

This time I would like to show how can you connect an external UltraWide SCSI hard disk to your Digi 002 system. Obviously, it would be easier to use a FireWire external hard drive, but it is good to know how you can implement a faster drive using an UltraWide SCSI disk. Of course, to use a SCSI drive, you must install an UltraWide SCSI card in your computer. Visit www.digidesign.com for more information on this card.

1. Connecting an external hard drive in your system.
   - Using a short UltraWide SCSI cable, connect the UltraWide SCSI card in your computer to one of the UltraWide SCSI ports of the external hard Disk #1. Don't forget to assign a valid SCSI ID number on your external drive.
   - If this is the last disk drive in the chain, terminate it as seen in Diagram 9.4.
   - If using an external FireWire drive instead, simply connect the FireWire port of the drive to an available FireWire port in the computer.

2. Connecting the Digi 002 to the computer.
   - Using a FireWire cable, connect the "FIREWIRE 1394" port on the rear panel of the Digi 002 to an available FireWire port located on the back of the computer.

3. Connecting the Digi 002 to a MIDI patcher.
   - Using a MIDI cable, connect the MIDI output 1 of the MIDI patcher to the MIDI IN of the Digi 002.
   - Using another MIDI cable, connect the MIDI OUT #1 of the Digi 002 to the MIDI input 1 of the MIDI patcher.

4. Connecting the synths and drum machine to the MIDI patcher. Using six MIDI cables, make the following connections:

- MIDI OUT #2 of the MIDI patcher to the MIDI input of Synth #1.

- MIDI OUT #3 of the MIDI patcher to the MIDI input of Synth #2.

- MIDI OUT #4 of the MIDI patcher to the MIDI input of the drum machine.

- MIDI OUT of synth #1 to MIDI IN #2 of the MIDI patcher.

- MIDI OUT of Synth #2 to MIDI IN #3 of the MIDI patcher.

- MIDI OUT of the drum machine to the MIDI IN #4 of the MIDI patcher.

5. Connecting the synths and drum machine audio outputs to the Digi 002 audio interface. Using six ¼"-TRS-male-to-male cables, make the following connections:

- "OUTPUT L" of synth #1 to "LINE IN 4" of the Digi 002 audio interface.

- "OUTPUT R" of synth #1 to "LINE IN 3" of the Digi 002 audio interface.

- "OUTPUT R" of synth #2 to "LINE IN 5" of the Digi 002 audio interface.

- "OUTPUT L" of synth #2 to "LINE IN 6" of the Digi 002 audio interface.

- "OUTPUT L" of the drum machine to "LINE IN 8" of the Digi 002 audio interface.

- "OUTPUT R" of the drum machine to "LINE IN 7" of the Digi 002 audio interface.

6. Connecting the Digi 002 audio interface to an analog audio mixer for monitoring and submixing.

- Using a ¼"-TRS-male-to-¼"-TRS-male cable, connect "MAIN L/1" of the Digi 002 audio interface to "LINE IN 1" of the audio mixer.

- Using another ¼"-TRS-male-to-male cable, connect "MAIN R/2" of the Digi 002 audio interface to "LINE IN 2" of the audio mixer.

7. Connecting the speakers to the analog audio mixer for monitoring and submixing.

- Connect the "MONITOR OUT L" of the audio mixer to the left speaker, using a ¼"-TRS-male to whatever type of connector your speaker has.
- Connect the "MONITOR OUT R" on the audio mixer to the right speaker, using a ¼"-TRS-male to whatever type of connector your speaker has.

Note: Generally, speakers use XLR or ¼" connectors, but it would be a good idea to consult the speaker's documentation for detailed information.

Software Setup

Assuming all the connections are correctly done, follow these steps to configure your MIDI devices and to be able to record and play MIDI information in a Pro Tools LE session using your Digi 002.

- Create a new Pro Tools Session.
- Create a MIDI track.

- If you are working with Pro Tools version 5.x.x, you will need to configure your OMS studio setup. First make sure Pro Tools is recognizing your MIDI interface, in this case, the Digi 002. To do this, go to the Setups pop-up menu and select the "OMS MIDI Setup" command. Create a "New Easy Setup" and follow all the instructions until you see your MIDI interface being recognized by Pro Tools. Now configure your OMS studio setup to define all your external MIDI devices by going to the Setups pop-up menu and selecting the "OMS Studio setup…" command. Follow the instructions and define all your MIDI devices.

- If you are working in Pro Tools 6.0 or higher, go to Setups > Edit MIDI Studio Setup. A new window with two tabs will appear on your screen. Make sure the "MIDI Devices" tab is selected.

  - Click on "Add Device."

  - Double-click on the newly added device icon on your screen.

  - Select the "Manufacturer" and "Model" of your devices.

  - Click on "More Properties," make sure you are on the "Basic" tab, and select the channels you want to use to transmit and receive MIDI data from and to Pro Tools LE.

  - Go to the Mix window and assign the appropriate MIDI inputs and outputs with their respective MIDI channels on a MIDI track or tracks. Don't forget to make the respective MIDI channel assignments on your external MIDI devices as well.

- Record-enable the MIDI track (press the "rec" button), and press the Record button and then Play button in the Transport window.

- Once the recording starts, play on the MIDI synthesizer or MIDI controller's keys to enter the MIDI data into Pro Tools.

- When you finish recording, you will notice the data recorded in the MIDI track.

- Click on the Play button of the Transport window to playback the MIDI information you recorded in Pro Tools. If all your connections and MIDI assignments are correct, you should be able to hear sound coming out of your synthesizer or MIDI sound module.

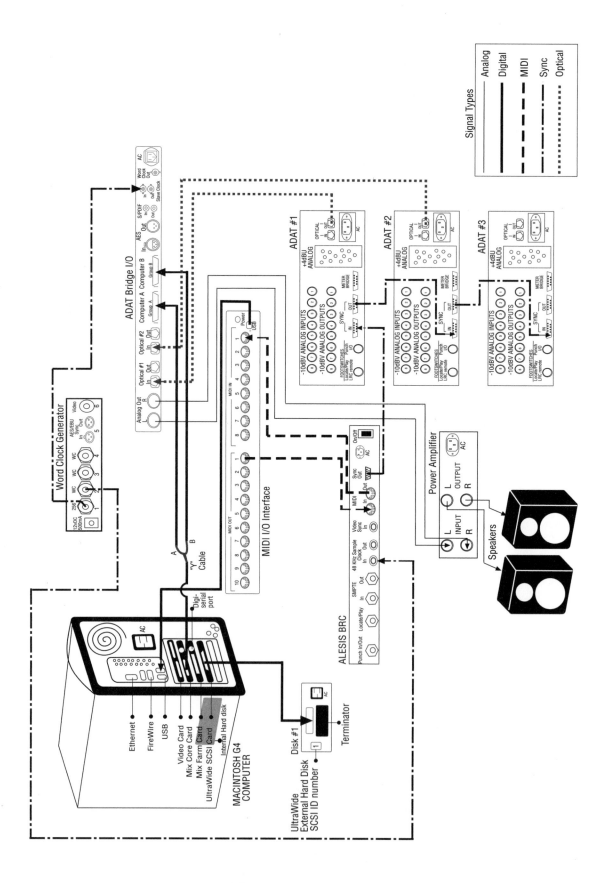

Diagram 9.5 A MIDI setup with a Mix system.

Explanation of the hardware MIDI connections using a Pro Tools MIX TDM system

Diagram 9.5 shows an example of a 24-track digital transfer from ADAT machines to a Pro Tools 24 MIX TDM system. In this scenario, a Digidesign's ADAT Bridge I/O is used for the digital transfer. Since the ADAT Bridge I/O can only transfer 16 tracks at the time, MIDI is needed to carry the necessary time code (MIDI Time Code or MTC) to synchronize the third tape (tracks 17 to 24) once the first 16 tracks have been transfered.

Connections:

1. Connecting an external hard drive in your system.
    - Using a short UltraWide SCSI cable, connect the UltraWide SCSI card in your computer to one of the UltraWide SCSI ports of the external hard Disk #1. Don't forget to assign a valid SCSI ID number on your external drive.
    - If this is the last disk drive in the chain, terminate it using an UltraWide SCSI terminator as seen in Diagram 9.5.

2. Connecting the ADAT Bridge to the MIX Core PCI card in the computer.
    - Using a Digidesign "Y" cable, connect the single-side connector to the MIX Core PCI card in the computer.
    - Connect the "A" side of the "Y" cable to the port labeled "Group A" located on the rear panel of the ADAT Bridge I/O.
    - Connect the "B" side of the "Y" cable to the port labeled "Group B" located on the rear panel of the ADAT Bridge I/O.

3. Connecting the ADAT machines to the ADAT Bridge I/O.
    - Using an optical cable, connect the "OPTICAL OUT" port of ADAT #1 to the "Optical In #1" port of the ADAT Bridge I/O.
    - Using another optical cable, connect the "OPTICAL OUT" port of ADAT #2 to the "Optical In #2" port of the ADAT Bridge I/O.

4. Connecting a USB MIDI interface to the computer.
    - Using a USB cable, connect the USB port on the rear panel of your USB MIDI interface to an available USB port on the back of your computer.

5. Connecting a USB MIDI interface to the Alesis BRC.
   • Using a MIDI cable, connect the MIDI OUT of the Alesis BRC to the MIDI IN #1 port of the USB MIDI interface.
   • Using another MIDI cable, connect the MIDI OUT #1 port of the USB MIDI interface to the MIDI IN port of the Alesis BRC.

6. Connecting a Master Word Clock generator to the ADAT Bridge I/O.
   • Using a BNC cable, connect the 256x clock output of a Master Word Clock generator to the "SLAVE CLOCK IN" of the ADAT Bridge I/O.

7. Connecting a Master Word Clock generator to the Alesis BRC.
   • Using a BNC cable, connect the 48kHz Word Clock output of a Master Word Clock generator to the "48kHz Sample Clock In" of the Alesis BRC.

8. Connecting the BRC and ADATs together.
   • Using a shielded dual-male "9-pin D connector" cable, connect the "Sync Out" port of BRC to the "Sync In" port of ADAT #1.
   • Using a second shielded dual-male "9-pin D connector" cable, connect the "Sync Out" port of ADAT #1 to the "Sync In" port of ADAT #2.
   • Using a third shielded dual-male "9-pin D connector" cable, connect the "Sync Out" port of ADAT #2 to the "Sync In" port of ADAT #3.

9. Connecting the audio output of the ADAT Bridge I/O to a power amplifier.
   • Using a ¼"-TRS-male-to-male cable, connect the "Analog OUT L" on the ADAT Bridge I/O to the left input of your power amplifier.
   • Using another ¼"-TRS-male-to-male cable, connect the "Analog OUT R" on the ADAT Bridge I/O to the right input of your power amplifier.

10. Connecting the power amplifier to the speakers.
    • Connect the left output jack of the power amplifier to the left speaker, using a ¼"-male-to-XLR-male or ¼"-male cable. Note: This end of the cable depends on your speakers' input connectors.
    • Connect the right output jack of the power amplifier to the right speaker, using a ¼"-male-to-XLR-male or ¼"-male cable. Note: This end of the cable depends on your speakers' input connectors.

- If your speakers are powered, meaning they already have a power amplifier built-in, you do not need to connect them to an external power amplifier. In this case, you may just connect them directly to the ADAT Bridge I/O outputs.

Software Setup

Assuming all the connections are correctly done, follow the next software-setting steps to configure your MIDI devices and to be able to synchronize using MIDI Time Code, Pro Tools, and the BRC for a 24-track digital transfer.

- Create a new Pro Tools Session.
- Create 16 mono audio tracks.

- If you are working with Pro Tools version 5.x.x, you will need to configure your OMS studio setup. First make sure Pro Tools is recognizing your USB MIDI interface. To do this, go to the Setups pop-up menu and select the "OMS MIDI Setup" command. Create a "New Easy Setup" and follow all the instructions until you see your MIDI interface being recognized by Pro Tools. Now configure your OMS studio setup to define all your external MIDI devices by going to the Setups pop-up menu and selecting the "OMS Studio setup…" command. Follow the instructions and define all your MIDI devices, including the BRC, since it will generate the MIDI Time Code for synchronization.

- You need to assign in Pro Tools the audio interface you are using, in this case the ADAT Bridge I/O. For this, go to the Setups pop-up menu and select the "Playback Engine Setup" command. Since in this case a "Y" cable is being used, you need to select in the "Interface Port" dialog box "A." This means the MIX Core PCI card is connected to the "A" side of the "Y" cable. Assign the audio interface being used on the "A" side of the "Y" cable, in this case, the "ADAT Bridge I/O (tracks 1-8)." Since the MIX Core PCI card is connected to the "B" side of the "Y" cable as well, click on the "Interface Port" dialog box to select the "B" side of the "Y" cable. This time assign the audio interface as "ADAT Bridge I/O (tracks 9-16)." The other assignments you must do for both sides of the "Y" cable (A and B) in the "Playback Engine Setup" command before the digital transfer can be accomplished are: set the "Sample Rate" to 44100 or 48000, depending on your session; the "Sync Mode" needs to be set to "ADAT Optical"; and "Ch 1-2 Input" needs to be set to "ADAT."

- To make sure you have chosen the right assignments, go to Setups pop-up menu and select the "Hardware Setup" command. The options should be: Card "MIX Card #1," "Interface Port: A," "Sync Mode: ADAT Optical," and "Ch 1-2 Input: ADAT." Then select "MIX Card #1," "Interface Port: B," "Sync Mode: ADAT Optical," and "Ch 1-2 Input: ADAT"

- Now, since we are transferring from the ADATs to Pro Tools, make sure the ADAT's sync is set to "Internal," the "Ext. Sync" on the BRC is off, and press the "Gen Sync" button. This enables the BRC to generate the MIDI Time Code.

- One more thing before you have a successful synchronization between the machines: Go to the Setups pop-up menu, select the "Peripherals" command, choose the "Synchronization" tab to select "Generic MTC Reader" from the "Device" pop-up menu, and choose "BRC" from the "Port" pop-up menu of the same window.

- Next, make the proper input and output assignments in Pro Tools' Mix window. You should have the following assignments:

Type of track (mono)	Inputs	Outputs	Inst/Source
Audio tracks # 1–8	A 1-8	A 1-2	(ADAT #1)
Audio tracks # 9–16	B 1-8	A 1-2	(ADAT #2)

- To be able to record any track for the transfer, you must record-enable (press the red "rec" button) the first 16 audio tracks in your Pro Tools Session. You need to set the "Session Start" time in the "Session Setup" window located in the Windows pop-up menu. This is so when you transfer the last eight tracks (17–24) there will be a time reference which Pro Tools can use to start the recording.

- Test if you are getting audio coming from the ADATs on each Pro Tools audio track by pressing Play on the BRC so the ADATs start playing back.

- Once you know audio is coming in, click on the "Online" button in the Transport window. This will allow Pro Tools to accept time code to be able to synchronize with the ADATs.

- If you are ready to transfer the first 16 tracks, then press the Record button in the Transport window. You'll notice it will start flashing. Press the Play button on the BRC. If everything is fine, Pro Tools will be in a "Pause Record Mode" and won't start recording until it reaches the time you specified as the "Session Start" time in the "Session Setup" window. Once it reaches that time location, Pro Tools will start recording.

- To transfer the last eight tracks from the ADATs, create eight more audio tracks in Pro Tools, make the proper assignments such as inputs and outputs, and test to find out if audio is coming in from tracks 17–24. If everything is fine, then press Record in Pro Tools' Transport window and Play on the BRC, and that is it—you successfully digitally transferred 24 tracks from ADAT to Pro Tools in synchronization. Congratulations!

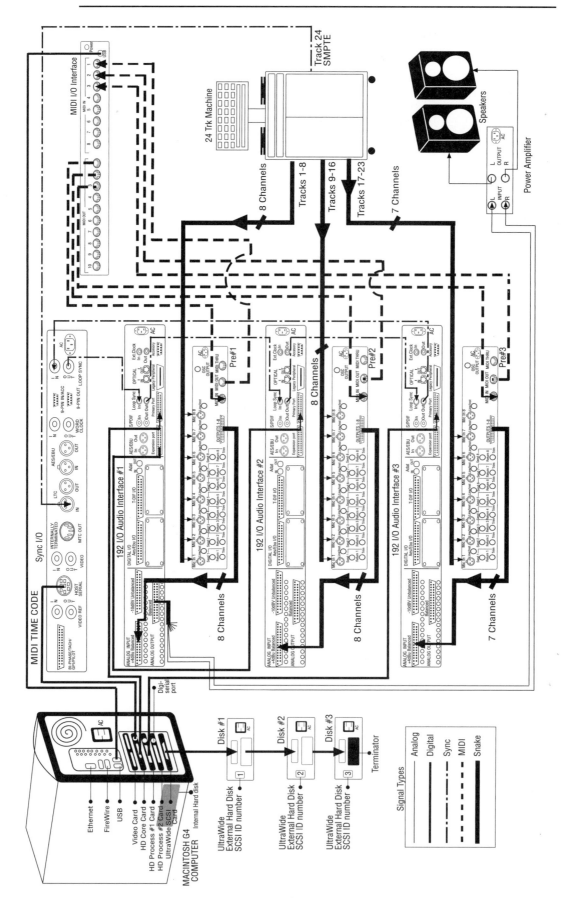

Diagram 9.6 A MIDI setup with an HD System.

Explanation of the hardware MIDI connections using a Pro Tools HD 3 TDM system

So far, I have shown different MIDI scenarios for every Pro Tools system available; this time it's a Pro Tools HD 3 system's turn. The situation is that an analog 24-track transfer needs to be done from a two-inch tape machine to Pro Tools. A Digidesign microphone preamplifier ("PRE") is used to boost the analog audio signal coming from the two-inch tape machine (Diagram 9.6). Also, in this system notice three 192 I/O audio interfaces, a SYNC I/O and a USB MIDI interface (Digidesign's MIDI I/O), and three UltraWide SCSI hard drives are used. The MIDI application in this situation is that since the PRE's parameters, including its input level, can be controlled via MIDI from Pro Tools, a MIDI interface and its connections are necessary.

Connections:

1. Connecting the external UltraWide SCSI hard drives in your system.

- Since three UltraWide SCSI drives are used in this situation, use a short UltraWide SCSI cable and connect one side to the UltraWide SCSI card in your computer. Insert the other side of the UltraWide SCSI cable to one of the ultra wide SCSI ports of the external hard "Disk #1" (SCSI ID #1).

- Using a second UltraWide SCSI cable, connect the other available SCSI port of "Disk #1" to one of the SCSI ports of "Disk #2" (SCSI ID #2).

- Using a third UltraWide SCSI cable, connect the other available port on "Disk #2" to one of the SCSI ports of "Disk #3" (SCSI ID #3)

- Since "Disk #3" is the last hard disk of the chain, make sure to terminate it using an UltraWide SCSI terminator, and plug it into the available SCSI connector on "Disk #3" (see Diagram 9.6).

- Don't forget to assign a valid SCSI ID number on each external hard drive.

- If this is the last disk drive in the chain, terminate it using an UltraWide SCSI terminator as seen in Diagram 9.6.

2. Connecting the 192 I/O audio interfaces to the computer.
- Using a DigiLink cable, connect the HD Core PCI card in your computer (on the back side of your computer) to the "PRIMARY PORT" on the rear panel of the "192 I/O audio interface #1."
- Using another DigiLink cable, connect the "EXPANSION PORT" on "192 I/O audio interface #1" to the "PRIMARY PORT" of the "192 I/O audio interface #2."
- Using a third DigiLink cable, connect the HD Process PCI card #1 in your computer (on the back side of your computer) to the "PRIMARY PORT" on the "192 I/O audio interface #3."

3. Connecting the Loop Sync on the 192 I/O audio interfaces.
- With a BNC cable, connect the "LOOP SYNC OUT" on the "192 I/O audio interface #1" to the "LOOP SYNC IN" connector of the 192 I/O audio interface #2."
- Using another BNC cable, connect the "LOOP SYNC OUT" on the "192 I/O audio interface #2" to the "LOOP SYNC IN" connector of the "192 I/O audio interface #3."

4. Connecting the Sync I/O to the 192 I/O audio interfaces.
- Using a BNC cable, connect the "LOOP SYNC OUT" of the SYNC I/O to the "LOOP SYNC IN" connector of the "192 I/O audio interface #1."
- Using another BNC cable, connect the "LOOP SYNC OUT" of the "192 I/O audio interface #3" to the "LOOP SYNC IN" of the "SYNC I/O."

5. Connecting the Sync I/O to the computer.
- Using a serial cable provided with the Sync I/O, connect the "DigiSerial" port on the HD Core PCI card inside of the computer to the "HOST SERIAL" port on the Sync I/O. This connection is for sending or receiving MTC.

6. Connecting the USB MIDI I/O interface to the computer.
- Using a USB cable, connect the USB port on the back of your computer to the USB port on the MIDI I/O interface.

7. Connecting the SMPTE time code track from the two-inch tape machine to the SYNC I/O.

   - Using an XLR-female-to-male cable, connect the output of track #24 of the tape machine to the "LTC IN" XLR connector in the SYNC I/O. Of course, this assumes there is SMPTE time code on track #24 of the tape machine.

8. Connecting track 1–8 of the 24-track machine to PRE #1.

   Using an eight-channel XLR-female-to-male snake, connect the following:

   - "TRACK 1 OUT" on the 24-track machine to "MIC IN 1" of PRE #1.
   - "TRACK 2 OUT" on the 24-track machine to "MIC IN 2" of PRE #1.
   - "TRACK 3 OUT" on the 24-track machine to "MIC IN 3" of PRE #1.
   - "TRACK 4 OUT" on the 24-track machine to "MIC IN 4" of PRE #1.
   - "TRACK 5 OUT" on the 24-track machine to "MIC IN 5" of PRE #1.
   - "TRACK 6 OUT" on the 24-track machine to "MIC IN 6" of PRE #1.
   - "TRACK 7 OUT" on the 24-track machine to "MIC IN 7" of PRE #1.
   - "TRACK 8 OUT" on the 24-track machine to "MIC IN 8" of PRE #1.

9. Connecting tracks 9–16 of the 24-track machine to PRE #2.

   Using an eight-channel XLR-female-to-male snake, connect the following:

   - "TRACK 9 OUT" on the 24-track machine to "MIC IN 1" of PRE #2.
   - "TRACK 10 OUT" on the 24-track machine to "MIC IN 2" of PRE #2.
   - "TRACK 11 OUT" on the 24-track machine to "MIC IN 3" of PRE #2.
   - "TRACK 12 OUT" on the 24-track machine to "MIC IN 4" of PRE #2.
   - "TRACK 13 OUT" on the 24-track machine to "MIC IN 5" of PRE #2.
   - "TRACK 14 OUT" on the 24-track machine to "MIC IN 6" of PRE #2.
   - "TRACK 15 OUT" on the 24-track machine to "MIC IN 7" of PRE #2.
   - "TRACK 16 OUT" on the 24-track machine to "MIC IN 8" of PRE #2.

10. Connecting tracks 17–24 of the 24-track machine to PRE #3.

    Using an eight-channel XLR-female-to-male snake, connect the following:

    - "TRACK 17 OUT" on the 24-track machineto "MIC IN 1" on PRE #3.
    - "TRACK 18 OUT" on the 24-track machine to "MIC IN 2" on PRE #3.
    - "TRACK 19 OUT" on the 24-track machine to "MIC IN 3" on PRE #3.
    - "TRACK 20 OUT" on the 24-track machine to "MIC IN 4" on PRE #3.

- "TRACK 21 OUT" on the 24-track machine to "MIC IN 5" on PRE #3.
- "TRACK 22 OUT" on the 24-track machine to "MIC IN 6" on PRE #3.
- "TRACK 23 OUT" on the 24-track machine to "MIC IN 7" on PRE #3.
- "TRACK 24 OUT" on the 24-track machine to the SYNC I/O's "LTC IN" connector.

11. Connecting PRE #1 to the "192 I/O audio interface #1."
    - Using a DB25-to-DB25 cable, connect the "Outputs 1–8" on PRE #1 to the "ANALOG INPUT +4dBu Balanced" DB-25 connector of the "192 I/O audio interface #1."

12. Connecting PRE #2 to the 192 I/O audio interface #2.
    - Using a DB25-to-DB25 cable, connect the "Outputs 1–8" on PRE #2 to the "ANALOG INPUT +4dBu Balanced" DB-25 connector of the "192 I/O audio interface #2."

13. Connecting PRE #3 to the 192 I/O audio interface #3.
    - Using a DB25-to-DB25 cable, connect the "Outputs 1–8" on PRE #3 to the "ANALOG INPUT +4dBu Balanced" DB-25 connector of the "192 I/O audio interface #3."

14. Connecting MIDI between the PREs and the MIDI I/O interface.
    - Using a MIDI cable, connect the "MIDI OUT 1" port from the MIDI I/O interface to the "MIDI IN" of the PRE #1.
    - Using a second MIDI cable, connect the "MIDI IN 1" port from the MIDI I/O interface to the "MIDI OUT" of the PRE #1.
    - Using a third MIDI cable, connect the "MIDI OUT 2" port from the MIDI I/O interface to the "MIDI IN" of the PRE #2.
    - Using a fourth MIDI cable, connect the "MIDI IN 2" port from the MIDI I/O interface to the "MIDI OUT" of the PRE #2.
    - Using a fifth MIDI cable, connect the "MIDI OUT 3" port from the MIDI I/O interface to the "MIDI IN" of the PRE #3.
    - Using a sixth MIDI cable, connect the "MIDI IN 3" port from the MIDI I/O interface to the "MIDI OUT" of the PRE #3.

15. Connecting the "192 I/O Audio Interface #1" to the power amplifier.
    - Since only with the "192 I/O audio interface #1" can we monitor the overall output of the HD 3 system, you can simply use a DB25-to-¼"

TRS-male snake to connect the "ANALOG OUTPUT-Balanced" jack on the "192 I/O audio interface #1" to the left and to the right inputs of the power amplifier.

16. Connecting the speakers to the power amplifier.
    • Connect the left output jack of the power amplifier to the left speaker, using a ¼"-male-to-XLR-male or ¼"-male cable. Note: This end of the cable depends on your speakers' input connectors.
    • Connect the right output jack of the power amplifier to the left speaker, using a ¼"-male-to-XLR-male or ¼"-male cable. Note: This end of the cable depends on your speakers' input connectors.

Software Setup

Assuming all the connections are correctly done, follow the next software-setting step to accomplish a successful 24-track analog transfer from a two-inch tape machine to a Pro Tools HD 3 TDM system. These settings will also allow you to configure the MIDI devices used in this scenario, including Digidesign's "PRE" and the MIDI I/O interface.

- First, create a new Pro Tools Session.
- Create 24 mono audio tracks.

- If you are working with Pro Tools version 5.x.x, you will need to configure your OMS studio setup. Make sure Pro Tools is recognizing your USB MIDI interface. To do this, go to the Setups pop-up menu and select the "OMS MIDI Setup" command. Create a "New Easy Setup" and follow all the instructions until youf see your MIDI interface being recognized by Pro Tools. Now configure you OMS studio setup to define all your external MIDI devices by going to the Setups pop-up menu and selecting the "OMS Studio setup…" command. Follow the instructions and define all your MIDI devices including the preamplifiers ("PRE"), since you will be controlling the PRE's parameters via MIDI from the Pro Tools software.

- If you are working in Pro Tools 6.0 or higher, go to Setups > Edit MIDI Studio Setup. A new window with two tabs will appear on your screen. Make sure the "MIDI Devices" tab is selected.

  - Click on "Add Device."

  - Double-click on the newly added device icon on your screen.

  - Select the "Manufacturer" and "Model" of your devices.

  - Click on "More Properties," make sure you are on the "Basic" tab, and select the channels you want to use to transmit and receive MIDI data from and to the Pro Tools software.

  - Make sure the preamps ("PRE") are defined on your OMS Studio Setup properly to be able to control them remotely from Pro Tools. In other words, when you are defining the "PREs," after entering the name of the device (which in this case would be PRE #1 for the first preamp, for example), the only other options needed to be checked in this window are the "Is controller" and the "Receive Channel" number that is going to be used for the first PRE. You can select it to receive on MIDI channel 1. Un-check all the other options such as: "Receive and Send boxes for MIDI Time Code," "MIDI Beat Clock," "MIDI Machine Control," and all the other Receive channels that are not going to be used.

- Repeat the above steps for each PRE configuration, and make sure to assign a different "Receive Channel" to each PRE; otherwise, their controls will operate in a "linked" fashion, i.e., changing the settings on one unit will change the settings on all of them. You might choose MIDI channel 2 for PRE #2 and MIDI channel 3 for PRE #3 to maintain a certain order.

- While still in the OMS studio setup window, click and drag the second PRE icon to the first PRE, and the third PRE to the second PRE. These are basically arrows between the PREs and the MIDI interface signifying that a connection has been made.

- Once you have defined the preamps in the OMS Studio Setup and save them, you must assign the MIDI channel on which each preamp will receive the MIDI commands. You can assign them through the preamp's front panel. To assign a MIDI channel on a PRE, press the "MIDI CHAN" button. Use the "GAIN/PARAM" knob to select the desired MIDI channel. The display underneath the "GAIN/PARAM" knob will display the current MIDI channel (1–16). To exit the MIDI channel mode, press "MIDI CHAN" again.

- Before being able to control the PREs, you must be "declare" them in Pro Tools through the "Peripherals" command located in the Setups pop-up menu. Once in the Peripherals window, click on the "Mic Pre-amps" tab. From the "Type" selection menu, choose "PRE." From the "Receive From" and "Send To" selection menus, choose the PRE's source MIDI port number and a MIDI channel on which to send and receive the MIDI data. Remember three steps ago how we defined the PREs on the OMS Studio Setup configuration? Well, according to our example the settings in the "Peripherals" window for receiving and sending MIDI should be:

PRE #1 = "PRE 1–1" (port #1 and MIDI channel #1)
PRE #2 = "PRE 1–2" (port #1 and MIDI channel #2)
PRE #3 = "PRE 1–3" (port #1 and MIDI channel #3)

- After making the proper "Peripherals" settings, click OK.

- The last step to successfully set up your PREs will be shown later, when configuring the I/O Setup.

- Since the SYNC I/O is being used in this system, it also needs to be "declared" in the "Peripherals" window. So go to Setups > Peripherals and click on the "Synchronization" tab. Under "Device," select "SYNC I/O," and under "Port," select the "DigiSerial" port.

- Once the SYNC I/O has been "declared," now the "Positional and Clock References" need to be set. You can set them in the "Show Session Setup" window located in the Windows pop-up menu. While in this window go to the "SYNC I/O Setup" section, and under the "Clock Reference" pop-up menu, select "Loop Sync," since the SYNC I/O and the 192 I/Os are attached through the "LOOP SYNC" connectors. Also, since the SYNC I/O will be reading SMPTE time code send out from the two-inch tape machine, set the "Positional Reference" option to "LTC."

- As I mentioned earlier, in this particular system setup there are three 192 I/O interfaces. The 192 I/O #1 is attached to the HD Core PCI card inside of the computer, so it will appear in the Peripherals list of the Hardware Setup menu. The same goes for the 192 I/O #3, which is attached to the HD Process #1 PCI card. For the 192 I/O #2 things are different—since it is connected through the "Expansion Port" of the 192 I/O #1, it needs to be declared. To do this, go to Setups > Hardware Setup and highlight the 192 I/O #1 in the Peripherals list, and click on the "Expansion I/O" option. Double-click on <No Interface> in the Peripherals window and declare the new 192 I/O. Set the Inputs 1–8 of the three of them to "Analog 1–8" and make sure the Clock Source is set to "Loop Sync." Then, click "OK."

- Now it's time to make the I/O setups. Go to Setups > I/O Setup. Select the "Input" tab and the click on the "Default" button. Do the same for the "Output" tab. This is so you'll be able to see the default names of your inputs and outputs when you assign the ins and outs in the Mix window. The I/O Setup window can also be used to type your own inputs, outputs, insets, and bus names so they make sense to you.

- While still in the I/O Setups window, select the "Mic Preamps" tab and click on the "Default" button. Each mic preamp channel will appear under the first eight input channels of the 192 I/O audio interface icon. Do the same for all three of them. Assuming that you made the right setting assignments and connections for the PREs, you should be able to remote-control the preamp's parameters through the Mix window.

- After making all the proper software settings for MIDI, for the synchronizer, and for the audio interfaces, it is time to make the input/output assignments in the Mix window. You can follow the next assignments for this example:

Track(mono)	Input	Inst/Source	Output
Audio track # 1–8	A 1–8	(192 I/O #1. Ch.1–8)	A 1–2
Audio track # 9–16	B 1–8	(192 I/O #2. Ch.9–16)	A 1–2
Audio track #17–23	C 1–8	(192 I/O #3. Ch.17–23)	A 1–2

- To be able to record any track for the transfer, you must record-enable (press the red "rec" button) all the 24 audio tracks in your Pro Tools Session. You need to set the "Session Start" time in the Session Setup window located in the Windows pop-up menu. This is to have a time reference in Pro Tools for feature tasks needed to be done after the transfer; you never know.

- Test to see if you are getting audio coming from the two-inch tape machine on each Pro Tools audio track by pressing Play on the tape machine to start the playback.

- Once you know audio is coming in, click on the Online button in the Transport window. This will allow Pro Tools to accept time code to be able to synchronize with the two-inch tape machine.

- If you are ready to transfer all the 23 tracks (track 24 is the SMPTE track, remember?), press the Record button in the Pro Tools Transport window. You'll notice it will start flashing. Then press the Play button on the two-inch tape machine. If everything is fine, Pro Tools will be in Pause-Record Mode and won't start recording until it reaches the time you specified as the Session Start time in the Session Setup window. Once it reaches that time location, Pro Tools will start recording, and the analog audio transfer will be completed once you press Stop in Pro Tools' Transport window. Congratulations!

CHAPTER TEN

Plug-Ins

10

Regardless of what your application with Pro Tools is, music production, audio for video post-production, broadcast, etc., sooner or later you will have the need to add effects such as reverb, delay, compression, etc., to your projects. These effects are added by means of what is known as "plug-ins."

This chapter is exclusively dedicated to "plug-ins" in which you will learn:

- What is a plug-in?

- Types of plug-ins

- The plug-in window controls

- How to assign plug-ins in a track

What is a plug-in?

A plug-in in the Pro Tools world is a software digital signal processor (delay, reverb, compressor), which you can use it to digitally alter the sonic characteristics of any audio source such as vocals, instruments, sound effects, etc. Depending of the type of plug-in or effect you are using—let's say a compressor, for example—it functions the same way and have the same control buttons as a compressor in a hardware version.

There are in existence an extensive number of software signal processors (plug-ins) on the market today which you can use in your Pro Tools projects. The various types of signal processors available are: EQs, delays, reverbs, guitar amp simulators, pitch correctors, software synthesizers and samplers, and compressors/limiters, among others. Some of these plug-ins were developed and are distributed by Digidesign, others by Digidesign's developer partners. Some of the developer partners are Antares, Metric Halo Labs, GRM Tools, Waves, Line 6, Eventide, Universal Audio, Focusrite, and Sony, among others. Figures Fig. 10.1a–c show some examples of their plug-ins.

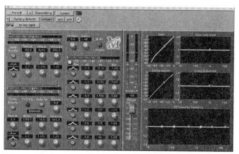

Fig. 10.1a Channel Strip from Metric Halo Labs.

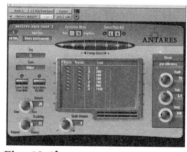

Fig. 10.1b AutoTune from Antares.

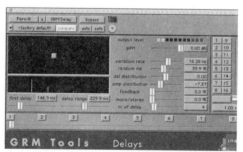

Fig. 10.1c A delay processor from GRM Tools.

When you purchase a Pro Tools system (TDM or LE), a basic set of real-time and non-real-time digital signal processors or plug-ins is provided with it. Digidesign refers this basic set of effects (EQs, dynamics, delays) as "DigiRack" plug-ins. However, you may get more plug-ins than the basic set, it all depends on the promotional offer Digidesign has at the time of your purchase. As I mentioned above, you can also purchase other available plug-ins from third-party developers.

Types of plug-ins

There are four different types of plug-ins that can be used in a Pro Tools TDM or LE system:

• AudioSuite plug-ins

• RTAS plug-ins

• HTDM plug-ins

• TDM plug-ins

AudioSuite plug-ins

An AudioSuite plug-in is what is considered a "file-based" type of plug-in, which means that in order to alter the sonic characteristic of a selected audio file or region, it must first be processed. This makes it a "non-real-time" type of plug-in. In other words, every time you adjust a parameter on an AudioSuite plug-in while in the "preview" mode (Fig. 10.2a), you will hear the change occurred, but not instantly since is a non-real-time type of plug-in. Once you are satisfied with the sonic result after adjusting the parameters, you must commit to the selected audio region alterations by pressing the "process" button in the actual plug-in window (Fig. 10.2b).

Fig. 10.2a Previewing the AudioSuite D-Verb plug-in on a selected audio Region.

Fig. 10.2b Pressing the "process" button to alter the sound with a reverb effect of a selected audio region.

You could permanently alter (destructive option) the original audio file you have selected by choosing the "overwrite files" option in the AudioSuite plug-in window (Fig. 10.2c). If you prefer to create and save the processed file under the same name, but with an "extension" with the name of the AudioSuite plug-in used, you can do that as well. For example, suppose you would like to "normalize" an audio region called "A. Guit-01." After processing the file using the "Normalize" Audio-Suite plug-in, a new audio file will be created with the same name, and it will appear in the Audio Regions List as "A. Guit-NORM_01-01." Notice the "NORM" name (for normalization) extension was added. As a second example, say you added a reverb AudioSuite plug-in on a vocal file named "BGRD Vox II-02." After processing the file, a new file will be created with the name "BGRD Vox II-Dvrb_02-02," and it will appear on the Audio Regions List as well (Fig. 10.2d).

Fig. 10.2c Selecting the "overwrite files" option in the AudioSuite plug-in to permanently change the selected audio file.

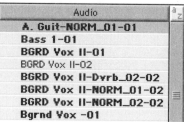

Fig. 10.2d Shows the Audio Regions List with audio files processed with AudioSuite plug-ins. Notice on the processed file names an "extension" name was added after its original name. For example, the name "A. Guit-NORM" means that an acoustic guitar sound was "normalized".

If your Pro Tools session contains a high number of tracks, too many real-time plug-ins, too much signal routing, etc., you may end up running out of DSP resources, i.e., DSP power, on either your host computer (for LE systems) or on your Digidesign PCI cards that contain the DSP "chips" (for TDM systems). This is when you might consider using AudioSuite type of plug-ins, which are found in the "AudioSuite" pop-up menu. By using AudioSuite plug-ins, you will be able to conserve some of the DSP resources needed to accomplish other important tasks in your session, such as auto-tuning an important vocal track among other tasks.

To process an audio file or region using an AudioSuite plug-in:

  a) First select a portion or the entire audio region you would like to process. In this example, suppose you would like to "normalize" a particular sound (audio region) that was originally recorded at a low volume level (Fig. 10.3a), and you need to optimize or normalize it to bring the level up.

  b) Go to the AudioSuite pop-up menu and select the "Normalize" plug-in (Fig. 10.3b).

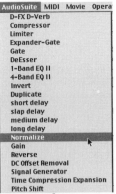

Fig. 10.3a Selecting a low-level audio file to be optimized.

Fig. 10.3b Choosing the "Normalize" AudioSuite plug-in from the AudioSuite pop-up menu.

c) After you have adjusted the right amount of normalization ("Max. Peak at:" slider), press the "process" button on the plug-in (Fig. 10.3c).

d) You will notice the "normalized" audio region has increased in volume level (Fig. 10.3d).

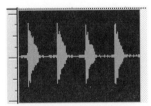

Fig. 10.3c Pressing the "process" button to optimize the audio region.

Fig. 10.3d Shows the selected audio region was normalized.

RTAS plug-ins

RTAS stands for Real-Time AudioSuite, which is the real-time version of an AudioSuite plug-in. RTAS plug-ins are included as well in the DigiRack basic plug-in set provided on each Pro Tools system. You don't have to limit yourself to using only the DigiRack plug-ins for your projects, since there is a wide variety of RTAS plug-ins offered by Digidesign developer partners. I highly recommend you visit Digidesign's web site at www.digidesign.com to learn more about the RTAS plug-ins available from other companies.

Continuing with our RTAS plug-in discussion, this type of plug-ins use the computer's CPU to digitally process the audio in a real-time manner. In other words, the changes you make on its parameters occur instantly. For example, if you are using an RTAS reverb plug-in, as you are increasing or decreasing the "decay time" parameter of the reverb plug-in, you can hear the change in the reverberation effect right away. Whereas, in a reverb AudioSuite type of plug-in, the change does not happen instantly; it takes a half of a second or more, depending on the plug-in complexity and how fast your computer does the processing.

You can differentiate between an AudioSuite (non-real-time) plug-in and a Real-Time AudioSuite (RTAS) plug-in by just looking at their windows. For instance, let's take a look at the compressor plug-ins in Fig. 10.4a and Fig. 10.4b. Notice in Fig. 10.4a the plug-in has parameters such as "auto" for automation. That is right, you can actually automate all the parameters in an RTAS plug-in. Also, it has an insert assignment pop-up selector, and it has the RTAS letters written in the window, right above the "bulls eye" icon. On the other hand, an AudioSuite plug-in doesn't have the features I just mentioned; instead, it has "preview" and "process" buttons to process the selected audio file or region (Fig. 10.4b).

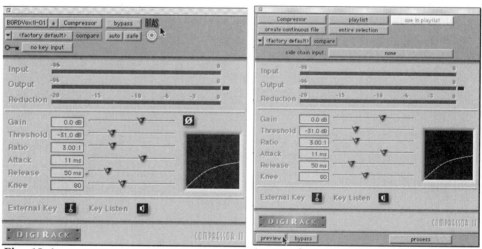

Fig. 10.4a An RTAS compressor plug-in.   **Fig. 10.4b** An AudioSuite compressor plug-in.

To use an RTAS plug-in, it must be assigned on any of the five inserts (Fig. 10.5a) on an audio track, aux input track, or master fader track (Fig. 10.5b). One of the benefits of using RTAS plug-ins, especially on a LE system, is that it is a faster way to try and audition any effect at any time on an audio track. The best part of using RTAS plug-in effects is the fact that you can always remove the effect on the track if you don't like it (Fig. 10.5c). In other words, the effect is not recorded in the actual audio file as in the case of an AudioSuite plug-in. To understand better the difference between RTAS and AudioSuite plug-ins read the following analogy. Suppose you are wearing a hat on your head, then you take it off, and then you decide to put it back on, and so forth. This is the same concept as on RTAS plug-ins where you can add the effect and then take it off and then put it back on, etc. On the other hand, let's say you put glue in the hat, then you put it on, and then you want to take it off, but this time, you cannot take it off anymore since it is glued onto your head. And this is what happens with Audio-Suite plug-ins in the event that you select the option in the plug-in itself to permanently alter the original sound (the "overwrite files" option).

Fig. 10.5a The five inserts (a, b, c, d, e) on an audio, aux input, or master fader track.

Fig. 10.5b A "4-Band EQ" RTAS plug-in assigned to insert "a."

Fig. 10.5c Removing the EQ effect from insert "a."

TDM Plug-Ins

A TDM (Time-Division Multiplexing) type of plug-in uses the DSP chips (Fig. 10.a) located on the PCI cards of a Pro Tools MIX or HD-Series TDM system to be able to support their more intensive processing algorithms. They do not share the host computer processing power to achieve their high performance and complex processing tasks. These plug-ins process the audio in real time and in a non-destructive way, and they only work on TDM systems. The number of TDM plug-ins you can use in a single Pro Tools session is limited by the number of DSP chips you have on your TDM system. If you need to add more plug-ins, either you can use RTAS, HTDM, and AudioSuite type of plug-ins to free some of the DSP chips on the PCI cards, or purchase additional PCI cards to increase the number of DSP chips in your TDM system (Fig. 10.6b).

Fig. 10.6a The DSP chips on a Pro Tools TDM PCI card.

Fig. 10.6b An HD Process PCI card containing nine DSP chips.

419

Similar to RTAS, in order to use a TDM plug-in, it must first be assigned on any of the five insert points of any audio, aux input, or master fader track (Fig. 10.7a). There are many TDM plug-ins that are not available in an RTAS version such as the guitar amp simulator from Line 6, the "Amp Farm" (Fig. 10.7b). Please check Digidesign's web site to find out if a particular plug-in is available in both versions, RTAS and TDM.

Fig. 10.7a Assigning the "Amp Farm" TDM plug-in on insert "a" of an audio track.

Fig. 10.7b The "Amp Farm," a guitar amp modeler TDM plug-in from Line 6.

Using TDM and RTAS plug-ins in the same audio track

If you use a combination of TDM and RTAS plug-ins in the same audio track, you will soon find out that sometimes you can and sometimes you cannot select an RTAS plug-in when using it in conjunction with a TDM plug-in. The reason for this is if you have assigned a TDM plug-in on the first insert of a track (Fig. 10.7a), for example, then you try to assign an RTAS plug-in on the insert right underneath where the TDM plug-in is, you will notice a small window reading "n/a because active TDM plug-in precedes" (Fig. 10.8b). What this means is that an RTAS plug-in must be assigned on an insert before (on top of) any TDM plug-in in the same audio track.

Fig. 10.8a A TDM GRM Delay plug-in assigned to insert "a" of an audio track.

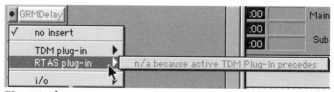

Fig. 10.8b Since a TDM plug-in is assigned before an RTAS plug-in, the list of RTAS plug-ins does not show when trying to select one.

Referring to the example in Fig. 10.8a, a TDM plug-in was selected on the first insert ("a") of an audio track. In order to be able to insert an RTAS plug-in in that same audio track, the TDM plug-in should be moved to insert "b" first. You can do this by clicking, holding, and dragging the plug-in with the mouse to the insert below, in this case, to insert "b" (Fig. 10.8c). Once you have an empty insert available before an already assigned TDM plug-in on the track, you can select an RTAS plug-in (Fig. 10.8d). Very important to remember: you can only use RTAS plug-ins on audio tracks in a Pro Tools TDM system; you cannot use them on aux input and master fader tracks.

Fig. 10.8c The TDM GRM Delay plug-in was moved to insert "b" of an audio track.

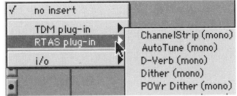

Fig. 10.8d The RTAS plug-in list is available to select a plug-in after the TDM plug-in was moved to insert "b."

HTDM *plug-ins*

HTDM stands for "Host Time Division Multiplexing" and refers to plug-ins with a fusion of TDM and RTAS technologies. This type of plug-in functions like a regular TDM plug-in (in real-time), but it does all the audio processing on the host computer processors as opposed to the DSP chips on a Pro Tools PCI card. When you add an HTDM plug-in in a session, one DSP chip on your TDM system is shared by the HTDM plug-ins to allow all audio from the host plug-in processes to be send and received to and from your TDM system. The number of plug-ins you can use in your system depends on how fast your computer is to do the digital processing.

There are a few reasons why you should use HTDM plug-ins:

a) Since this type of plug-in uses the computer or CPU to do all the audio processing, DSP chips in your TDM system will be available for other important, more complex tasks.

b) Unlike RTAS plug-ins on a TDM system, which can be used on audio tracks only, HTDM plug-ins can be inserted on any track (audio, aux input, and master fader tracks).

c) HTDM plug-in parameters can be automated and controlled by external control surfaces for hands-on control.

Bear in mind that HTDM plug-ins can only be used on MIX-series and HD-series TDM systems. If you have a Digi 001, Digi 002/002R, Mbox, Toolbox, Pro Tools III, or Pro Tools 24, don't try to use them.

Some examples of HTDM plug-ins available on the market are: GRM Classic Tools from GRM, T-RackS from IK Multimedia, MachFive from MOTU, NI Studio Collection (B4, Battery, and Pro-52) from Native Instruments, HTDM Software Instruments from Emagic, and Altiverb from Audio Ease, among others (Fig. 10.9a–e). I recommend you visit www.digidesign.com for more information of the availability of HTDM plug-ins on the market.

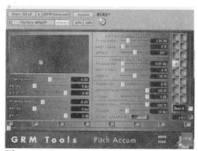

Fig. 10.9a GRM's Pitch Accum.

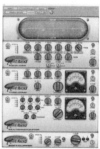

Fig. 10.9b 1K Multimedia's T-RackS.

Fig. 10.9c Audio Ease's Altiverb.

Fig. 10.9d MOTU's Mach Five.

Fig. 10.9e Native Instruments' B4.

The plug-in window controls

Whenever you click on an insert button of any track containing a plug-in (Fig. 10.10a), whether you do it through the Mix or Edit window, the corresponding plug-in window will appear (Fig. 10.10b). This floating window (Fig. 10.10c) is used to edit or alter any parameter you desire.

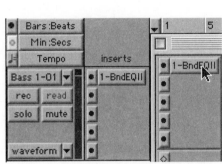

Fig. 10.10a Clicking on an insert button with the "1-Band EQII" plug-in on it.

Fig. 10.10b The "1-Band EQII" window appears.

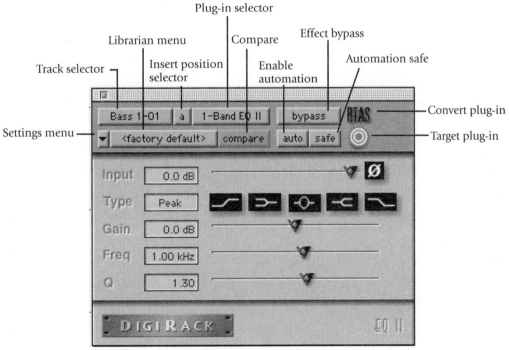

Fig. 10.10c Plug-in window.

Plug-in controls

Most plug-ins have the following common controls:

- Track selector: This pop-up menu (Fig. 10.11a) allows you to select a plug-in on any other audio, aux input, or master fader track (Fig. 10.11b) without leaving this window.

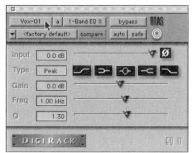

Fig. 10.11a

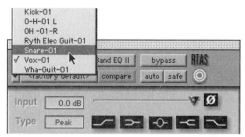

Fig. 10.11b

- Insert position selector: This little button (Fig. 10.12a) allows you to select another insert of the five available in the same track to be able to assign a different plug-in without leaving the plug-in window (Fig. 10.12b–c).

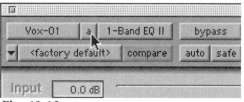

Fig. 10.12a

Fig. 10.12b

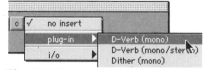

Fig. 10.12c

- Plug-in selector: This pop-up selector (Fig. 10.13a) allows you to change the type of plug-in on the specified track from the plug-in window (Fig. 10.13b).

Fig. 10.13a

Fig. 10.13b

• Effect bypass: This button (Fig. 10.14a) lets you bypass (Fig. 10.14b) or disable the plug-in, so you can compare the track with and without the corresponding effect of the plug-in.

Fig. 10.14a

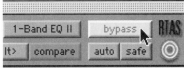

Fig. 10.14b

• Convert plug-in: This function allows you convert an insert from a TDM plug-in to an RTAS plug-in of the same type and vice-versa. In order to use this feature, the plug-ins must be available in both TDM and RTAS formats.

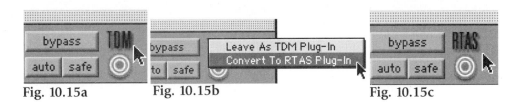

Fig. 10.15a   **Fig. 10.15b**   **Fig. 10.15c**

• Target plug-in: When you have multiple plug-in windows open in your session Fig. 10.16a), if you click on the "target" button on a desired plug-in, that plug-in will be selected as the target for any keyboard commands.

Fig. 10.16a

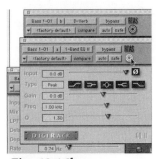

Fig. 10.16b

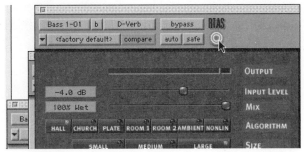

Fig. 10.16c

• Automation Safe: If you have "written" plug-in automation on your mix, the Auto Safe button (Fig. 10.17a) will allow you to prevent the any existing plug-in automation from being overwritten when enabled (Fig. 10.17b).

Fig. 10.17a

Fig. 10.17b

• Enable Automation: The Enable Automation button (Fig. 10.18a) enables the individual plug-in parameters for automation. When you click on this button, a dialog window will appear allowing you to select the plug-in parameters you would like to automate. In Fig. 10.18b notice the first five parameters (Master Bypass, Input, Inv, Type, and Gain) of the EQ plug-in were selected. By clicking on the "Add" button, the selected parameters will move to the column on the right (Fig. 10.18c) meaning that those parameters will be the only parameters you will be able to automate when the "Auto Write" automation mode is selected on the track the plug-in is inserted in. When you click "OK" in the dialog window, the perimeter of the plug-in parameters you selected to be automated will turn green or red depending on the automation mode the track is in, "auto read" or "auto write," respectively (Fig. 10.18d).

Fig. 10.18a

Fig. 10.18b

Fig. 10.18c

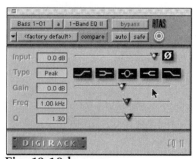

Fig. 10.18d

- Compare: When you edit some of the parameters in a plug-in, clicking on the Compare button will toggle between the original settings (Fig. 10.19b) and the ones made by you (Fig. 10.19b), so you are able to compare them.

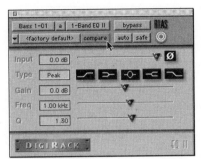

Fig. 10.19a

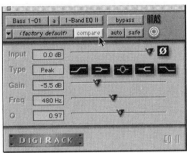

Fig. 10.19b

- Settings menu: Let's say you are editing the EQ plug-in parameters of one of the tom drum's audio tracks you have in your Pro Tools Session for mixing. Also, suppose you love the sound of the tom with EQ and you want to add it to another tom track in your session, no problem. If you click on the Settings pop-up menu (Fig. 10.20a), a list of functions such as copy, paste, save, and import plug-in settings, among others, will be displayed. Since in this case you want to have the same EQ parameters of the first tom in the second, you can select the "copy" function in the Settings menu list to copy the first tom parameters. Then, click on the second tom's EQ plug-in and go to its Settings pop-up menu and select the "paste" function. You will notice the first tom EQ parameters will be in the second tom's EQ settings. Try it—it's easy to do.

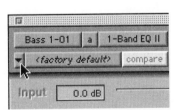

Fig. 10.20a

Fig. 10.20b

- Librarian menu: The Librarian menu pop-up selector (Fig. 10.21a) allows you to recall or select plug-in preset settings that were preprogrammed from the factory. You can also create your own settings by clicking on the Settings pop-up menu and selecting the "Save Settings As" function (Fig. 10.21a). A dialog window will appear prompting you to name the setting and save it by clicking on the "Save" button (Fig. 10.21c). The new setting name will appear now in the Librarian menu pop-up list for you to select it (Fig. 10.21d). This is a good way to create your own favorite plug-in programs so you can use them anytime you are recording, mixing, or mastering with Pro Tools.

Fig. 10.21a

Fig. 10.21b

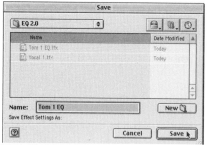

Fig. 10.21c

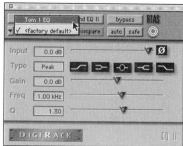

Fig. 10.21d

How to insert a plug-in into a track

Regardless of what type of track (audio, aux input, master fader) you want to insert a RTAS, HTDM, or TDM plug-in into, the process is the same and very simple.

To insert a plug-in into a track follow these next steps:

a) Go to the Mix window and position the cursor over one of the five insert points ("a" to "e") available on each track in the "insert section" (Fig. 10.22a).

b) Click and hold the mouse over the desire insert point. You will see a pop-up list appearing prompting you to select the type of plug-in (TDM or RTAS) and the plug-in itself (Fig. 10.22b).

c) While still holding down the mouse, select the desire plug-in by sliding the cursor to the right. In the example in Fig. 10.22b I have selected the "AmpFarm" TDM plug-in from Line6..

d) Release the mouse and the plug-in window will appear on your screen and the insert point you have selected will contain the plug-in name, which in this case is the "AmpFarm" (Fig. 10.22c).

Fig. 10.22a Positioning the cursor over insert "a."

Fig. 10.22b Selecting the "Amp Farm" TDM plug-in.

Fig. 10.22c The "Amp Farm" TDM plug-in is assigned on insert "a."

e) If you want to remove a plug-in from the insert point, click and hold the mouse over the "dot" icon on the insert point. You will see a pop-up list prompting you to select a TDM or RTAS type of plug-in, or to select "no insert." Select the "no insert" option by sliding the cursor up to that option (Fig. 10.22d).

f) Release the mouse and you will notice the plug-in is no longer assigned on the insert (Fig. 10.22e).

g) By the way, if you are a Pro Tools user who likes to keep the Mix window controls in the Edit window, then you can assign a plug-in on any of the five inserts available through the Edit window as well (Fig. 10.22f).

Fig. 10.22d Selecting the "no insert" option to remove a plug-in from a track.

Fig. 10.22e The plug-in has been removed.

Fig. 10.22f The "insert section" displayed in the Edit window.

CHAPTER ELEVEN

Cables and Connectors

Pro Tools systems utilize a variety of audio, digital, and fiber-optic cables and connectors.

In many cases, you can identify these cables by the connectors used at each end. But in some cases, you may need to know a few more details about these cables, such as length limitations, impedance, etc.

This chapter will introduce to you the most commonly used cables and connectors needed to connect a Pro Tools system. These include:

- DigiLink interface cable
- TDM II FlexCable
- TDM ribbon cable
- 50-pin interface cable
- 16-ch peripheral cable adapter
- 60-pin interface connectors
- Expansion chassis cable
- Digi 001 I/O cable
- BNC slave clock cable
- ADAT optical cables
- DB-25 connectors

- RCA connectors
- Cannon or "XLR" connectors
- ¼" plug connectors (TRS and TS)
- 5-pin DIN connectors
- USB connectors
- FireWire connectors
- Ethernet connectors
- Telephone connectors
- SCSI connectors
- 68-pin UltraWide SCSI connectors
- Serial connectors

DigiLink interface cable

If you purchase a Pro Tools | HD 1, HD 2, or HD 3 system, you will need at least one DigiLink interface cable to connect the HD PCI card in your computer (labeled HD Core) to your audio interface (a 192 or a 96 I/O).

A 12-foot-long DigiLink cable is included with the system. To add a second audio interface, either to another 192 or 96 I/O, you will need another short DigiLink interface cable. A 1.5-foot-long DigiLink cable is included with the 192 I/O and 96 I/O. Fig. 11.1 is an example of a DigiLink interface cable.

Fig. 11.1 DigiLink interface cable.

TDM II FlexCable

A multi-card HD system (HD2, HD3) will need a TDM II FlexCable (Fig. 11.2) to connect the cards. This is a short, flat, custom cable used to connect HD PCI cards together inside your computer or expansion chassis. You will not need a TDM II FlexCable if you own a single-card system (HD1). A Pro Tools | HD 2 system will include one cable, and a Pro Tools | HD 3 system will include two.

Fig. 11.2 TDM II FlexCable.

TDM ribbon cable

If you have a Mix Series Pro Tools TDM system, you will need to interconnect all the Mix Core and Mix Farm series PCI cards inside your computer or expansion chassis using a TDM ribbon cable as shown in Fig. 11.3. A 5-node TDM ribbon cable is included in a Pro Tools | 24 MIX Plus system. Expanded systems that require an external expansion chassis, either 7 or 13 slots, will need a 7, 8, or 10-node TDM ribbon cable from Digidesign.

Fig. 11.3 TDM ribbon cable.

50-pin interface cable

MIX systems use a 50-pin audio interface cable (Fig. 11.4) to connect their interfaces, like the 888|24, to the Pro Tools PCI cards. They are the MIX Core, MIX Farm, DSP Farm, the d24 and/or the Disk I/O card.

Pro Tools HD systems also enable the use of 50-pin audio interface cables to connect "older" MIX equipment to the "legacy" ports of the newer 192 or 96 I/O units. Supported I/O interfaces include the 888|24 I/O, the 882|20 I/O, the 24-bit ADAT Bridge, the 16-bit ADAT Bridge, and the 1622 I/O. Older interfaces, such as the 16-bit 888 I/O or 16-bit 882 I/O, are not supported by the Pro Tools | HD-series.

Fig. 11.4 50-pin interface cable.

16-channel peripheral cable adapter or "Y" cable

Pro Tools MIX-series PCI cards (MIX Core or MIX Farm) can support up to 16 simultaneous inputs and outputs. Although the normal 60-pin interface cable connects to a single eight-channel audio interface, you can use a 16-channel "Y" cable (Fig. 11.5) to connect two eight-channel interfaces.

When you use a 16-channel peripheral cable adapter, you must assign one audio interface to the "A" side of the adapter, and the other audio interface to the "B" side.

These assignments are made in the "Playback Engine" window, located in the "Setups" menu. HD-series PCI cards can support up to 32 simultaneous inputs and outputs without the need of a "Y" cable.

Fig. 11.5 16-channel peripheral cable adapter or "Y" cable.

60-pin interface connectors

MIX-series systems use a 60-pin cable (Fig. 11.6) to connect the 1622 I/O interface to the MIX Core card (in a Pro Tools 24 MIX system) or the d24 card (in a Pro Tools | 24 system).

Be careful not to confuse this 60–pin connector with the 50-pin connector used to connect the 888 I/O or the 882 I/O audio interfaces to the Pro Tools PCI cards.

Fig. 11.6 60-pin interface connector.

Expansion chassis cable

If your system has more cards than your host computer allows, you will have to expand it using a 7- or 13-slot external chassis. Check www.digidesign.com for the latest compatibility information.

An Expansion chassis cable (Fig. 11.7) connects the chassis host card in the computer to the chassis controller card. A short expansion chassis cable (no more than two or four feet long) will improve your chances for a trouble-free performance.

Fig. 11.7 Expansion chassis cable.

Digi 001 I/O cable

This six-foot-long I/O cable (Fig. 11.8) is used primarily to connect the Digi 001 PCI card to the Digi 001 audio interface. The Digi 001 PCI card must be installed in an available PCI slot of your computer. This card includes optical digital inputs and outputs for digitally transferring eight channels of ADAT-format audio source or two channels of S/PDIF audio source to and from Pro Tools LE.

Fig. 11.8 Digi 001 I/O cable.

BNC slave clock cable

BNC cables are used to convey "clock" information between pieces of equipment in your studio. In essence, this timing information allows your electronic components to march in step with one another.

BNC cables (Fig. 11.9) are used to make slave clock in/out, word clock in/out, or loop sync in/out connections between the audio interfaces and synchronizers used in your Pro Tools studio.

Combining an HD-series interface with a MIX-series interface will require extra care in order to avoid clocking problems . Timing issues are critical in the digital realm.

BNC cables are included with every Digidesign audio interface—such as the 192 I/O, 96 I/O, 888 I/O, ADAT Bridge I/O, etc.

Always use high quality 75-ohm RG-59 cable, and keep the length of these cables under nine feet because of the crucial timing data passing through them.

Fig. 11.9 BNC connectors.

ADAT optical cable

ADAT optical cables (Fig. 11.10) use laser pulses to digitally transfer information through a thin fiber-optic cable with Toslink connectors at both ends. Avoid looking at the red laser light coming out of the Toslink connectors when your equipment is turned on. ADAT optical cables are used by Pro Tools for both digital transfers between ADATs and Pro Tools, and for S/PDIF digital transfers. When used for ADAT transfers, these cables use the Lightpipe format to transfer up to eight channels of digital audio. When used for S/PDIF transfers, they transfer two channels of digital audio.

The 192 I/O has both Lightpipe and S/PDIF connections on its back. You can reconfigure the 192's S/PDIF connectors to work as Lightpipe connectors in the "Hardware Setup" menu in Pro Tools. This allows you to hook up a second ADAT, and transfer a total of sixteen tracks of ADAT audio at a time.

Fig. 11.10
ADAT optical cables.

DB-25 connectors

DB-25-pin connectors, a.k.a. 25-pin D-sub multi-pin connectors, are used in a wide range of computer applications—from SCSI connections to printer cables.

HD-series Pro Tools systems use a special cable with DB-25-pin connectors (Fig. 11.11) to do digital transfers using the AES/EBU and the T-DIF digital formats between Pro Tools and other digital devices. These connectors are also used to plug all your analog inputs and outputs to a patchbay or other analog device. You can buy the DB25 "DigiSnakes" from Digidesign, which are custom-made colored and labeled cable snakes to connect your Pro Tools HD system.

Fig. 11.11 DB-25 connectors.

RCA connectors

All Pro Tools audio interfaces, including the Mbox, Digi 001, and the Digi 002, use RCA connectors (Fig. 11.12) for digital transfers using the S/PDIF digital format. Make sure the cables you use for S/PDIF transfers have an impedance rating of 75 ohms. You will be fine if your cables have gold-plated RCA connectors.

If you have to choose between analog or digital transfer, you should stay in the digital domain. Connecting a CD player, DVD player, or any external signal processor via an audio interface will degrade your audio with each transfer. Your original signal will be preserved when kept in the digital domain. Never plug a digital output into an analog input; the results will be loud, unpleasant, and perhaps even damaging to your equipment.

Fig. 11.12 RCA connectors.

XLR or Cannon connectors

XLR connectors, a.k.a. Cannon connectors (Fig. 11.13), are typically used for microphone cables. Although there is no industry standard for the assignment of the three pins on these connectors, usually pin 1 is connected to ground, pin 2 is the "hot" or the "+" signal, and pin 3 is the "cold" or "–" signal. You should study the pinout arrangements whenever you connect any professional equipment. Some companies assign pin 2 to be the "–" signal, and pin 3 the "+" signal. If you don't pay attention to this, you could end up with signals 180° out of phase.

In the Pro Tools TDM world, the only audio interface that uses XLR connectors for analog connections is the 888 I/O. All other Pro Tools TDM hardware (192 I/O, 96 I/O, 888 I/O, and the ADAT Bridge) uses XLR connectors for digital transfers using the AES/EBU digital transfer format. When you use XLR cables for AES/EBU digital transfers, be sure they have an impedance of 110 ohms.

Fig. 11.13 XLR or cannon connectors.

¼"-Plug connectors (TRS and TS)

¼"-plug connectors are used almost exclusively for analog audio transfers, and come in two configurations. TS or *Tip-Sleeve* connectors (Fig. 11.14a) are used for unbalanced audio lines (–10dBV), such as the signal from an electric guitar. You will find this type of connector on all Digidesign audio interfaces except the 888 I/O, where you would have to use a direct box to convert your line level (hi-Z) signal to a mic level (lo-Z) signal.

TRS or *Tip- Ring-Sleeve* connectors (Fig. 11.14b) are used for balanced line analog inputs and outputs (+4dBu), insert points (in/out) for effect loops, and for headphone outputs (stereo). The Mbox, Digi 001, and Digi 002 use both TS and TRS connectors.

Fig. 11.14a ¼" mono or TS plug.

Fig. 11.14b ¼" stereo or TRS plug.

5-pin DIN or MIDI connectors

The 5-pin DIN connector (short for Deutsche Industry Norm) is usually called a MIDI connector (short for Musical Instrument Digital Interface), and is used exclusively for MIDI applications (Fig. 11.15 and Fig. 11.16).

Only the Digi 001 (one in and one out) and the Digi 002 (one in and two outs) include MIDI connectors. Pro Tools TDM systems require an external MIDI interface, such the Digidesign MIDI I/O, to hook up MIDI equipment.

MIDI is used by Pro Tools to control MIDI sequencers and synthesizers, as well as to utilize MIDI controllers, such as the CM Labs Motor Mix, the JL Cooper CS 10 Square, the JL Cooper MCS3800, and the HUI from Mackie, among others.

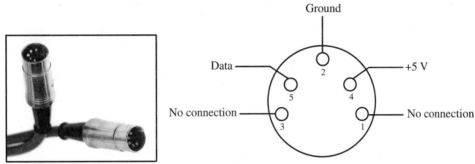

Fig. 11.15 MIDI connectors.

Fig. 11.16 MIDI connector pinout.

USB connectors

The Universal Serial Bus or USB (Fig. 11.17) is easy to use. USB devices can be connected and disconnected without having to power your computer off and/or on.

If your computer runs out of USB ports, you can add ports by buying a four- or seven-port USB hub. USB lets you connect up to 127 external devices such as keyboards, computer mice, and storage devices. USB provides data transfer rates up to 12 megabits per second, which is over 50 times faster than traditional serial ports, and over 1,000 times faster than Apple's Desktop Bus (ADB).

In the Pro Tools world, only the Mbox and the MIDI I/O use this type of connector. If you want to connect your Mbox after you have turned on your computer system, just plug it into any available USB port.

Fig. 11.17 USB connector.

FireWire connectors

FireWire external hard drives are becoming a viable alternative to SCSI UltraWide drives. The FireWire data transfer rates are up to 400 Mbps, 30 times faster than the USB standard, and up to 63 FireWire external devices can be chained together.

As of this writing, the Digi 002 is the only Digidesign product that uses FireWire. Like the Mbox's USB connection, the Digi 002's FireWire connection can be made and broken without powering your computer off and ón, which can be a real time saver. FireWire also allows you to connect other hardware, such as digital audio and video devices, and other high-speed peripherals, to your computer (Fig. 11.18).

Fig. 11.18 FireWire connector.

Ethernet connectors

Ethernet connectors (Fig. 11.19) are widely used in local area networks (LANs) to connect computers together and to share devices. If you have Internet cable or DSL connection, this is the connector you use to connect your computer to the modem. If your computer does not have an Ethernet port, you could buy and install an Ethernet 10baseT card. This would use up one of your computer's PCI slots, and would reduce the number of PCI slots available for your Pro Tools PCI cards. If you can afford it, you would be better off buying a computer that has the Ethernet port built in. Digidesign uses Ethernet cables to connect Pro Tools to their control surfaces (such as ProControl or Control|24). After plugging one end of the Ethernet cable into your computer, and the other end into the control surface, you need to define the control surface you are using within the Pro Tools software.

Fig. 11.19 Ethernet connector.

Telephone jacks

If you don't have access to a high-speed Internet connection, such as DSL, cable, or T1 line, you may still be able to connect to the Internet using a standard telephone line. The telephone jack (Fig. 11.20) is similar to the Ethernet jack. There are a number of good reasons for connecting your computer to the Internet. Downloads of software updates, software authentication, and technical support are only a few. Today, the Internet is becoming a way of collaborating with other musicians, producers, and engineers all over the world. Transferring files over the Internet can be greatly superior to overnight delivery services, and a lot less expensive. Digidesign now also offers a service called DigiStudio, designed to improve long-distance musical collaborations. If you need more information about DigiStudio accounts, you should contact www.digidesign.com.

Fig. 11.20 Telephone jack.

SCSI connectors

SCSI, pronounced "scuzzy," stands for Small Computer Systems Interface, and is used in the Pro Tools world for recording, playback, and storing all your audio files on an external hard drive. You can use the internal hard drive of your host computer to record music data, but Digidesign highly recommends the use of external hard drives for better performance.

SCSI hard drives are designed for heavier duty cycles than standard hard disks, and are expected to maintain high levels throughput for sustained periods of time, in contrast to the short bursts of activity required of typical computer operations. Whenever you need to connect one or more external SCSI hard drives to your Pro Tools system, you will need some type of SCSI connector and cable. Regular SCSI is a bit slow by today's standards, but is still used for data backups, CD burning, scanning, and printing. A number of connectors have been used for this type of SCSI, including the DB-25 and Centronix 50-pin connectors shown in Fig. 11.21.

Fig. 11.21
SCSI connectors.

68-pin UltraWide SCSI connectors

Today, the 68-pin UltraWide SCSI connector, also known as SCSI-3 connector, has become the standard (Fig. 11.22). SCSI-3 can support data transfers up to 160 MegaBytes per second, and employs a 16-bit bus width, making it a good match for hard drives with rotational speeds of 10,000 rpm and higher. Digidesign highly recommends using UltraWide SCSI bus hard drives with a Digidesign-approved SCSI host adapter.

Fig. 11.22 68-Pin UltraWide SCSI Connector.

Serial connectors

The standard Macintosh serial connector was used on older Apple computers to connect printers and/or modems to the computer.

This serial connector (Fig. 11.23) is now used by Pro Tools to connect Digidesign's Universal Slave Driver (USD) or SYNC I/O with the DigiSerial ports on the MIX Core card (in the Pro Tools MIX-series) or on the HD Core card (in the Pro Tools HD-series).

This connection enables Pro Tools to synchronize with external video or audio devices via SMPTE time code. The DigiSerial port also supports the use of a 9-pin device with the Pro Tools Machine Control option.

Fig. 11.23 Serial connectors.

CHAPTER 12

Step-By-Step Exercises

12

In this section, you will have a chance to put into practice all the techniques you have learned in previous chapters, while continuing to learn more skills. Two interactive exercises are included in this chapter for use with the accompanying CD-ROM, and two more exercises are found on the CD-ROM. I want to thank my friends, Hillary Beth, Gary Glass, Don Quentin Hannah, Fernando Cavazos, Anthony Fung, Cory Barker, and James Grey, who graciously allowed me to use their music for you to practice with and enjoy. Please use this music solely for your own educational purposes and do not abuse it by utilizing it in any other way. All contributing artists' credits and contact information can be found in this book.

Exercise #1 Session

In this first exercise you will be able to practice:

- Opening a Session
- Saving a Session
- Creating an audio track
- Renaming a track
- Importing an audio track
- Importing an audio file from the Audio Regions List
- Changing the View Size of a Track
- Playing back an Audio Track
- Various techniques for selecting a Region
- Capturing a region
- Separating a region
- Duplicating a region
- Inserting a region within a region

1) To access the "Exercise #1 Session" file in this chapter, you must first insert the CD-ROM titled "Pro Tools Book" included at the end of this book. Once you have inserted the CD-ROM in your computer's drive and see it appearing on your computer screen, double-click on its icon. You will notice several folders in it, among them, a folder named "Pro Tools Exercises" containing four different exercise folders named "Exercise #1 Session," "Exercise #2 Session," "Exercise #3 Session," and "Exercise #4 Session" (Fig. 13.1).

2) To work on Exercise #1, click and drag the "Exercise #1 Session" folder into the hard drive you will be using to practice Pro Tools; this can be your internal or external hard drive.

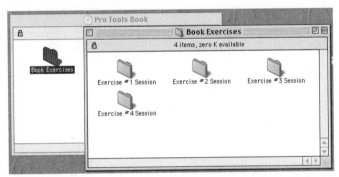

Fig. 12.1 The "Book Exercises" folder containing four different exercise folders.

Opening a Session

3) If you double click on the folder named "Exercise #1 Session," you will see three items in it: an Audio Files folder, a Pro Tools Session ("tape reel" icon), and a Fade Files folder.

4) Position the cursor over the Pro Tools Session named "Exercise #1 Session" and double-click on it to open it (Fig. 12.2).

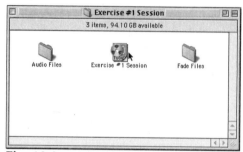

Fig. 12.2 Positioning the cursor on the Session's "tape reel" icon to open the Session.

5) If you have the Pro Tools application already opened, the "Exercise #1 Session" file will be displayed right away on your screen; otherwise, it will take a little bit longer, meaning that the Pro Tools application was not launched yet.

6) Once you have double-clicked on the "tape reel" icon of "Exercise #1 Session," a dialog window will appear on your screen prompting you to select either "Edit Stationery" or "New Session," since this exercise file is a Session template. This was done so you don't overwrite the original file on your drive when practicing on the exercise. In the event that you decide to click on the "Edit Stationery" option to overwrite the original exercise session, you can always get it back by making a copy of the file using the "Save As" command in the File pop-up menu while the Session is opened, or simply by dragging the file from the CD-ROM onto your hard drive.

7) Click on the "New Session" option to continue with the exercise (Fig. 12.3).

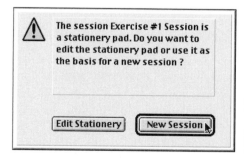

Fig. 12.3 Clicking on "New Session" to create your own Session for practice.

Saving a Session

8) As soon as you click on the "New Session" button, another dialog window
will appear prompting you to type a new name and to save the Session. Type
your name—or any other name you desire—in the "Name" box and then
click on the "Save" button (Fig. 12.4a). The session will be saved in the
"Exercise #1 Session" folder.

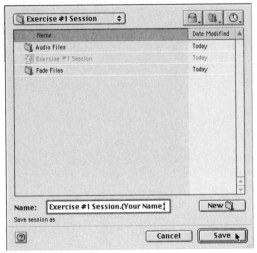

Fig. 12.4a Renaming the "Exercise #1 Session"
and saving it.

9) A new folder will be created with the name you gave the Session when you
.pressed the "Save" button in step #8 (Fig. 12.4b).

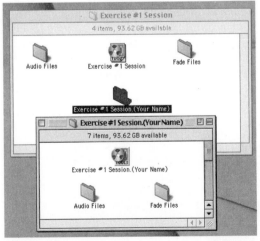

Fig. 12.4b A new folder was created with the name
you typed when you saved Exercise #1 Session.

10) After saving the Session, an empty Pro Tools Edit window (no tracks in it)
will show on your screen (Fig. 12.5).

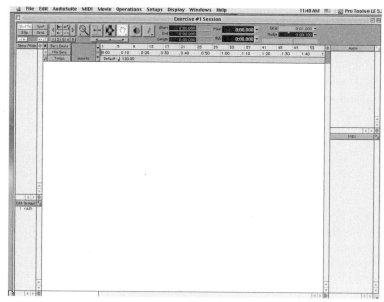

Fig. 12.5 An empty Edit window.

Creating an audio track

11) Choose the File pop-up menu and select the "New Track" command (Fig. 12.6).

Fig. 12.6 Selecting the "New Track" command.

12) Create one stereo audio track by selecting the "Stereo" and "Audio Track" options and clicking on the "Create" button (Fig. 12.7).

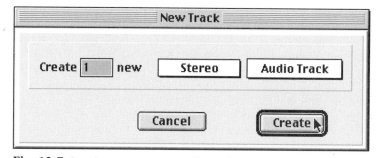

Fig. 12.7 Creating a new stereo audio track.

Renaming a track

13) A new stereo audio track named "Audio 1" will appear in the Edit window. Position the cursor on the track's name (the small box that says "Audio 1" in blue) and double-click on it to rename the track (Fig. 12.8).

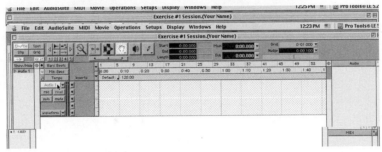

Fig. 12.8 Positioning the cursor on the track's name to rename it.

14) As soon as you double-click on the track's name box, a dialog window will appear on your screen prompting you to rename the audio track. Type "Africali" in the "Name the track:" box (Fig. 12.9), and type "This is a stereo song." in the "Comments:" box and click on "OK." You might be wondering why I asked you to type "Africali." Well, because "Africali" is the name of the stereo audio file you are about to import from the Audio Files folder later on in the exercise. Also, remember I asked you to type a note in the "Comments:" box? This is so you get in the habit of writing a comment on each track to keep your session organized. This is sort of like a "track sheet" when working on a Session in a recording studio. Believe me, this is a good habit to have since it is visually very helpful, especially when working on large Pro Tools Sessions.

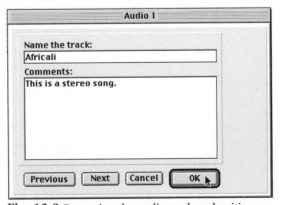

Fig. 12.9 Renaming the audio track and writing comments about the track.

15) By now, you should have a stereo audio track named "Africali" (Fig. 12.10).

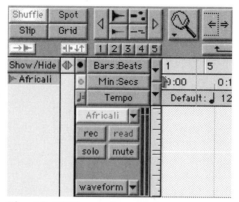

Fig. 12.10 The newly created stereo audio track renamed as "Africali."

Importing an audio track

16) Next, position the cursor on the Audio pop-up menu located on the upper-right-hand side of the Edit window (Fig. 12.11a). Click on it and drag the mouse down to select the" Import Audio" command (Fig. 12.11b).

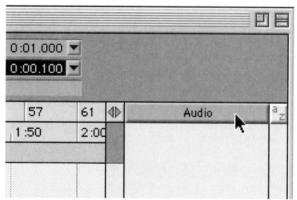

Fig. 12.11a The Audio pop-up menu.

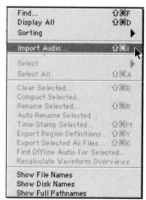

Fig. 12.11b Selecting the Import Audio command.

17) After releasing the mouse, the "Import Audio" dialog window will appear on your screen (Fig. 12.12a). Double-click on the "Exercise #1 Session" folder first (the one you saved on your hard drive), and then double-click on the "Audio Files" folder to select the audio files to be imported in this exercise (Fig. 12.12b).

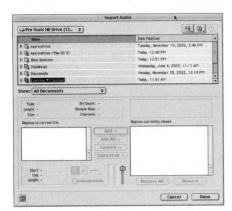

Fig. 12.12a Clicking on the "Exercise #1 Session" folder to select the audio files to be imported in the exercise Session.

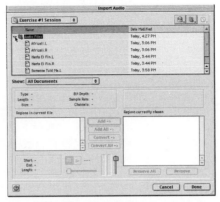

Fig. 12.12b Selecting the Audio Files folder to import the desired audio files.

18) Once you have the Session Audio Files folder open, select the audio file named "Africali L" and click on the "Add" button to add the audio file to the right-hand list (Fig. 12.13).

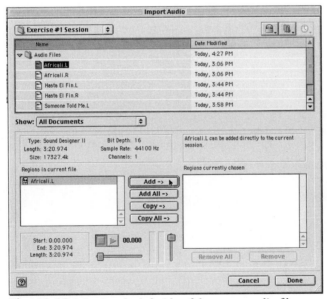

Fig. 12.13 Selecting the left side of the stereo audio file named "Africali."

19) Now, click on the "Africali R" audio file in the Audio Files folder to select it, and then click on the "Add" button to add it to the right-hand list of the dialog window. When finished adding the files, press the "Done" button to execute the importing of the audio files into the Session (Fig. 12.14).

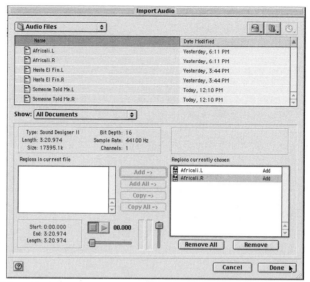

Fig. 12.14 Selecting the right side of the stereo audio file to be imported.

Importing an audio file from the Audio Regions List

20) You should see the "Africali" stereo audio file in the "Audio Regions List" by now (Fig. 12.15).

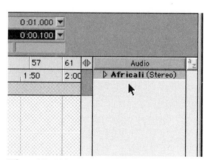

Fig. 12.15 The imported stereo audio file in the Audio Regions List.

21) Click on the audio file in the Audio Regions List and drag it into the stereo audio track you created earlier. Make sure you are in the Shuffle edit mode (i.e., "Shuffle" is highlighted in the upper left-hand corner of the screen) when you drag the file into the track (Fig. 12.16).

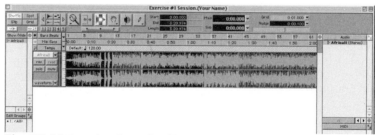

Fig. 12.16 Dragging the audio file into the stereo audio track.

Changing the View Size of a track

22) Position the cursor over the "track height" selector to enlarge the track for better editing view (Fig. 13.17a). Click and select the "large" size option (Fig. 12.17b).

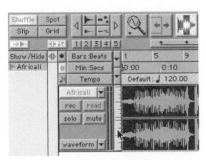

Fig. 12.17a Positioning the cursor on the "track height" selector.

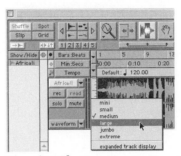

Fig. 12.17b Choosing the "large" height option for the track.

23) Now you have a better view to start editing the audio file (Fig. 12.18).

Fig. 12.18 The Edit window with the stereo audio track enlarged for better editing view.

Playing back an audio track

24) Play back the track using the Play button in the Transport window or simply press the spacebar on your computer keyboard. If you forgot how to display the Transport window, go to the Windows pop-up menu and select the "Show Transport" command (Fig. 12.19a). The Transport window will appear in the Edit window (Fig. 12.19b). If you wish to stop playing the track, press the Stop button on the Transport window, or simply press the spacebar again.

Fig. 12.19a Selecting the Transport window command.

Fig. 12.19b The Transport window.

Selecting regions

In order to perform edit functions such as: trimming, capturing, separating, consolidating, locking/unlocking, muting/unmuting, deleting, and moving regions, among other functions, you must first make a region selection in the Edit window. There are several techniques for making region selections, which I will discuss shortly and at the same time, you can practice them. But first, to keep track of the same screen shots appearing in this exercise on your computer screen, please follow the next steps. Of course, this is assuming you have the "Exercise #1 Session" opened at this time.

25) While in the Edit window (see steps 21–24 above), go to the upper left-hand corner of the audio track and position the cursor on the down arrow (Fig. 12.20a).

26) Click and hold down the mouse and select the "Markers" ruler (Fig. 12.20b).

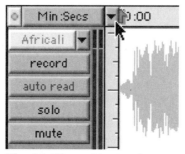

Fig. 12.20a Positioning the cursor to show the "Markers" ruler.

Fig. 12.20b Selecting the "Markers" ruler.

27) You will see two "Markers" appearing on the ruler section, on top of the audio track (Fig. 12.20c).

28) Select the Zoomer tool and position it on the track, to the left of "Marker 1" (Fig. 12.20d).

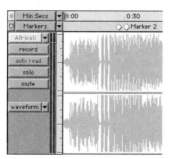

Fig. 12.20c The "Markers" ruler.

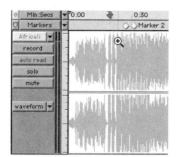

Fig. 12.20d Positioning the Zoomer tool to expand the track view.

29) Click and drag the mouse passing "Marker 2." Notice you have a better view of Marker 1 and Marker 2 to practice the selection techniques I am about to discuss (Fig. 12.20e).

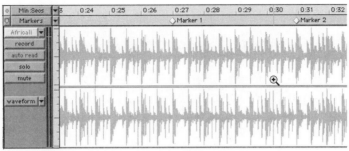

Fig. 12.20e Expanded view of Marker 1 and Marker 2.

Region selection techniques

1) Visual region selection

 a) Again, referring to "Exercise #1 Session," using the Selector tool, position it right on "Marker 1" and click on it (Fig. 12.21a). Over the audio file, you will see a flashing line over the audio file, which, by the way, is referred as the "edit cursor." On the other hand, the solid line that moves along the track when clicking on the Play button of the Transport window or pressing the spacebar is called the "playback cursor." From now on, I will use these two terms, OK?

 b) Once the edit cursor is flashing over "Marker 1," click and drag the Selector tool to "Marker 2" (Fig. 12.21b). You see? You have just visually selected a region between "Marker 1" and "Marker 2." It's that simple!

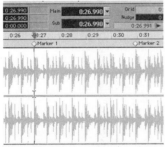

Fig. 12.21a Positioning the Selector tool on "Marker 1."

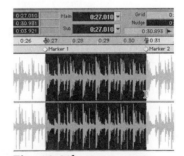

Fig. 12.21b Clicking and dragging the Selector tool to "Marker 2."

Now push the return key to go back to the beginning of the track.

2) Using the "Start" & "End" selection indicators

a) While you still have the "Exercise #1 Session" opened, double-click on the Zoomer tool (Fig. 12.22a) to view the entire track in the Edit window (Fig. 12.22b).

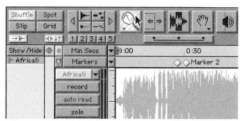

Fig. 12.22a Double-clicking on the Zoomer tool.

Fig. 12.22b Viewing the entire track in the Edit window.

b) Set the Main counter to "Min:Secs" and type "0:00:000" in the "Start" selection indicator box, in either Edit window (Fig. 12.22c) or the Transport window, and then press the return key. This sets the start time of the desired region selection.

c) Type "0:10:000" in the "End" selection indicator box, in either the Transport (Fig. 12.22d) or Edit window and press the return key. This sets the end time of the desired region selection.

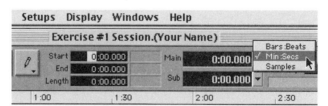

Fig. 12.22c Setting the Main counter to "Min:Secs" and the selection start time in the "Start" indicator box of the Edit window.

Fig. 12.22d Selecting the end time of a region in the "End" selection indicator box of the Transport window.

d) By typing "0:00:000" and "0:10:000" you will select the first ten seconds of the entire audio file from the beginning of the track (Fig. 12.22e).

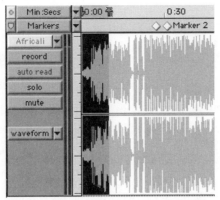

Fig. 12.22e The first ten seconds of the entire audio file was selected.

3) Selecting a region "on-the-fly"

You can make a region selection "on-the-fly" while playing back a track using the down and up arrow keys on your computer keyboard. To accomplish this on the "Exercise #1 Session":

a) Select the "Show Memory Locations" command located in the Windows pop-up menu (Fig. 12.23a).

b) Once the memory location window appears, click on the memory location named "Location 2" to show a good view area of the audio file that contains "Marker 1" and "Marker 2" (Fig. 12.23b).

Fig. 12.23a Selecting the "Show Memory Locations" window.

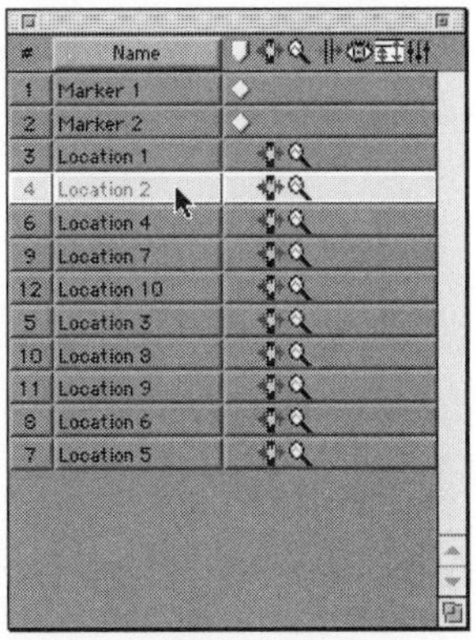

Fig. 12.23b Clicking on memory "Location 2."

c) Press the spacebar on your computer keyboard or the Play button of the Transport window to start playing back the track. As soon as you get close to the "Marker 1" location, click on the down arrow key located on the lower right side of the alphanumeric section of the computer keyboard. The edit cursor will continue flashing right on the spot where you pressed the down arrow key, which makes it the start point of the selection (Fig. 12.23c).

d) At this point, the track will still be playing, so get ready to click on the up arrow key when the playback cursor gets closer to the "Marker 2" location. As soon you click on the up arrow (end point of the selection), the area between "Marker 1" and "Marker 2" will be highlighted (Fig. 12.23d).

e) Once you have the selection made, stop the playback by pressing the spacebar on the keyboard or clicking on the Stop button in the Transport window.

f) Play back the track again by pressing the spacebar. You will be able to listen to the region selection over and over again until you stop the playback. This means the playback is in loop mode. If you experience the opposite (i.e., when you play back the track, it plays the selection only once and then it stops), then you need to enable the "Loop Playback" command located in the Operations pop-up menu (Fig. 12.23e).

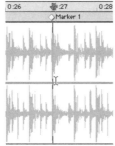

Fig. 12.23c Setting the start point of a region selection "on-the-fly" using the down arrow key.

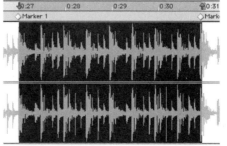

Fig. 12.23d Setting the end point of a region selection "on-the-fly" using the up arrow key.

Fig. 13.23e Selecting the "Loop Playback" command

g) After enabling the "Loop Playback" command—a circle will appear on the Play button of the Transport window—you should now be able to listen to the region selection repeatedly. If you feel that your selection was not perfect, meaning the loop playback is not seamless, you need to fine-tune the selection on either the start or end point depending on where it needs it. You can stop playback by pushing spacebar or by pushing the Stop button in the Transport window.

4) Adjusting a selection using the "blue up/down arrows"

h) While you still have the exercise Session opened, click on the memory location named "Location 6." You will notice the start point of the selection is not quite on "Marker 1" (Fig. 12.24a).

i) Click and drag the blue down arrow (located right above "Marker 1") to the left until you line it up with the yellow diamond icon (Fig. 12.24b). Zoom in to make the adjustment with precision (Fig. 12.24c).

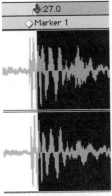

Fig. 12.24a The start point selection is not quite on "Marker 1."

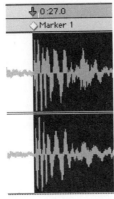

Fig. 12.24b Moving the blue down arrow to "Marker 1."

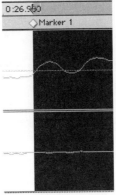

Fig. 12.24c Making fine-tune adjustments by zooming in.

j) Now, let's adjust the end point of the selection or "Marker 2." Go to the "Show Memory Locations" window and click on the location named "Location 8."

k) Notice the end point of the selection passed the "Marker 2" location (Fig. 12.25a).

l) Click and drag the blue up arrow right above "Marker 2" and line it up with the yellow diamond icon (Fig. 12.25b).

m) Zoom in using the Zoomer tool and adjust the blue up arrow to end the selection at the "zero crossing" point (Fig. 12.25c).

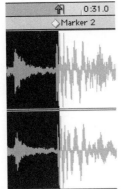

Fig. 12.25a The on-the-fly end point selection passed the "Marker 2" location.

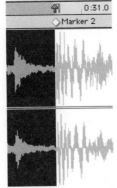

Fig. 12.25b Moving the blue up arrow to adjust the selection.

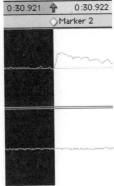

Fig. 12.25c Zooming into the region selection for a fine-tune adjustment to "Marker 2."

5) Selecting a region using the "Tab to Transients" function

Perhaps making a selection using the "Tab to Transients" function with the tab key on your computer keyboard is the easiest and most precise method to make region selections to create perfect loops. So let's practice, shall we?

a) First, go to the "Show Memory Locations" window and click on the location named "Location 2."

b) Position the cursor on the "Tab to Transients" button located right underneath the Slip mode button in the Edit window (Fig. 12.26a).

c) Click on it to enable the function (Fig. 12.26b).

Fig. 12.26a Positioning the cursor to enable the "Tab to Transients" button.

Fig. 12.26b Enabling the "Tab to Transients" button.

d) Place the edit cursor right before the "Marker 1" location (Fig. 12.26c).

e) Press the tab key on your keyboard several times until you see the edit cursor has moved exactly to the "Marker 1" location. Notice the edit cursor flashing right on "Marker 1" (Fig. 12.26d).

f) Press and hold down the shift key and start pressing the tab key until the selection has reached the "Marker 2" location (Fig. 12.26e).

g) Click the Play button in the Transport window to begin playing back the selection. Assuming the "Loop Playback" function is enabled, you should be able to listen to a perfect loop. Notice you did not have to zoom into the region to make any fine adjustments to the selection; you just have to use the tab key, and that is it. Don't forget to keep "Tab to Transients" active when trying to select seamless loops; otherwise, clicking on the tab key will move the cursor all the way to the end of the region you are in.

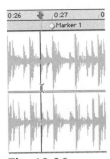
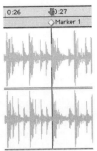
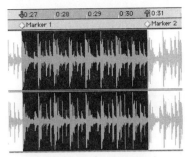

Fig. 12.26c Positioning the edit cursor right before "Marker 1."

Fig. 12.26d The Tab key was pressed (one click at the time) until the edit cursor reached the exact "Marker 1" location.

Fig. 12.26e The region selection from "Marker 1" to "Marker 2" was achieved.

6) Selecting a region using "Markers" locations

As you may have already noticed, there are many techniques to make region selections. It all depends which of them you like best and which one fits your needs according to the edit task you are performing at the time. Let's take a look at one more technique. This time we will use marker locations already in the exercise session, and the shift key.

  a) Click on "Location 2" in the memory locations window. You should see "Marker 1" and "Marker 2" shown in the Edit window (Fig. 12.27a).

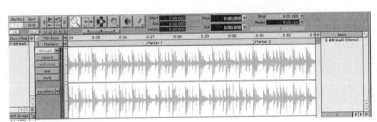

Fig. 12.27a "Marker 1" and "Marker 2."

  b) Position the cursor on "Marker 1" and click on it. The edit cursor will start flashing right on "Marker 1" (Fig. 12.27b).

  c) Next, hold down the shift key and click on the "Marker 2" location. As soon as you click on "Marker 2," the selection from "Marker 1" to "Marker 2" will be made (Fig. 12.27c).

  d) Play the selection back, and notice the selection is a perfect loop. Of course, you must pre-insert the markers at the exact right locations in order to achieve what I just showed you.

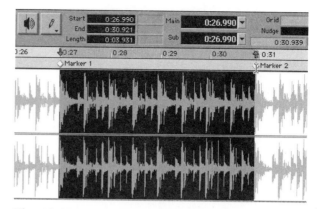

Fig. 12.27b
Clicking on the
"Marker 1" mem-
ory location."

Fig. 12.27c Clicking on "Marker 2" to make an instant
region selection.

Capturing a region

30) Now that we have a perfect loop selection, let's capture it, i.e., save it as an
audio region in the Audio Regions List of the Edit window so we can import it
back into the audio track as many times as we desire. As I mentioned earlier, in
order to capture, separate, delete, etc., a region, you must first select it. Since we
already have the selection made, let's do the following:

  a) Before we capture the selected stereo region, take a look at the Audio
  Regions List and notice that there is only one audio file (in bold type)
  named "Africali" (Fig. 12.28a).

  b) Now, since we already have a region highlighted, select the "Capture
  Region" command in the Edit pop-up menu (Fig. 12.28b).

  c) A dialog box will appear prompting you to give a name to the new captured
  region. Let's name it "Loop" and click on the "OK" button (Fig. 12.28c).

  d) Take a look at the Audio Regions List now and note that a stereo file named
  "Loop" was created. Notice the "Loop" file is not bold. This means the file is
  not an "audio file" document (the original sound recording), but is what is
  considered an "audio region," which is a derivative of the original audio or
  sound recording.

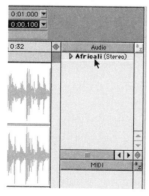

Fig. 12.28a A
stereo audio file
(original sound
recording) in the
Audio Regions
List.

Fig. 12.28b
Selecting the
"Capture Region"
command.

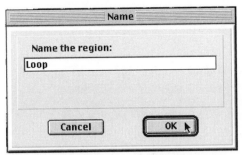

Fig. 12.28c Naming the captured region.

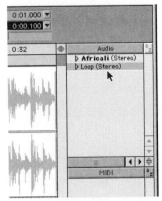

Fig. 12.28d A stereo audio region (a derivative of the original sound recording) was created in the Audio Regions List.

Separating a region

31) Proceeding with our exercise, let's now insert the stereo audio region named "Loop" somewhere in the stereo audio file in the track. But first, we need to create a separation in the audio file in order to insert the loop.

    a) Click on "Location 13." The edit cursor will be flashing right on "Marker 14" (Fig. 12.29a).

    b) Select the "Separate Region" command in the Edit pop-up menu (Fig. 12.29b).

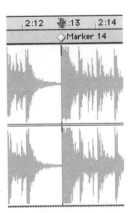

Fig. 12.29a The edit cursor is positioned on "Marker 14."

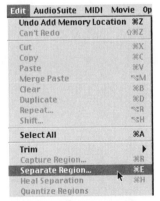

Fig. 12.29b Selecting the "Separate Region" command.

    c) You will see a line across the stereo file meaning the region has been separated (Fig. 12.29c).

    d) Click on the Tab key four times and select the "Separate Region" command one more time. As you can see in Fig. 12.29d, the small selected region has been separated from the main audio file region.

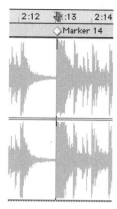

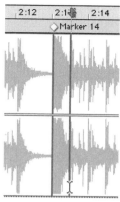

Fig. 12.29c The region has been separated.

Fig. 12.29d A small selected region was separated from the main audio file.

Duplicating a region

32) Since we separated a small section of the audio region, let's experiment by duplicating it.

    a) Set Pro Tools in Shuffle edit mode.

    b) Using the Grabber tool, click on the separated audio region to highlight it (Fig. 12.30a).

    c) Select the "Duplicate" command from the Edit pop-up menu (Fig. 12.30b).

    d) An exact replica of the separated audio region will be made (Fig. 12.30c). Notice that the rest of the audio file moved to the right. This is because you set Pro Tools in Shuffle mode.

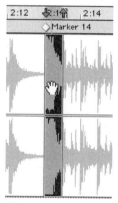

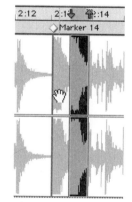

Fig. 12.30a Highlighting the separated region.

Fig. 12.30b Selecting the "Duplicate" command.

Fig. 12.30c The highlighted region was duplicated.

Inserting a region within a region

33) Let's keep experimenting, shall we? Now that we have separated and duplicated the highlighted audio region, let's insert the already captured region (the "Loop") right after the duplicated one.

a) Click on "Location 13" in the memory locations window.

b) Select the Shuffle edit mode (Fig. 12.31a).

c) Go to the Audio Regions List and click on the "Loop" audio region to select it (Fig. 12.31b).

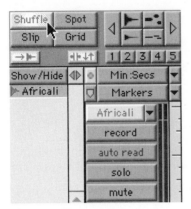

Fig. 12.31a Choosing the Shuffle edit mode.

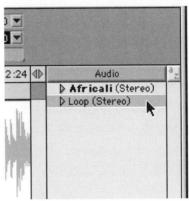

Fig. 12.31b Selecting the "Loop" by clicking on it.

d) Once you click on the region, hold it and drag it to the separation where the "Marker 19" location is. Notice the "loop" was inserted right after the duplicated audio region (Fig. 12.31c).

e) Click on "Marker 17" and press play to listen to the edits we just made (Fig. 12.31d).

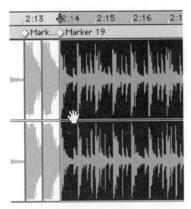

Fig. 12.31c Inserting the "Loop" in a separated section.

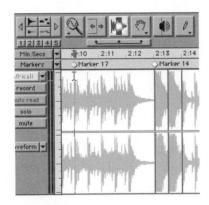

Fig. 12.31d Playing back the edit from "Marker 17."

Congratulations! You just completed the first exercise. What you just did was an experiment using the various functions I have been discussing throughout this book. Understanding the concepts behind the edits, you can do just about anything you desire. Remember it is the experimentation and the practicing that will make you proficient in Pro Tools, so don't be afraid to do or change anything, since almost all the functions are undoable.

Exercise #2 Session

This second exercise covers basic techniques for approaching a simple post-production task using a QuickTime movie and several sound effects.

In this exercise you will be able to practice:

- Opening a Session
- Saving a Session
- Importing a QuickTime movie
- Setting Pro Tools in Spot mode
- Importing audio files into a track from the Audio Regions List in Spot mode
- Playing back a Session

Opening a Session

1) If you double-click on the folder named "Exercise #2 Session," you will see four items in it: an Audio Files folder, a Pro Tools Session ("tape reel" icon), a Fade Files folder, and a QuickTime movie (Fig. 12.32).

2) Position the cursor over the Pro Tools session named "Exercise #2 Session" and double-click on it to open it.

Fig. 12.32 The "Exercise #2 Session" folder.

3) If you have the Pro Tools application already opened, the "Exercise #2 Session" file will be displayed right away on your screen; otherwise, it will take a little bit longer, meaning that the Pro Tools application was not launched yet.

4) Once you have double-clicked on the "tape reel" icon of "Exercise #2 Session," a dialog window will appear on your screen prompting you to select either "Edit Stationery" or "New Session," since this exercise file is a session template. This was done so you don't overwrite the original file on your drive when practicing on the exercise. In the event that you decide to click on the "Edit Stationery" option to overwrite the original exercise session, you can always get it back by making a copy of the file using the "Save As" command in the File pop-up menu while the session is opened, or simply by dragging the file from the CD-ROM onto your hard drive.

5) Click on the "New Session" option to continue with the exercise (Fig. 12.33).

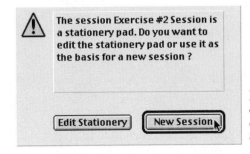

Fig. 12.33 Clicking on "New Session" to create your own Session for practice.

Saving a Session

6) As soon as you click on the "New Session" button, another dialog window will appear prompting you to type a new name and to save the Session. Type your name—or any other name you desire—in the "Name" box and then click on the "Save" button (Fig. 12.34). The Session will be saved in the "Exercise #2 Session" folder.

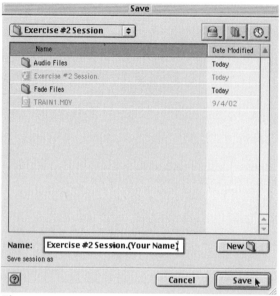

Fig. 12.34 Renaming the "Exercise #2 Session" and saving it.

7) A new folder will be created with the name you gave the Session when you clicked the "Save" button in step #6 (Fig. 12.34b).

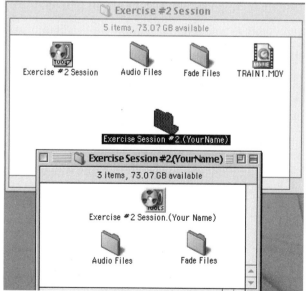

Fig. 12.34b A new folder was created with the name you typed when you saved the Exercise #2 Session.

8) After saving the Session, a Pro Tools Edit window with five stereo audio tracks and five stereo audio files in it will show on your screen (Fig. 12.35).

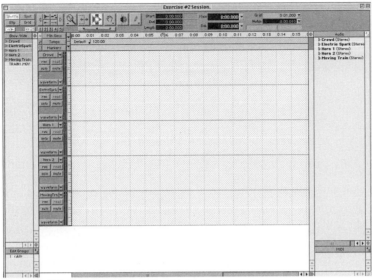

Fig. 12.35 The opened Exercise #2 Session.

9) Go to the Movie pop-up menu and select the "Import Movie" command (Fig. 12.36).

Fig. 12.36 Selecting "Import Movie" from the Movie menu.

10) After releasing the mouse, a dialog window will appear. Click on the QuickTime movie file entitled "TRAIN1.MOV" (Fig. 12.37a) and then click "Open" (Fig. 12.37b).

Fig. 12.37a Clicking on the file "TRAIN1.MOV."

Fig. 12.37b Clicking on "Open."

11) You will notice that a new window appears in your Session displaying the image of a subway train in the station (Fig. 12.38a). Click on the new window and drag it to the bottom right-hand corner of your screen so that you have a good view of your Edit window (Fig. 12.38b). You may also notice that a new track has been created at the bottom of your Edit window with the same name as the movie you imported. This is the actual QuickTime movie being shown as a movie track (with the initial part shaded gray).

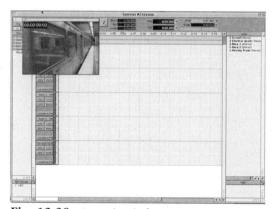

Fig. 12.38a A movie window appears.

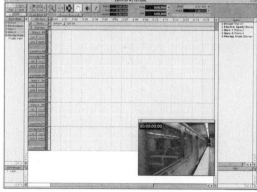

Fig. 12.38b The window has been moved to the bottom right-hand corner of the screen.

12) Now look at the Audio Regions List in the upper right-hand corner of the screen and notice that there are several stereo audio files listed (Fig. 12.39). These are sound effect files that we will be matching up with the movie you imported.

Fig. 12.39 Stereo audio files in the Audio Regions List.

13) Set Pro Tools in "Spot" mode by positioning the cursor over the word "Spot" in the upper left-hand corner of the screen and clicking on it (Fig. 12.40a). Also, make sure you have set "Min:Secs" in the Main counter (Fig. 12.40b).

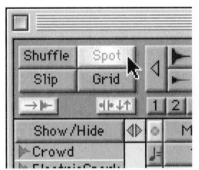

Fig. 12.40a Setting Pro Tools in "Spot" mode.

Fig. 12.40b Selecting "Min:Secs" in the Main counter.

14) Position the cursor over the first audio file listed, "Crowd" (Fig. 12.41a), and drag it into your Edit window in line with the track named "Crowd" on the left.

15) As soon as you release the mouse, the Spot Dialog window will appear. In the space labeled "Start:" type in 0:00:000 (Fig. 12.41b) and click "OK."

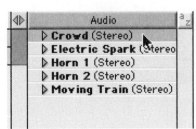

Fig. 12.41a Positioning the cursor over the file called "Crowd."

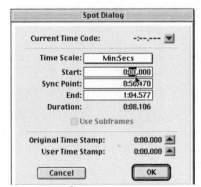

Fig. 12.41b Selecting "Min:Secs" in the Main counter.

16) This will automatically position the "Crowd" sound effect at the start of the track named "Crowd" (Fig. 12.42).

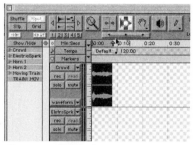

Fig. 12.42 The file "Crowd" has been positioned at the beginning of the track.

17) Similarly, we are going to sequentially drag each of the audio files from the Audio Regions List into their respective tracks in the Edit window. For example, the track called "Electric Spark" will be dragged into the track named "Electric Spark" in the Edit window, "Horn 1" into the track named "Horn 1," and so on. But each of them will need to be positioned in a particular place using the Spot Dialog window, so please follow along carefully with the next instructions. When you drag the file called "Electric Spark" into its track, enter 0:04:513 in the space labeled "Start:" in the Spot Dialog window and then click on "OK." For the file called "Horn 1," enter 0:00:333; for "Horn 2," enter 0:06:675; and for "Moving Train," enter 0:00:000.

You should end up with something that looks like Fig. 12.43:

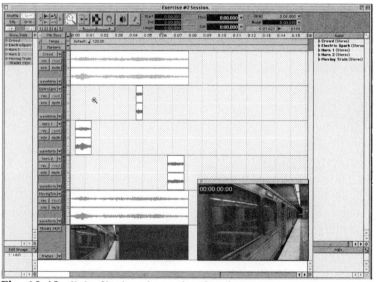

Fig. 12.43 All the files have been placed in their proper positions.

18) Now all you have to do is press the return key, followed by the spacebar or the Play button in the Transport window and notice the QuickTime movie playing with synchronized sound effects. Play it back as many times you desire and mix it—go ahead, have fun with it! You may add other sound effects as you wish to continue practicing the art of post-production in Pro Tools using QuickTime movie files.

Shortcuts

Whenever you find more than one picture to explain a shortcut, keep in mind that these follow a certain order. The picture closest to the left edge of the page shows what you should see before applying the shorctut, and the picture closest to the right edge of the page shows what you should see after applying the shortcut. Sometimes you might see three pictures in order to explain the shortcut because the process takes three steps to complete. Look at them from left to right. The first picture will be what you see before applying the shortcut, the second, what you see after applying the shortcut but before it is completed, and the third will be the result of applying it.

Not all the shortcuts are easy to explain on paper, so it is always a good idea to practice with Pro Tools while you look at these pages. Some of them will be much easier to understand if you see the result on your screen.

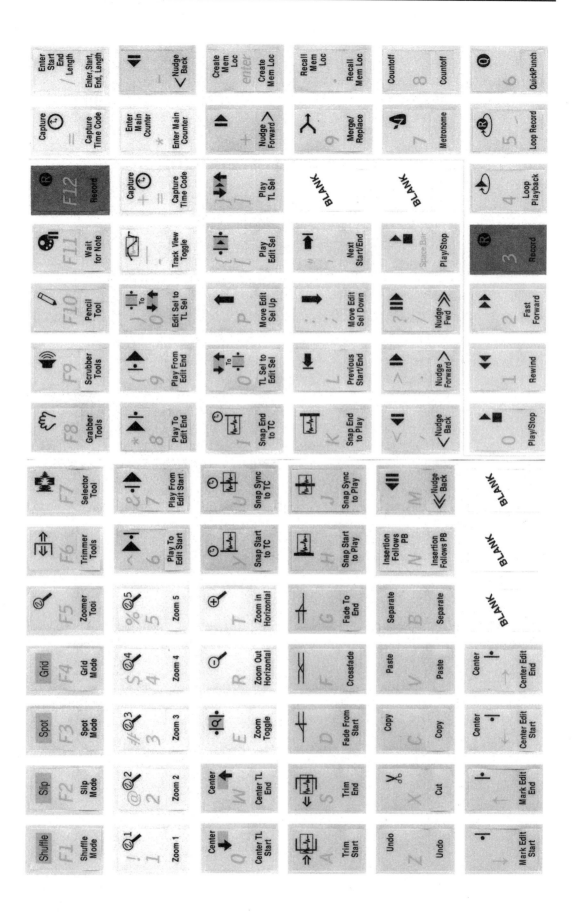

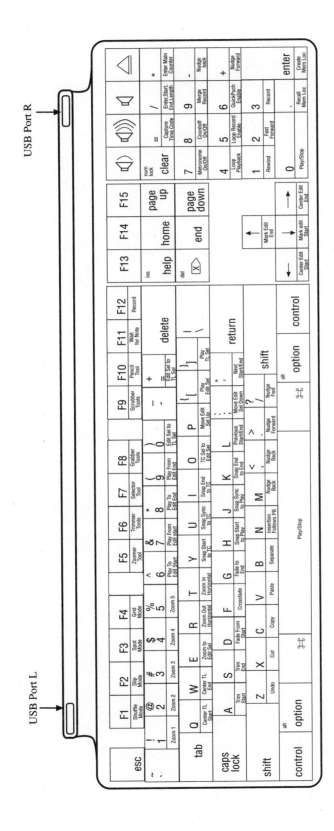

USB Port R

USB Port L

The following 16 pages show shortcuts for some of the most frequently used tasks in Pro Tools. For a complete set of the Pro Tools shortcuts, a companion book titled *The Complete Pro Tools Shortcuts* is available. It features 88 pages of shortcuts—over 250 different functions in all! For further information please see:

http://www.backbeatbooks.com/protools

RECORD AND PLAYBACK OPTIONS

Return
PC: Enter

← __Go to Start of Session__

Start of Session (Note the counter: 0.00.000)

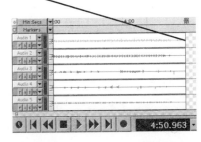

Option + Return
PC: Ctrl + Enter

← __Go to End of Session__

End of Session (Note the counter: 4.50.963)

* (Numeric) and typing a number

←__Enter Cursor Location__

Note that the counter is highlighted

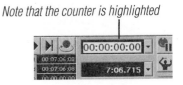

Spacebar or ø (Numeric)
PC: Spacebar or ø (numeric)

←__Playback/Stop__

479

Half-Speed Playback→

Shift + Spacebar

PC: Shift + Spacebar

Rewind→

1 (Numeric)

PC: 1 (numeric)

Fast Forward→

2 (Numeric)

PC: 2 (numeric)

Loop Playback →

4 (Numeric)

PC: 4 (numeric)

3 (Numeric) or Command + Spacebar or F12 ← <u>Record</u>
PC: Ctrl + Spacebar or F12 or 3 (numeric)

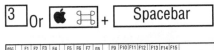

Shift + Command + Spacebar ← <u>Half-Speed Record</u>
PC: Ctrl + Shift + Spacebar

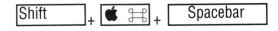

5 (Numeric) ←<u>Loop Record Enable</u>
PC: 5 (numeric)

6 (Numeric) ←<u>Quick Punch Enable</u>
PC: 6 (numeric)

Note the "P" inside the Record button

Metronome On/Off →

7 (Numeric)
PC: 7 (numeric)

Metronome

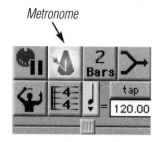

7

Count On/Off →

8 (Numeric)
PC: 8 (numeric)

Count

8

Merge Record →

9 (Numeric)
PC: 9 (numeric)

Merge Record

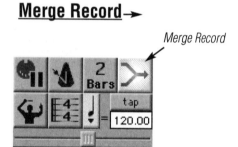

9

Stop Record and Discard Take →

Command + . (Numeric)
PC: Esc or Ctrl + . (numeric)

Recording process view

Applying the shortcut, notice that nothing has been erased

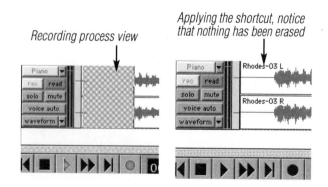

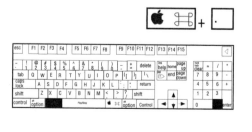

Option + Command + Click on Play button
PC: Start + Spacebar or Alt + click on Play button

←**Pause (Pre-prime deck for instant playback)**

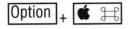

Option + Command + Click on Record button
PC: Start + Spacebar or Alt + click on Play button

←**Pause (Pre-prime deck for instant Record)**

Command + J
PC: Ctrl + J

← **Online/Offline**

Online button

Shift + Command + J

←**Movie Online**

Enable/Disable Online Record →

Option + Command + Spacebar
PC: Ctrl + Alt + Spacebar

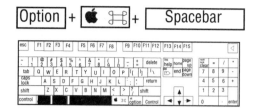

Enable/Disable Online Playback →

Option + Spacebar
PC: Ctrl + J or Alt + Spacebar

Toggle Record Modes: →
Normal/Destructive/
Loop/QuickPunch

Control + Click on Record button
PC: Right mouse click on Record button

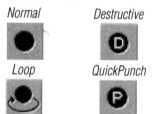

Normal   *Destructive*

Loop   *QuickPunch*

Loop Playback Toggle →

Shift + Command + L or Control + Cilck on Play button
PC: Start + Click or Right mouse click on Play button

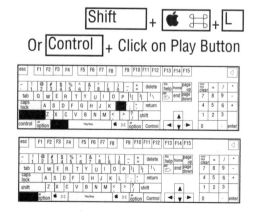

Command + Click on Record Enable button
PC: Ctrl + click on Record Enable button

← Record Safe Track

 + Click on Record Enable button

Notice that the Record Enable button looks darker than the rest

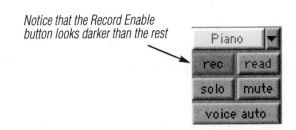

Command + Click on Solo button
PC: Ctrl + click on Solo button

← Solo-Safe Track

 + Click on Solo button

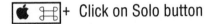

Notice that the Solo button looks darker than the rest

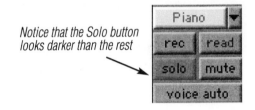

Shift + Command + P
PC: Ctrl + Shift + P

← QuickPunch

Shift +  + P

Command + Spacebar or
Command + Click on Record button
PC: Ctrl + Spacebar or Ctrl + click on Record button

← Enter/Exit Record during playback in QuickPunch

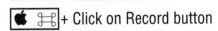 + Spacebar Or

 + Click on Record button

Enter Record   *Exit Record*

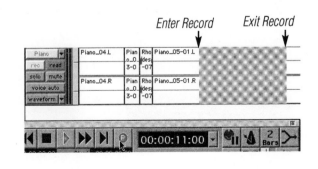

Enable/Disable Pre & Post-roll Time→

Command + K

PC: Alt + click within selection closer to front/back

Pre & Post-roll time buttons are enabled when they are highlighted

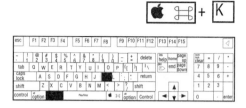

Set and Enable Pre-roll Time→

Option + Click with selector before selection

PC: Alt + click with selector before selection

Option + Click with selector before selection

Set and Enable Post-roll Time→

Option + Click with selector after selection

PC: Alt + click with selector after selection

Option + Click with selector after selection

Disable Pre-roll Time→

Option + Click within selection closer to front

PC: Alt + click within selection closer to front

Option + Click with Selector closer to front

Option + Click within selector closer to back  **<u>Disable Post-roll Time</u>**
PC: Alt + click within selection closer to back

Option + Click with Selector closer to back

Command + Click on Record Enable button  **<u>Toggle Transport Master</u>**
**PC: Ctrl + ** (Pro Tools/Machine/MMC)

+ Record Enable button

VIEW OPTIONS

<u>Zoom In</u>→   Select the Zoom tool and click on the waveform

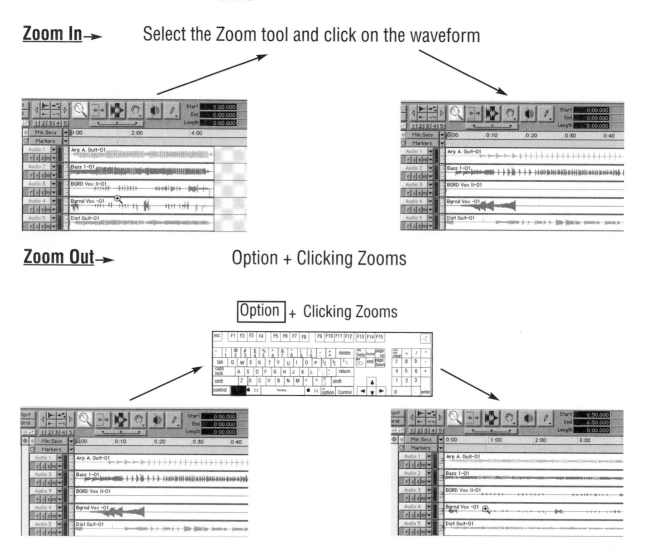

<u>Zoom Out</u>→   Option + Clicking Zooms

<u>View Entire Session</u>→ Option + A or Double-click on Zoomer

PC: Double-click on Zoomer

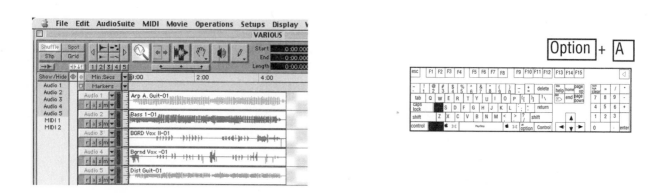

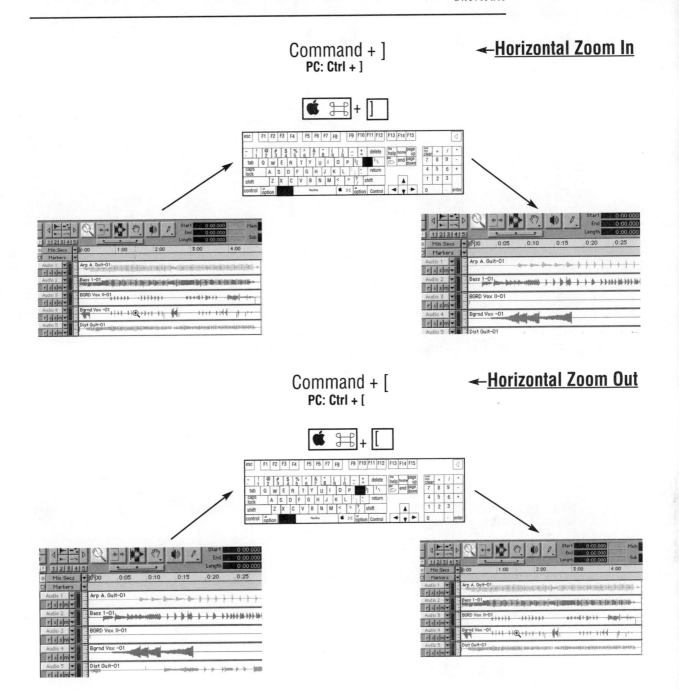

Command +]
PC: Ctrl +]

← **Horizontal Zoom In**

Command + [
PC: Ctrl + [

← **Horizontal Zoom Out**

Vertical Zoom In (Audio) → Option + Command +]
PC: Ctrl + Alt +]

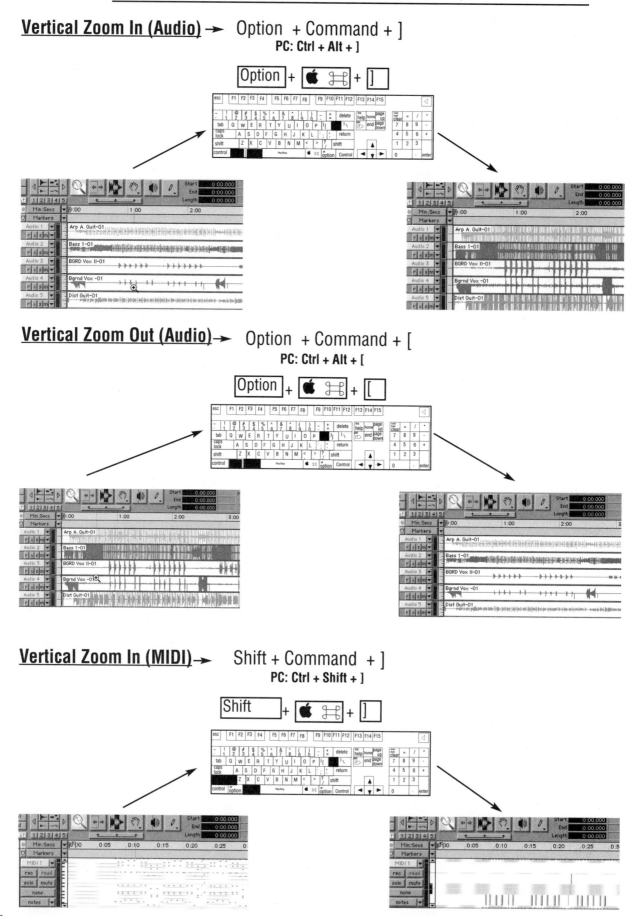

Vertical Zoom Out (Audio) → Option + Command + [
PC: Ctrl + Alt + [

Vertical Zoom In (MIDI) → Shift + Command +]
PC: Ctrl + Shift +]

Shift + Command + [←**Vertical Zoom Out (MIDI)**
PC: Ctrl + Shift + [

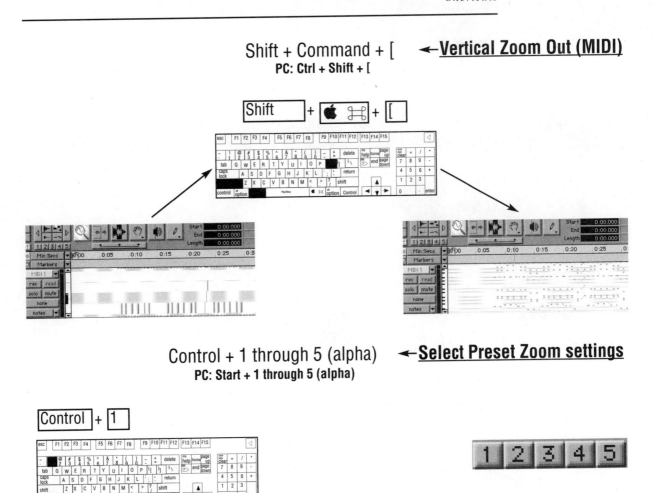

Control + 1 through 5 (alpha) ←**Select Preset Zoom settings**
PC: Start + 1 through 5 (alpha)

←**To store your own settings**

Control + Command + Click on an upper-left-hand-corner numeral
(it will blink several times to indicate that the new setting has been stored)

PC: Ctrl + click on an upper-left-hand-corner numeral (it will blink
several times to indicate that the new setting has been stored)

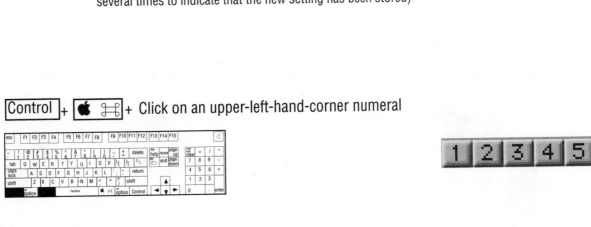

SHOW/HIDE WINDOW OPTIONS

Transport →

Command + 1 (numeric)
PC: Ctrl + 1 (numeric)

Session Setup →

Command + 2 (numeric)
PC: Ctrl + 2 (numeric)

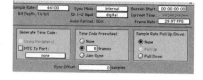

Big Counter →

Command + 3 (numeric)
PC: Ctrl + 3 (numeric)

00 : 00 : 00 : 00

Automation Enable →

Command + 4 (numeric)
PC: Ctrl + 4 (numeric)

Glossary

The following is a glossary of frequently used professional music and post-production studio terms.

ADC (Analog-to-Digital Converter): A device that converts an analog input signal (analog) into a series of binary numbers (digital).

AES/EBU (Audio Engineering Society/European Broadcast Union): A digital audio transfer format used between professional-quality audio devices. An AES/EBU connection typically uses an XLR-type connector to send and receive two channels of digital audio at the same time.

BNC: A type of plug and socket used to connect video equipment to professional RGB monitors. Pro Tools uses this type of plug and socket for word clock, super clock, and loop sync connections among its audio interfaces and synchronizers.

Control surface: An external hardware mixing interface for digital audio software such as Pro Tools that allows you to control your software mixing process with controls similar to those on analog mixing consoles.

DAC (Digital-to-Analog Converter): A device that converts digital audio information into an analog signal.

DAE (Digidesign Audio Engine): Operating system that provides for Digidesign's real-time hard disk recording, editing, digital signal processing, mix automation, and MIDI sequencing.

DAW (Digital Audio Workstation): A digital audio production system based on the computer's hard drive used for post-production, recording, editing, mixing, and mastering.

DSP (Digital Signal Processor): DSP usually refers to software programs ("plug-ins") that provide the ability to apply complex mathematical operations to digital audio data for the purpose of altering sounds. DSP is the digital equivalent of analog outboard equipment such as reverb units, compressors, and equalizers.

Ethernet: A networking system that allows linked computers to transfer data at relatively high speeds.

Latency: The time delay experienced during the processing of digital audio data within a computer, such as inserting signal processors in a track in Pro Tools.

Lightpipe: A digital audio transfer format created by Alesis, that is able to receive and transmit eight channels of digital audio through a Toslink-type connector (optical).

MIDI (Musical Instrument Digital Interface): A protocol that allows recording, editing, and playback of keyboard synthesizer events on a hardware or software sequencer.

MIDI module: A non-keyboard MIDI synthesizer unit which produces sounds based upon MIDI information received from a MIDI keyboard or sequencer.

MIDI Time Code (MTC): A high frequency digital signal encoded as MIDI data that allows synchronization among audio, MIDI, and video devices; it is the MIDI equivalent of SMPTE time code.

OMS (Open Music System): A "MIDI operating system" developed by Opcode for Macintosh computers. A collection of software tools to handle the flow of MIDI information between music applications and MIDI hardware.

RCA connector: Unbalanced audio connector that is typically colored either red or white and is most often used to connect consumer electronics such as home audio components.

Sampling: The process of taking previously recorded audio files and using them as insertable sounds in contexts other than their original context.

Serial port: A computer connector for input and output of digital information in series (as opposed to SCSI transmission, which is a parallel transmission). For example, through these connectors, printers, modems, and other computer peripherals may be connected. Until recently, when working with MIDI, the MIDI interface had to be connected to this port.

SCSI (Small Computer Systems Interface): An electronic information protocol and interface that is used in a computer to communicate with a hard disk or any other external peripheral with SCSI, such as a printer, scanner, CD-ROM, sampler, etc.

S/PDIF (Sony/Phillips Digital Interface Format): A digital audio transfer format used between "consumer" audio devices. A S/PDIF connection typically uses an RCA- or Toslink-type connector to send and receive two channels of digital audio at the same time.

Synchronization: The unifying of the audio events of multiple hardware pieces so that they consistently operate (playback and/or record) in unison, known as "locking" together.

T-DIF (Tascam Digital Interface Format): Tascam's digital audio transfer format for sending and receiving eight channels of digital audio via a 25-pin D-sub connector.

TDM (Time Division Multiplexing): TDM is a 24-bit, 256-channel "data highway" that provides digital mixing and real-time DSP capabilities in a Pro Tools system.

Toslink: A connector type for fiber optic communication, frequently used on consumer audio equipment for S/PDIF digital transfers as well as for Lightpipe digital audio transmission.

TRS (Tip-Ring-Sleeve): A quarter-inch connector typically used for balanced audio lines, stereo signals, and "effect loop" audio adapters.

UltraWide SCSI: A 16-bit version of Wide SCSI with data transfers at up to 40 Mb/second. UltraWide SCSI is commonly used, by Digidesign's recommendation, in a Pro Tools TDM system for higher performance.

Voices: Recorded tracks currently available for simultaneous playback. In a Pro Tools environment, the number of voices is the equivalent of the number of audio tracks; in other words, it is Pro Tools' polyphony. A Pro Tools session can have more tracks than the total number of available voices, but only the maximum number of voices will concurrently sound.

XLR: A three-pin connector usually used with professional equipment, especially for balanced lines. It is also typically used for microphones.

CD-ROM Credits

The following are credits for the composers, musicians, producers, and engineers who collaborated on the Pro Tools exercises in the CD-ROM:

Song used in "Exercise #1 Session"

"Africali"

Written, performed, and produced by

Don Quentin Hannah for

Parallusion Music BMI ©2003

Contact: www.audiographintl.com

Movie clip used in "Exercise #2 Session"

Anthony Fung (Commercial Director)—movie clip

anthony.fung@verizon.net

Loren Henry—sound editor

Christopher Rawson—sound effects editing

Contact: www.audiographintl.com

Songs used in "Exercise #3 Session"

Song #1: "Someone Told Me" ©2003

Written and performed by Unclear:

Johnny Scalco—lead vocals/rhythm guitar

Luca—lead guitar/ vocals

Gary Glass—bass/vocals

Shaunlemagne—keyboards/vocals

Noriyuki Kitagawa—drums/percussion

Produced and engineered by Gary Glass

Song #2: "Africali"
Written, performed, and produced by Don Quentin Hannah
For Parallusion Music BMI ©2003

Song #3: "Hasta El Fin Del Tiempo" ©2003
Music and lyrics by Fernando Cavazos
Produced and Engineered by Fernando Cavazos
Vocals—Luis Arias
Contact: www.audiographintl.com and fernando_cavazos@excite.com

Song #4: "Gotas de Verdad" ℗©2002
Music and lyrics by Hillary Beth
Produced by Ben Yonas at Studio Y, El Cerrito, CA
Mixed and mastered by Dave Greensberg
All vocals—Hillary Beth
Piano and organ—Ben Yonas
All guitars—Gowian Matthews
Bass—Curtis Ohlson
Drums—Dave Tweedy
Contact: hillary@hillarybeth.com

Song used in "Exercise #4 Session"

"Shogun"—Instrumental
Composed, produced, and engineered by Cory Barker ©2003
Contact: barkercory2002@yahoo.com

Song used in Chapter 8

"Love Changes Everything"
Words and music by James Grey ©2001
Produced and performed by James Grey
On *Shadows In Light*, New World Records, NWR 1006-2
Publisher: Greysongs (SESAC)
Contact: james@jamesgrey.com and www.jamesgrey.com

Acknowledgments

I would like to express my thanks and appreciation to those who collaborated with me on this book, and to all my friends and family who patiently supported me and helped me in one way or another throughout the completion of this important project.

First of all, to my wife, Marina Zapata Valenzuela, for her patience and understanding, and for believing in me and the project. Secondly, to Matt Kelsey, Publisher of Backbeat Books, for giving me the opportunity to publish this book and for his patience. Thanks, Matt. To my right hand, Ana Lorente Izquierdo, for her invaluable time, talent, effort, and persistence.

To the AudioGraph International team: Ma. del Refugio Valenzuela, Andre Oliveira, George Madaraz, Debbie Green, Luis Alberto Capilla, Oscar Elizondo, Gary Glass, Giovanna Imbesi, Abel Chen, Hillary Beth, Mark Dawson, Don Quentin Hannah, Vivian Khor, Christopher Rawson, Saskia Tracy, Fernando Cavazos, James Grey, Severine Baron, Jonathan Valens, Loren Henry, Gabe Kubanda, Sarah Israel, and Cory Barker.

To Backbeat Books: Nancy Tabor, Karl Coryat, Richard Johnston, Amy Miller, Kevin Becketti, Nina Lesowitz, and the late Jay Kahn.

To Digidesign: Christopher Bock, Paul Floecker, Sirpa King, Claudia Cursio, Mary Stevens, Andy Cook, Jon Connolly, Victoria Faveau, Mark Kirshner, Boe Gatiss, Dusty DiMercurio, Bill Lackey, Jerry Antonelli, Alex Steinhart, José "Pepe" Reveles, Adinaldo Neves, and Felipe Capilla.

To Steve Gorski from The SG Group (SLS Speakers); Marcus Ryle, Sue Wolf, and Mike and Carol Hatzinger from Line6; Dennis Yurosek for his support and friendship; Michael Papp, Erik P. Papp, and Damon Gramont from Summit Audio; Hank and Joan Waring from FDS; Mark McCrocklin from StorCase, Kay Dorrough from Dorrough Electronics; EveAnna Manley from Manley Laboratories, Inc.;

Richard Wilson from Quantegy, Kirk Johnson, Joey Heredia, Richard Schulenberg, Daniel Votino, and the rest of "The Flash Brothers" team; Eric Gibson, Regi Collins, Patty Aguilera, Len Naemark, Troy Morris, and Dave Elvenia; Jim Cooper, Chuck Thompson, Danny O'Donnell from JL Cooper Electronics; Terry Hardin and Michael Logue from Antares; Raul Elizondo from Soundabout Music; Benjamin Chadabe from GRM Tools; Woody Moran and Chris Adams from M-Audio; Scott Ray from Waves; Wynton R. Morro and Brad Zell from Avalon Design; Claudia Castro and the rest of the Alejo's crew; and Felix Rosario and Ali Nasri from Mac 911 in Santa Monica for fixing my computer to write this book.

Thanks to all of you!
Chilitos

About the Author

José "Chilitos" Valenzuela is a recording, mixing, electronic music, and computer engineer born in Tijuana, B. C., Mexico. He graduated in Audio, Electronic Music and Computer Science Engineering from Baja California's Institute of Technology (ITR #21), California State University Dominguez Hills in Carson, CA, and UCLA.

Valenzuela has worked as an audio engineer for Oberheim Electronics (a synthesizer manufacturer) and for the ABC TV Network during the 1984 Olympic Games held in Los Angeles, CA. He also worked as design engineer for Fast Forward Designs (now Line 6) where he collaborated in the design of several Alesis Corp. and Digidesign products, among others.

As a recording, mixing, and mastering engineer, Valenzuela has worked for internationally renowned artists and producers such as Whitney Houston, Elton John, The Go Go's, Jay Graydon, Alejandro Lerner, Keith Emerson, Pepe Aguilar, Marcelo Cezán, John Waite (The Babys), and Michael Sembello, among others.

In the post-production world, Valenzuela has worked as a sound-effects designer and synthesizer programmer in feature films such as *Star Trek: Generations*, *Dark Devil*, and others.

He has been the editor of *Guitar Player* magazine's Spanish edition, editorial director of *Latin GRAMMY* magazine, and collaborator of *Mix* magazine Spanish edition.

In addition to writing several books, Valenzuela has given professional audio conferences in United States, Spain, and several countries in Latin America.

Valenzuela is a UCLA Professor, Pro Tools consultant, and President of Audio-Graph International, which is a Spanish Information Center for Music and Technology, and a training center certified by Digidesign for Pro Tools in English and Spanish.

Valenzuela has started a music production company in Los Angeles, where he will develop and produce new and already established Latin and American artists, in both English and Spanish.

Index

WHEN IT COMES TO MAKING MUSIC, WE WROTE THE BOOK.

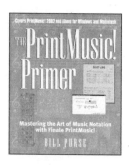